Praise for *The Evening Star*

"Faye Haskins masterfully gives us both the history of this greatest of American afternoon newspapers and captures the spirit of its unique role for more than 150 years in the life of the Capital of the United States."—**Carl Bernstein**

"Important reading for anyone who has an affection for journalism or Washington or both."—**John Kelly,** Metro Columnist, *The Washington Post*

"The rise and fall of the *Washington Star* stands as a morality tale for modern journalism. Faye Haskins' careful history reveals how the *Star* became a great paper, how well it covered the news of its day, and why it failed to survive."—**Donald A. Ritchie,** author of *Reporting from Washington: The History of the Washington Press Corps*

"The life and death of an institution like the *Washington Evening Star* is painful enough to live through—to believe that a great paper's and a great city's fates were intertwined. Reading this history leaves one with the realization that a dying publication was not indicative of a dying city. Faye's recapitulation forces one to wish the *Evening Star's* fate had mirrored that of Washington. And that is a painful reminder for all of us exes who were so Star Struck."—**Paul Delaney,** former *New York Times* National Editor

The Evening Star

The Evening Star

The Rise and Fall of a Great Washington Newspaper

Faye Haskins

ROWMAN & LITTLEFIELD
Lanham • Boulder • New York • London

The *Evening Star* newspaper was established in 1852. The paper's name was changed to the *Washington Star-News* in 1973 after the Noyes, Kauffmann, and Adams families, who owned the paper, purchased The *Washington Daily News*. In 1974 when Joseph Allbritton bought the paper, its name was changed to The *Washington Star* on the masthead, where it remained until the paper closed in 1981. The more common term for the paper was the *Star*, which is most often used in the text of this book.

Published by Rowman & Littlefield
An imprint of The Rowman & Littlefield Publishing Group, Inc.
4501 Forbes Boulevard, Suite 200, Lanham, Maryland 20706
www.rowman.com

6 Tinworth Street, London SE11 5AL, United Kingdom

British Library Cataloguing in Publication Information Available

Library of Congress Cataloging-in-Publication Data

Names: Haskins, Faye, author.
Title: The Evening star : the rise and fall of a great Washington newspaper / Faye Haskins.
Description: Lanham : Rowman & Littlefield, 2019. | Includes bibliographical references and index.
Identifiers: LCCN 2019006064 | ISBN 9780742548725 (cloth : alk. paper) | ISBN 9781538105764 (electronic)
Subjects: LCSH: Washington star—History.
Classification: LCC PN4899.W32 W355 2019 | DDC 071.53—dc23 LC record available at https://lccn.loc.gov/2019006064

∞™ The paper used in this publication meets the minimum requirements of American National Standard for Information Sciences—Permanence of Paper for Printed Library Materials, ANSI/NISO Z39.48-1992.

Contents

Acknowledgments

I wish to thank a number of people and institutions that helped me in researching and writing this book.

I am grateful to the staff of the Washingtoniana Collection, Special Collections Division at the D.C. Public Library for their research assistance and unfailing support for the book. Research in collections held in Washingtoniana were crucial to writing an accurate account of the *Star* and the city in which it was published. I especially want to thank Derek Gray, who helped with extensive research in the papers of the *Washington Star*, and Michele Casto and Lisa Warwick, who assisted with photographs used in the book from the *Star* photo collection. I also want to thank Jerry McCoy, Mark Greek, John Muller, and Ayana Reed for their help and support.

Thanks to the many staff at archives and libraries for their research help, including Jennifer King, manuscripts librarian, Special Collections, George Washington University; staff in the Manuscripts and Periodicals Divisions of the Library of Congress; archivists Amy DeLong and Christina Jones at the National Archives and Records Administration, College Park, Maryland; librarian Jane Sween at the Historical Society of Montgomery County, Maryland; Jeffrey Schlosberg and other staff at the National Press Club Archives; reference archivist at the Wisconsin Historical Society; and Barbara Cline at the LBJ Presidential Library and Museum, Austin, Texas.

Without the reporters, editors, other *Star* staff or their family members who were open to discussing their memories of the *Star*, I could not have written this book. Many continued to be supportive and open to helping throughout the process. Persons who I interviewed appear in the notes and bibliography. Former *Star* staff who were also helpful but not specifically listed include: Joan Anderson, Carl Bernstein, Bernie Boston, Alan Bruns, Chuck Conconi, Phil Evans, Phil Falcone, Sara Harrison, Bruce Kinsey, Cody Pfanstiehl, and Carl Sell.

Newbold (Terry) Noyes III graciously offered me access to some of the personal papers of his father, Newbold Noyes. Terry also shared personal memories of his father and the Noyes family with me. His help provided important insights into his father's professional and personal life as well as the Noyes family.

Thanks to professional colleagues, including Jane Levey, Mara Cherkasky, and Roxanne Deane, who provided advice and encouragement. I am also very grateful for the patience and support of my family and friends during the many years I was preparing this book. Lastly, thanks to the staff at Rowman & Littlefield, including Christopher Anzalone (formerly with Rowman), who suggested I write this important book, and Jon Sisk, Kate Powers, Chelsea Panin, and Elaine McGarraugh for bringing it to final publication.

Introduction

O n Pennsylvania Avenue in Washington halfway between the Capitol and the White House stands an iconic building that reminds us of a bygone era when powerful and influential city newspapers thrived. The Evening Star Building is a classic nineteenth-century Beaux-Arts structure built at the dawn of the twentieth century as a testament to the success and wealth of the *Evening Star* newspaper (later the *Washington Star*). The *Star* was established in 1852 when the capital city was a backwater southern town. By 1900 the paper was the most financially successful newspaper in Washington and among the top ten in the nation, and would remain so for many decades into the twentieth century.

In the first five decades of the twentieth century, Washingtonians could choose to read news from at least four different daily newspapers published in the morning and afternoon in the city. Dailies were delivered to city homes, or Washingtonians bought them at newsstands or from newsboys who hawked them on city streets from dawn to dusk. City dwellers read their print newspapers at home and to and from work on streetcars that laced through the city. It was an era of large editorial staffs, reporters who wrote copy on typewriters and called in stories from telephone booths to dictation desks, dedicated local news beat reporters, and newsprint that rolled off pounding printing presses set by typesetters and delivered by union truck drivers or boys and girls with paper routes as their first jobs. Daily newspapers wielded great power and prestige in their hometowns and were more often trusted and respected than not by residents. The *Star* was at its pinnacle in this era at the heart of news

1

and history in the nation's capital. The paper's history is the quintessential story of an earlier breed of city newspapers and a kind of journalism slowly disappearing. Yet it is also the singular story of the rise and fall of a once-great evening newspaper, its oft-told legends, and the famous and quirky people who passed through its noisy, untidy newsroom. The *Star* earned a unique reputation among journalists as a "reporter's paper," where reporters' independence and judgment were encouraged—not suppressed—over an editors'. Among the scores of journalists who flourished and were mentored at the paper were liberal syndicated columnist Mary McGrory, Pulitzer Prize winner Haynes Johnson, respected political reporter David Broder, and a young Maureen Dowd and Howard Kurtz, who started their careers there.

The *Washington Star*'s history is irrevocably intertwined with the history of the city of Washington too. Yet few Washingtonians today know the story of one of the most respected and successful newspapers and publishing dynasties in the capital city and the nation. The paper's success was due in large measure to its unique devotion to local news from its inception, its many highly respected journalists, and the historic times in which it was published from the dawn of the Civil War to the election of Ronald Reagan. The Noyes and Kauffmann families who owned and operated the *Star* for a century also played a crucial role in the paper's great successes and also its eventual decline. Patriarch Crosby Noyes's legacy and life is the most inspiring. Noyes, who exerted a great deal of influence on both the paper and the city's early development, came from very modest roots. Noyes was born the illegitimate son of a Maine farmer who through hard work and native intelligence became a respected newspaper publisher and member of Washington's influential elite by the time of his death in 1908. In 1974 his descendants, however, were forced to sell the once-great newspaper Noyes had built to Joseph Allbritton. Allbritton and then Time, Inc. tried to save the *Star* but failed.

The Evening Star Building, ca. 1930s. D.C. Community Archives, *Washington Star* Papers, D.C. Public Library.

1

✢

Nineteenth-Century Roots

On a cold night in December 1859, "newspaper folks, artists, and other vagrant Bohemians" crowded in Room 13 at Carter's Hotel in the remote mountain village of Charles Town, Virginia (now West Virginia), "under military durance till daylight," wrote Crosby Noyes, a reporter for the *Evening Star*. The newspapermen were there to witness and report the hanging of the notorious John Brown, the biggest and most explosive news story of their time. Noyes, a transplant from a hardscrabble New England background with talent and an indefatigable, up-from-your-bootstraps ambition was in the throes of making a name for himself in the newspaper business. Noyes, at age thirty-four and six years at the *Star*, was among a select group of reporters who had made it to Charles Town. Among them were "Fulton of the *Baltimore American*, Wingate of the *Sun*, Sultzer of the *Clipper* [and] . . . Hays of the *New York Herald*." Noyes had traveled in fits and starts by train from the city of Washington in a jammed railcar full of reporters, curiosity seekers, and other suspicious characters. All along the route, railroad guards and soldiers continually stopped trains and horse-drawn wagons to check and sometimes eject suspected vigilante groups sympathetic to Brown and purported to be bent on freeing the prisoner. Many correspondents were sent home, and Noyes wasn't sure he would make it in time or at all for the hanging, but he did. When Noyes arrived in Charles Town, he found the small Virginia town in the Blue Ridge Mountains transformed into a heavily guarded fortress with over 1,500 military troops who were larger than the town's population. Dr. Rawlings, special illustrator for *Leslie's Pictorial*, fed the reporters sardines and sandwiches and entertained them all night with "puns and poetical quotations ad libitum," wrote Noyes. There were no beds in the room, so the men stood or paced while those lucky enough to have a chair occasionally nodded off only to be roused by laughter, a kick, or a rough shake urging them to join in the night's entertainment and conversation. Shortly after sunrise, Noyes and other correspondents met with General William Booth Taliaferro to obtain permission to visit the grounds where the gallows were being erected. That morning Noyes observed Brown and some of his accused co-conspirators at their cell windows from the jail yard below, among them Albert Hazlett, "whiling away the time by squirting tobacco juice with considerable accuracy at the shed-roof below," wrote Noyes, but he never saw accused assassin John Cook, whom Noyes judged looked "forward to his fate with the least fortitude." Two hours before the scheduled execution at 11:00 am, the newspapermen were escorted by military guard to the location picked for them to view the hanging. Reporters had negotiated with local authorities for a better spot, and although Noyes thought the new location was slightly better, it was still too far away from the gallows to see or hear clearly. Virginia authorities wanted to keep the press as far as possible from the gallows so they couldn't report anything provocative Brown might say or do. The winter day was unseasonably warm and balmy as Brown, with hands bound, made the short trip from the jail to the hanging grounds in a small, wooden cart seated atop his coffin. Despite the reporters' obstructed and distant location with hundreds of soldiers encircling the grounds, Noyes's account of Brown's hanging draws in words an intimate and gruesome picture of a stoic Brown facing his last minutes of life.

Brown descended from the cart and mounted the platform with the same imperturbably, wooden composure which had distinguished him at every step of his progress. He was dressed in a well-worn suit of black cassimere—the same which he wore on first entering Harpers Ferry—white woolen stockings, red figured carpet-slippers . . . and it was noticed that his neck and breast were as white as a woman's. The sheriff and jailor mounted the platform with Brown, and quickly adjusted the white cap over his head and the rope round his neck, and tied his feet securely. Then occurred another remarkable exhibition of nerve by Brown. He was requested to take his place on the drop (trap door) "I cannot find it; guide me to it" he answered in the same even tone of voice as if asking for a chair. He was placed in position, and then there was an unpleasant pause of some eighteen minutes . . . which the prisoner stood without tremor, at a quarter past 11, Col. Smith called out audibly "All ready, Mr. Campbell." The sheriff touched the spring, the flooring dropped beneath the prisoner's feet; down he shot through the trap, then up, then down, there was a quick convulsive movement of the hands, a slight muscular tension of the limbs, then they straightened, and the body swung perpendicular, turning slowly round and round . . . with the fluttering of the coat shirts in the breeze, giving it singularly the appearance of a cornfield scarecrow.

Brown's violent raid and end on the gallows are emblematic of the strong passions that festered and grew into an unbridgeable chasm between political extremes in the country over slavery in the years before the Civil War. Brown was a murdering madman to "slavery men" and a martyred hero to abolitionists. As the sectional divide over slavery pulled the country wider apart, the middle way for reasonable debate vanished and the drumbeat toward a fierce sectional conflict grew louder. These were the tumultuous and historic times from which the *Evening Star* newspaper arose.[1]

Captain Joseph Burroughs Tate, a printer by trade and captain in the local Washington militia, established the *Evening Star* newspaper at age

"The Birth of The *Star*." Drawing by Newman Sudduth for the *Star*'s Centennial Anniversary Edition, December 16, 1952. Owner-Editor Joseph Tate stands reading the *Star*'s front page with his only reporter Bill Tucker to the left and pressman Frank Sage at right, December 16, 1852. DC Community Archives, *Washington Star* Papers, DC Public Library, Neg. #21495.

thirty-four with a loan of $500 from friends. The first regular edition of the *Star* was issued on December 16, 1852, and totaled one thousand copies of a single sheet folded in the middle to make four pages printed on a flat-press press. It included telegraphic news, an editorial, a poem, a dramatic yarn, court news, and fifty-four paid advertisements. The staff consisted of Tate, editorial writer Rev. Charles W. Denison, reporter W. W. Tucker, pressman Frank Sage, four compositors, and two apprentices. Type was set by hand and pages manually turned to print both sides. Offices and equipment were housed in two locations on a half floor at 8th and D Streets, NW and at 6th Street, between Missouri and Pennsylvania Avenue, NW. Tate was a small, sinewy man with angular features and a profundity of whiskers whose modest appearance and demeanor matched his simple but unique desire to be the publisher of a successful nonpartisan penny newspaper devoted to local news, a rare commodity in the city of Washington and most American cities at the time. In the first three decades of the nineteenth century, American newspapers were party organs—advocates for political parties and candidates they openly and aggressively supported. Early nineteenth-century American newspapers depended heavily on the patronage of political parties to obtain lucrative government printing contracts in exchange for being party mouthpieces. Newspapers devoted little space to local news and were too costly for an ordinary working man to buy. James Gordon Bennett Sr. established the *New York Herald* as the first successful and independent penny newspaper in 1835, which was followed by the *Philadelphia Public Ledger* in 1836 and *Baltimore Sun* in 1837. One year before founding the *Star*, Tate made his first attempt at publishing an independent penny newspaper he dubbed the *American Daily Telegraph*, but it folded after he unwittingly supported the Whig presidential candidate General Winfield Scott, who lost the election. Tate tried again, and in the *Star*'s first edition he promised to keep it "free from party trammels and sectarian influences . . . [which] will preserve strict neutrality, and whilst maintaining a fearless spirit of independence." In 1852 four daily newspapers were published in Washington—the *Intelligencer*, a Whig paper; *The Republic*, a vocal supporter of President Polk's Democratic Party; and the *Washington Union*, which traditionally was also an organ of the Democratic Party. Most Washingtonians depended on the *Baltimore Sun* to read about local news, but the *Star* was hoping to change that.

In 1852 a Whig administration occupied the Executive Mansion headed by President Millard Fillmore, and on the streets of Washington you might see John Quincy Adams, John Breckinridge, or Jefferson Davis, as well as other lesser-known statesmen, legislators, and ordinary people walking the muddy thoroughfares of the city. Stephen Douglas, who introduced the Kansas–Nebraska Act of 1854, four years later would engage in historic debates over slavery when his Senate seat was challenged by the young and less well-known Illinois politician Abraham Lincoln. Despite all the powerful men and important news emanating from the capital, Washington was still a backwater southern city. In the early 1850s, the city of Washington, as it was then known, was a ten-mile square bounded on the north by Boundary Street (now Florida Avenue) and to the South by the Potomac River. The city was a provincial country town with unpaved streets, open sewers, shanty dwellings, and a few half-finished federal buildings scattered throughout. Pigs, geese, and cows grazed the muddy streets and open fields, residents took their water from pumps and springs, and a scarce few police and firemen protected the city. Pennsylvania Avenue was a combination of macadam, cobblestones, and gravel, which only extended from the White House to the Capitol, and Tiber Creek divided one section of the city into an island. The federal government officially moved the capital city to the banks of the Potomac in 1800 but invested little in building a respectable city. Less than a dozen routes led north out of the town beyond Boundary Street, where large farms, wooded forests, hunters, fishermen, and an occasional farmhouse dotted the landscape. Long Bridge was the only bridge that crossed the Potomac to Virginia. Under construction was an extension to the Capitol and grounds, additions to the Patent Office, the beginnings of the Washington Monument, and a soldier's home for returning veterans of the Mexican War. The total population of Washington by 1850 was around fifty thousand, of which approximately ten thousand were free blacks and four thousand slaves. Washingtonians worked as artisans and laborers on federal projects, ran boarding houses for the capital's many visitors and temporary residents, owned small shops, or held modestly paid but stable jobs as clerks, janitors, and messengers with the federal government. A few professionals, diplomats, and successful businessmen owned mansions near Lafayette Square or west of the President's House at 1600 Pennsylvania Avenue. Most residents, however, lived in small frame or brick houses primarily in the central core of the city not far from work. City dwellers found public entertainment at the National Theater at 14th and E Streets as well as taverns and gambling houses. The nation's capital was a hodgepodge of grand structures and monuments, rural landscapes, wooden shacks, boarding houses, taverns, scattered building projects, stately mansions, a swarm of laborers, transients, grand ladies, and statesmen. This was the city the *Star* wrote about and the advertisers and residents it hoped to attract to be a successful newspaper in the city of Washington.

In May 1853 the *Star* moved to a building at Sixth and Pennsylvania Avenue but was not there long. Tate was not a fearless or experienced businessman, so he soon sold the *Star* to William H. Hope and William

Douglas Wallach and took a secure salaried position as the *Star*'s cashier until his death in 1858. The new owners moved operations to a two-story building on D between 12th and 13th Streets, whitewashed the walls, and installed a small business counter on the ground floor where a carriage shop once was. Printers and reporters climbed a back staircase reached through an alley next to Flynn's blacksmith shop to work in a second-story room they all shared with a hand press that printed 250 editions per hour. The *Star*'s offices were among a half dozen shops and private homes in the sparsely populated neighborhood, which included Curtis Graham's lithograph shop, Lepreux grocery, Mrs. Annie Hughes's boarding house, and the homes of colored violinist Andrew Henson and a local Democratic officeholder, C. Sengstack. Reporters wrote their stories with quill pens surrounded by dingy walls and ink-stained floors lit with kerosene lamps and tallow candle tips, since most modest proprietors could not afford expensive gas light. The new owners in 1854 moved to yet another home, a three-story brick building with an attic at Pennsylvania Avenue and 11th Street, which was formerly a hotel. The paper would remain at this location until 1881. The *Star* shared the building with an auction parlor, a bookstore, and the stage to an adjoining variety theater, which served as a ceiling to the pressroom. The composing room on the third floor was heated by a cylinder stove around which the printers gathered on cold mornings to warm their hands and the steel sticks they used to set type.[2]

Hope and Wallach dissolved their partnership in 1855, leaving Wallach as the sole owner. Doug Wallach was a colorful character, vivacious, demonstrative, socially and politically connected, and outspoken. He was trained as a civil engineer but preferred the newspaper business, and for awhile published the Matagorda *Texas Gazette* in the 1840s and then moved back East to write for northern newspapers, including the *Daily Union* in Washington. By the 1850s, Wallach was a rotund, middle-aged man of forty-one who sported a stylish top hat, cravat, and frockcoat on the streets of Washington and aspired to be a country squire. Despite his gentlemanly aspirations, his strong opinions and temper often led him into heated quarrels and even a few fistfights on the streets of Washington. His brother Richard Wallach was mayor of Washington from 1861 to 1867, so he had important connections to local politicians. Wallach wrote strong editorials opposing the radical abolitionist press, the anti-Catholic Know-Nothing Party, and Lincoln's election but remained a staunch supporter of the Union during the Civil War. A year after the *Star* was established, Wallach hired twenty-eight-year-old Crosby S. Noyes to establish a route carrier system in 1853, and two years later he became a full-time *Star* reporter. In the decades that followed, Noyes, with hard work, talent, and vision, would make the *Star* the preeminent newspaper in Washington and one of the most successful newspapers in the country by the start of the twentieth century. Noyes would also become a prominent leader and philanthropist in Washington and would establish the Noyes family publishing dynasty that lasted almost a century. Noyes's rise to prominence is a classic American rags-to-riches nineteenth-century story.

Crosby Noyes began his life as a farm boy in Minot, Maine, in 1825 in a hilly, cold country in the southwest part of the state surrounded by mountains through which the Little Androscoggin River ran. Noyes was born to Miranda Noyes and a Quaker farmer, Samuel Hilborn, to whom she was not married, according to family lore. Miranda's father, Nicholas Noyes, and stepmother Susan sent twenty-three-year-old Miranda to work as a live-in housekeeper and nanny of three children for Susan's recently widowed brother-in-law Hilborn at his nearby farm. Miranda returned relatively soon to her father's farm feeling ill, and a local doctor diagnosed her as pregnant. Nicholas Noyes was reported to have sought revenge or marriage for Miranda at gunpoint. Instead, Nicholas's eldest daughter, Nancy, at age twenty-nine, stepped in to work in her sister's place, and several months later Hilborn married Nancy when she was four months pregnant. In 1835 when Crosby was ten years old, Miranda's stepmother Susan maneuvered her husband to banish Miranda from their household. Miranda first worked as a housekeeper in her uncle Peter Noyes's house and then eventually moved to Lewiston, where she earned her living as a nurse and housekeeper. Eventually Miranda married twice. Noyes, as an illegitimate heir in his grandfather Nicholas's household with three adult male legitimate sons, had few prospects. A few years after Crosby's mother was forced to leave her father's home, Crosby moved to Lewiston to be near her and find employment. With wages Noyes earned at the Lewiston cotton mill and a harness shop, he paid for his education at the Lewiston Falls Academy. Noyes also taught school for a short time at the same academy he attended. One month before Noyes's fifteenth birthday, he self-published a weekly he called *The Minot Notion*, which didn't last long. Noyes continued to write, and eventually his humorous sketches about work in the Lewiston mill and Maine life were published in the *Boston Yankee Blade, Harp of a Thousand Strings* (a literary magazine), and other New England newspapers that picked up the original stories. Noyes was not fond of the cold winters in Maine, and when Alonzo Garcelon, publisher of the *Lewiston Journal* (later governor of Maine), promised Noyes a dollar for each letter sent from Washington, he decided to move to Washington to take his chances as a newspaper correspondent. With few savings and slim prospects for a reliable or substantial income, at age twenty-two Noyes made his way to Washington.[3]

Noyes traveled from Lewiston to Boston then onto New York and Philadelphia by train, but upon arriving in Baltimore his money ran out, so he proceeded on foot without an overcoat on a cold December evening in 1847. In Beltsville, Maryland, just outside of Washington, he caught a ride on the back of a wagon with a farmer taking his produce to the Marsh Market at Seventh and Pennsylvania Avenue. Noyes remembers the ride as welcomed but still pretty dismal as the evening wore on and the weather turned colder. To make matters worse, the trip was made even longer and colder by his host, who stopped at every grog shop on the way to market. The farmer asked Noyes to join him in a drink which, according to Noyes, was a mortal sin to refuse. Noyes managed to maintain his sobriety by emptying his spirits surreptitiously in a spittoon while the driver grew more inebriated and "more stupid," according to Noyes. After a long trip, they arrived at midnight to hear the New Year's bells welcoming in 1848. Noyes's first impression of the city was of a "set of tumble-down sheds, moss covered, doorless and the lodging place for tramps and vagrants" that served as a market, with a "a filthy old canal, the city cesspool, and receptacle for all the offal of the city" behind it. He spent the night in a room above a tavern on 7th Street opposite a lane called Cattail Row. Noyes found permanent lodging the next day at 3rd Street and Pennsylvania Avenue at Michael McDermott's boarding house. McDermott's was a rowdy place that housed workmen who bantered constantly at mealtimes and made constant demands upon the black slave cook named Sally, whom retorted back in kind with her own "sauciness," Noyes later wrote. Noyes looked for work immediately and found his first job at Joseph Shillington's bookstore on Pennsylvania Avenue at 4½ Street. Shillington was a distributor for the *Baltimore Sun*, so Noyes worked both as a clerk in the store and route agent for the *Sun*. Shillington later admitted he only intended to give Noyes a temporary job because the gaunt young man to him looked too frail and sickly to last more than a few weeks. The slim Noyes was sturdier than he looked, and he worked a number of odd jobs to make ends meet, including as a theater usher at night.[4]

Noyes earned a solid reputation in newspaper circles during his first years in the capital city as a correspondent for the *Lewiston Journal*, the *Yankee Blade*, *New York Spirit of the Times*, and the *Philadelphia Saturday Evening Post*. Noyes also freelanced for the *Washington News* in the spring of 1848 not long after arriving in D.C. When Wallach hired Noyes in 1853 as a route carrier, the once sickly young man was still thin, but he now sported a full, clipped beard and short hair, a fashionable but modest suit of clothes and cape, and the gaze from his clear but piercing eyes and comely face was direct and steady. Noyes became part of a dozen or so correspondents in that era who, seated on a single row of stools in the Capitol's galleries, reported on the slavery debates in Congress. Noyes befriended men like Francis J. Grund of the *Philadelphia Ledger*, whom he described as "stout, oily, smiling, vivacious," unlike Eliab Klingman of the *Baltimore Sun*, who was a quiet and serious, tall, spare man, or Dr. Wallis, who wrote for James Gordon Bennett's famous *New York Herald* and whom Noyes judged "a hustler." In 1855 as an unattached bachelor, Noyes tramped by foot through Europe for three months and reported on his travels in the *Portland* (Maine) *Transcript*. When he returned in late 1855, Wallach hired him as a full-time reporter.[5]

In those very early years, Noyes on many days ran the *Star* single-handedly as editor, reporter, printer, and manager. Wallach, reporter Bill Tucker, and Noyes constituted the full-time reportorial and editorial staff. When Wallach was away, Noyes put out editions alone with Tucker, who was frequently not much assistance because he suffered epileptic fits at the "most inopportune moments," according to Noyes. Noyes's work-day generally started at 7 am and often ended at midnight. He began at the Central Guard House (jail) reporting on crime and arrests the night before, then later the executive departments, Congress, community meetings in the evening, and social news and visitors to the capital at night. During the day he clipped reports from the local morning press and other papers for "The Spirit of the Press" section and often wrote the editorial as well. Noyes supervised layout, proofread, and made sure the sometimes drunken pressman printed the paper. He was paid $12 per week for seven fifteen-to-eighteen-hour days. Noyes characterized Wallach as a "wonderful newsgatherer" but "exceedingly parsimonious in regard to expenditures for the paper," and Wallach eventually became less and less interested in the newspaper business than in running his farms and plantations in Virginia and Maryland. Doug Wallach hired more staff as circulation increased, but he still refused to pay adequate salaries to hire and keep a larger, more capable staff. Talented reporters who wrote briefly for the *Star* but did not stay included Ben Perley Poore, who had an illustrious association with the *Boston Journal*; James O. Clephane, who helped develop the Merganthaler press; and L. A. Gobright, who had a long career with the Associated Press. After a year at the *Star*, Noyes earned enough of a stable and sufficient income to wed his childhood sweetheart, Miss Elizabeth S. Williams, daughter of the Reverend and Mrs. Thomas Williams of Lewiston, Maine.[6]

By the opening of the Civil War, Washington was no longer a south-ern backwater capital, but was on the verge of becoming the epicenter of events and decisions that would change and shape the future of the nation. The number of reporters populating the Congressional Gallery and Newspaper Row increased from barely a dozen when the *Star* was founded to more than sixty-three in the years just before the Civil War. They included historic journalists like Joseph Medill of the *Chicago Press and Tribune*, Whitelaw Reid of the *New York Tribune*, L. A. Gobright of the

Associated Press, C. G. Halpine of the *New York Times*, D. W. Bartlett of the *Springfield Republican*, and Crosby Noyes of the *Evening Star*. William Wallach was a southerner whose family had strong ties to the Democratic Party, but he understood that undue support and influence from political parties had undone many of Washington's local newspapers, so he bristled when a reader accused the *Star* of speaking for the Democratic administration of Franklin Pierce. Wallach responded, "We treat the present national administration just as we would feel it to be our duty to treat it were the Whigs in power." The *Star*'s November 7, 1860, editorial read, "We are forced to the lamentable conclusion that Abraham Lincoln has been elected President . . . we see in the immediate future only gloom and doom." Wallach as publisher made no attempt to hide his displeasure with Lincoln's election nor his affection for the Democratic Party in the *Star*'s opinion columns. During the presidential campaign of 1860, the *Star* had supported Stephen Douglas's election and warned if Lincoln and his campaign for containing slavery in the South was victorious, southern states would split from the Union and bring the country to war. As the paper predicted, in December South Carolina seceded from the Union with other southern states after Lincoln's election. As the threat of war hovered in March 1861, Lincoln traveled east and then south to Washington for his inaugural in disguise to avoid assassination attempts. Washington, sandwiched between Maryland and Virginia, had its share of Confederate sympathizers in the streets, taverns, hotel lobbies, private homes, halls of Congress, and Newspaper Row of Washington. Before the Civil War the city of Washington was a small town heavily controlled by the money power of wealthy southern property owners in the Democratic Party. Lincoln attracted "Western men" and other strangers new to the city, wrote a reporter for the *Star* on the eve of Lincoln's inauguration. "The hack drivers and porters . . . complain that the new-comers are mainly of the carpet-bag order. . . . and exhibit mental throes of the deepest on being called on to disburse a quarter dollar" wrote a *Star* reporter of Lincoln's supporters. The Willard, Brown, and Kirkwood hotels as well as smaller hotels and boarding houses ordered extra mattresses to allow the overflow of guests to sleep on any spare floor space they could find to accommodate the out-of-town guests for the inauguration. Lincoln, who was staying at the Willard, emerged from the lower 14th Street exit before the inaugural parade and was greeted by a swelling and surging crowd. Lincoln rode in an open carriage despite the number of soldiers and mounted police guarding him from rooftops and on foot along the parade route of Pennsylvania Avenue. Vice-president-elect Buchanan took no chances and rode in a closed carriage. Lincoln delivered his inaugural speech and handed a draft with handwritten corrections to Crosby Noyes. The *Star* published the full text of Lincoln's first inaugural address and six columns describing the inaugural proceedings. The paper boasted that crowds jammed its doorways waiting for a copy of the inaugural edition until individuals were trapped and the glass shattered, releasing the crowd into its offices to find copies.[7]

On the morning of April 12, 1861, guns manned by Confederate forces at Fort Moultrie opened fire on Union forces at Fort Sumter in Charleston Harbor. The *Star*'s afternoon edition said no news of the battle had arrived by seaboard telegraph, but it expected "within 24 hours we shall have news of the commencement in Charleston Harbor of the direst calamity—civil war—that ever the world experienced." The next day the *Star* reported that news of hostilities in Charleston had reached the city, and "it is safe to say that the people of this city have never been brought up to such a feverish statement of excitement by any event with the memory of this generation." On April 16, 1861, a *Star* editorial scolded, "Nothing could more strongly illustrate the madness which rules the hour than the fact that a considerable number of citizens of Washington, some of them holders of real property, are rabid Secessionists. . . . who seek not only the ruin of their country, but also their individual ruin." Washington was militarily fortified and protected from attack throughout the Civil War, but open hostility among residents with divided loyalties and anxiety over the future of the city and the country in the first year of the war was palpable. As the seat of federal power, no other city had more intrigue behind closed doors, angry debates on city streets, and powerful people in government responsible for the course of the war. The next four years would only intensify the thirst for war news. The *Star* had the largest circulation and was the most popular of the two dailies in the city at the time. The *National Intelligencer* would last only to the end of the Civil War. For two weeks at the start of the Civil War, the *Star* was cut off from deliveries of newsprint from the North and published only two pages on half sheets. When the shortage ended, it published two daily editions with frequent extras for the remainder of the war using a staff of four reporters, stringers for various newspapers on the battlefield, the telegraph, and wire news services.

The next big battle of the Civil War the *Star* covered was much closer to home. The First Battle of Bull Run raged from July 16 to 22, 1861, across the Potomac a few miles from the capital. The windows of the *Star*'s office rattled from the cannons and gunfire from the battle as Crosby Noyes, Doug Wallach, James Croggon, and Billy Tucker compiled the July 16, 1861, edition. In the *Star*'s July 20 first edition a special correspondent to the *Star* predicted a Union victory after the enemy's batteries were captured the previous night at Bull Run, but by the second edition the reporter was vilifying General Tyler and Richardson under General Irvin McDowell's command for what appeared to be a Union retreat. Congressmen and their wives as well as ordinary Washington residents took picnic baskets in a celebratory mood to view the battle in Virginia, expecting a spectacle of certain victory. In the end, there was no triumph, but instead a humiliating retreat to Washington over Long Bridge packed with carts of dead and wounded soldiers, and scores of bedraggled Union troops in disarray returning in defeat on July 21. The next day's edition described in long detail the chaotic scene of the previous day sent by a correspondent on the battlefield between Fairfax Court House and Centreville, Virginia, who heard or witnessed conflicting accounts. The reporter wrote, "We began to meet carriage loads of civilians, newspaper men, Congressmen, just from the scene of conflict who in elated terms shouted . . . the news of glorious victory as they whirled past on their way to Washington. . . . Then the perturbed faces of some sweaty newcomers from nearer the scene of conflict showed that something was going wrong." When the correspondent saw "squads of dust begrimed, exhausted, spiritless looking soldiers" overflowing into the fields on their way to Fairfax Court House, he realized it was a stampede of federal troops from the battle. Private carriages with civilians were overturned in the retreat to Washington, and in many instances panicked teamsters cut lose horses when their movement was blocked and drove on. The next day the *Star* had to print a number of apologies for, among other things, erroneously killing off a "Senator Foster" and mistakenly charging regiments, brigades, and officers with bad judgment and cowardice in its rush to judgment.

During the Civil War, Noyes and Wallach developed relationships with top military and political leaders who could help them report the war, including Secretary of War Edwin Stanton and Secretary of State William Seward. Crosby Noyes's descendants have claimed that Secretary Stanton was a mentor to Noyes on the intricacies of Washington politics, and during the Civil War Stanton sometimes shared strategic information with Noyes few reporters received. Secretary Seward sometimes dined with Wallach at the publisher's country farm and valued his support and insight into southern sympathies. As the war progressed, Stanton wrested exclusive control over the telegraph lines and warned newspapers if they published military information not authorized by the War Department, they would lose the privilege of receiving telegraphic news. In the days leading up to the battle at Gettysburg, the War Department, General Hooker, and Stanton were hypervigilant that intelligence about Union troop movements through Pennsylvania, Maryland, and Virginia not pass into Confederate hands. Despite Wallach's friendship with Seward, he couldn't avoid the wrath of Stanton when he was arrested after publishing a letter that gave the whereabouts of various regiments of the Army of the Potomac in June 1863. It is unclear what happened after Wallach's arrest, but the *Star* never stopped receiving telegraphic news.[8]

Despite Wallach's politics and initial reservations about Lincoln as a southern Democrat, he produced an editorial page during the Civil War that reflected a balance between Noyes's admiration for Lincoln's policies and Wallach's commitment to reunifying the country. Noyes with his New England roots had always been cool to local Democratic Party politics. When the Republican Party held secret meetings in the mid-1850s at the antislavery newspaper the *New Era*, Noyes attended those meetings and became a convert. Noyes even ran for office on the Unconditional Union Party ticket (a fusion party of the Republicans), serving from 1863 to 1864 during the Civil War as alderman from Washington's Ward Seven. Even Wallach's brother, Richard, adapted to the city's new political landscape, split from the Democratic Party, and won as an independent mayoral candidate, serving two terms from 1861 to 1867 with a number of Republicans, including future *Star* owners Noyes and Alexander Shepherd, later territorial governor of the district. By the end of the war, the *Star* was solidly behind Lincoln, who had steadfastly led the nation through a horrific war that restored the union and ended slavery. The *Star*'s March 4, 1865, edition expresses a very different view of Lincoln's second inaugural than the gloom and doom expressed before his first term: "Since the inauguration of George Washington no similar event has so stirred the popular heart of the country . . . the people with comparatively few exceptions emphatically approve the policy and measures by which he is suppressing the rebellion, and have universal confidence in his energy, capacity, and patriotism." Crowds had swelled all morning around the Capitol on muddy streets in a steady rain shadowed by clouds waiting for Lincoln to appear. Just as Lincoln stepped out through the columns of the east portico with his entourage, the sun broke through, and when the president "in his unassuming way came into full view of the throng, a loud, long and enthusiastic cheer welcomed him, with many repetitions, that seemed as though they would not be checked . . . finally the tumult subsided . . . and in the universal hush, the President addressed the people." Lincoln's call for "us to strive on to finish the work we are in; to bind up the nation's wounds; . . . to do all which may achieve and cherish a just and lasting peace" was not to be. On the same day Washington celebrated Lincoln's second inaugural, the city's roads and bridges were heavily guarded to protect against radical southern sympathizers rumored to be hell-bent on violent retaliation against the Lincoln administration. In barely a month, Lincoln and his dreams for the nation's future were gone forever.

At 1:30 pm on April 15, 1865, the first of five *Star* editions reported the shooting of President Lincoln the previous evening at Ford's Theater and the text of a letter signed by Secretary of War Stanton, predicting the president would probably not live through the night. An eyewitness who was at Ford's Theater wrote in the *Star* what he saw and heard that night:

> In the third act, and only a single performer on stage, I heard a pistol which appeared to be coming from the direction of the stage, to the right of the audience . . . from the range of the theatrical wardrobe room . . . and therefore attracted no particular attention until a person emerged from the State stage box who stepped upon that portion of the balcony rail covered by the blue portion of the American flag with which the box front was draped. On mounting to the front of the box he raised his right hand, flourished a dagger in theatrical style, and in the same style uttering the words "Sie simper tyrannis." At the same time he sprang to the stage and on striking it seemed a little staggered by the concussion but rising almost instantly rose to his feet and ran across the stage to the prompt side . . . and disappeared.

After the assassin's disappearance, a bewildered crowd was quiet for a moment until Mrs. Lincoln's "piercing screams" were heard and then an unknown voice announced that the president had been shot. Some people began to move toward the president's box to offer help. An actress from the stage called for the pursuit of the assassin and help for the president. The reporter heard someone ask for brandy for the president, and then everyone was directed to leave "and the audience in compliance surged first towards the door and then in a new passion of grief, horror, and terrible white-face wrath, back towards the stage." In the *Star*'s second edition, Stanton's letter to General Grant named John Wilkes Booth as the president's assassin and reported Booth's horse had been found on a road near Washington. For the next twelve days the *Star* reported Booth's pursuit, Jefferson Davis' escape west, a letter purportedly written by Booth, arrests of suspected co-conspirators in the city, as well as the continued surrender of Confederate troops in the South and West. On April 27 the *Star*'s bold headline heralded "THRILLING NEWS!!" that Booth and his co-conspirator David Herold were "pursued yesterday morning to Garrett's farm, near Port Royal, Virginia, on the Rappahannock" River and when Booth attempted to escape from the barn where he was hiding, he "was shot through the head and killed, lingering about three hours." Herold was captured alive. The Civil War had ended, and the country mourned the loss of President Lincoln. The Union was restored, chattel slavery abolished, and the city of Washington transformed. The city's most popular local newspaper would be transformed too after the war ended.

Wallach was tired of running the newspaper and worried that a possible economic panic after the war ended might drastically reduce advertising to support the paper. One spring evening in 1867, Noyes found a note on his desk from Wallach, with the first option to buy the paper for $100,000 within forty-eight hours. Wallach asked Noyes to "please have George [possibly a servant] place your reply on my mantelpiece by Monday night . . . so that I may know your determination on my arrival here." Over the next two days, Noyes prodded newspapermen that might have the cash and ambition to own a newspaper as well as his friend and successful local Washington politician and businessman Alexander Shepherd to invest in the *Star*. Noyes succeeded in convincing Shepherd and three other investors—Samuel H. Kauffmann, former Ohio newspaper publisher; George W. Adams, respected Washington correspondent for the *New York World*; and Clarence Baker. As confirmed in a letter from Noyes to Wallach dated October 7, 1867, Noyes agreed to purchase a press and other property worth only about $15,000 for $100,000, and on October 9, Wallach agreed to the terms of the letter. The investment was an expensive and risky proposition with the *Star*'s subscription base hovering around seven thousand. At the first board meeting Noyes was chosen editor and Samuel Kauffmann president. Kauffmann came to Washington in 1861 during the Civil War after Treasury Secretary Salmon Chase appointed him to a position at the Treasury Department. Not long after investing, Samuel Kauffmann wrote his youngest brother, Benjamin, in Peru about his hopes and reservations, explaining that his "share ought to yield from $5 to $6,000 per year" but "still, we may 'slip up,' as all human calculations and expectations are likely to fail" still if the owners stick with their "idea . . . to run it as a non-partisan, independent business paper . . . with its present patronage and prestige, it can hardly fail to be successful." Kauffmann's primary role at the *Star* was to build a large advertising base "to support the *Star*'s editorial work."[9]

A month after the new owners took charge, new subscribers increased by nearly 1,100. The new owners published under the name Noyes, Baker & Co., until October 13, 1868, when Congress chartered the *Star* under a special act of Congress. Two years after Baker invested in the *Star* a $9,000 shortfall appeared on the books, forcing Baker as treasurer to sell his shares. In 1874, Shepherd sold his shares too after becoming entangled in a political scandal during his term as Washington's territorial governor, leaving Noyes, Kauffmann, and Adams as the three remaining owners. George Adams's only role during his lifetime was serving as the *Star*'s president for seven years, from 1879 to 1886. Noyes, Kauffmann, and Adams divided their shares of stock in the *Star* equally into thirds. Kauffmann and Noyes's descendants would own and take primary responsibility for running the *Star* for more than one hundred years. By 1877 the *Star*'s circulation had increased to 17,500, and two years later, the paper purchased one of the city's first telephone exchanges with special lines to the office of the Capitol and City Hall. Copy boys continued to bring stories from City Hall by bicycle to the newsroom at first, but eventually reporters started calling in stories that dictationists typed on the latest time-saving invention—the typewriter. In 1877 when Crosby Noyes's oldest son, Theodore Noyes, began working at the paper, he claimed "the over-grown rowdy newsboys" that gathered in the back alley full of sewer rats leading to the composing room were held in check by men in the business office with "a long whip and firearms." In the nineteenth century, newsboys that sold *Star* editions on Washington streets were a colorful lot of street urchins turned entrepreneurs essential to the newspaper's profitability. During the Civil War, hundreds of only white newsboys hawked the many daily *Star* editions of breaking war news to the soldiers in town. By the end of the nineteenth century, a mix of black and white adolescents gathered around noon in a space provided on 11th Street to buy their papers for two cents and sell them for five cents, a goodly profit. Sometimes the boys would sing in harmony to attract buyers.[10]

Harry Godwin was named the *Star*'s first city editor in 1881. "Dear old Godwin," as he was affectionately known by staff, sported a fetching walrus mustache and was a "clumsy, untidy man but a veritable wizard for finding the inner facts of a news story, a marvelous reporter," a young *Star* protégé recalled. Tom Noyes, Crosby's youngest son, became city editor in 1898. "Uncle Billy Collins," who was a young printer's apprentice when the first edition was printed, by the 1890s was an old man with a craggy, gray beard extending down to midchest. Uncle Billy was a devoted and indefatigable employee who continued to edit copy until his death in 1891.William B. Bryan joined the staff in the 1880s and became a prolific editorial writer with a special interest and expertise in district affairs. In 1916 Bryan resigned from the *Star* to devote full time to writing the first authoritative history of the District of Columbia, a two-volume, 1,400-page tome. In 1897 the *Star* hired Philander Johnson as a humorist to write its new "Shooting Star" column full of witty stories, poems, and anecdotes. Gideon Lyon, who came in the 1880s, would cover the story of Coxey's army of unemployed men that staged the first protest march in Washington in 1894. Clifford Berryman began his stellar career with the *Star* in January 1907 as its first cartoonist. For nearly forty years Berryman's prize-winning, memorable cartoons appeared on the paper's front page. Noyes and Kauffmann realized the importance of keeping a quality editorial and production staff, so they paid some of the highest salaries in the business. In 1890 a *Star* Dining Club was initiated by management for monthly gatherings of *Star* employees to celebrate anniversaries, retirements, farewells, and other accomplishments. According to Rudolph Kauffmann, however, one pleasure his grandfather, Sam Kauffmann, and his partner Crosby Noyes never allowed employees to do was smoke at the *Star*'s offices, although most sneaked a cigarette when the bosses were not around.[11]

In the 1870s, Walt Whitman, as a former newsman himself, was a frequent visitor to the *Star*'s newsroom and was well liked by almost everyone, including his old friend Sam Kauffmann, with whom he had worked at the Treasury Department, and fellow newspaperman Crosby Noyes. Whitman used the *Star* to print his poems or to promote his latest book or himself. The *Star*, realizing the increasing importance of Washington's social scene to its readers, hired freelance women writers in the late 1880s to thoroughly cover it. Sketches and long, gossipy news of the first wedding in the White House of Grover Cleveland and Francis Folsom appeared in its June 2, 1886, edition. Both the killer flood in Johnstown and the simultaneous rampant flooding of the Potomac in Washington streets were reported with graphic photographs in the June 1, 1889, edition. The *Star* sent reporters for the first time outside the United States to Cuba during the Spanish–American War after the sinking of the *Maine* in Havana Harbor. *Star* reporter George Harries covered the massacre at Wounded Knee, sending dispatches from Omaha and Chicago in 1890 and the Homestead strike from Homestead, Pennsylvania, in 1892. Under Noyes and Kauffmann, the newspaper in the last two decades of the nineteenth century editorially stepped up its campaigns for civic improvement. As progressive Republicans, Crosby Noyes and his son Theodore as editors supported business interests and philanthropy and prodded the federal government to provide its fair share of money to improve the capital city's infrastructure.[12]

Flush with success and cash, Noyes and Kauffmann in 1881 moved the *Star*'s operations across Pennsylvania Avenue on the northwest corner at 11th Street to a marble-front, four-story building that had served as a drugstore and a candy store. They immediately began making plans to remodel the building. The remodeling included adding cherry rails and balustrades with a frescoed stairway in the rear leading to the editorial and telegraph departments. The floors were covered with black-and-white dappled marble, and the fourth-floor composing room had sixteen-foot ceilings. In just a few years, the building was no longer large enough to hold the printing presses and staff required to meet the demand of the expanded edition and circulation, so the owners secured a lease on a lot just north of the current building on 11th Street, and by 1889 they had built an annex for the composing room, advertising, and business operations. On April 13, 1892, a fire occurred in the boiler room of the main building, which forced the staff to move print operations temporarily to a neighborhood print shop. The *Star*, however, never missed an edition.[13]

During the 1890s, the owners purchased additional buildings fronting on Pennsylvania Avenue to accommodate the paper's growth, but by the end of the decade, they realized the hodgepodge of buildings and annexes were inadequate. In 1899 Frank Noyes, Crosby Noyes's second

Star **delivery truck parked in front of the Evening Star Building's 11th Street entrance, 1913. Reprinted with permission of the D.C. Public Library,** *Star* **Collection,** © *Washington Post.*

son and business manager at the time, personally oversaw plans for the construction of what he hoped would be a stunning, ten-story modern building overlooking Pennsylvania Avenue at 11th Street in the heart of the city. The Evening Star Building opened to the public on June 30, 1900. The white marble, ten-story Beaux-Arts building's exterior was adorned with carved scrollwork and ornamental friezes. The hallmark of its interior design were the murals designed by Frederick Dielman, who at the time was president of the American Academy of Design and was the famous designer of the classical murals at the Library of Congress. Dielman's murals, which spanned the walls of the first-floor entry hall and the public business office, were drawn with classical motifs meant to represent the best ideals of the newspaper business—commerce, advertising, the dissemination of knowledge, justice, art, history, literature, and the printing trades. The Evening Star Building would become a historic landmark in Washington and a testament to the *Star*'s success as it opened at the dawning of the twentieth century.[14]

The *Star* was born in the nineteenth century, and its character and successes were shaped for years to come by its first fifty years. By 1900, the *Star* had built and moved into an impressive new Beaux-Arts building on Pennsylvania Avenue as a symbol of its success and powerful presence in the city. In 1902 the *Star* celebrated its fiftieth anniversary and enormous successes. By 1908 Crosby Noyes and Samuel Kauffmann, who were largely responsible for the rise of the *Star* to prominence in its first fifty years, were both dead. Crosby Noyes's sons, Theodore Noyes and Thomas C. Noyes, were editor and city editor, respectively, and Samuel H. Kauffmann's sons, Rudolph Kauffmann and Victor Kauffmann, were managing editor and literary editor. Like other newspapers, the *Star* benefited from the tragic and transformative news stories of the nineteenth century generated by a horrific civil war, fiery populist politics, a booming Industrial Revolution, scientific breakthroughs, and compelling historical figures. By the start of the twentieth century, the *Star*'s popularity with readers was also to a great degree the result of its consistent dedication to reporting local news and its ability to exert a powerful influence on the city both for good or ill. By the twentieth century, no one would disagree that the *Star* was a solid Washington institution, a community builder, nationally respected, and a bright star in its hometown, America's capital city. The future looked bright.

2

The Hometown *Star*

By the start of the twentieth century, Washingtonians most often reached for a copy of the *Evening Star* when they wanted to read about news of the latest shenanigans of local politicians that squared off in rough political contests commonplace in American cities. The *Star* was also the paper most city dwellers read to find out about local amusements, society, sports, crime, and civic meetings. By 1900 the *Star* was the most successful newspaper in the District of Columbia primarily because as founder Joseph Tate promised in the first edition, it remained "devoted in an especial manner to the local interests of the beautiful city of Washington." The *Star*'s early owners and editors, however, sometimes found it hard to remain true to Tate's other admonition to be "free from party trammels and sectarian influences." Tate's experiences with newspapers had taught him that partisanship and an inability to "preserve strict neutrality" had doomed many newspapers to failure. By nineteenth-century standards, the *Star* was certainly independent and its news columns were generally objective, but as Democrat William Wallach, its second owner, once quipped, any newspaper he owned would never be "neutral" just "independent . . . neutrality implies being undecided" and "no one can really fancy that it is in our nature to fail to have an emphatic opinion upon every subject worth forming an opinion about."[1]

Crosby Noyes trumpeted balance and fairness, but as part owner and editor, he sometimes strayed from those principles. Noyes was a progressive Republican that saw the paper he owned as a vehicle for promoting his political views, especially in local affairs. Noyes and successful businessman-turned-politician Alexander "Boss" Shepherd were good friends and political allies by the end of the Civil War. They both served as city alderman and became active in the local Republican Party. Shepherd was one of three men Noyes persuaded to help him purchase the *Star*, and both men were never shy about using the paper to promote their political interests and aspirations for the city. The imposing, gregarious, 225-pound Shepherd, who stood over six-feet tall and spoke with a booming, sonorous voice, was a natural politician. In February 1871 President Ulysses S. Grant signed legislation establishing a territorial government for the District of Columbia and appointed fellow Republicans Henry D. Cooke, brother of successful financier Jay Cooke, its governor and Shepherd its vice president of the Board of Public Works. Grant also appointed a majority of Republicans to seats in city government. Shepherd, as de facto head of the Board of Public Works, proposed an ambitious plan for infrastructure improvements sorely needed in the city. The Republican Party majority in city government angered wealthy Democrats who were now out of power. Democrats, who were large property owners, bitterly opposed not only the racial and political changes Republicans were making in the city but also the risky loans and property tax increases proposed to finance infrastructure improvements. Democrats obtained an injunction to stop Shepherd's plan for financing the improvements and at the same time financed the *Citizen*, a newspaper to publicize their views. The *Star* in its news columns called for an immediate election to vote on a referendum supporting Shepherd's plan, and when the election was held the referendum passed. The *Star* crowed at the time that the "old anti-improvement fossils . . . planked down their money to start" the *Citizen*, a Democratic Party–backed newspaper, but despite efforts to "run the *Star* off the track, demolish the Board of Public Works, and defeat the four million loan [it] has gone dead." The *Citizen* lasted barely a month. More than a century after Shepherd headed the district's territorial government, *Star* reporter Tom Dowling wrote that Shepherd was "an absolute dictator" who held the "Republican Press in his hip pocket" and used the *Star* as "his direct publicity organ." Dowling gleaned from the historical record that the *Star* and *National Republican*, the two Republican-leaning newspapers at the time, dominated the market and were so closely aligned they sometimes shared stories and reporters.[2]

Shepherd's unbridled use of his power to make needed improvements, however, started to dismay city residents beyond his natural opponents. Board officials undertook the dismantling of the unsightly Northern Liberties Market near Mount Vernon Square by making an unannounced raid, which put scores of merchants out of business and a young boy dead during the melee. Residents and officials also awoke one morning to find the tracks of the Alexandria and Washington Railroad gone after workmen hired by the board had worked all night to remove them. In January

1872, Democrats sent a memorial to Congress charging the board with fa-
voritism and corruption, but Congress found no proof of wrongdoing. An
economic panic hit the nation in 1873 and dried up Shepherd's financial
backing. One year later, Congress investigated Shepherd again and found
no evidence of corruption but concluded the board had grossly misman-
aged and overspent funds. Congress decided to curb Shepherd's un-
checked power and recommended a temporary three-commissioner form
of government for the District of Columbia. In 1877 Congress passed the
Organic Act, which made the three-commissioner form of government
permanent and established a fifty-fifty formula with half of the city's annual budget coming from a federal appropriation and the remainder from
local tax revenues.[3]

Barely two decades after locally elected government ended in Washington, Crosby Noyes's oldest son, Theodore, ironically became a strong
and vocal supporter of the appointed three-commissioner form of government in the *Star*. The elder Noyes had largely retired from the *Star*'s
day-to-day operations by the 1890s and had relinquished most editorial
functions to Theodore. Crosby Noyes never expressed enthusiasm for
the three-commissioner form of government, but he never challenged it
much either or acknowledged his friend Shepherd's part in causing it.
The younger Noyes never practiced the bare-knuckled politics his father
and Shepherd did, but instead relished the power he and other local elites
had to influence an appointed local government and champion what
they judged was in their paternalistic view best for the city. Noyes attrib-
uted the appalling financial condition and political corruptness in many
American cities at the time "in the main to unlimited suffrage which has
given to non-taxpaying, irresponsible voters the power to expend, ex-
travagantly and corruptly" taxpayer's money. To Noyes the district had
a less corrupt and more efficient government than most American cities
because it did not have a locally elected government. Until the late 1960s,
generations of Noyeses would argue that congressional representation for
the district was more desirable than local suffrage on the *Star*'s opinion
page and its broadcast TV and radio stations. Noyes and Kauffmann family members used their powerful leadership roles on the Board of Trade
and other influential civic organizations to promote their views as well
for decades.[4]

Theodore Noyes at age fifty became editor after his father died in 1908
and gladly assumed the role of an influential civic leader in Washington.
Even before becoming editor, Theodore used the *Star* to champion many
local improvements. Noyes convinced Congress to pass legislation to
fund a free public library system in 1896 and helped persuade Andrew
Carnegie to donate $250,000 to fund the construction of a public library
in 1903. Noyes also advocated for the draining of James Creek, reclama-

tion of the Potomac and Anacostia rivers, Rock Creek Park, street paving, increased public school funding, modern jails, better sanitation, and a larger share of federal money for the city. For more than a decade Noyes fought the powerful Baltimore and Ohio and Baltimore and Potomac railroads to eliminate unsightly and dangerous rail crossings that injured or killed hundreds of people. Noyes accused Congress of lavishing "upon the local railroads privileges worth millions of dollars at the expense of the people of the Capital" and disregarding "infractions of the law by the railroads, and the disfigurement of the parks. . . . Might not an energetic spanking by Uncle Sam improve the morals and manners of these spoiled pets of the Nation?"[5] Noyes's complaints proved impotent against the powerful railroads of the era. The passage of time and political will on Capitol Hill were more crucial in winning concessions and the building of Union Station in 1907 than all the *Star*'s editorials and news coverage. In the early twentieth century, Noyes supported the City Beautiful movement in Washington, which helped bring an extension of parks and the development of the mall under the McMillan Plan, and campaigned to remove overhead trolley wires and to construct Memorial Bridge. Theodore Noyes's most ardent campaign, however, was for a constitutional amendment to give the district voting representation in Congress and the right to vote for president.

In 1888 Theodore Noyes published "Some of Washington's Grievances," a treatise that inaugurated hundreds of articles on congressional representation for D.C. In 1914, Noyes wrote a series of articles titled "A Political Square Deal," which argued against the repeal of the Organic Act, and in 1917 he convinced leaders of key civic organizations to establish the Citizens Joint Committee on National Representation to lobby for a constitutional amendment. The *Star* provided office space in the Evening Star Building for the Joint Committee, and its first chair, Jesse Suter, was a *Star* reporter. That same year Noyes also convinced the Board of Trade to establish a National Representation for D.C. Committee with him as chair. Noyes's protests during much of the early twentieth century focused largely on Congress's continual erosion of the Organic Act passed in 1877. In 1919, Congress appointed a Joint Select Committee to seriously consider repealing the Organic Act when local taxes began generating a surplus in the city's coffers. Two years later Congress effectively repealed the act, making a 60:40 ratio the law. From 1929 to 1932 the *Star*-owned radio station WMAL opened its airwaves to the cause of national representation, and in 1933 Suter began a regular Sunday column titled "Civic Problems, Civic Bodies" that discussed D.C. suffrage, national representation, home rule, and fiscal reforms. Congress consistently turned to the Board of Trade and the Joint Committee to recruit witnesses for hearings on proposed legislation for congressional representation and the federal share of the district's budget, but its lobbying proved ineffectual. In 1934 during the Great Depression, Congress reduced the lump sum federal contribution below 40 percent to 7.6 million, 2 million less than a decade earlier. Noyes protested with a series of articles titled "Fiscal Equity for Washington," but it did little good. The lump sum continued to decrease.

Nation editor and left-leaning journalist Oswald Garrison Villard, in his book on popular early twentieth-century newspapers, provides insight into why Theodore Noyes's editorial page failed to inspire the fiscal and political changes he wanted for the city. Noyes is a "fine character," wrote Villard, who is "profoundly interested in all local enterprises" and "is believed to be kindly and fair," but he is "so kindly that the editorial page suffers from it as well . . . which makes it intellectually without distinction and politically worthless." Grover Ayers, executive secretary of the Ten Miles Square Club, was not as balanced in his critique of the *Star* and Noyes. Ayers labeled the *Star*, the Board of Trade, and other Noyes's supporters unceasing arguments in support of national representation as the "noise organization." Ayers complained that Noyes "has plastered the streets of Washington with discontent in order that he might become its political boss," confused the public, and continued "irritating the members of Congress by heckling that body with preposterous demands." Ayers claimed Noyes's campaign for national representation was disingenuousness since one of the core reasons the *Star* opposed local suffrage was the fear that "negroes would dominate if municipal suffrage were granted the Capital City of the Nation." Ayers's claim was a common criticism leveled at opponents of home rule. Theodore Noyes often referred to such claims as the "bogeyman of Negro domination" and countered that the Board of Trade's opposition was present long before blacks were a significant part of the district's population. Benjamin McKelway, who succeeded Noyes as editor and had worked with him for more than forty years, did not believe race was a factor in Noyes's preference for congressional representation over home rule, either. McKelway thought Noyes believed blacks would vote in the same way as whites, divided equally between Democrats and Republicans, if they were given the right to vote.[6]

Katharine Meyer Graham, who witnessed the *Star*'s influence when her father, Eugene Meyer, and husband, Phillip Graham, ran the *Post*, said of the *Star*, "It appeared to have a heavy hand in running the government of Washington, D.C. . . . [and] members of the *Star* families served on some of the most important boards of banks and businesses in the city" during the first half of the twentieth century. The year the Washington Board of Trade elected Theodore Noyes as its president, the *Washington Times*, a newspaper begun by out-of-work trade union printers, quipped, "the brevet mayor of Washington, the chartered interferer with everybody's business but his own . . . will have the power to enforce . . . the thoughts he thinks in the *Star*" on the Board of Trade. Theodore's father, Crosby Noyes, was an original Board of Trade incorporator, and many Noyeses and Kauffmanns would serve as directors and officers over the next seventy years. The Board of Trade even maintained its offices in the Evening Star Building on Pennsylvania Avenue from its founding until 1954. An incident illustrative of how the *Star* used its political connections to promote its business and political interests occurred in 1902 when President Theodore Roosevelt had to appoint a new D.C. commissioner. Teddy Roosevelt wrote Theodore Noyes and his father, Crosby, asking for advice. Father and son agreed that no Democrat should be appointed by a Republican president, but if Roosevelt chose a "so-called Democrat," by custom, he should be "politically colorless and innocuous." They explained to Roosevelt that they were not in favor of either Henry Litchfield West, "a keen-witted newspaper man," nor Henry MacFarland, a Democrat appointed by President McKinley. Theodore Noyes objected to West because he was "not the candidate of business," had no association with the Board of Trade, and is "an ally of the [Maryland Democratic senator Arthur] Gorman Democrats and an injury to Maryland Republicans." Crosby Noyes objected to Albert Ferguson of "the democratic *Post*" as a "slap in the face to the *Star*," and Theodore complained that the *Post*, with its "democratic proclivities," would have better access to news sources than the *Star* if Ferguson was appointed and would "certainly affect the local prestige of the *Star*." Roosevelt appointed West, left McFarland in office, and did not appoint Ferguson.[7]

Katharine Graham in her autobiography harshly assessed many in the Noyes and Kauffmann clans as "snobbish and WASPish" and incapable of doing real newspaper work. She singled out Ben McKelway, however, for praise, calling him an "an outside professional, a nice man with fine credentials." McKelway was a protégé of Theodore Noyes, who chose McKelway to succeed him as editor when he retired rather than any member of the Noyes or Kauffmann families. McKelway was a southern gentlemen and hardworking newspaperman who inspired awe and respect from colleagues inside and outside the *Star* with his commanding presence. One *Star* reporter remembered McKelway even in the heat of Washington summers wore a coat and tie to work, and the famous columnist Mary McGrory insisted she would never call her revered editor anything but "Mr. McKelway." McKelway easily embraced his mentor's political views and inherited and cultivated the same influential and powerful associates who had been close to the Noyeses and Kauffmanns. In the late 1940s McKelway was elected the Board of Trade's president and remained a key leader in the organization for years. Starting in the 1950s, McKelway, through *Star* editorials and congressional testimony, consistently opposed the efforts of emerging liberal interests, including the *Washington Post*, liberal congressional members, and the Home Rule Committee established to give the district home rule. "The central source of opposition to the Home Rule bill is the directorate of the Washington Board of Trade," said Senator Estes Kefauver, chief sponsor of a home rule bill in 1951. "This little oligarchy," Kefauver continued, "has been the invisible government of the District of Columbia for many years," which works "hand and glove with the District Commissioners who do the bidding of the Board of Trade." The *Star* with Ben McKelway as editor called the senator's assertion "a form of shoddy nonsense" for assigning the board "with a sinister and selfish power which does not exist and which the Board has never possessed or sought."[8]

Until the late 1940s, most city residents and leaders were largely content with the commissioner form of government since it brought relative stability and prosperity to the city. Liberals who had come to Washington during the New Deal, however, challenged the city's existing power structure. In the late 1940s, Phil Graham was already advocating for D.C. home rule in the *Post* and was an early member of the Home Rule Committee, which was formed in 1952 as an elite grassroots lobbying organization. The Committee's members included influential progressives like attorney Lloyd Cutler, art collector Duncan Phillips, and Democratic Party activist Daisy Harriman. In 1954 Graham formed the Federal City Council as a counterweight to the powerful Board of Trade. At the same time political influence by liberals rose in the city, the *Star*'s market share of the newspaper business began its steady decline in 1954 after the *Post*'s Phil Graham made a strategically smart business decision to buy the *Times Herald*, the city's only other morning newspaper. The *Star*'s role in shaping city politics diminished slowly in post–World War II Washington. The balance of power and influence in local politics and the newspaper business was shifting and slipping away from the *Star* and its allies. At the same time, radical demographic changes were at work shaping the city's future course.

In 1945 Congress chartered the Redevelopment Land Agency to condemn slum properties and rebuild America's urban landscapes. In the 1950s, white, middle-class city dwellers increasingly moved to suburbia, leaving behind the problems of blighted areas in the city caused by neglect and poverty. This was especially glaring in the district where the worst of the slums were in plain sight of the Capitol building in southwest Washington. In January 1952 the *Washington Post*'s Chalmers Roberts wrote an eighteen-part series titled, "Progress or Decay? Washington Must Choose," as city officials considered redevelopment plans to clean up slums and rebuild low-income housing on a desegregated basis, mostly in southwest D.C. In the early stages of the planning in 1952 the *Star* appealed to investors to fund a "flexible plan that places more emphasis

on slum clearance than on attracting new and larger taxpaying groups."
Over time, however, this sentiment was overshadowed by an enthusiasm
among all of the city's major dailies for costlier plans by developers who
proposed building upscale apartment buildings, a shopping mall, office
buildings, and a new highway. By 1953 the *Star* was supporting a bolder
project proposed by Bush Construction near the Capitol building, which
held out the promise of greater tax revenues than the district had anticipated. In 1954 a crucial Supreme Court decision gave the Redevelopment
Land Agency the power to seize and condemn private properties in order
to clear blighted areas. Urban renewal was a hot news topic and the preferred cure for urban blight in postwar America. Although urban renewal
replaced unsafe and unsightly older structures with modern architecture,
it also often broke apart cohesive neighborhoods, as it did in southwest
Washington when low-income African American, Jewish, and white
families were forced to move to other parts of the city or the suburbs.
Few who reported on urban renewal for Washington's local dailies in its
heyday clearly saw the downsides.[9]

George Beveridge, the *Star*'s expert on metropolitan-wide planning issues, in 1957 won a Pulitzer for a series of articles titled "Metro . . . City
of Tomorrow," which described in detail comprehensive planning for
growth in Washington and its suburbs. The *Star*'s coverage of Virginia
and Maryland news was not a high priority until the late 1940s as *Star*
subscribers increasingly moved from the city to the suburbs. Until then,
the *Star* designated one reporter or hired part-time stringers as needed
to cover significant stories in Maryland and Virginia. In the postwar era,
Star reporter Alex Preston introduced readers to Northern Virginia and
was one of the first of any district newsman to cover the Virginia General
Assembly. Preston was a native Virginian, as were many of the reporters
assigned to the state desk. Ludy (Mary Lou) Werner (later Forbes) was
a teenager when the *Star* hired her as a copy girl during World War II.
In the late 1940s, Werner began covering the legislature, police, courts,
crime, and human interest stories in Virginia. Once as a cub reporter, the
tall, athletic, dark-haired young woman was sent to cover a contentious
meeting in Colonial Beach, Virginia, between Virginia and Maryland
Chesapeake Bay oystermen who had been shooting and killing each
other over trolling rights. When Ludy walked into the rustic hall that
night packed with crusty, fighting-mad men, the space grew dead silent
around her, and the only sound heard was the clicking of her high heels
on the wooden floor as she made a long walk to the front of the room.
Ludy recalled later with a chuckle, "I was very aware that night of being
the only person in the room in a skirt." John Barron, hired by the *Star* in
the late 1950s, worked closely with Ludy Werner on the State Desk. John
and his wife, Patty, moved to Virginia after the *Star* hired him, and the

Barrons and Ludy remained close friends long after Barron left the *Star*. Patty Barron characterized Ludy's style of mentoring as telling her husband as a novice reporter "where to go and how to part his hair." Barron was grateful for the help of the more experienced Werner, but for a man to willingly take orders in the 1950s from a woman was uncommon. In 1959 Werner covered massive resistance to desegregation in Virginia, and that same year at age thirty-two she became assistant state editor and in 1964 state editor. The civil rights movement would be a major news story for more than a decade for reporters like Werner and Barron. Civil rights leaders, including Dr. King, saw district residents' inability to vote for their locally elected officials a civil rights issue because a majority of Washington's population was black by 1960. At the start of the 1960s, a voting right for district residents the *Star* had long championed was realized. The legislation ironically rode on the coattails of the push for greater civil rights throughout the nation.[10]

In 1960 the Twenty-Third Amendment to the Constitution was passed, giving district residents the right to cast votes for the US president. *Star* editor Ben McKelway, through his friends in Congress, editorials, and political maneuvering, played a major role in the passage of the amendment, although no single person could rightfully take credit. McKelway was also helped by the political climate of the era. In 1957 Congress passed the first civil rights legislation since Reconstruction, which ironically opened the door to passage of the Twenty-Third Amendment. In the summer of 1959, Senator Spessard Holland of Florida introduced a constitutional amendment to end the poll tax in federal elections as a way to curb more drastic civil rights legislation. Holland, however, couldn't get it out of the Judiciary Committee for a vote on the Senate floor because the committee chaired by Mississippi senator James Eastland opposed it. Senator Holland told *Star* editor Ben McKelway about his plan to attach the poll tax amendment to legislation that had already passed in the Judiciary Committee in order to thwart Eastland blocking it in committee. Once on the Senate floor, Holland was sure he had the votes to pass it. McKelway suggested an alternative to Holland, which he presented in an August 10, 1959, *Star* editorial titled "Amend the Amendment." McKelway proposed adding the phrase "by reason of residence in the Capital of the United States" to the end of the amendment. The revised amendment would remove not only the poll tax and property requirements already spelled out in the amendment but also residence in the District of Columbia as barriers to voting for president and vice president in federal elections. McKelway then continued to write a series of editorials throughout August to generate support, which he also titled "Amend the Amendment." Grace Bassett was most often the *Star*'s young beat reporter on Capitol Hill covering congressional politics behind the scenes as the amendment moved through Congress. District politics in the 1950s and early 1960s was rapidly changing, and she negotiated well the inner workings of local and national politicians to get the story right. Home rule supporters who were working to move their own bills through Congress were taken by surprise by the proposal, but in the end the amendment was universally supported in the city. Political haggling continued until the House passed a final resolution in June 1960. After the amendment's ratification, the *Star* wrote in a March 30, 1961, editorial: "It is historical fact rather than vain boasting that enables us to say with some assurance that no amendment ever received the tender, watchful care of a newspaper, from the time of its birth and pains of growth to its final admission to the Constitution, that this one received from the *Star*." The *Star*'s rival, the *Post*, strongly

Benjamin McKelway, first *Evening Star* editor not a member of the Noyes or Kauffmann families. McKelway was an influential Washington political elite and a highly respected editor among his colleagues, ca. 1963. Reprinted with permission of the D.C. Public Library, *Star* Collection, © *Washington Post*, Neg. #2496.

supported home rule for the district. *Post* reporter Morton Mintz in a news article—not an editorial—soon after the amendment's ratification wrote he thought supporters proposed the amendment "to serve as a diversionary attack on district home rule" and its passage has "made the nation more aware than ever of the lack of self-government here."[11]

In 1961, political scientist and scholar Martha Derthick, after conducting a study of district politics for Howard University and the Washington Center for Metropolitan Studies, reached a number of revealing conclusions about the influence of the city's top two rival daily newspapers. Derthick confirmed the commonly held notion that the *Star* was far more interested in local affairs than the *Post*, which resulted in greater coverage of local issues and influence in local government. Derthick also weighed in on the perennial criticism leveled at the *Star* and its top leadership for having undue control over local government through its close association with powerful civic associations, especially the Washington Board of Trade. Derthick judged that although the *Star*'s leadership had been cozy with the city's local conservative government for many years, "nobody can be sure that it has been the team's most valuable player." For six decades Theodore Noyes championed the cause of national representation and the presidential vote for D.C. in the columns of the *Star*, yet in his lifetime his crusade bore no real fruit. Despite Noyes's unceasing efforts to win congressional representation for D.C., the goal to this day remains unmet. The posthumous victory of passage of the Twenty-Third Amendment was successfully pushed in the *Star*'s columns by his successor Ben McKelway more than a decade after Theodore Noyes died. In 1964 when McKelway gave the keynote speech at a luncheon commemorating the seventy-fifth anniversary of the Board of Trade, he touted the board's many achievements since its founding but also took the opportunity to answer its growing critics in the liberal establishment. McKelway was unapologetic about the board's political influence and questioned why anyone should complain "if a President of the United States wishes to select a qualified person for Commissioner, well regarded in the community for his ability and trustworthiness rather than for his activities as a political partisan is there anything evil or self-serving" if the board's directors give him names to consider. McKelway told a sympathetic audience that he saw no "unworthy motives" or "sinister" objectives in the board's influence and power in city government, and the board's critics instead simply resented "the use of a power in which they do not participate." McKelway had already retired as the *Star*'s editor one year before he made the keynote speech. As Washington entered the 1960s, the *Star* was still the city's establishment newspaper and a player in local politics, but by decade's end, demographics and new local power brokers meant the *Star*'s fortunes and influence would substantially diminish.[12]

In 1965 Marion Barry Jr. came to Washington to head the D.C. chapter of the Student Non-Violent Coordinating Committee (SNCC). In January 1966 he conducted a successful boycott of D.C. Transit to stop a bus fare hike. Building on this success, a month later Barry, according to a *Star* February 1 editorial, engaged in "a soaring flight into the wild blue yonder" with the announcement of a "massive boycott" and picketing of individual members of the Metropolitan Washington Board of Trade. Barry's primary objective was organizing activists to picket retail stores that refused to post orange stickers supporting his newly formed Free D.C.'s home rule platform. As part of the campaign, Barry directly attacked the Board of Trade. The *Star* defended the board against attacks by Free D.C., SNCC, and the Congress of Racial Equality, editorializing "even a member of the Board of Trade, is entitled to take an uncoerced position on any political question" and "CORE's invasion of last week's Board of Trade dinner," the *Star* wrote, "adds up to a great deal less than a persuasive argument for home rule." Barry's campaign could have been a solid success, but he went too far. Allies like John Diggs, chair of the Merchants and Business Committee of Free D.C., and Joseph Rauh, District Democratic Central Committee, withdrew their support from Free D.C., as did many progressive organizations, upon learning that Barry asked volunteers to pressure merchants for financial donations for Free D.C. or face pickets. *Star* reporters Walter Gold and Sheldon Fahnestock on March 10 attended a press conference called by Barry to announce Free D.C.'s success with H Street, NE merchants and its plans to move on to larger downtown department stores. After the press conference, the reporters decided to talk with local H Street merchants who chose not to display the stickers and faced pickets. Proprietors of larger chain stores simply said they were prohibited from engaging in political activity. One African American businessman who owned an employment service center at 13th and H Streets, NE, told the reporters, "I am not against home rule . . . but I am against this pressure . . . I don't feel that a few people can set my destiny or open or close my business." The young reporters also spotted the sign of one business owner who displayed the sticker supporting home rule but scribbled on it "not the Free D.C. Committee."

When the Free D.C. boycott escalated in March, the Board of Trade struggled to keep a united front because wavering retail merchants fearing the effects of the boycott were ready to jump ship. Harry N. Hirshberg, executive vice president of the Hecht Company and head of its retail bureau, complained to board president Elwood Davis that "our public image on home rule is poor and our Public Relations inept." Hirshberg explained to Davis that most retailers actually did not oppose home rule and wrote, "I state categorically and unequivocally that the Retail Bureau, if asked, to vote would vote overwhelmingly against the present position of the Board on this subject." Hirshberg told Davis for now he had deliberately postponed asking the retail bureau to vote on the matter but suggested the board study the issue carefully and soon because "Rome is burning." The same day Davis received Hirshberg's letter, he ran into the *Star*'s city editor Sid (Sidney) Epstein at a party. Epstein told Davis about published news reports that Isaac Frank of the Jewish Community Council had withdrawn his support of the boycott and that Roy Wilkins of the national NAACP preferred congressional action over the boycott. Epstein counseled Davis not to say anything publicly about the matter in order to avoid bad publicity and thought the board so far had handled the situation well. Retailers eventually came out with a message of neutrality on home rule, stating, "We public service corporations have no corporate view on political issues." The Monday after speaking with Epstein, Washington businessmen Leonard Doggett, William Calomiris, Harry Merrick, Larry Hogan, and Victor Gold met at the board, where Davis shared Epstein's advice. They decided to stop the direct publicity campaign started the previous year. The board chose to publicize popular programs it sponsored, such as job creation and training for city youth rather than continue to work behind closed doors with friends in Congress that opposed home rule. On April 6, 1966, the *Star* and the *Post* published dueling editorials on the issue. The *Star* admitted that some store owners did support home rule but that most large stores had issued a statement of "corporate neutrality" weeks before. The *Star*'s editorial strongly lambasted Free D.C. for using "intimidation tactics" to coerce businesses to publicly support home rule and to close off legitimate political debate with its opponent on the issue as "just plain wrong." The *Post* editorial, "Speaking of Morality," questioned both the morality of the Board of Trade and Free D.C.'s actions, arguing "if it is immoral for the Free D.C. movement to coerce businessmen in supporting home rule, it seems quite as immoral for the Board of Trade to pressure businessmen into opposing home rule."[13]

In 1967 President Lyndon Johnson proposed a reorganization of D.C. local government, which allowed him to appoint one commissioner, a mayor, and a nine-member city council. Congress only had to say no to the legislation, so it passed. The *Star* strongly supported President Johnson's pick of Walter E. Washington for mayor. The *Star*'s top leadership cultivated the new Washington administration. *Star* president Jack Kauffmann lunched regularly with the mayor and was friendly with key leaders in the Washington administration. In addition, managing editor Charlie (Charles B.) Seib and city editor Sid Epstein in 1967 started looking for black reporters to cover the city's new government headed by a black mayor. Seib made the initial call to Paul Delaney, who worked at the *Dayton Daily News*, to come for an interview. Epstein hired Delaney

and two other black reporters, Ernie Holsendolph and Paul Hathaway, in
1967. Delaney grew to admire Epstein as a "great editor . . . terrific newsman who knew his craft well" and "was very supportive" of Delaney's
work. Epstein teamed Delaney with Ron (Ronald) Sarro, who was white
and had covered local city hall news at the *Providence Rhode Island Journal*.
Sarro had also covered the National Crime Commission's investigation of
the Washington Metropolitan Police Department before Delaney arrived.
Sarro understood Epstein and the *Star* were, as he described it, "buddy-
buddy" with the Metropolitan Police Department and the district courts,
but when Sarro began writing bold investigative pieces critical of police
abuse in black neighborhoods and race bias in its ranks and leadership,
Epstein never interfered. Epstein had friends at the Board of Trade and
the police department, and "maybe Sid got grief but he supported me,"
recalled Sarro, and besides, he continued, "it's not like the *Star* invented"
the department's problems. Sarro knew the *Star* was an "establishment
paper," but he also discovered it was "a reporter's paper," which meant
that "most of the ideas or stories were generated by reporters who were
out in the field interacting with people and digging up their own stories." When Sarro was joined by Delaney to cover the Walter Washington
administration, "the *Post* was beating our brains out," Sarro recalled, by
a young Robert Kaiser, who was covering city hall. The *Post* reassigned
Kaiser to another beat, and from then on "it was all mine and Paul's . . .
we started beating the socks off the *Post*," Sarro boasted. Delaney viewed
Kaiser as "an intellect who didn't care that much for local government"
and instead rose through the *Post*'s ranks to become its managing editor in the 1990s. Sarro saw a "revolving door" of *Post* city hall reporters
come and go after Kaiser, including a young Carl Bernstein, who when
caught napping by the *Post*'s city editor, Sarro told him "he always does
that" and Bernstein was reassigned. Delaney recalled that they "worked
the building" every day when it was fairly easy to develop sources and
get the latest news because the new administration was full of people
who were "honest, amateur politicians who wanted to do good . . . were
so friendly and told us everything." Delaney and Sarro took someone at
city hall to lunch almost every day, drank with them after hours, or met
informally with city officials in their offices. As a team they got lots of
exclusives or offered to leak news stories the administration wanted out
often while sitting with the mayor in his city hall office having a drink after a long workday. Sarro and Delaney's journalistic style meshed so well
they often ended each other sentences and others mixed up their names,
calling Paul by Ron's name and vice versa. Sarro and Delaney became
known as the *Star*'s "I Spy Team," borrowing the moniker from a popular
TV drama with the black and white detective team of Robert Culp and
Bill Cosby. The *Star* promoted its "I Spy Team" in advertising campaigns

with a full-page photo of Sarro and Delaney on Mayor Washington's desk to entice the city's diverse readership. Delaney left the *Star* in 1969 but Sarro remained, covering urban politics through the early 1970s. As a result of that experience, Sarro developed a rapport and trust among black politicians that gave him an expertise on the *Star* staff for urban black politics and civil rights. In 1972, staunch segregationist, chair of the District Committee, and longtime foe of home rule John McMillan lost his reelection to Congress, and activist Marion Barry was elected a school board member. In December 1973 Congress passed the District of Columbia and Self Rule and Government Reorganization Act, and in November 1974 Walter Washington became the city's first elected mayor in more than one hundred years. Then civil rights activist Marion Barry became a member of the city council. That same year, the Noyes and Kauffmann families, who were sinking under the weight of debt, sold Joseph Allbritton, a wealthy Texas businessman, a 10 percent share in the newspaper. Allbritton hired James Bellows from the *New York Herald Tribune* as editor. By 1976 Allbritton owned the newspaper outright. The nearly century-old power structure led by old establishment Washington, of which the Noyeses and Kauffmanns were a part, was less powerful, and the *Star*, the establishment newspaper, was now run by a Texan trying to save it from bankruptcy.[14]

Beginning in November 1974 the *Star* published a series of profiles on Mayor Walter Washington and city council members before they officially took office, which were largely positive. After the newly elected officials started running local government, however, they faced closer scrutiny from the city's two newspapers. One of the *Star*'s more controversial news stories was its investigation of Joseph Yeldell, whom Mayor Washington had appointed to head the large and unwieldy D.C. Department of Human Resources (DHR) in 1972. Yeldell, as head of DHR, was responsible for overseeing Forest Haven. Barely four months after the mayor's term began, *Star* reporter Diane Brockett began a series on Forest Haven after the court ordered an evaluation of its educational programs for 240 mentally disabled residents. Brockett claimed Mayor Washington hired Roland Queene in 1974 to improve the facility "as a result of a public outcry over deplorable conditions at Forest Haven first uncovered by the *Star* in October 1973," but that conditions according to Queene had only worsened. In one of Brockett's first articles, she described a disturbing scene at Forest Haven of "old-looking young men, most clad only in shorts but one naked and holding his diaper in his hand" who "sat on benches and hard chairs around the barren room. One lay on the floor. There were puddles under two chairs." Across the hall students with similar IQs, however, were able to dress, feed themselves, and engage in various educational activities. The difference in the quality of care was the

result of student-to-teacher ratio in each classroom. A year-and-a-half after Yeldell hired Queene, Brockett reported that Queene was discouraged
that his repeated requests to the DHR for more staff had been ignored
at worse and at best answered with overtime approvals for an already
overworked staff. When Brockett asked Yeldell why the city could not
hire more staff at Forest Haven, his only reply was that the city's budget
deficit precluded more hires, and when she pressed him on why other
city agencies had been allowed to break their hiring freeze, he could only
answer that those agencies had additional funds in their budgets. Brockett found Forest Haven, like many institutions for the mentally disabled
at the time, as a "depressing, often filthy" place where residents were
"condemned to the barest of existences until death." By the spring of 1976,
House District Committee Chair Charles Diggs called for a hearing on
conditions at Forest Haven, and then several district committee members
asked Joseph Califano, US Health and Human Service (HHS) director, to
conduct an independent review. Brockett continued to report on abuse
and neglect at the center. A month after Queene left Forest Haven for a
position at HHS in October 1976, Brockett conducted an exclusive interview with him. Queene confided to Brockett that after speaking to the
press, he was cut out of decision making and became, wrote Brockett, a
"persona non grata with the District Government." Brockett was awarded
the grand prize in writing from the Washington-Baltimore Newspaper
Guild for her nearly two-year-long series, but problems persisted at Forest Haven until it closed in 1991. Yeldell continued to stay in the headlines
for his mismanagement of DHR agencies like Forest Haven, D.C. General
Hospital, and St. Elizabeth's Hospital as well as misuse of public funds
for personal perks.[15]

On November 18, 1976, *Star* reporter Ned Scharff wrote an exclusive
story about Yeldell that revealed four members of his family were on
DHR's staff payroll in possible violation of federal law, including his wife
and two other relatives. Scharff got the tip about rampant nepotism in
Yeldell's administration from Councilwoman Polly Shackleton during a
casual phone conservation and immediately took the idea to *Star* editor Jim
Bellows, who gave him his blessing. Scharff spent weeks reviewing public
records and made repeated attempts to contact Yeldell, but the DHR director's only response to apparent "instances of nepotism and cronyism on
his staff" was a terse response from Susan Truitt, a city government press
officer. Truitt told Scharff, "The Director chooses not to participate in your
story because . . . we don't view it as a scandal" since the claim "that nobody who's a friend of anybody can work in the D.C. government? is not
realistic . . . if that were true, I couldn't have gotten my job." When the news
broke, the mayor asked City Administrator Julian Dugas to investigate
the charges. Before Dugas completed the investigation, Yeldell supporters

called a rally at his family church, the Turner AME Church at 6th and I Streets, NW where Yeldell planned to speak in his defense. *Star* reporter Philip Shandler reported when the mayor learned of Yeldell's plans during a Sunday cabinet meeting at the mayor's press aide Sam Eastman's home, the mayor phoned Yeldell urging him not to attend. When Yeldell refused, an unnamed source told Shandler the mayor "pleaded with Joe at least not to get into specific cases, and not to get into a fight with the press." Despite the mayor's warnings, Yeldell singled out Ned Scharff and the *Star* for his harshest attacks. The *Star*'s banner headline for the story read "Yeldell Defense: Everybody Does It; 'Racist Vendetta.'" Kenneth Walker and Gloria Borger described Yeldell's speech as "an aggressive and wide-ranging speech interrupted several times by applause," when he defended his hiring of relatives and friends because he claimed it was "exercised by every executive" in all branches of local and federal government. Yeldell specifically took aim at the *Star*, claiming "the highly personalized attack seems to obscure the real motives of the *Washington Star*, and to legitimize its continuing attack upon the integrity of black leadership in the District of Columbia." Yeldell then personally attacked Scharff by telling rally attendees that a "well-informed source" told him that Scharff's brother David, a local respected psychiatrist in private practice, had told his friend Dr. Mark Lawrence, a former DHR mental health officer who left DHR after a dispute with Yeldell, "Don't worry, Mark, my brother Ned, and Alice Bonner (a *Washington Post* reporter) are going to get that Yeldell." Yeldell then asked the audience, "Would you conclude that Ned Scharff is less than objective . . . but then I wouldn't really say such things." Scharff was forced to answer reporters' questions about Yeldell's accusations besmirching his reputation. Scharff told his colleagues, "I started this story on my own initiative and have never received any information or assistance from any member of my family." Scharff felt burned by the accusations but certain of his own integrity—the story came from an anonymous source inside city government he couldn't name at the time, and his brother never discussed the story with him. To add to Scharff's woes, he mistakenly identified Eloise Turner as Yeldell's niece rather than his first cousin's former wife, which Scharff did later correct in print. Turner sued the *Star*, but the case went on so long that Scharff was told by *Star* lawyers that it eventually settled for an unspecified amount. Mayor Washington placed Yeldell on administrative leave the day after the rally and eventually appointed him to an innocuous job as chair of the Board of Appeal and Review. Michael Kiernan, whose beat since 1973 had been City Hall, reached out to his contacts in City Hall to write a follow-up story. Those closest to Walter Washington told Kiernan that the mayor's primary goal was to stop speculation that "cronyism is a way of life in the city and that anyone who challenges the concept is a racist." Kiernan wrote that "several city officials" knew when Yeldell instigated a "public brawl pitting a black-dominated city government against two white-dominated newspapers and a white dominated Congress" the mayor had to remove him to stop "the enemies of home rule" from benefiting.[16]

Across the city's borders in Maryland, old-fashioned political corruption by seasoned politicians was making big headlines too. *Star* reporters James Rowland had covered Maryland politics since 1973, and Jerry Oppenheimer, who came later, waited with a glut of news media outside the federal courthouse in Baltimore to hear the grand jury's decision on whether or not to indict Maryland governor Marvin Mandel and five co-defendants on charges of mail fraud, bribery, and racketeering. Rowland and Oppenheimer spent as much time explaining the press frenzy as the twenty-four-count indictment itself in their report in the next day's *Star*. Reporters ate sandwiches at the courthouse snack bar, and prosecutors ordered hot dogs at Jake's Deli while Mandel and his wife, Jean, lunched at the Auberge de France on veal and bourbon. The press ran for the telephones to call in their stories as the US Attorney Jervis Finney gave the assembled newsman copies of the indictments and press releases. Radio bulletins went out even before the governor was phoned about the indictments. When Mandel stepped out of his office into the governor's reception room to face the huge mass of reporters, he remarked, "Aw, look at them all," he said, and then read a prepared statement. Mandel was a popular governor that the *Star* praised in an editorial the day after his indictment as "an able administrator and a progressive innovator not given to demagoguery or pontification" and cautioned the public not to rush to judgment of Mandel since "he has been accused, not convicted; the presumption of innocence still is his." The profile of Mandel that Rowland wrote the same day was more nuanced. After Rowland talked with those closest to Mandel, he described Mandel as a politician whose success can be "credited to a mixture of opportunism, refusing to be wedded to a fixed ideology and helping persons who later felt indebted and anxious to repay favors." Mandel's close friends also saw a big change in the governor who, after his divorce and second marriage to divorcee Jeanne Dorsey, began "living it up."[17]

Prosecutors in the US Attorneys office asked Judge Herbert Murray for a gag order on pretrial publicity to stop statements to the press from Mandel's office, which they claimed were prejudicing the jury. Judge Murray disagreed and denied the order after attorneys for media organizations and the defendants argued against it on First Amendment grounds. While the threat of a gag order existed, reporters and photographers found it difficult to get candid photos or statements from Mandel at his staged press conferences overseen by vigilant state security forces. Mandel told reporters at one of his press conferences outside the courtroom even before the gag order was lifted that US Attorney Finney had facts that could prove his innocence but wouldn't reveal them. Mandel also told reporters he vowed to fight the gag order and would not plea bargain because he was innocent. When reporters asked Mandel if he had problems being questioned outside the courtroom, he responded, "Not at all, as long as you print the truth . . . when the truth comes out there'll be a lot of embarrassed people." Judge Murray was asked to recuse himself before the first trial began because of a possible conflict of interest, and a mistrial was called. The case was then assigned to Judge John Pratt to start in September 1976. Allan Frank, who came to the *Star* in 1973 and had previous local reporting experience at the *Pittsburgh Post-Gazette* and the *Anchorage Daily News*, was assigned to cover the trial.[18]

Judge Pratt issued an order sealing court records in the Mandel case and chose not to sequester the jury despite an anticipated long trial and extensive publicity surrounding the case. Both actions would prove misguided. On December 2, 1976, Allan Frank reported that a juror had reported to the judge after returning from the Thanksgiving holiday that someone had attempted to bribe him. The judge made a decision to sequester the jury, but it was too late and a mistrial was called on December 7, 1976. In addition, the press learned that Judge Pratt had kept from the media and trial attorneys a previous attempt in early November to bribe a juror. In an editorial two days after the mistrial, the *Star* said an attorney in the case told its reporter David Pike, "I'm afraid Pratt blew it. He should have sequestered the jury after the first bribery attempt," and in a closed session Pratt admitted he had "goofed." Another court observer told a *Star* reporter, "There was somebody out there who wanted to abort the trial at all cost" and "even sequestering the jury might not have worked." After two years and three trials Mandel was finally convicted and served nineteen months in prison, but his conviction was overturned a decade later. Allan Frank would win the Washington-Baltimore Newspaper Guild's first prize for his interpretative coverage of the Mandel trial.[19]

Mayor Walter Washington looked for ways to improve his reputation with potential voters after the press' relentless scrutiny of his administration revealed corruption in its ranks, financial mismanagement, alleged illegal use of campaign funds in the mayor's 1974 campaign, and a general malaise in city government. In January 1977 Mayor Washington granted *Star* reporter Michael Kiernan an exclusive interview in hopes of improving his image. The mayor attempted to highlight his accomplishments, including the start of a subway system, a decrease in unemployment, and the building of more city housing units, but as Kiernan looked across the desk he observed, "Washington looks like a beaten man these days." Kiernan talked with other district officials about the mayor's record. One official told Kiernan that Washington was a lame-duck mayor that wasn't accomplishing much, and a council member said he liked the mayor but despised his closest aide Julian Dugas, who "had the attitude that he knew everything and we were baboons." Kiernan and Philip Shandler got a second interview with the mayor in September on the tenth anniversary of Washington's appointment as mayor in 1967. Washington had hoped again to use the two-hour interview to put a positive spin on his time in office. Julian Dugas and the mayor's press secretary Sam Eastman remained in the mayor's office during the interview. The mayor reminded readers he had kept calm during the many riots and protests in the city over the decade, put people back to work, and tried to bring a divided city together to work for the good of all. Kiernan observed Washington had "clearly prepared for the interview" by referring often to prepared notes on his desk, but when the mayor was asked why his popularity had eroded with the press, the black clergy, liberal Democratic leaders, and Washington's business community, the mayor didn't have much of an answer but could only agree. Washington blamed his unpopularity on his perceived lack of charisma, which he didn't think was that important in the city. Kiernan would win the Washington-Baltimore Newspaper Guild's grand prize in the general news category in 1977 for his series of articles on local election politics.[20]

City Council chair Sterling Tucker and at-large councilman Marion Barry were Mayor Washington's main rivals in the 1978 mayoral campaign. In August Michael Kiernan echoed the words of one candidate who described the campaign from every quarter as pretty "tame" and "dull." In July Kiernan wrote sardonically after visiting Walter Washington's campaign headquarters, "The mayor is so behind in his campaign. What, one wonders, is the mayor preparing for? A large birthday party or the District's toughest political contest in recent memory?" Behind the scenes, however, Kiernan and another *Star* reporter were working on a story that summer that had the potential for shaking up the mayor's race. Based on an anonymous tip from a rival campaign about a possible scandal in Barry's personal life, they talked with sources and investigated public records for several weeks to corroborate the story. When the reporters presented their evidence to Barry, he denied all wrongdoing, threatened to sue the *Star* if it printed the story, and hired a tough attorney to back up his threat. Barry knew the story had the potential for eroding his growing electoral support in more affluent and white neighborhoods in the city. Then witnesses, who had confirmed facts in the story, said they would deny their previous statements to the reporters. Managing editor Sid Epstein decided that without more solid evidence, like signed witness affidavits that could stand up in court, he couldn't risk printing the story with the pile of lawsuits already on his desk and the paper's finances in free fall. The *Star* endorsed Sterling Tucker because it wrote Tucker had "the personal and intellectual qualities . . . that are most apt to meet the city's requirements for change." It praised Mayor Washington for his years of service but thought it was time for him to step aside for new leadership. The *Post* endorsed Barry because as they wrote he had the "energy, nerve, initiative, imagination, toughness of mind, an active concern for people in distress" that is "conspicuously absent from the present administration" and all other candidates in the race.[21]

During Barry's first term as mayor, he used his skills and magnetic personality to improve city government and attract fresh talent to help run it. Barry, however, was plagued by a number of mini scandals as the city's dailies scrutinized his personal and professional life more closely when he became mayor. Among them, the *Star* scooped an embarrassing story about a preferential discounted mortgage Barry and his wife, Effi, received from Independence Federal Savings and Loan as a perk for Mrs. Barry's board membership at Independence. In the 1970s the *Star* hired a number of young reporters, many of whom were increasingly black or female, to staff the metro desk. Editors needed the perspective of a young and diverse staff who understood the changing politics and demograph- ics of the city better than their elders. Many of these young reporters would go on to long, successful journalistic careers. Among the new hires were hard news women reporters like Mary Ann Kuhn, Diane Brockett, Maureen Dowd, and Gloria Borger; young white newsmen like Michael Kiernan, Howard Kurtz, and Ned Scharff; and male and female black re- porters like Kenneth Walker, Michael Davis, Jackie Trescott, and Lurma Rackley. Metro desk reporters at the *Star* had covered Marion Barry as an outspoken and charismatic activist on his way to the highest office in the city for a decade. Lurma Rackley, however, knew nothing about Marion Barry or his activism when she came to the *Star* in 1970 as a twenty-one- year-old young black woman through a Ford Foundation–Columbia Uni- versity master's degree program designed to help integrate the nation's newsrooms. Sid Epstein, who hired Rackley, initially assigned her to the Women's Department to take Jackie Trescott's place while Trescott was in the *Star*'s obligatory training program for novice reporters. Rackley waited her turn to enter the paper's training program so she could work on the metro desk covering hard news. When a mini riot erupted on 14th Street and with no available reporter on the metro desk, she was sent to cover it. There she encountered Barry as she stood inside the "House of Jerry's" talking with its proprietor and taking notes. The tall, handsome Barry dressed in a dashiki and followed by "an entourage of brothers" asked Rackley who she was and what she was doing there. Rackley in- troduced herself, politely extended her hand, and told Barry in her best professional manner that she was a *Star* reporter, in hopes of getting some quotes from the group of men. Barry responded, "The *Evening Star* doesn't have any black reporters" and then insinuated, she later recalled, "something to the effect of how do I know you weren't sent from the CIA or FBI." The petite cub reporter without a press badge on her first assignment was a bit shaken by his remarks but retained her composure and disputed his claim that the *Star* had no black reporters by rattling off a few names. Barry interrupted her in midsentence and asked for her press badge, and without one she instead offered to show him her *Star* building ID, to which he replied, "You could be a janitor at the paper and have an ID." Lurma, embarrassed and near tears, thanked the man she had been interviewing before Barry arrived and left to call in her story. Hank Wilson, who was in Barry's group that night, followed her to apologize for Barry's comments by explaining he was "just playing with you." She also learned from Wilson that Barry was the head of Pride, Inc., was actually pleased the *Star* had black reporters, and extended Barry's invitation to her for drinks that night at the Pitts Hotel. Lurma would come to like and understand Barry for both his weaknesses and strengths. After leaving the *Star*, Rackley took a job in Barry's Office of Communications and was his press secretary during his infamous trial on drug charges in the 1990s.[22]

Black Washingtonians saw the two white-owned newspapers' negative press coverage of the district's first two black mayors as undermining black leadership in city government. The city's African American population saw the bad publicity through the lens of the city's racial history and the role the white press had played in perpetuating or ignoring racism in Washington for decades. The *Star*'s reporting on race and the black community in Washington and the nation is a crucial part of the paper's history.

3

The Race Beat

In 1919 as soldiers returned from the war in Europe and President Wilson negotiated peace in Paris, civilians, soldiers, native Washingtonians, federal workers, and southern migrants of all races jockeyed for scarce jobs and housing. Residents drank illegal liquor in pool halls and private homes, crammed into clanging streetcars along Pennsylvania Avenue, 9th Street, or New York Avenue and rode to Center Market on Pennsylvania Avenue to buy flowers, fish, and produce, or work in temporary and permanent federal offices that had bulged with wartime work but were now thinning. In the spring of 1919 an extreme radical element in the country carried out a series of bombings that exacerbated rumors about communists plotting to undermine American democracy. On June 2, the façade of Attorney General A. Mitchell Palmer's house in Washington was bombed. Into this mix of uneasiness and fear, Washington residents suffered through a succession of hot, humid, sweaty summer days. Then in late June stories began appearing in the local newspapers about "Negro Assailants" attacking young white women. On June 30 and July 1, the *Star* reported two separate assaults on white women who accused a Negro of attacking them in Ray's Wood located on Nicholson Street, NW near the sleepy residential subdivision of Brightwood Park on a streetcar line.

In the cooler month of February, the *Star* had welcomed home the Separate First Battalion of the National Guard with a front-page headline that honored approximately two hundred colored soldiers who had lost their lives on the battlefields of France, thirty of whom were district residents. No other local daily in the city took notice of the all-black battalion's service. In a 1918 editorial, Washington's African American weekly newspaper, the *Washington Bee*, praised the *Star*, writing, "The *Star* has made a notable record of fairness to the colored race and there have been instances where it has waived the rule of proportion to help our race." Oswald Garrison Villard, liberal editor of the *Nation*, largely agreed, writing of the *Star*'s editor Theodore Noyes, "The coloured people trust him as they do no one else in the District's public life." Villard also claimed that the *Star* was the one "exception" among Washington newspapers that were not interested in the news of "them and their doings, except that Negro crime is always news." By summer the courage of the Negro battalion was old news, and the rapes of white women by an alleged black assailant dominated local newspaper headlines. When black soldiers returned home from the trenches in Europe, they became less willing to resume a subservient role in white society because of their service to the nation. Unfortunately, their deserved pride was often met with a harsh brutality and racism in parts of white society. In 1919 more than seventy blacks were reported lynched, many of them returning veterans, and twenty-six race riots broke out in cities across the nation, which became known as "The Red Summer." The District of Columbia seemed the least likely place for a race riot as the nation's capital and home to a substantial elite and middle-class Negro population who lived in fine homes, ran profitable businesses, and held secure federal jobs or academic positions at Howard University. Despite this reality, in the summer of 1919 Washington's deadly race riot made big headlines. Washington's newspapers would play a key role in the violence that erupted that year in the city.[1]

For two weeks in July, the *Star* published twenty-six news stories about attacks on white women, descriptions of police suspects, and the public's reaction. It also ran advertisements announcing cash rewards totaling almost $2,000 for clues leading to the capture of the suspected assailant. The *Star*'s July 8 headline read, "Woods Scored in Hunt for Negro" by vigilante committees that are "reminiscent of the days when the Ku Klux Klan rode to protect white women from brutal attacks," along with a description of white men who "terrorized" blacks with a knotted rope in Bethesda. A *Star* reporter wrote that anyone in "possession of a gun, rifle, revolver or automatic weapon" has "oiled, cleaned and loaded" them "for use on a second's notice." Despite the hyperbole of news accounts, a *Star* editorial in early July appealed for the home guard to abide by the law, even though "the heat of indignation is natural in the circumstances but calm thoroughness of investigation and search is more effective" because "innocent people may be accused" and the guilty go free. On July 9 the local branch of the NAACP wrote in a letter to all four daily Washington newspapers "that they were sowing the seeds of a race riot by their inflammatory headlines, featuring 'Negro' in all sorts of unnecessary ways." The NAACP acknowledged the *Star* as the only newspaper to respond to "the justice of the Association's complaint" while "the other papers ignored our warning." On July 9, the *Star* published excerpts from a letter sent to Theodore Noyes by the *Washington Bee* reminding readers that "there was a time when unprotected females, white and black, could run to the black man for protection without fear" and that "colored citizens are as much in favor of bringing violators of the law to justice as any class of American citizens."[2]

On Saturday, July 19, both the *Washington Post* and *Star* reported two young black men allegedly attempted to grab a young woman as she walked home from work on Friday evening but were frightened away by a car of white men. The young woman was married to a naval aviator, and as restless sailors and soldiers on leave crowded the streets of downtown Washington on Saturday, the news accounts reached them that an enlisted man's wife had been attacked the previous night by a "Negro fiend"—a term repeatedly printed in local newspapers to describe suspects. By nightfall a white mob of hundreds of uniformed men and some civilians armed with clubs and bats went to the black section of southwest Washington and indiscriminately beat and injured a number of its residents. According to the *Star*, by the time the police and military personnel arrived most of the servicemen had fled. Officers arrested two white servicemen from the mob and eight black men.[3]

From Sunday evening through the early morning hours of Monday, a large mob of white servicemen and civilians attacked blacks in downtown Washington, near the White House, and as far as the American Baseball League Park near Howard University and the affluent black neighborhood of LeDroit Park. They pulled African Americans from streetcars, bloodied pedestrians with stones and fists, and almost lynched a suspect after snatching him from police officers. Black Washingtonians fought back. The *Star* reported during the early hours of Monday a "big touring car" with four Negro men shot at marines and sailors at the Navy Yard. After Sunday night's violence, the *Washington Post* reported in its Monday morning edition that "a mobilization of every available service man stationed in or near Washington or on leave has been ordered" to the Knights of Columbus hut on Pennsylvania Avenue at 8 o'clock "to 'clean-up' that which caused the events of the last two evenings to pale into insignificance." The *Washington Post*'s article was a thinly veiled call to arms by an unattributed source. The violence on Monday evening was the most deadly of the three days of rioting. After the riots ended, John Shillady, secretary of the NAACP, sent a letter on July 25 to US Attorney General Palmer asking him to initiate legal action against the *Washington Post* "on the ground of incitement to riot." Louis Brownlow, chairman of the D.C. Board of Commissioners and an experienced journalist, in his autobiography claimed that although he had no real proof, he "always believed that these white ex-service men were frauds, paid to provoke the trouble they began." One fact, however, he knew was "indisputable"—the *Washington Post* ran "an alarming article with inflammatory headlines announcing" that ex-servicemen gather Monday night "for the purpose of cleaning up the Negroes," which led to even worse violence that night. The *Star*'s Monday afternoon edition ran an editorial urging law-abiding citizens of both races to stay indoors and expressing regret that white servicemen were by far the largest contingent of men involved in the weekend's violence. Anticipating the worse, Commissioner Brownlow had asked Secretary of War Newton Baker, Army Chief of Staff Peyton March, and Secretary of the Navy Josephus Daniels on Monday morning for troops to quell the escalating riots and to cancel the leave of sailors and soldiers at local military camps.[4]

On Sunday twenty local NAACP members, which included Washington attorneys L. Houston and James Cobb, had urged Brownlow to hire black police officers and warned him that black men were ready to take up arms to defend themselves and their families. Brownlow offered to add three hundred soldiers to the police force but rejected their request to add black officers. These meetings were never reported in the white press. By Monday evening, the NAACP's warnings became a reality. African American men armed themselves with pistols, hand grenades, and machine guns to protect their own. The *Star* described Monday night's riot as the "wildest and bloodiest night since the civil war times" with "race sentiment that rose to unprecedented heights . . . all night . . . as angry men swept up and down usually peaceful thoroughfares, bent upon beating or killing some dark shadowed figures which scurried ahead of their shouts." The "backbone of a centralized white mob attack," a *Star* reporter estimated in the thousands, was barely stopped by a troop of cavalry until they drove their horses "rearing and careening" directly into the "mob scattering its members in every direction." Armed black men full of fear mixed with rage and revenge shot at whites from touring cars, pulled whites from streetcars, and stabbed a white marine in front of the White House. *Star* reports emphasized police and soldiers were severely outnumbered and overwhelmed by the mobs. On Monday night a police officer, two African Americans, and one white were killed; eleven civilians were seriously wounded, including six whites and five blacks. Nearly three hundred men, most of whom were black, were arrested as seven hundred police officers and four hundred soldiers attempted to control the violence. President Wilson finally ordered Major General William Haan on Tuesday to detail a special military guard of two thousand troops from Quantico and Fort Myers. Tuesday night's sporadic mob violence continued, but by Wednesday the riots were over. General Haan, who oversaw the troops, said of his strategy to end the riots, "When I got them [the newspapers] to agree to say approximately what I wanted them to say, which was the truth, then soon everything was over," since he felt it was mostly "a newspaper war." The *Star* disagreed with other local dailies that blamed the riots on the ineffectiveness of the Washington police force. The *Star*'s editorials agreed that increasing police officer pay and passing a new pistol law would help, but it wrote the country should be "far more concerned about the development for the first time in this community in half a century, of murderous race antagonism" than police ineffectivness. To find the "cure it is necessary to seek the cause," the *Star* wrote, which "undeniably" it warned was an "intense race animosity that has been developing for some time." It defended "good law-abiding colored citizens" while recognizing "there are bad negroes, as there are bad white men," but "to pursue all men of color without provocation is just as unjust and tyrannical as though the negroes were to turn upon all whites and without discrimination or cause attack all they met."[5]

As a result of the riots, the *Star* and Washington's four other local white-owned newspapers—the *Washington Post, Washington Daily News, Washington Times,* and *Washington Herald* (both Hearst papers)—modulated their reporting of black crime and ignored much of what was happening in segregated black neighborhoods between the two world wars. Elite black society and the black church were sometimes covered as well as gatherings of national Negro organizations in the *Star*. Occasionally positive human-interest stories about men and women of color attracted the attention of a white audience and made front-page news, like boxer Joe Louis's win over Max Schmelling in 1938 or acclaimed Negro contralto Marian Anderson's concert on the National Mall in April 1939 after the District of Columbia School Board denied her request to sing at white Central High School and then the Daughters of the American Revolution (DAR) at Constitution Hall. All Washington newspapers condemned the DAR's decision in editorials. On April 9, 1939, the *Star*-owned WMAL radio broadcasted Miss Anderson's concert on the national mall at 5 pm. A *Star* reporter who covered the concert described seated dignitaries rising to their feet as Miss Anderson crossed the stage to stand before a phalanx of mics, and then the "singer took off the fur-trimmed hat she had been wearing and her long mink coat hung free over her trailing velvet gown as she clasped her hands before her and with closed eyes started 'America' . . . there wasn't a stir in the crowd as the rich voice was amplified across the park," and as she finished singing "a ripple, resembling a sigh, went over the crowd as the voice died away." The story of Miss Anderson's concert was placed deep inside the *Star*'s edition, however. African Americans would remain largely invisible to white reporters in newsrooms at white-owned newspapers where white reporters wrote primarily for a white audience segregated from blacks. In the post–

World War II years, however, bolder tactics by those involved in the black civil rights struggle attracted greater attention from the mainstream white press. It was a key tactic of the new civil rights movement to bring change.[6]

The first official attempt to integrate the races in Washington that made front-page news began when the D.C. Board of Recreation in June 1949 sanctioned the Society of Friends to run two interracial playgrounds. A majority of playgrounds in the district were run by the Interior Department, and no federal facility could legally segregate under federal law. From June 25 to 28, white Quakers encouraged young African American men to attend free morning swim programs to challenge de facto segregation at the Anacostia and McKinley swimming pools. When a group of young black men attempted to enter the Anacostia pool in southeast Washington, an equal number of whites taunted and heckled them. Staff at both facilities refused to work because they claimed they feared more violence if Negroes were allowed to enter the pool. The D.C. Board of Recreation voted to withdraw its personnel from operating the morning program, and federal employees of General Services Inc. remained to run the program. The *Star*'s June 28, 1949, editorial supported the board's decision and argued, "Secretary Krug and his aides may believe that there is no serious danger of trouble. . . . But if the judgment of a Federal official is going to be substituted for the judgment of local officials in a matter of this kind," then the responsibility for more violence rests squarely with the Interior Department. On the afternoon of June 28, mounted police officers disbursed a riotous crowd of whites estimated at nearly five hundred by the *Star* and made five arrests at the Anacostia pool. The Interior Department then closed all district pools. *Washington Post* reporters Jack London and Ben Bradlee covered the June 28 incident and considered the story front-page news. According to Bradlee, the *Washington Post* editors struck a "big deal" with Interior Secretary Krug to downplay the Anacostia story in order to quell the violence in exchange for Krug's promise that the pools would open in a year on an integrated basis. There is no proof of any deal with the *Star*. The *Star* ran a page-one story and photo on June 30 of the June 28 confrontations. The *Star*'s editorial of the same day blamed the violence on Secretary Krug's "own rashness" in not realizing that "abolishment of segregation in the pools is too long a step to take right now." The *Post* left the door open to integrating the pools but believed for now it was in the best interest of all district residents to postpone the experiment. The pools reopened a year later on a desegregated basis.[7]

In 1947 when the gentlemanly and well-respected Ben McKelway became the *Star*'s editor, he retained most of his predecessor and mentor Theodore Noyes' moderate views on race. Noyes had always been a strong supporter of education and fair treatment for Negroes in the city but had never questioned the wisdom of racial segregation. Under McKelway's leadership, the *Star's* editorial page argued for a gradual end to segregation to allow Washingtonians of all races to adjust to a new status quo. Such moderate views came under greater scrutiny in the post–World War II years. The same year McKelway became editor, the *Washington Post's* publisher, Eugene Meyer, retired and his younger protégé and son-in-law Phil (Phillip) Graham became publisher. Phil Graham pushed the *Washington Post* to take more progressive stands on racial justice. From that time forward, the *Star* and the *Washington Post's* editorial opinions on race often diverged. In 1948, the *Post* was the first white-owned newspaper in the city to stop identifying blacks as either "Negro" or "colored" in print and began advocating for an end to segregation in public accommodations, housing, and schools. In 1952 Phil Graham also made a stab at integrating the *Post's* newsroom when he hired Simeon Booker as its first black reporter. Booker, however, left after two years of being repeatedly stymied in his efforts to obtain access to sources or the chance to write news stories about the district's white leaders, especially the Washington Metropolitan police. The *Star* would not seriously recruit or hire black staff reporters until the mid-1960s, although most district weeklies had paid freelance Negro stringers to cover stories in the city's black neighborhoods for years. Since the 1920s, the *Star* employed blacks in low-level production jobs in the press room or as route carriers, but they were still excluded from many jobs at the paper because of their race until the 1960s. As far back as the 1930s, the *Star* experienced public challenges to its racially discriminatory policies. In 1933 the New Negro Alliance met with the *Star's* personnel staff and threatened it with a boycott if it didn't start hiring black newspaper boys. The *Star* couldn't afford to lose money from its Negro subscribers or street sales, so in three weeks it agreed. It didn't always bend to change. Twenty years later, the *Pittsburgh Courier*, an out-of-town black newspaper distributed in Washington, in 1952 reported that when a local black pastor asked a *Star* official why the paper had advertised for only white high school–aged young men as section inserters, a step above a route carrier in pay, and not Negroes, he replied, "Yes, it is the policy of the *Star*, and we don't care whether you like it or not." Editor Ben McKelway confirmed the official's statement when asked by the NAACP. The *Star* also played an important role in keeping Washington's neighborhoods racially segregated in the first half of the twentieth century. The *Star* had a tacit agreement with the white Washington Board of Realtors not to accept advertisements that offered properties to black purchasers restricted by racial covenants to whites. The US Supreme Court ruled the practice unconstitutional in 1958. The *Star's* newsroom remained white until the mid-1960s, but to the paper's credit and consistent with its best traditions, each reporter had the freedom to write the story of the black civil rights movement as it emerged in the 1950s without interference from editors, management, or editorial board decisions.[8]

On May 17, 1954, the *Star* carried an image of Spottswood Bolling, a wide-eyed, clean-cut black teen with a big, dimpled smile dressed in a button-down white sweater. Like most young men who tend to shy away from their mother's physical affections, his head leans slightly away from the hug of his matronly looking mother, Sara. Spottswood was a student in the colored schools of Washington and the lead plaintiff in *Bolling v. Sharpe*, a companion case to *Brown v. Board of Education*, which ruled that school segregation in the nation's capital was unconstitutional based on the due process clause of the Fifth Amendment. The *Star*, true to its moderate stand on ending segregation, was critical of the federal power of just nine men to impose "this momentous policy determination" on local authorities based upon what it considered were "obscure" constitutional grounds, and "if ever a decision 'made' law at the expense of States' rights, this one does." The *Star*'s editorial writer, however, believed the decision "finds much support in wisdom and fairness" because it ends the separate but equal doctrine that "has not produced equal school facilities for colored, especially in the south." The *Washington Post* in contrast was unequivocal in its support of a decision that "affords all Americans an occasion for pride and gratification." The *Daily News* called it a "just and wise decision" and hoped good will among the races would prevail, but cautioned that "no court, however right, can rule out prejudice from a man's heart, any more than it can rule out the color of a man's skin." The black-owned *Pittsburgh Courier* was ecstatic, writing the decision was "the most powerful affirmation of the ideals of our country since the Emancipation." All four newspapers agreed that the hardest part now would be implementation. Except for efforts to slow school desegregation by the white Federation of Citizens Associations and a few brief protests by white students at D.C. high schools in October, schools were desegregated without much fanfare in the school year of 1954. The response was quite different across the Potomac in rural Virginia.[9]

Virginia's conservative senator Harry F. Byrd Sr. and his formidable political machine were fashioned from an entrenched oligarchy of Black Belt politicians representing the interests of white constituents living in Virginia's Tidewater and southside counties. The alliance was politically powerful and strongly opposed school desegregation. Byrd, a robust and graying Virginia gentleman, who had been in elective office since 1925, promoted the passage of "massive resistance" legislation to oppose desegregation. In August 1956 the Virginia General Assembly passed a bill that gave the governor the authority to close integrated schools and cut off state funds to any jurisdiction that chose to operate them. NAACP attorneys filed lawsuits against the state of Virginia, and lawyers in the Virginia Attorney General's office filed countersuits. For two years litigation snaked its way through state and federal courts until a showdown took place in 1958. *Star* reporters Ludy Werner and Alex Preston, who had covered Virginia since the 1940s, took the lead on the "massive resistance" story. Preston, the more senior of the two, started at the *Star* in the 1930s, and as a native Virginian, he had friends and connections in the highest levels of Virginia state government. Werner was also a native Virginian, who by 1958 had become a familiar and friendly face in police stations, courts, and the Virginia General Assembly. Ludy's ability to cultivate contacts and friends on both sides of Virginia's racial divide enabled her to write a fair and objective story. Judge Albert Bryant Sr.'s clerk in the Fourth Circuit Court of Appeals, where many of the desegregation cases were decided, called Werner personally after each decision was issued. NAACP attorney Oliver Hill described her as "an excellent reporter, very objective and fair in her stories on cases in which we have been involved," and Virginia governor Lindsay Almond characterized her reporting as "accurate and unbiased with no effort to color her report." Werner held moderate to liberal views on Virginia's racial politics, but as she later said, "No one had any idea what your politics were" at the *Star* in those days because you made sure to never reveal them and instead just "stick to facts and make it straight" if you wanted to be a good reporter. Ludy began at the *Star* in 1944 when she answered a want ad for a job as a bookkeeper at the paper, mostly because the *Evening Star* building on Pennsylvania Avenue was at the end of the bus line from her home in Alexandria. Ludy was hired instead as a copy girl at age seventeen during World War II when the *Star* was short on men to fill jobs. She had intended to return to the University of Maryland to study nuclear physics when the war ended. However, as she later said, "I had fallen in love with news" and found her true calling. In Werner's first year, a few of her stories got on the *Star*'s front page, but when a payroll clerk informed editors that it was illegal to send a seventeen-year-old minor alone to evening civic meetings, Ludy was forced to take a year's hiatus from reporting. Werner was a tall, statuesque brunette with an athlete's grace, a booming voice, sharp wit, and easy laugh who exuded maturity even at an early age. The few women reporters at the *Star* in the 1940s usually ended up writing for the "women's pages" as Ludy remembered, but she coveted hard news. For her "the *Star* was a meritocracy," so when she asked to continue covering hard news after reporters returned from World War II, she got her wish.[10]

On February 4, 1958, Werner reported that State Senator Armistead Boothe of Alexandria, and Ted Dalton, a Republican from Radford, had introduced a bill to substitute a local pupil placement program for the state's school closing laws. Boothe was part of a group of young moderate Democrats that entered politics after World War II sensitized by their wartime experiences to racial and social inequities. In 1948 Boothe was elected to the House of Delegates from Alexandria, and he along with like-minded reformers began cautiously to introduce legislation that challenged Byrd's conservative agenda. Boothe shared representation of Alexandria with State Delegate Jim Thomson, a leading segregationist and a staunch supporter of massive resistance. Ludy characterized Alexandria where she lived as a city with "a split personality" that Boothe and Thomson epitomized. Werner's vivid memory of a live interview with Thomson on *Star*-owned WTOP-TV to her exemplified the worst racial attitudes held by white Virginians. Werner and her counterpart at the *Washington Post*, Bob (Robert E. Lee) Baker, had covered race stories in the South since the mid-1950s. The two reporters were returning to Washington from Roanoke after attending the state Republican convention where Ted Dalton was nominated the Republican gubernatorial candidate when they were forced to abandon their stalled train near Lynchburg around midnight. The two reporters hiked along the railroad ties to the closest rental car place and rented a car to arrive on time for a TV interview with Thomson and Albert Smith, Democratic Party candidates for the Virginia House of Delegates. They drove the 185-mile trip to Washington in three hours, arrived just after noon, and after makeup and a quick breakfast, the two exhausted reporters began their interview. Ludy and Bob Baker, a big, tall, imposing man, peppered both candidates with tough questions. When Thomson pulled out a glass and poured in some kind of white substance, Ludy's first thought was that maybe he was getting sick from their grilling. Instead Thomson poured ink into the glass of milk and then turned to face the TV cameras to say "once you've mixed the races, you can never unmix them." Ludy found it pretty hard to contain her disgust and maintain her professional composure in front of the cameras after that remark, but she did.[11]

In the fall of 1958, the federal courts ordered public schools to desegregate in Charlottesville, Norfolk, and Warren County. Werner wrote a three-part series before the start of the school year to clarify the complex web of lawsuits, legislation, racial issues, and historical context of school desegregation in the three jurisdictions ordered to desegregate. Lindsay Almond had previously handled Virginia's desegregation cases as a former Virginia attorney general and was now the state's governor. On the campaign trail, Almond would dramatically raise his arm above his head, and with palm outstretched like a knife make a chopping motion to his arm and swear he'd rather cut off his arm than let black and white children go to school together. Despite Almond's racist demagoguery designed to win conservative southern white votes, he privately expressed doubts that the massive resistance ultimately would succeed. Almond asked his attorney general, Albertus Harrison, to file a case in the Virginia Supreme Court in September to test the validity of Virginia giving parents state tuition grants to send their children to private, segregated schools. Charlie Alexander in the *Star*'s newsroom answered a call from Harrison to Werner the day the case was filed. Charlie walked to Werner's desk and said loudly so the entire newsroom could hear, "Ludy, the Attorney General of Virginia wants to talk to you." As she later recalled, Harrison informed her, "Mary Lou, I just want you to know that I filed suit in the Virginia Supreme Court of Appeals to check the legality of these tuition grants; we don't want to be paying out these things if they are illegal." Ludy already knew the NAACP had filed a test case in federal court for the same reason, and her first reaction was "Oh, come on, Albertus, isn't this just another delaying tactic, you know what the end is?" Harrison was silent for a moment and then spoke. "I will deny that I ever said this if you ever put it in a story, but let me ask you one question, if we have to get rid of these stupid laws, is it better to let the federal courts or our own state supreme court decide?" She only said, "Enough said," and prepared to write her lead. Ludy wrote a front-page story for the September 14 afternoon edition that she described later as "straight down the middle," which essentially paraphrased Harrison's aim to get a clear ruling from the state court. The next morning "the powers that be," as Werner later referred to her senior editors but did not name, rewrote her lead without consulting her. Werner's editors at the time included national news editor Charlie Seib, managing editor Herb Corn, and associate editor Newby Noyes. The editors were persuaded by a *New York Times* front-page story by John Morris that the suit was a delaying tactic by Virginia "to ward off a possible Federal Court injunction against the closing of the Warren County High School at Front Royal." Werner felt her editors had "betrayed" her and protested that they put her lead back because Harrison as a reliable source had trusted her to write a straight story, and she argued they were "drawing an inference that wasn't there," she later said. She won her argument, and the final lead read, "The State of Virginia has initiated a test of its own school closing fund cut-off and tuition grant laws which were adopted to bar integration." As she said later, she wasn't going to let a "high placed doofus" undermine her judgment or rewrite her story.[12]

On September 15, 1958, Governor Almond seized and closed the white high school in Front Royal, then Charlottesville and finally Norfolk on September 29. According to Werner, Almond "followed the Byrd machine, but he knew the end was in sight." Almond later admitted, "I never felt there was any way short of violence that would nullify a final decision of the Supreme Court." Within weeks, white parent groups in Charlottesville and Norfolk began voicing their opposition to the unworkability of public school closings. Both the *Star* and the *Washington Post* reflected the sentiment of most of its moderate Northern Virginia readers in opposing the bankrupt policy of massive resistance. By October, even conservative newspapers like the *Richmond Times Dispatch* and *Lynchburg News* began to editorially oppose the closings. Finally, in January 1959, the Virginia Supreme Court in a three-judge court ruled that the school closings were unconstitutional and ordered schools reopened. In January 1959 Governor Almond addressed the Virginia legislature, calling for an end to massive resistance to school desegregation. Mary Lou Werner won a Pulitzer for her coverage of Virginia's "massive resistance" to school desegregation in 1959.[13]

The headline news stories about "massive resistance" in the late 1950s shared the *Star*'s front-page columns with stories about more violent opposition to desegregating schools in the Deep South. In 1957 the *Star* sent Bill Hines and later Cecil Holland south to cover Arkansas governor Orval Faubus's use of the State National Guard to block nine black students from attending Little Rock's all-white Central High School at the opening of the 1957 school year. Hines was seen as an interloper and troublemaker, like other members of the northern press by white southerners in the crowds that protested school desegregation in Little Rock. Hines was a native Californian but had worked as city editor at the *Chattanooga Times* in his twenties in the 1930s, so he knew something of southern culture. On the morning of September 9, Hines faced an angry white mob in North Little Rock that jeered and used racial epithets directed at him and Benjamin Fine of the *New York Times*. Some in the crowd had seen Hines grill Governor Faubus as part of an ABC-TV news panel broadcast the night before. When a man spotted Hines in the crowd, he yelled, "That's the man who made Faubus look like a fool last night." Hines stood silently for a time next to a National Guardsmen, but as the jeers continued to mount at newsmen in the crowd, he left to find a telephone booth. In Hines's customary style, he dictated the story at breakneck speeds that few other reporters could match, as one young reporter discovered during his obligatory time on the *Star*'s dictation bank. Hines's article on September 9 reported that six black students and two ministers were "met near the top of the steps by a solid phalanx of several hundred white students" that stopped their entry to the North Little Rock High School. Finally, President Eisenhower federalized the National Guard on September 24 to protect black students attending Central High. Cecil Holland, who came to the *Star* in 1939 and was a native Tennessean, would return to Little Rock after Hines left to cover the continuing story of desegregating Little Rock's high schools.[14]

Just a barely a month before Little Rock became a national news story, Haynes Johnson joined the *Star*'s news staff. In the 1940s Johnson's father,

Malcolm, had won the Pulitzer for his coverage of trade union corruption and crime on the New York City waterfront for the *New York Sun*. The series was later fictionalized in the classic movie *On the Waterfront*. When Johnson arrived at the *Star*, there were no black reporters, but he took little notice of it, as he recalled later. Johnson was promoted to night city editor by the late 1950s, and like other *Star* editors he directed reporters to ignore news leads, even crime stories that originated in black neighborhoods, as was the accepted custom then. By the 1960s Johnson's perspective had been changed by the fight for racial justice in the country, and he viewed it as the most important news story of his generation. Johnson also saw that Washington had a majority black population with little or no economic and political power by 1960. Despite the removal of legal barriers to segregation in public spaces, most black Washingtonians still experienced small, everyday indignities when they left their racially segregated neighborhoods and had little economic or political power. The white press had been complicit in ignoring or distorting ordinary black voices, and Johnson wanted to bring their stories into the light. Johnson was on a track to move up in the editorial ranks, but as an academically trained historian, he wanted to research and write investigative pieces. In 1961 Johnson asked Newby Noyes for time off to do an in-depth investigation of how the Negro lived in Washington, and national news editor Charlie Seib agreed to release Johnson from daily reporting. Johnson produced a fourteen-part special series titled the *Negro in Washington*. For six months Johnson talked with black Washingtonians from all walks of life when they were willing to invite him into their homes. Letters to the *Star* commenting on Johnson's series ran the gamut. Some readers praised his writing as "objective," "honest," "timely," "commendable," "forward looking," "articulate," and "well done," but others were critical, like the white man who asked for a comparable series on "Whites in Washington," or another reader who asked, "What kind of an editor are you to let that trash to press?" Most African Americans praised Johnson's frank analysis, but some questioned whether a white reporter could translate the black community's voice. One reader asked that the series be reprinted in booklet form, and two years later Johnson published the series as a book titled *Dusk at Dawn*.[15]

On May 4, 1961, the *Star* and *Washington Post* sent one reporter each to a press conference where thirteen black and white members of the Congress of Racial Equality (CORE) announced they were traveling as racially integrated groups by bus through the South, starting in Washington. Their purpose was to directly challenge southern states that refused to abide by the US Supreme Court's decision ruling segregation in interstate travel unconstitutional. The story appeared with a photo buried deep inside the *Star*. At first reporters from black newspapers like Moses Newson of Baltimore's *Afro-American* or Simeon Booker of *Jet* and *Ebony* magazines as well as reporters from local southern newspapers were the only news-men directly witnessing and reporting the story of the "Freedom Riders." The *Star* generally relied on the Associated Press for civil rights stories unless federal intervention occurred. As the Freedom Riders journeyed further into the South, news of white mob violence against them came over the wire services to the *Star*'s newsroom. When Klan-led beatings in Birmingham bloodied Freedom Riders and news photographers, and injured dozens of black bystanders, CBS broadcaster Howard K. Smith and a handful of reporters fearlessly covered the story and brought it to a wider audience. Alabama state officials did little to protect the Freedom Riders but instead arrested them and transported them across state lines to avoid the press. The Freedom Riders returned to Birmingham unde-terred. When the Freedom Riders finally reached Montgomery on May 20, white mobs again attacked them, and members of the press at the bus terminal. Among the injured was Attorney General Robert Kennedy's administrative aide John Seigenthaler, who was beaten unconscious as he attempted to aid two female activists. Attorney General Robert Kennedy ordered five hundred federal deputies to Montgomery after Saturday's violence. Cecil Holland was already on his way to Montgomery.[16]

On Sunday evening Holland gathered with other reporters outside a rally at Dr. Ralph Abernathy's church where Dr. Martin Luther King Jr. was scheduled to speak to a large audience. An angry white mob was there too. As Holland reported in the Monday, May 22 *Star*, late Sunday evening he witnessed "a rampaging mob which besieged about 1,500 Ne-groes attending a church meeting" and "overturned automobiles and set them afire, smashed windows and hurled fire bombs." Alabama governor John Patterson did not order the National Guard to the scene until the violence was out of control. Back in Washington, Robert Kennedy called a late-night press conference at the Justice Department to announce he was ordering more federal marshals to Montgomery. *Star* reporter Miriam Ottenberg had been at the Justice Department most of the weekend. In 1937 the *Star* had hired Ottenberg at age twenty-three when she returned to her hometown of Washington after earning a degree in journalism from the University of Wisconsin and working at newspapers in Chicago and Ohio. Ottenberg became the *Star*'s first hard news female reporter. By 1961 Ottenberg had been a savvy police reporter for two decades and had developed key sources at the Justice Department, including a close association with Attorney General Robert Kennedy. Ottenberg saw a frustrated Kennedy "with shirt sleeves rolled up" and "slowed down by a sleepless week end" tell reporters that Patterson was "resentful" that fed-eral marshals were in his state, but she observed that "Mr. Kennedy had a touch of resentment in his own voice." Finally, that night Governor Pat-terson was pressured to declare martial law and bring in eight hundred

National Guard to control the crowds. When the Guard arrived, Holland saw them push rioters down the street and explode tear gas to disperse the crowd, but the crowd just "jeered at the tear gas saying 'Whee, I love that smell.'" Governor Patterson seemed more concerned with federal authorities in the state than local violence when he told reporters that if "any federal people violate any of our State laws, we will arrest them," reported Holland. On Tuesday Holland attended a news conference where Dr. King along with student leaders John Lewis and Diane Nash told the press that the freedom rides would continue. On Wednesday a black and white group of Freedom Riders left in two buses with newsmen in tow "under a massive military and police guard" for Jackson, Mississippi, observed Holland. Ottenberg reported on negotiations between Governor Patterson, Mississippi governor Ross Barnett, and Robert Kennedy. Local authorities agreed to protect marchers from violence in exchange for Kennedy removing federal marshals and not interfering with local police arresting activists. The next day the freedom marchers were jailed in Jackson but refused bail. Among the marchers was CORE's national director James Farmer, who decided to ignore the attorney general's request for a "cooling off period," wrote Holland. Holland summarized his view of the violent week he had just experienced by comparing the two cities he covered. "When the racially mixed 'freedom riders' defying Southern segregation customs came to Jackson . . . they were treated firmly but politely," wrote Holland, and "when they went into the white waiting room, they were arrested and jailed." Jackson now "continues in its easy Southern way," while Montgomery suffers because of the violence. After Montgomery, cities along the Freedom Riders' route followed Jackson's model, and authorities arrested protesters quickly and quietly to tamp down any violence or bad press. As the violence subsided, so did the media's interest in the Freedom Riders.[17]

A year later in September 1962, Holland with the help of *Star* reporter Jerry O'Leary Jr.—a tough, crew-cut World War II marine, native Washingtonian, and plainspoken newsman—came to Oxford, Mississippi, to cover the showdown between Mississippi governor Ross Barnett and federal authorities who were there to enforce a federal court order to enroll twenty-nine-year-old student James Meredith at the University of Mississippi as its first black student. The Fifth Circuit Court of Appeals held Barnett in contempt with the threat to arrest and fine him $10,000 a day if he continued to use Mississippi state police to block Meredith's enrollment after Tuesday. On Saturday, September 29, Miriam Ottenberg joined a phalanx of newsmen outside the attorney general's office waiting for hours for him to emerge and answer questions about the standoff in Mississippi. When Kennedy finally came out of his private office that night, Ottenberg observed, he "obviously intended to say nothing, but only to respond to the insistent demands for pictures." Newsmen shouted questions at Kennedy, but he answered none and said only "in a quiet, almost offhand voice 'He's going to be enrolled at the University of Mississippi'" as he walked back into his office. Neither Kennedy's press secretary Ed Guthman nor the attorney general explained to reporters how, why, and when Meredith would be admitted, so Ottenberg wrongly concluded that "the Governor and the Government had agreed on a week-end truce." On Sunday Holland in Oxford, witnessed "a night of wild and uncontrolled rioting on the nearby Old Miss campus" that "left two dead and scores injured" and endangered reporters and bystanders alike after white crowds rioted when the Mississippi State Highway Police left. By Monday federal troops had poured into Oxford to clear the "marauding gangs," still in the city, reported Holland and Meredith enrolled at "Ole Miss." David Broder, who knew Holland when he worked at the *Star* in the early 1960s, once referred to him as a "deep-dyed southern conservative." Holland's civil rights coverage was thorough and impartial, and as Broder observed, despite his southern roots, he had a "kind of honesty and independence" that is "the rarest, most precious commodity in the news business." As a trenchant example, Broder recalled when Holland was sent to investigate charges of corruption by Harlem politician Adam Clayton Powell, he concluded that Powell indeed was a controversial figure but found no evidence of corruption.[18]

Paul Hope and John Barron would be the *Star*'s newest recruits to cover the black civil rights movement. Paul Hope and John Barron had both worked under state editor George Porter and with Ludy Werner on the *Star*'s state desk covering Virginia and Maryland since the mid-1950s, including school desegregation. Barron was a Korean War veteran and former naval intelligence officer in Berlin who had received his journalism degree from the University of Missouri before coming to the *Star* in 1957. Paul Hope was hired in 1955 by the *Star* and was a World War II veteran with a few more years of reporting experience than Barron. Barron's wife, Patty, knew both men and said they had different temperaments but saw that as a key reason they got along so well. Patty Barron characterized Paul as even tempered while her husband was a tough fighter that boldly took on anyone, powerful or not, when investigating a story. Before Barron went to the Deep South, he would cover racial violence closer to home in a small town on Maryland's eastern shore just eighty-five miles east of Washington, D.C., beginning on the night of June 11, 1963. That night Barron, a husky white man, clean shaven, with a buzz haircut, and conservatively dressed in a white shirt and pencil-thin tie, found himself in the thick of a race riot in Cambridge, Maryland. Barron's article about the Cambridge racial disturbances appeared just below an Associated Press

bulletin announcing that civil rights leader Medgar Evers had been shot
dead in his carport that same day and a showdown was brewing between
Alabama governor George Wallace and the federal government.[19]

Paul Hope had reported from Tuscaloosa since June 8 in anticipation
of a confrontation between federal authorities and Alabama governor
George Wallace over a federal court order to admit Vivian Malone and
James Hood to the University of Alabama. On June 11, 1963, Hope along
with more than three hundred newsmen, photographers, and TV crews
with scores of microphones, cameras, and press equipment stood in
the hot summer sun ringed by Alabama state troopers. Wallace staged
a drama of defiance for his southern supporters and the media, but he
knew eventually he would be forced to admit the students. Hope saw
Wallace waiting in the shade of the auditorium's doorway as Deputy
Attorney General Nicholas Katzenbach, President Kennedy's personal
envoy, arrived by car with the two black students. Katzenbach mounted
the steps to the auditorium with Macon Weaver, US attorney for the
district, and a US marshall to confront Wallace and ask him to make an
"unequivocal" promise, wrote Hope, not to block the entrance. Wallace's
long-winded speech was printed in the *Star*, in which he pontificated
that it was his "solemn obligation and duty" to stand against the "un-
welcomed, unwanted, unwarranted and forced induced intrusion upon
the campus" by federal authorities. Hope and other reporters stood in
the boiling one-hundred-degree weather on the Foster Auditorium steps
waiting for the next showdown while Wallace alternated between retreat-
ing to the cool indoors and coming outside to speak to reporters. When a
brigadier general of the Alabama Guard returned that afternoon, Wallace
called for peace and order and then stepped aside and left the campus.
That same evening President Kennedy introduced a civil rights bill in a
speech to the nation. The *Star* called Kennedy's speech "a good speech,"
but "if it goes unheeded, the consequences will be unimaginably serious,"
because as the president said the "fires of frustration are burning." Hope
then headed for Jackson, Mississippi, to report the news surrounding
Medgar Ever's murder.[20]

By June 15, Hope was in Jackson to witness and report on an imposing
procession of five thousand mourners following Evers's gasket from the
Masonic Temple to the funeral home nearby. After the body was placed
inside, a crowd of angry, black mourners gathered outside the funeral
home to sing freedom songs. As their numbers grew, they marched toward the business district to face solid lines of police three-to-four-feet
deep. Then Hope observed as "more Negroes gathered and soda bottles
began to fly" in response to the police presence, and a "massive race
clash" began brewing. Further violence was prevented when John Doar,
the "number 2 man in the Civil Rights Division" at the Justice Depart-

ment, bravely appeared as a lone, white face among a sea of angry black protesters and took bottles out of their hands. Doar pleaded with them to "go back, you can't win this way . . . don't throw bottles that's what they want you to do," observed Hope. Medgar Evers's body was flown to Washington and buried with honors as a veteran in Arlington Cemetery four days later. The same day Hope was in Jackson and John Barron was back in Cambridge, Maryland, to report that talks to bring racial peace had failed.[21]

The one peaceful and healing break in violence in 1963 was the March on Washington for Jobs and Freedom in August. President Kennedy would praise the march after it occurred, but as organizers planned the march, the Kennedy administration and many in the press expressed concerns about the safety of such a large civil rights demonstration in Washington after so much violent resistance to ending racial segregation. The *Star* opposed the march for much the same reason, writing in a July editorial "there is a nightmarish unreality in the plans being laid out for the march" and arguing if organizers believe the march might spur Congress to pass Kennedy's civil rights bill, they are misguided and have "everything to lose and nothing to gain." During August, Clarence Hunter, the *Star*'s first full-time African American reporter, reported on local plans for the march, including reports on D.C. Police Chief Robert Murray's crowd-control strategy, local civil rights organizers' meetings, the communications center at the District Building, and parking arrangements for demonstrators. By August 26 the *Star*'s opinion was the march was still an "ill-advised" risk despite it being for "a good cause," but now that "the march is on . . . it cannot be allowed to fail. It must be peaceable and dignified" because "this Capital City of ours finds itself now in the burning glass of world attention, the symbol by which the national character will be judged." In the judgment of history, the 1963 March on Washington was a high point in the civil rights movement's history. *Star* columnist Mary McGrory, who walked among the crowd, found "a spirit of gentleness and mutual consideration . . . as though each one present had decided that the whole future of the race depended on his own self-discipline." McGrory gave the reader an intimate view of the people there as she wandered through the crowd talking and listening to the people, like the elderly Negro couple who marched in their Sunday best, leaders on the podium who greeted each other with kisses and hugs, and a white South Carolinian tourist who didn't agree with the march's cause yet told McGrory, "But I must say they can teach this Nation a lesson in good manners." McGrory heard Bayard Rustin apologize to a choir leader for a bad microphone, saw a Brooklyn CORE captain fall asleep beneath a tree on the mall, and whites and blacks march hand in hand. Jerry O'Leary reported the orderly leaving of the crowd, Myra MacPherson attended a party for march leaders and celebrities at Senator Jacob Javits's home after the march, and *Star* cameraman captured the day with photographs of celebrity marchers and entertainers like Joan Baez, James Garner, Paul Newman, James Baldwin, and Charlton Heston, as well as the not-so-famous marchers that cooled their feet in the reflecting pool, listened to speeches on the mall, and proudly marched with picket signs. Photographer Gene Abbott shot panoramic views of the historic throngs on the mall from a helicopter. Political reporter David Broder wrote a front-page political analysis of the event in the August 29 edition. A. Philip Randolph, the seventy-four-year old elder civil rights leader and chairman of the march, emphasized to Broder and other reporters that there was no violence or disorder as many predicted but a peaceful interracial march the world thought was not possible. Despite the march's emotional uplift for the movement, Broder as an astute political reporter noted that the march's major goal of influencing Congress to pass the civil rights bill was still in doubt. In a late afternoon press conference called by march organizers after meeting with congressional leaders, they admitted that passing the bill would still not be easy. Broder also uncovered controversy in the ranks of the march's leaders when he revealed that Patrick O'Boyle, Roman Catholic archbishop of Washington, had refused to give the invocation unless the speech of twenty-five-year-old Student Non-Violent Coordinating Committee (SNCC) leader John Lewis was revised. The changes made to Lewis's speech were printed in the *Star*, including the omission of the original statement, "in good conscience we cannot support the administration's civil rights bill, for it is too little too late." Stepping outside of politics, Broder saw the broader significance of the moment, writing "the voices of the Negro leaders counseling their people never to abandon their fight, never to lose hope that the freedom they seek will soon be theirs" rose above it all. He then quoted generously from the "I Have a Dream" section of Dr. King's speech and let his readers know that those phrases were an extemporaneous outpouring from Dr. King not found in the printed version the press received. The lull in violence lasted barely three weeks when one of the most heinous crimes during the civil rights movement took place in Birmingham, Alabama.[22]

On September 15, 1963, four young black girls were killed in the bombing of the 16th Street Baptist Church in Birmingham as they attended Sunday school. The week before the church bombing, two other teenagers were mysteriously shot. Paul Hope attended and reported on the funerals of seven children in one week in Alabama, he remembered later. Hope spoke to white Birmingham residents that said they were shocked by the killing of innocent children but had no answers to stop the violence. "One of the city's few liberals" told Hope their town was a "dead city," and black leaders "say their people are getting short on patience and harder to keep in check." Hope attended fourteen-year-old Carol Robertson's funeral held at St. John's AME Church because her 16th Street Baptist church was still in shambles. Paul heard "four girls in soft green and white dresses" sing hymns, and the Reverend Fred Shuttlesworth indict the State of Alabama for allowing "children to be blown to pieces rather than turn evil men out of office." The *Star*'s editorial writer the day after the bombing too found George Wallace complicit in the children's murders, writing he "will not be cleansed because he has offered a $5,000 reward for apprehension of the bombers. Incitement remains incitement and the deaths of these children must lie heavily upon his conscience."[23]

By the summer of 1964 President Johnson was in a tough war with congressional leaders of both parties to pass the civil rights bill he inherited from President Kennedy that he now had made his own cause. At the same time, SNCC the Student Non-Violent Coordinating Committee, Dr. King's Southern Christian Leadership Conference (SCLC), the NAACP, and CORE formed the Council of Federated Organizations (COFO) to recruit and train hundreds of student volunteers for "Freedom Summer." In the summer of 1964 COFO mounted a large-scale drive with trained volunteers to register black voters in Mississippi and provide legal services and education. On June 21 Freedom Summer volunteers Michael Schwerner, James Chaney, and Andrew Goodman had gone to investigate the burning of a black church in Philadelphia, Mississippi, but had not returned to COFO's offices in Meridian, Mississippi, by that evening. Schwerner and Goodman, two white New Yorkers, and Chaney, a black Mississippian, were released from a Philadelphia, Mississippi, jail late in the evening on June 21 after being stopped for an alleged traffic violation but had not been heard from since their release. John Barron was sent to Neshoba County to cover the story of their unexplained disappearance. Barron's southern roots in Houston, Texas, and his time as a Cold War spy in Berlin in the 1950s magnetically drew him to investigate the story behind the disappearance of these three young activists on a lonely back country road in the Deep South. When Barron arrived in Philadelphia, Mississippi, a week after the three activists went missing, local Neshoba County residents he interviewed told him "'outside agitators' from the north" were causing all the trouble and locals saw "the disappearance of the trio . . . being distorted by a malicious press dedicated to the defamation of Mississippi and the creation of trouble where none exists." Barron chose not to edit out the racial epithets some Mississippians used when sharing with him their view of local customs that they thought outsiders did not understand. Meridian businessman Woody Warren told Barron, "the local niggers are well content unless somebody starts stirring them up," and hotel proprietor C. B. Sanderson believed "a good nigger can go to any white man he works for and if he needs money, he can borrow it."[24]

Barron rented a car and traveled the road the three young civil rights workers were on the night they went missing. When he stopped at a roadside diner for a meal that evening, he talked with local whites that were not hostile to Barron but, out of fear for their safety or southern loyalty, refused to tell him anything they knew about the disappearance of the three young men. Barron would tell his wife, Patty, later after returning to Washington, he had decided not to travel too far down the road that night when the diners expressed genuine concern for his safety on a stretch of road they knew had a dark history of unexplained violence. On June 30, Barron talked with an African American couple in Philadelphia, Mississippi, that attended the black church the three civil rights workers had visited to investigate a suspected arson before they were murdered. The night the church was burned, Mr. and Mrs. Junior Roosevelt Cole told Barron they were stopped by a truckful of white men armed with rifles and shotguns around 10 pm on their way home from a church meeting. Despite the Coles's denial that they had ever attended a civil rights meeting, armed men pulled them from their car, searched them, and then hit Mr. Cole unconscious with a large metal object, and threatened Mrs. Cole but did not strike her. The church was torched later that evening. Barron, highly critical of all he had seen and heard for the last few days, singled out the *Meridian Star*, which had "objectively reported the recent racial news . . . from Philadelphia, Mississippi," but had printed no stories "about the activities of 20 to 30 heavily armed men traveling in cars without license plates together with the burning of a church which would seem to be a subject worthy of newspaper stories and police investigation." Barron concluded that "had it not been for the subsequent disappearance of three civil rights workers and the arrival of the FBI," the earlier vigilante violence would never have come to light. On July 2, 1964, President Johnson signed the Civil Rights Act after tough negotiations with members of Congress and urgings from civil rights leaders as the FBI searched for the three young civil rights workers. Johnson's support for the bill was strong, but he worried it might trigger more violence in the South. The day after the bill's passage, the *Star*'s editorial lauded it for ending "prejudiced actions which infringe on the citizenship rights of the minority" but predicted the struggle for racial justice was not at an end. After searching the surrounding area of Neshoba County for more than a month, the FBI finally found the bodies of the three young men buried under an earthen dam near the scene of the murders. When Mississippi authorities refused to charge anyone for the murders, federal charges were brought against eighteen local Ku Klux

Klan members, including the Neshoba County sheriff, but none served more than six years for the crime.[25]

In early 1965 Dr. King and Ralph Abernathy turned SCLC's attention to an ambitious drive to register voters in Selma, Alabama. Local civil rights leaders James Bevel and his wife, Diane Nash, recruited prospective black voters to march to the county courthouse to register to vote starting in early January 1965. For nearly a month the quick-tempered Dallas County sheriff Jim Clark arrested hundreds of demonstrators and regularly billy clubbed, cattle prodded, and jailed them, including Dr. King, for the smallest provocation. Haynes Johnson, who wanted to go to Selma and report on the story firsthand, traveled to Selma in early February around the time of King's arrest. Reporters who covered civil rights and were familiar to Johnson, like John Herbers of the *New York Times* and Jack Nelson of the *Los Angeles Times*, were already in Selma as well as a few other intrepid reporters. In the early months, however, there was not a huge press presence. Johnson found Selma's public safety director Wilson Baker the most approachable among the city's white leadership. Baker told Johnson he was sure King and Ralph Abernathy had targeted their small, impoverished town because they knew that Clark would give them the publicity they wanted. A member of the white Chamber of Commerce told Johnson the town expected trouble when Congress passed the Civil Rights Act. The day after Dr. King was released from jail, Johnson asked him why had he had chosen Selma for the voting rights campaign. King replied, "Because it is considered the capital of the Black Belt," but an unnamed source revealed to Johnson another reason—King had a "master plan" to bring attention to Alabama's voter inequities by provoking mass arrests. Johnson was well aware that King was using the press in Selma to further the movement's mission, writing, "It has been obvious that Negroes in some instances here have sought to be arrested to bring national attention to the need for stronger voting rights legislation." Johnson met King for the first time in Selma, and over the next few years he often traveled with him to cover his work as King added opposition to the Vietnam War and northern racism to his causes. Haynes Johnson returned to Washington in March to report on President Lyndon Johnson's decision to start bombing North Vietnam.[26]

During the next month, official violence and terror continued in Selma and nearby Marion County in response to marches and efforts to register voters. Not only were marchers beaten, hospitalized, and jailed repeatedly, but the press, particularly cameramen and TV crews, were attacked too. John Lewis of SNCC and Josea Williams of SCLC led marchers on Sunday, March 7 over the Edmund Pettus Bridge, but they never made it across. Governor Wallace ordered Alabama state troopers to turn the marchers back at all costs on what became known in history as "Bloody

Sunday." Johnson was not in Selma that Sunday, but when he flew into
Montgomery airport the next day, he recalled later that he could hardly
believe what he was seeing. Scores of volunteers that included priests,
rabbis, students, housewives, and ordinary Americans were so moved by
the violence they had seen on TV and in newspapers, they came to Selma
to help. Johnson offered stranded travelers at the airport unable to rent a
car a ride to Selma in his own rented car. After Bloody Sunday, Johnson
viewed Selma in hindsight as "the biggest story in the world," as huge
numbers of journalists from both the international and national press
came to Selma. Clarence Hunter, the *Star*'s first black full-time reporter,
joined Johnson in Selma, and they integrated a Selma hotel. The *Star*'s
liberal columnist Mary McGrory came later as well. Remembering Selma
years later, Johnson would characterize it as "a Perfect Story," because
it was so "simple, black and white and I don't mean race, but a struggle
between good and evil. . . . When people are being beat before your eyes,
stopped in the streets, ten blocks from the courthouse just to register to
vote—not to put their heads on spikes and create a revolution—this was
the challenge of America . . . and it all came alive in those streets." That
night Johnson witnessed hundreds of civil rights workers gather at the
historic Brown AME Church in Selma to sing Negro spirituals and freedom songs as they waited for Dr. King to speak. Those nightly meetings
at the church, Johnson recalled later, were "the most emotional experiences I have ever experienced . . . there was an electric and emotional
quality to them" when folks forged by hardship in the streets gathered for
communion and refuge. From Selma Johnson wrote of watching whites
and blacks gather together and sing as they poured into the church near
midnight until they "were packed to the very rafters." The congregation
rose spontaneously and began singing "Battle Hymn of the Republic" to
signal the arrival of Dr. King while the jeers and threats of hostile whites
erupted outside the church.[27]

On Tuesday, March 9, Johnson met James Reeb, a Unitarian minister he
knew from Jim's years working at All Souls Church in Washington, D.C.,
and two other clergymen for a cup of coffee after dinner at an integrated
cafe. Johnson had no idea that would be the last time he saw his friend Jim
alive. Johnson parted company with Reeb and two clergy friends at the
door and went back to his hotel. Reeb and his companions on their way
back to Brown Chapel for the night were met on the street by three white
men that taunted and mercilessly beat them with a baseball bat. Reverend
Reeb died of his injuries two days later. Johnson's anger over his friend's
death and the violence surrounding him in Selma pushed him one night
to cross a line he knew a journalist never should to remain objective. It
was a cool, spring evening, so Johnson dressed for the weather in a black
raincoat to go out for a walk with no specific purpose in mind and found

himself alone and in an isolated area, when a group of inebriated whites began heckling him from across the street. Their taunts fueled Johnson's anger, and thinking like the ex-soldier he once was, he stepped off the sidewalk and began moving toward them convinced that if they started punching, he could hold his own. Halfway across the street he shouted at them in anger, "You sons of bitches, I'm not non-violent," but before they reacted, he realized his odds were probably not that good after all, so he turned, walked back across the street, and back to his hotel. Fortunately, they did not follow him. President Lyndon Johnson that same evening spoke before Congress on national TV urging its members to pass strong voting rights legislation that he was introducing that day.[28]

On March 21, 1965, with the protection of the National Guard, US military, and other federal law enforcement, civil rights workers in Selma began their march to Montgomery from the Brown Chapel after a federal court lifted an injunction prohibiting the march. Clarence Hunter walked with the marchers for five days in the rain and mud or on sunny crisp days while helicopters flew overhead to protect them from violence. At the end of the day a driver would pick up the *Star* reporters and take them to the nearest phone booth to call in their stories, often two a day. At night reporters like Johnson and Hunter spoke with marchers as they huddled around fires in below freezing temperatures, and on the final night they were entertained by celebrities like James Baldwin, Harry Belafonte, Sammy Davis Jr., and Peter, Paul and Mary. Washington Carter, a twenty-eight-year-old black farmer, told Hunter at the end of the march in Montgomery, "It just looks like everything we do make the white man madder . . . Unless the President and the world do something, our marching won't change much." The marchers did not know yet that Mrs. Viola Luizzo, who came from Detroit to join the demonstrations, had been killed that night and that the FBI had swiftly identified and arrested her murderers. After the march things didn't change much in Selma for blacks, and it wouldn't for years. Four months later Haynes Johnson would write critically about the disarray, criminal arrests, and scandals among some Negro leaders in the Selma movement. Despite the transgressions of the movement's leaders, Johnson could still say "as a result of what the Selma Negroes and their white friends did last spring, the Deep South will never be the same. The demonstrations and the march lifted the spirits of Negroes everywhere." A respected black man in Selma later explained to Johnson even more poignantly why Selma was not a failure: "It hasn't been lost—the march and what happened in Selma gave the Negro a sense of dignity he didn't have . . . I don't know if you know this but you can't deal with a man as a man unless he regards himself as a man. And this is what has happened, and I rejoice in it." Haynes Johnson was awarded the Pulitzer Prize for distinguished national reporting in

Haynes Johnson in the *Star*'s newsroom smiles as he learns he
has earned the Pulitzer for distinguished national reporting for
his coverage of the civil rights movement's campaign for voting
rights in Selma, Alabama, in 1965. D.C. Community Archives,
Washington Star Papers, D.C. Public Library.

1965 and especially cited for his coverage of the civil rights struggle in
Selma, Alabama.[29]

City editor Sid Epstein and managing editor Charlie Seib in 1967 make
a concerted effort to recruit more than one black reporter at a time to
better cover a majority black city. In the early 1960s, the *Star* had hired
Hunter and then Larry Still to cover mostly local black issues, but by 1967

Hunter and Still were gone. Paul Delaney was among three black reporters Epstein hired in 1967. The two others were Ernie Holsendolph and
Paul Hathaway. Delaney had worked as a journalist for eight years first,
at the black-owned *Atlanta Daily World* and then the *Dayton Daily News*
in Ohio. Delaney was specifically hired to team with Ron Sarro, a white
reporter familiar with city hall, to cover Walter Washington's administration as the city's first black mayor. Delaney and Sarro became good
friends and a superb news team on the *Star*'s city desk. In addition to
Delaney's reporting duties, Epstein asked him the summer he arrived at
the paper to frequent bars, restaurants, corner stores, and other hangouts
in black neighborhoods and talk with residents to find out anything he
could about the mood there. The thirty-four-year-old tall, husky African
American blended easily into the district's inner city neighborhoods. On
the street, Delaney heard blacks express an increasing militancy to what
they perceived as indignities and abuse by police officers. Years later
Delaney recalled he sensed a racial tension in the city he had never experienced elsewhere. Paul found a police force dominated by white officers
from rural towns in surrounding states whose immediate response was
to overreact with force and violence to the increase in crime and militancy
in the city. Police Chief John Layton, as Delaney observed him, was "old
school . . . a straight laced southern gentleman" that Delaney thought was
"totally out of sync with the changes occurring in the city."[30]

On July 27, 1967, H. Rap Brown, after being released from jail in Virginia, held a rally at St. Stephens and the Incarnation Church in Washington. *Star* reporters Ernie Holsendolph and Michael Adams heard Brown
tell a crowd that the reporters estimated at "nearly 1,000 Negroes and a
sprinkling of whites" to "arm themselves for a rebellion in the city" because "freedom . . . won't be given to you, you must seize it." Less than
a week later on August 1, 1967, violence erupted as police tried to move
hundreds of spectators away from a two-alarm fire at a furniture store
near Seventh and M Streets. Delaney and *Washington Post* reporter Jesse
Lewis were at the intersection of 14th and T streets when black youths
began torching buildings and smashing windows until events escalated
to near "riot condition," as Delaney described it. As police moved in to
quell the violence, gunfire erupted, which was followed by a melee of
demonstrators and police shooting and swinging at each other down 14th
Street. In the ensuing chaos, the three reporters did not know whom to
fear more—the police or the rioters. As each reporter called in his story,
the other one kept a lookout for rioters or police to warn the reporter in
the phone booth when to duck. That summer reporters referred to the
many lootings and rampages of black youths as "mini-riots." The mini riots were a prelude to Washington's second major race riot one year later.
Despite the historic significance of the district's 1968 riots after Dr. King's

murder, for Delaney the mini riots were far more scary and dangerous for reporters than the one in 1968.[31]

Martin Luther King Jr. spoke at the National Cathedral four days before his assassination about SCLC's plans for a Poor People's Campaign in Washington. Before the tragic news of King's death on April 4, 1968, the *Star*'s afternoon edition that day carried an editorial by Crosby S. Noyes, the great grandson of the Noyes patriarch, complaining that "King's plans for massive demonstrations and civil disobedience in Washington will create conditions that could lead to a tragic riot," and if they do "it is fair to ask whether the cause of social justice and civil rights will not be the first and most important victim." Local and federal politicians and law enforcement were anxious too about King's "Poor People's Campaign" but believed they were well prepared for the confrontations that might take place. By 7 pm on April 4, the *Star*'s last edition was on the streets, so Delaney, Sarro, and Holsendolph joined *Star* reporters David Braaten and Woody West at the Hawk and Dove Restaurant in the Capitol Hill neighborhood to relax over a few drinks and dinner. As the sun lowered on a balmy spring day and cherry blossoms bloomed, the biggest news in Washington was President Johnson's recent announcement that he would not seek another term in office and instead devote his time to peace talks with Hanoi. The reporters placed their dinner order and were settling into food and drinks and hashing over the day when the waiter returned with the shocking news that Dr. King had been shot. They peppered the waiter with questions but learned few details except that Dr. King had been shot by an unknown assassin at a Memphis hotel earlier that day. The reporters arrived to a mostly empty *Star* newsroom to get more details from the national wire services about King's condition and the city's reactions. The *Star*'s offices on Virginia Avenue and 2nd Street, SE were isolated from the city's core in a rundown neighborhood surrounded by warehouses, a city dump, and the Carrollsburg Dwellings public housing project. A little after 8:00 pm word came from the national wires that Dr. King was dead. The dozen or so reporters in the newsroom gathered around a small black-and-white TV in the newsroom to listen to President Johnson address the nation to ask that all Americans join him in mourning the death of Dr. King but reject the violence that struck down a leader who preached and lived nonviolence. Delaney was deeply troubled by the death of King but kept his feelings to himself, as did others in the newsroom. As journalists, they understood the significance of King's death and the need to focus on events to follow in order to write fair and objective news stories.[32]

Sarro and Delaney chose to go together to 14th and U Streets, NW, a popular gathering place for black Washingtonians most nights. By the time they arrived at the intersection, the People's Drug Store at the corner was closed, its windows smashed, and bystanders were helping themselves to whatever they could find. Over the course of the next two hours, the two reporters witnessed groups of black youths strolling through the 14th Street commercial corridor, smashing windows, looting, and setting fires as they went. Earlier in the evening the twenty-six-year-old tall, black militant Stokely Carmichael, wearing dark shades and army fatigues, led young black men from store to store, asking owners to close in honor of King's death. Many business owners did comply, but Carmichael failed to control the angry crowds when they turned violent. The two reporters never saw Carmichael, and by most accounts, he had left the neighborhood by 9:45 pm. Fire alarms were going off, smoky fires were blazing, rocks and bottles hurled pass the reporters, and breaking glass was under foot. Police were in total disarray and outmanned by the rioters. Jim (James) Clarke, a white reporter at WMAL news, began tagging along with Delaney and Sarro as a kind of protection. The three reporters decided to leave the riot area and capitalize on Delaney and Sarro's friendship with the mayor and see what they could learn from him. The three made their way to the mayor's home in LeDroit Park at 4th and T streets, NW, arriving around 11:00 pm. The mayor's home was surrounded by squad cars and a crowd of onlookers, but the newsmen managed to talk their way past security. The mayor invited them into watch TV news coverage of the riot. Corporation Counsel Charles Duncan, Julian Dugas, and their wives had been dinner guests at the Washingtons's home that night when the riots broke out. Around 11:30 pm, the mayor decided to take a tour of the riot area and agreed to let Delaney come along. Sarro had to return to the newsroom to write his story, and Clarke left too. Duncan offered to drive his brand new gray metallic Ford Tempest. Mayor Washington and Dugas sat in front while Mrs. Duncan, Delaney, and a police officer rode as passengers in the back. In a light rain they drove west toward 14th Street. When they reached the riot area, Delaney observed that Mayor Washington shook his head in disgust but only "looked on in silence" while looters casually walked away with stolen merchandise. "There was a sort of holiday gaiety about it all, people laughing and talking," Delaney wrote, and although the looters were not hostile, small crowds of bystanders on street corners "heckled motorists" and "shouted obscenities" at passing cars. Young teenagers moved unimpeded, stealing anything they could from nearby stores. The air was filled with the deafening sounds of people shouting, burglar alarms blaring, police sirens screaming, and squad cars "streaking by." Occasionally the police would hurl a tear gas canister, but for the most part, they were so outnumbered by the rioters and could do little to stop the large-scale looting without using their service revolvers. Mayor Washington and Public Safety Director Patrick J. Murphy, strongly backed by the US Justice Department, had ordered the police not to shoot at the mostly nonviolent looters. Local and federal officials wanted to prevent a large number of gun deaths in the nation's capital that had occurred in other riot-torn cities. Store owners hit hard by the riot's destruction would later bitterly complain about the lack of more forceful police protection from looters and arsonists, but the mayor's decision was credited for saving many lives. The mayor ended the tour around midnight at the 13th Police Precinct temporary command post. Around 3 am Friday, the mayor conducted an impromptu news conference to announce the crisis was not over but felt the police had it under control.[33]

Sid Epstein as city editor sometimes sent photographers where even veteran reporters might not go to tell the story with the camera lens. *Star* cameramen Bernie Boston and Ray Lustig were in the riot area late Thursday night through Friday morning soon after the riots began, and Ken Heinen shot images of some of the first looters on 7th Street on Friday morning. Lustig's photography ended when his D.C. National Guard unit was called to duty the next day. Boston and Heinen were relatively new recruits to the *Star*. Delaney had worked with Boston at the *Dayton Daily News*, and when he showed Sid Epstein samples of Boston's work, the city editor hired the talented photographer right away. After Boston had been at the *Star* for only a few short months, Epstein asked Delaney if he

Photograph taken by *Star* photographer Bernie Boston of police in riot gear at the intersection of 14th and U Streets, NW, in Washington on April 4, 1968, just hours after the announcement of Dr. Martin Luther King Jr.'s assassination. Reprinted with permission of the D.C. Public Library, *Star* Collection, © *Washington Post*.

knew anymore black photographers as good as Bernie, to which Delaney replied, "I don't know of any white cameraman as good as Bernie." In the darkest hours of Friday morning, the cameramen shot dramatic scenes of the riot area backlit by neon lights, and images of tear gas exploding behind rioters fleeing from a line of police officers in full riot gear that blocked a large swath of 14th Street. Three of the many images Heinen, Lustig, and Boston shot that night were picked for the front page of the *Star*'s Friday edition. Boston's gifted eye and talent moved him up the ranks at the *Star* to become director of photography during the 1970s.[34]

Star staff nearly doubled in size as reporters from other departments volunteered to lend a hand to cover breaking news all over the city as the riot progressed throughout the weekend. Boris Weintraub postponed his vacation and manned the city desk on Friday night; Harry Bacas, Sunday editor but once assistant city editor, returned to help out; sportswriter Steve Hershey and Dick Heller joined their editor Bill Peeler to walk the riotous streets and call in what they saw and heard to the city desk; and Emerson Beauchamp in the drama department took charge of the city desk on Saturday night. Some staff found it easier to remain at the *Star*'s offices, like dictationist Anne Groer, who slept in the editor's office, or production manager Bin (Wilmott) Lewis, who stayed Friday and Saturday night to make sure everything ran smoothly. Photographers and reporters caught naps in the newsroom, the employees lounge, or wherever they could. Woody West, who had been with the group at the Hawk and Dove on Thursday night, was in the newsroom Friday morning gathering stories from newsmen and photographers covering breaking news for Friday's edition all over the city. West, a husky man in his early thirties with a wry smile, tattoos from his US Navy service, and an unruly mop of curly hair was a seasoned reporter and an exceptional rewrite man. From behind thick, black-framed glasses, West reviewed copy, edited, and prepared the front-page story for Friday's edition. The *Star* hit the streets before noon, with three more editions to follow, each giving updates on the developing story. The lead story on the front page of the Friday afternoon edition read "Widespread riotous looting and arson broke out again this afternoon in near Northwest Washington as bands of rampaging youths raced with their stolen goods" while "police appeared largely to have abandoned efforts to halt the pillage." One reporter described hearing an "anguished voice over the police radio pleading 'Send in the National Guard, for God's sake,'" and another asking, "Won't someone please tell us what to do." The *Star* reported nine major fires, two hundred persons arrested, one white Virginian beaten to death, 155 looting incidents, several firemen injured, and 233 broken store windows.[35]

Stokely Carmichael called a press conference at the New School for Afro-American Thought just a few blocks north of the heaviest hit part of the city at 14th and U Streets for 11 am on Friday morning. As the press arrived, including veteran *Star* cameramen Randolph "Ranny" Routt, they were met by "50 to 75 young Negroes standing on the sidewalk" who "frisked" them and checked their credentials. Carmichael had been characterized in the press as encouraging violence but told the press, "Last night's violence . . . was 'light stuff' compared with what's about to happen." When Winston Groom showed up in the *Star*'s newsroom on Friday morning for his first day as a bona fide reporter for the paper after a night of rioting in the city, he thought, "This is going to be a very interesting day." Groom had just completed his obligatory stint in the *Star*'s probationary training program the day King was shot. Bill Hill, managing editor of the *Star*, had met Groom at a wedding in Point Clear, Alabama, in 1967 just six months after Groom returned from Vietnam after serving a year as a sergeant in the 4th Army Division. During the wedding reception, Groom wandered out to a pier nearby for a fortuitous encounter with Hill standing alone on the pier smoking a cigarette. Groom would later joke that when he saw Hill's brown shoes jutting out beneath his black tuxedo he guessed his new acquaintance was probably a newsman. The two men struck up a conversation, during which Groom told Hill he wanted to be a writer rather than a lawyer, which his father, a judge advocate general, expected him to be. Hill suggested Groom write a letter of introduction to the *Star*, and the young, aspiring writer took his advice and was eventually hired. Police radios were blaring in the newsroom while the always impeccably dressed, tall, World War II US Marine veteran, and city editor Sid Epstein sat at the city desk bellowing for reporters, cameramen, copy boys, and editors as news was breaking all over the city. Epstein would later claim directing the coverage of the 1968 riots was the most difficult assignment of his career. With deadlines approaching, Epstein yelled from his desk, "Groom, you and Fahnestock go over to 14th and U Streets and see what's going on." Sheridan Fahnestock, a native Washingtonian and Harvard graduate, sported a red beard and drove a red sports car to match. Around 12:30 pm, the two reporters drove north up 16th Street until they met heavy traffic and chose to park the car in a no-parking zone in front of the Italian embassy and walk up 16th Street to Harvard Street, where they met a line of helmeted officers with squad cars blocking their way east. When they showed an officer their press passes, he stepped aside but warned them the area was not safe for anyone. As they walked east to 14th Street, sirens grew louder, the smell of tear gas stronger, and bricks and broken glass littered the street. Groom recalled later that he never really felt in danger because people in the street "were too busy hauling away loot to be very dangerous." Groom saw exhausted and outnumbered police officers protect firemen while they put out fires but had to stand by and watch while looters ransacked stores. Police called for reinforcements, but none were available.

The reporters tried to conduct "man in the street" interviews, but Groom never felt he ever got "much of a sensible answer" from anyone, although anger and frustration was palpable among the rioters, looters, business owners, and residents. The reporters searched for a phone booth and called in their stories to the newsroom, then stuck around until late afternoon. When the looting subsided and the violence got "ugly," as Groom described it, they left before night fell on the city. A cavalry regiment was sent in later that afternoon to control the crowds, but it managed only to push the rioters into the side streets.[36]

On Saturday morning, April 6, at 2:00 am a platoon of soldiers arrived to guard the Star Building, and fires could be seen blazing in various parts of the city from its third-floor newsroom. *Star* maintenance staff installed metal screens on the building's windows to protect employees from the possibility of flying glass from bottles or bricks thrown by rioters. The riots continued despite three thousand police officers and four thousand federal troops on city streets, and a 5:30 pm to 6:30 am curfew. The Saturday afternoon *Star* reported the death toll had risen to five, more than two thousand people had been arrested, and six hundred cases had been processed in a Friday night marathon at the Court of General Sessions. Groom showed up for his second day in the 14th Street riot area in his own car that still carried Alabama tags. The streets "looked like a damn fair," he remembered later. When Groom returned to his car a few hours later, "three or four black guys were sitting" on the hood. Groom ignored their jeers as he approached, until one of the men reached up and smashed a beer bottle across his head. Groom opened the car door and strategically pushed his assailant back and away from the door, slammed the door shut, and while a trickle of blood ran down the side of his face he turned the ignition and drove away. Groom's cut was minor but head wounds bleed profusely, so when he appeared in the *Star*'s newsroom, Sid Epstein croaked loudly, "What the hell happened to you, Groom," to which the reporter responded in his southern drawl, "Well sir, could I have one of those *Star* cars next time." After leaving the *Star* nine years later, Groom would write novels and histories, including *Forrest Gump*, later made into a popular major Hollywood film.[37]

On Saturday Haynes Johnson returned to Washington from Memphis after covering the hunt for Dr. King's assassin. The last time Johnson saw King alive was in August 1967 while questioning him about his views on the Vietnam War as a panelist on *Meet the Press*. At the time, Johnson had been "shocked with how King had aged." Johnson heard that King was shot in Memphis just before he was scheduled to appear on *Washington Week in Review* at Howard University. Everyone on the show agreed not to mention King's death during the live broadcast. Immediately after the show ended, he and *Star* reporter Chuck Conconi met and managed to catch a ride on an 82nd Airborne military plane going to Memphis. When Johnson overheard soldiers on the flight cracking jokes about Dr. King, his anger boiled until he stood up and shouted to shame and silence them. "I used to wear the uniform myself and you are a disgrace to the uniform." As Johnson drove to his home from National Airport on Saturday, he could see the smoke rising in the distance and headed toward it instinctively to see what was happening. As he drove deeper into the 14th Street riot corridor and passed row after row of burned and looted stores, he was startled by "a young Negro boy—he couldn't have been more than 6," wrote Johnson, that "leaped toward the car, pointing his fingers and shouting: 'Bam! Bam! Bam!' Then he drew back his hand and hurled an imaginary brick." The Korean War veteran and civil rights reporter who had witnessed far worse violence during his life and career was shaken by the incident and violence taking place in his own hometown. Soon after Johnson arrived, he flew back to Atlanta to report on Dr. King's funeral, which was attended by an estimated 150,000 mourners.[38]

By Sunday the fires were smoldering, the anger subdued, and most of the damage already done. US Attorney General Ramsey Clark, Mayor Washington, and Public Safety Director Patrick Murphy, LBJ's hand-picked law enforcement officer for the city, all agreed that using deadly force against looters would have led to worse violence. Local retail store owners, however, complained bitterly about the loss of their businesses because of the policy. The *Star* praised Mayor Washington, his top aides, and the police for their response to the riots and the humanitarian aid afterward but criticized those who thought the police should have taken more forceful action to curb the looters because to do so "might only have spread the bloodshed and the death toll." The riots ended, but it would take decades for the city to rebuild. In response to the National Advisory Commission on Civil Disorders' conclusion that the press had failed to "provide white readers with an accurate picture of the black community," the Baltimore-Washington Chapter of the American Newspaper Guild invited top executives of the three local white-owned dailies to a seminar on June 15, 1969, to hear from community leaders and residents. *Star* editor Newby (Newbold) Noyes, *Washington Post* editor Ben Bradlee, and associate editor of the *Washington Daily News* Nicholas Blatchford represented their newspapers. During the four-hour meeting, outspoken activists such as Marion Barry and Julius Hobson criticized the papers for a lack of "honesty and accuracy" in covering the black community. Etta Horn, first vice-chair of the National Welfare Rights Organization, had a harsher assessment. Ms. Horn called the white publishers "a racist bunch of bastards." Noyes admitted newspapers had made mistakes but took issue with the "notion that editors meet to decide how every story should be written as 'absolute baloney.'" At the time that meeting took place, Lyndon Johnson, who had championed civil rights legislation and Great Society programs to reduce poverty and inequality, was no longer president. Johnson's successor Richard Nixon pivoted his attention to the concerns of the "silent majority" that elected him to bring law and order back to a nation they felt was awash in violence.[39]

By 1973 the *Star*'s editorial support for Nixon's record on reducing violence, alleviating urban poverty, and bringing peace in Vietnam was sorely tested. This turn in opinion was especially difficult for Newby Noyes, who had supported and respected Nixon since the 1950s. In January 1973 Noyes privately wrote Nixon to express his concerns, not as a traditional adversary "who wants to score a few brownie points with the Georgetown set," but as a friend and fellow conservative. Noyes wrote that he agreed with Nixon's views that "theoretical expensive answers" offered "by 'liberal' sociologists and politicians" to alleviate poverty in the past haven't always worked. Noyes, however, was more concerned by Nixon's tone than his policies. In response to Nixon telling the *Star*'s White House correspondent Jack Horner after his reelection "that the main thing this country needs is a more responsible attitude on the part of its disadvantaged citizens," Noyes wrote in his letter to the president, "Do you really believe this" is the solution for ending poverty? Instead, Noyes counseled that the president "more than anyone else is responsible for the moral tone, the mood of spirit of the American people, and right now that spirit is not good." Noyes asked for a meeting with the president, and on March 8 Nixon and his domestic policy advisor John Ehrlichman met with Noyes in the Oval Office to discuss his concerns further. At the meeting Noyes prodded the president to appeal "to the higher sense of duty and opportunity of the citizen, not just to take care of himself but to take care of his neighbor," and not to "the very deep and dangerous current running now in the national consciousness" of the "middle-American, the little man who . . . feels he has somehow been had by all these liberal schemes to do good—that it's time to put an end to all that nonsense." Noyes told Nixon he was concerned that an "anti-black, anti-poor mood in the middle class" is building and could result in a "very ugly, very unhealthy, something" Nixon "would have cause to regret bitterly." Nixon's response was defensive. The president complained that blacks want him to attack those "goddamn rednecks and segregationists," but he thinks that strategy would be counterproductive, and besides, the black community has not given him enough credit for the concrete actions he has taken to reduce inner city poverty. These divisive sentiments and tensions have not abetted. They continue to fester in American society even now.[40]

By 1970 race relations in the city had improved in some ways but deteriorated in others during the half century since the riots of 1919. In 1919

Washington's white-owned dailies unfairly and incorrectly linked race and crime together with disastrous results. Newspapers by 1970 were at least aware and attempting to address the problem of racial bias in crime reporting, but the effort was only in its infancy. The problem would not be solved in the *Star*'s lifetime. Crime always will be with us in all segments of society, among all races and genders, and in cities and hamlets across the country and world. The news of crime and natural or man-made disasters are a perennial and integral part of the daily news. The *Star*, like any good newspaper, knew their readers wanted and needed to know about the titillating and tragic stories of mayhem, murder, and disasters, and the paper from its inception did not disappoint.

4

+

Murder and Mayhem

On a clear, cold Sunday afternoon in February 1859, New York congressman Daniel E. Sickles repeatedly shot Philip Barton Key II at close range on a sidewalk in an upscale neighborhood near Lafayette Square across from the White House. Key, attorney general of the District of Columbia and son of the famous composer Francis Scott Key, would soon die of his wounds in a backroom of a men's social club. *The Evening Star*'s February 28, 1859, edition devoted a substantial part of its four-page newspaper to Key's murder and issued nearly three thousand copies. An unnamed *Star* reporter, most likely Crosby Noyes, interviewed eyewitnesses to the crime and relayed their accounts and what he had learned of Key's murder. The bystanders believed Sickles's action was in response to his wife Teresa Sickles's confession of infidelity after her husband presented to her an "anonymous note stating that his wife had held criminal intercourse with Mr. Key at an assignation house." The young and beautiful Teresa Bagioli Sickles and the dashing Key had carried on an illicit sexual affair for many months in a secret hideaway—a house Key rented from a free Negro, John Gray, at 15th Street between K and L Streets close to the Sickleses's residence. Soon after Teresa's confession, the brooding and betrayed Sickles saw the unsuspecting Key strolling in the street below the Sickleses's home waving a white handkerchief to summon Teresa to their love nest. An enraged Sickles raced downstairs, retrieved his gun, and confronted Key in the street. Sickles's friend Samuel Butterworth told Captain Goddard that he heard Sickles call Key by name and then say, "You Scoundrel, you have dishonored my home or my family I do not know precisely which." Sickles then fired his gun at Key, who simultaneously pulled something from his pocket that police later learned was an opera glass—not a pistol. Sickles shot Key three more times while Butterworth stood by his side. Key was taken to the Washington Club where the dead man was laid on the backroom floor, as Noyes described in grim detail, "denuded of all clothing except . . . shirt and pantaloons . . . the face calm and unruffled as if in sleep . . . save the unnatural position of the left arm and the appearance of blood upon the apparel." Sickles, a prominent politician and friend of President James Buchanan, was arrested for the crime but acquitted by a jury of men who judged him temporarily insane for killing his young wife's lover in a jealous rage.[1]

In the 1850s, only sensational crime stories or those involving high-profile personalities, like the murder of Key, made headlines in Washington's local dailies. James Croggon, who covered local courts for the *Star* from 1863 until the 1890s, remembered in the very early years "there were no court reporters, but simply news gatherers, who, as occasion seemed to require, ascertained what was going on by glancing over the minute books of the clerks." Reports published from the daily police log and clerk of the court were usually short but colorful and sardonic descriptions of a panoply of petty vices and occasionally more serious crimes. A sampling from an 1859 *Star* edition includes Robert Wilson, who "was fished up in the streets in a condition of overflowing hilarity, induced by the strong temptations of the corner grocery," or Francis and Mary Robinson who "had committed sundry disturbances of the public peace." Those who could not pay the fines were sent to the "corporation farm" in the country or workhouse in the city. Some reporting from the courts contained more violent or tragic accounts, like the "body of a very large new born female infant, supposed to be a mulatto" found in the streets with "marks upon it [that] indicated a violent death." Croggon was joined by Dan Curry and then Howard Brooks in the 1880s in helping to chase down crime and how society exacted justice.[2]

On May 9, 1865, Jim Croggon reported that the trials of the co-conspirators accused of assassinating President Lincoln would soon take place in a makeshift courtroom in the old Penitentiary Building where the prisoners were housed in separate cells and held in chains. By May 13 the press was allowed into the courtroom, and for nearly two months Croggon wrote regular accounts of the trial for the *Star* until the verdicts came down in late June. Of the co-conspirators, Mary Surratt, Lewis Powell, David Herold, and George Atzerodt were found guilty and hanged in Washington's Old Capitol Prison yard on July 7, 1865. Four months later on November 10, 1865, Captain Henry Wirz, the only man found guilty of war crimes during the Civil War, was hung from the same gallows in the same prison yard. Wirz was commander of the interior stockade at the Confederate prison at Fort

James Croggon (#7 leaning against railing at left) and Crosby Noyes (#6 seated on steps just above Croggon) waiting to view the hanging on November 10, 1865, of Captain Henry Wirz, who was the commander of the Confederate prison at Fort Sumter. Courtesy D.C. Public Library, Washingtoniana Division, Photo by Alexander Gardner, Neg. #7120.

Sumter in Andersonville, Georgia, where approximately forty-five thousand captured Union soldiers were imprisoned from February 1864 to April 1865. The provost-marshal and the Capitol prison's commandant oversaw the execution and issued only two hundred passes for civilian spectators to view Wirz's hanging. Among the witnesses were Noyes and Croggon. Alexander Gardner, assistant to Civil War photographer Matthew Brady, shot photographs for *Harper's Weekly* of the notorious hangings conducted in the prison yard. Among Gardner's photos that day was an image of members of the press gang who had gathered to pose for him. The reporters with pad and pen in their hands stood or sat on the rickety wooden steps leading into the prison yard. A young Noyes, smartly dressed in a fashionable brimmed hat, cravat, and full-length black winter cape with a velvet collar, sits on the stairs while Croggon, wearing just an ordinary frockcoat and bowler, stands next to Noyes and leans casually against the stair railing as he glances sideways at the camera. Others identified in the photo were Ben Perley Poore of the *Boston Daily Journal*, L. A. Gobright of the Associated Press, John Clagett Proctor, who would later write for the *Star*, and actor Frank Lawler. The dozen or so correspondents Gardner photographed rushed to see his negative but immediately scattered when notice came that the prisoner was on his way to the gallows. The *Star*'s account, headlined "Wirz Last Hours," gives excruciatingly florid detail of the very public end to Wirz's life, whose last months "must have been a rack of immeasurable agony" as he received "not one ray of comfort . . . in all the weary months from his capture to the present time" and who daily "had to face a crowd thirsting for his blood." The *Star* reported Wirz's last full meal was oysters and a large glass of whiskey the night before the execution, and only a swig of whiskey for his breakfast before being led to the gallows. Noyes and Croggon saw Wirz "with great ease and urbanity raising to his feet" to receive Major Russell, who placed a black gown on the prisoner but not handcuffs because Wirz's hands were swollen from a chronically injured wrist. Wirz mounted to the scaffold in a "quick step" with his head uncovered and a slight breeze blowing wisps of hair over his eyes. Noyes, who had observed Wirz at trial for many weeks, saw his familiar "sort of grim smile" as he mounted the gallows, but also in his visage "a sort of ghastly merriment on the very edge of the Great Shadow he was entering," as the crowd in the yard and spectators in the tops of houses and the trees nearby shouted, "Hang the Scoundrel" and hurled other vicious epithets at him. When Major Russell asked Wirz if he had any answer to the charges, the reporters heard him say, "No, sir, only that I am innocent and will die a man, my hopes being in the future, I go before my God . . . and he will judge between me and you." Then "at 10:30 o'clock when the drop fell with a 'thug' and the criminal was 'left dangling in the air,'" a loud cheer arose from the crowd. According to contemporaneous and historic accounts, the noose failed to break Wirz's neck immediately, and he slowly choked to death. Nearing retirement, Croggon claimed he had witnessed more hangings than any other man in Washington and often traveled far into Maryland and Virginia to witness and report on both legal hangings and illegal lynchings. Nearing retirement, Croggon admitted he finally "lost his nerve" and refused to cover another hanging after a prominent Washingtonian was sentenced to hang for his wife's murder—just two short of Croggon's self-imposed goal of fifty.[3]

As the divisions and violence of the Civil War faded from memory, a peaceable and proper middle-class Victorian ethos struggled to dominate late nineteenth-century America. Behind the Victorian façade, however, murder, prostitution, orphanages, opium dens, wife beating, child labor, and all manner of perennial vice and crime stubbornly remained a part of urban life. Newspapers like William Randolph Hearst's *New York Journal* flourished by sensationalizing the violence, human tragedy, and vice in American cities of the era. These so-called yellow journals had a large audience but were especially attractive to the growing immigrant and working-class populations whose causes also championed in their columns. The *Star*'s editor, Crosby Noyes, was a sharp critic of "yellow journalism." Although Noyes came from humble roots and had reported on his share of the violent and seedier sides of urban life, by the turn of the nineteenth century he too had embraced the Victorian values of the class to which he had risen. In an address before the National Editorial Association in 1907, Noyes characterized yellow newspapers as the "penny dreadful . . . devoted to lurid descriptions of the great scandal—murder cases . . . assassinations, rapes, elopements, divorces, frightful railroad wrecks, massacres of Jews in Russia, . . . cannibalism in China, and manifold horrors and atrocities" that did not have a chance against the "clean, sane, reputable journals like the *Star*." Noyes made every effort to keep the *Star*'s columns free of the worse kind of sensationalism and exploitation he deplored in yellow journals. Crime reporter Jim Croggon, with whom Noyes had worked closely in the *Star*'s early years, was not fooled by the Victorian pretenses of some Washingtonians, however. Rudy Kauffmann vividly recalled an angry Croggon coming into the newsroom one day after being splashed by a passing motorcar, and pounding his cane on the floor and with "blue eyes blazing" and "white beard jutting forward," loudly exclaimed that the "two dressy dames" in the car's back seat "who kept their noses stuck in the air and gave me not a glance . . . are very high and mighty today, but I can remember when their grandmother stood barefoot in old Center Market behind a plank spread across two barrels. From its top she sold fly-specked sweetmeats and from a bucket hidden underneath it she dispensed gin at 2 cents a dipperful." As Croggon's contemporary, Noyes too had written colorful and gruesome stories in his time, but as editor and owner, he passed on a legacy to the *Star* that encouraged editorial staff to shun sensationalism and stick to the facts. Still, melodramatic flourish that was the lifeblood of nineteenth-century prose persisted.[4]

In the spring of 1889, one of the deadliest natural disasters of the century became one of the press's biggest news stories. On Saturday, June 1, 1889, the *Star* reported the news sent over the telegraph wires that morning of a horrific flood in Johnstown, Pennsylvania. The same edition reported a less tragic but no less dramatic story taking place in Washington as a deluge of rain in the Mid-Atlantic region swelled the Potomac. The *Star*'s headline read, "Water, water everywhere! Muddy water, raging, boiling, racing whirling past the city to the sea, creeping up, inch by inch, foot by foot, a turbid, angry flood, showing its teeth and growling in its fury." On Saturday night and all day Sunday, *Star* reporters joined with throngs of residents along the Potomac in Quantico and Alexandria, atop the Aqueduct and Long Bridges, at the Analostan Island, and Pennsylvania Avenue to observe the flood and write copy. Copy boys like Thomas Harlow took copy from reporters and rowed a boat in waist-high water down Pennsylvania Avenue to the *Evening Star*'s newsroom at 11th Street for each edition. The *Star*'s Monday edition of June 3 reported that the previous night the Analostan Boat House came unmoored, the K Street Bridge broke apart, and homeowners upstream were living on their top floors or camped outside on higher ground. From Saturday to Sunday, throngs of people crowded in the center of the city to see Pennsylvania Avenue flooded from 2nd to 7th streets where the "market house stood in the center of a great lake" and boats instead of horse and buggies traversed city streets. Along the Potomac's banks or atop bridges, the *Star* estimated that thousands gathered to see the surging waters and hundreds went further upstream to see "Chain Bridge and the Little Falls, where the river rushed with a mighty roar in its pent-up channel, overflowing the bridge and sweeping great trees and wrecks of barns and houses along in its resistless flood." *Star* reporters talked to the owners of coal wharves, lumber yards, a steamship company, restaurants, hotels, and haberdashers about their efforts to save their businesses. Kurt Johnson, a local coal wharf owner whose business had suffered a fire the week before and a flood that week, told a reporter that despite the city's losses, Washingtonians "ought not to complain when we think of the awful disaster at Johnstown, Pa." Washington recovered quickly from its "Great Flood," but Johnstown took more than ten years to regain what was lost.[5]

The next big disaster in the city was caused by human failures at the site of the nation's first presidential assassination. At 9:40 am on the morning of June 9, 1893, as workmen excavated in the cellar of Ford's Theater, its rickety and deteriorating walls collapsed, killing twenty-two and injuring nearly fifty War Department employees. Ford's Theater had recently become an office for clerks of the Pension Records Division charged with copying Civil War muster rolls. Victor Kauffmann, son of owner Samuel Kauffmann, was on the balcony of the *Star* building barely

a block away from Ford's Theater when he heard a crash and saw a large
cloud of dust rise in his direction. Kauffmann, Will Chandlee, the *Star's*
artist of only a few months, and another half-dozen *Star* reporters went
to the crash site. Kauffmann wrote his story, which finally stretched to
sixteen columns, while Chandlee sketched the scene of the disaster from
an upstairs window across 10th Street from the theater. Kauffmann
dropped his copy and Chandlee's drawings from the window to a messenger who took them by bicycle to the newsroom. Chandlee drew ten
sketches that portrayed firemen removing the wreckage of timber, girders, broken desks, and the injured and dead just after the floors and walls
of the front of the theater collapsed. Crosby Noyes uncharacteristically
paced the almost deserted newsroom, worrying about the reporting
and getting the paper out, but city editor Harry Godwin assured him
he had things under control with copy coming from dozens of reporters
around town. The *Star* published four extras on the disaster the same
day. Among the half-dozen *Star* reporters who entered the building, one
managed to pass through an unblocked door on the south side of the theater, where he found an intact staircase held in place by a standing wall.
The reporter climbed the steps to the third floor and from a platform that
once was the third-floor threshold, he described thirty to forty feet below a mass of timber, girders, beams, rubble, and debris where no "man
could have lived long under that debris" without suffocating. Other
reporters talked with survivors, neighbors who opened their homes to
the injured, firemen, and physicians who helped at the disaster site, and
city hospitals. A "colored workman" who was part of the excavating
team explained to a *Star* reporter, "I told them yesterday that the arch-
way would fall, for every time any one walked over the floor it would
bend. There were twenty men at work with me. Deed, I don't know what
became of them." Some reporters made mistakes in the confusion. In
one instance when a reporter asked survivor Samuel McMichael about
casualties, he told him he had found his colleague A. L. Dietrick dead,
but later when McMichael saw Dietrick on the street, they went to the
Star's offices to correct the error. Without objectivity or restraint, Victor
Kauffman indicted those he believed at fault, writing, "Oh, the shame of
it to the government of a fair nation. It could not afford to provide a safe
building for its faithful employees . . . Will it go as a blot on the fair name
of the capital or will it be shown that the sin lies at the door of the federal government?" The June 14, 1893, *Star* headline read "HANG HIM!
HANG HIM!"—the "Him" referred to Colonel Fred C. Ainsworth, head
of the Record and Pension Division of the War Department. A grand
jury brought indictments against both Ainsworth and George Dent, the
contractor who oversaw the excavation. Ainsworth was never tried, nor
was the federal government ever held liable.[6]

Star editor Theodore Noyes, who came of age in the late nineteenth century, embraced the strict Victorian moral values of the era, and like his father he incorporated those values into the newspaper he ran. Theodore was always the proper gentlemen, wearing spats long out of style until he died in the 1940s and was a committed teetotaler and early supporter of temperance. In 1916 Theodore got a head start on the moral crusade against the evils of strong drink. Flush with advertising revenue, the *Star* boldly severed all its ties with the purveyors of evil spirits by banning liquor advertising in its columns. The Eighteenth Amendment was not officially passed until January 16, 1920, but Congress closed saloons in the nation's capital at midnight on Halloween 1917, and official prohibition began for the city. The day after the last official drink was served before prohibition, the *Star* wrote that "there were wakes to mourn," the passing of "King Booze," but "his friends in retrospect, had to admit for him the blame for heart-sore mothers and wives and tears of little children." *Post* publisher Ned McLean and heavy drinker himself, however, was not thrilled. On April 21, 1917, in the midst of World War I, a *Washington Post* editorial ridiculed the US Army for denying soldiers drink on the field when even George Washington had rewarded his soldiers with rum. During prohibition, Ned McLean kept illegal stocks of liquor at Friendship House, the family home on Wisconsin Avenue in Georgetown, where he and his wife, Evalyn Walsh McLean, entertained friends lavishly. Theodore Noyes was not among them. Noyes remained true to his convictions in both his business and personal life and refused to keep or serve hard spirits at his private residence. The *Star*'s columns predicted "the end of a glamorous romance that probably has passed from the city forever" when the Eighteenth Amendment passed, but they were wrong. In the 1920s Washingtonians had no trouble finding illegal spirits from the many bootleggers who operated in the city, at private parties, and speakeasies. Even Congress had its own official bootlegger, George L. Cassiday, known as "The Man in the Green Hat."[7]

Arrests for violation of the Volstead Act exacerbated overcrowding at the district jail in the 1920s, which, according to a *Star* news story, led to inmates being "penned up like animals." In March 1926, Philip Kauffmann, Samuel Kauffmann's second son, disguised as drunken hobo Pete Martin, spent ten days in the district jail, then located at 19th Street, SE near Congressional Cemetery on the eastern shore of the Anacostia River. Kauffmann hoped to get an unfiltered look at conditions inside the jail in order to write an honest exposé. In the jail's north wing, grand jury prisoners convicted of serious crimes lived in relative comfort in larger cells like "Wan, the Chinese," who was awaiting trial for his third murder. These more high-profile criminals had "the run of the place," observed Kauffmann, while derelicts and drunks like Pete and his companions were housed in the south wing in cramped and dirty cells. To get himself arrested like the "hardboiled and professional habitués of the District jail," wrote Kauffmann, he donned a tattered army overcoat, grew a scraggly beard and hair to his shoulders, and soaked his clothes in ashes. In a farcical sequence of events, Pete feigned drunkenness while sprawled on a curb in what he described as the "orderly community" of Brookland. The police officer, Kauffmann concluded, didn't seemed inclined to arrest him despite his drunken state but was finally convinced when Pete turned belligerent, broke a whiskey bottle, and told the officer, "'Go Take a jump in the Lake' or something to that effect." Kauffmann described the holding cell for defendants awaiting trial at police court as more suffocating than "the black home of Calcutta" where 125 men, mostly hungover from the previous evening, were crammed into a 20x20-foot room for hours. Living space for seven inmates was in three connecting 7x5 cells, one of which contained the lavatory and a bunk consisting of canvass stretched over metal piping or a straw mat on the floor. Kauffmann spoke with other inmates who told him that when prisoners misbehaved, they had their arms wrapped behind them around a pillar and were handcuffed or chained by their wrists to crosslike bars for hours. Other prisoners told him about solitary confinement, or the "hole," where the most difficult prisoners were sent. As a result of the *Star*'s undercover story, Frederick N. Zihlman, as head of the House District Committee, introduced legislation to build a new wing for women prisoners at a cost of $125,000. The wing was finished in 1927 and freed up space for the male inmates in the main facility, but it would still remain in poor and deteriorating condition for years.[8]

During the 1920s, law-abiding Washingtonians fell back on more simple pleasures when prohibition closed the corner saloon. They spent their leisure time dancing the Charleston at Marshall Hall, skating at the Coliseum skating rink above the Center Market on Pennsylvania Avenue, or attending vaudeville shows at Keith's Theater. Washingtonians could see silent movies at the Rialto and Loew's Palace downtown or the Knickerbocker Theater in the heart of the then-affluent D.C. suburb of Adams Morgan. The Knickerbocker, located at the intersection of Columbia Road and 18th Street, NW, was a large modern movie theater with a seating capacity of 1,700 designed in a neoclassical style by local architect Reginald Wycliffe Geare at a cost of $100,000. A smattering of residents in Adams Morgan and nearby neighborhoods had ventured out by foot on the evening of January 28, 1922, to the Knickerbocker, while a steady, blowing snow rained down on the city for nearly twenty-four hours. At 9 pm that night, the roof of the three-story limestone building collapsed under the weight of a twenty-seven-inch fresh snowfall that killed ninety-eight people and injured hundreds more. A *Star* reporter talked to a number of eyewitnesses and pulled their stories together for a vivid account of the tragedy at the Knickbocker that night. As the orchestra played, the reporter wrote, "The house lights suddenly dimmed, the organ stopped and a huge crack ran across the ceiling," and then "the rattle and clatter of falling timber, stone, steel and plaster" was followed by "a stillness, an unearthly pause . . . then a scream, an agonized cry, a moan," leaving men, women, and children buried under tons of steel and masonry. Raymond and Mildred Bowen, who were among the small crowd of theatergoers, described their memory of that night fifty years later to *Star* reporter Woody West. The Bowens told West that they had walked to the Knickerbocker to see the silent movie comedy *Get-Rich-Quick Wallingford* and remained in their first-row balcony seats at intermission when they heard a crack from above. In seconds the entire balcony where they were seated slid precipitously down into the crowd. The Bowens were trapped for nearly five hours surrounded by hundreds of screaming and injured persons beneath mounds of heavy debris as rescuers used acetylene torches to try to free them. Mildred Bowen's leg was broken and mangled, but she credited the "two pair of socks" she wore under her "stylish mid-calf laced shoes" for saving her leg. The first graphic images the public saw of the chaos and destruction was shot by *Star* staff photographers for the first edition. All Sunday afternoon, the *Star* printed extras with updates on the disaster and rescue efforts, including the names, occupations, and addresses of the dead and injured and detailed physical descriptions of unidentified victims to help families locate their loved ones. The *Star* reported forty-five deaths in the first edition, but by late afternoon the number had increased to eighty-five. More than two hundred soldiers, marines, police, and firemen conducted the rescue operation in a blinding snowstorm. Fifteen hours later, "cries of the injured," the *Star* reported, were still heard coming from the rubble. Within the next year, criminal manslaughter charges were brought against Geare, the architect; John McDonald, the contractor; and eight other men connected with the building's construction. Similar to the defendants in the Ford's Theater case, none of the men were ever tried on the charges because of insufficient evidence. Reginald W. Geare committed suicide by gassing himself at his home on August 20, 1927, followed by Harry M. Crandall, president of the Knickerbocker Theater, who ten years later died in the same gruesome manner. Crandall killed himself in a rented room at 13th and I Street in Washington on February 26, 1937, and left a suicide note that read only, "I'm so despondent and miss my theater." John L. McDonald, who remained head of the Federal Steel Erecting Company, never appeared to have suffered similar remorse. Ironically, McDonald was killed in 1936 when a steel girder fell on him at the Benning Road viaduct.[9]

Star newsman Cy Perkins years later recalled the frequent trips that he and staff reporter Johnny Mueller made with Internal Revenue service agents to photograph raids of illegal liquor stills in southern Maryland in the 1920s. IRS agents complained the reporters made too much noise helping to carry the large cases of dynamite, but Perkins joked, "There was no way to stop our chattering teeth and banging knees from the fright." Prohibition ended in December 1933, but violent crime remained. News about the numbers rackets, illegal gambling, prostitution, and gangland murders in D.C. and surrounding areas filled the daily news in the 1930s. One of the more sinister crimes of the 1930s was the murder of Allen Wilson, a thirty-two-year-old newspaper route carrier, who was shot in the head after delivering a newspaper to the Takoma Park, Maryland, home of Edward "Mickey" McDonald, a notorious gambler with suspected bookmaking interests in the area. Wilson was mistaken for McDonald, who slept soundly in an upstairs bedroom. After more than a year of investigating the murder, Montgomery County, Maryland, police in October 1935 gave the press the names of possibly five suspected gunmen hired to kill McDonald by rival gambler Albert S. Sutton, who ran numbers and gambling houses in D.C. *Star* reporter John H. Cline followed the story of racketeering and the so-called Tri-State Gang and mobsters with colorful names like Tony "the Stinger" Cugino, who county police chief Ernest Brown named the suspected "trigger man." Cline came to the *Star* as a general assignment reporter in 1928 in his early twenties and would go on to cover politics and the courts. Cline eventually became associate editor and then chief editorial writer before retiring. From October 1935 until February 1936, Cline followed up leads and prodded state's attorney Pugh in Montgomery County, who was keeping quiet as he worked with federal authorities to build a racketeering case against the Tri-State Gang that operated in the area from Philadelphia to Washington. On January 20, 1936, a grand jury was scheduled to convene at the Rockville, Maryland, courthouse to hear testimony from eleven witnesses against Wilson's suspected killers. Cline reported police "armed with shotguns and pistols were stationed in the corridor" to bar the press and the general public from the jury and witness rooms on the third floor. Out of the seven men accused of the murder, two had already met violent deaths in prison, and Albert McDermott, aka John "Slim" Dunn, was being transferred from Alcatraz, where he was serving time for his part in the "Heurich Brewery holdup." The next day, Cline reported that Dewey Jenkins, a member of the Tri-State Gang, was added as a fifth co-conspirator charged with attempting to murder McDonald and would be a witness for the state. Cline also named all the witnesses who had testified the previous day and that a defense fund for the four accused murderers was "being raised in the Washington underworld."[10]

Star crime reporter Carter B. Jones came to the *Star* in 1937 and focused on the numbers rackets not long after he arrived and produced a five-part series about it. In the first article, Jones let readers know that the numbers rackets were not an innocent crime but run by "murderers, con men, criminals," and he recounted the recent murder of the newspaper route carrier Wilson as a stark example. "*Star* witnesses have been taken for rides and silenced forever" in the Wilson case, wrote Jones, and "rival mobs shoot it out" over turf. Jones was "a small man with large brown eyes and elfin smile," as a fellow newsman remembered, and he seemed an unlikely man to bring numbers racketeers to heel in Washington. Jones believed the district was an easy city for corruption and crime, especially in the 1930s, when murders nearly doubled in the period from 1930 to 1937. Jones observed that a game of chance to gamblers, runners, and merchants at first appears harmless, but in time everyone involved will "sink lower and lower," and those who try to extricate themselves from the business or give testimony are silenced by fear, intimidation, or murder. Jones's series included an exclusive on the prosecution of the Warring brothers for tax evasion in March 1938 for not reporting gambling income from criminal racketeering. Mob lawyers representing Warring "assailed the press for building up a super racketeer who did not exist," wrote Jones. The *Star* was unimpressed, boasting in a full-page editorial display that the paper "has built no super-racketeers, existent or non-existent but . . . proudly claims credit for its part, as a newspaper . . . in bringing the light of publicity to bear on the vicious numbers racket and keeping it there." With shameless self-promotion, the *Star* wrote its "editorials and unceasing publicity" about the district's corrupt numbers game led to a Washington Metropolitan Police investigation and Congress finally pulling "stronger anti-numbers legislation from the dusty pigeonhole to which complacent legislators had consigned it years before," and "made it law" after Jones's series appeared.[11]

In 1936 *Star* crime reporter Rex Collier began a syndicated cartoon strip titled "War on Crime" that gave "authentic" descriptions of crimes solved by G-Men found in the Federal Bureau of Investigation (FBI) files. J. Edgar Hoover had complete control over the final product, and his friend Collier willingly drew G-Men and Hoover at the top as crime-fighting heroes who outwitted violent gangsters with their scientific methods. The truth was never that simple. The strip was a publicity tool orchestrated by Hoover, but its popularity waned rather quickly. Over the years certain *Star* reporters and editors cultivated close ties with the FBI and Hoover. The *Star* even has a loose connection to one of the biggest criminal pursuits by the FBI and other law enforcement officials in the 1930s—the hunt for Charles and Anne Morrow Lindbergh's kidnapped baby and the child's kidnappers. James Berryman, son of longtime *Star* political cartoonist Clifford Berryman, was hired by the FBI in 1934 to sketch a composite sketch of the suspected kidnapper based on information provided by John Condon, who negotiated with the kidnappers. The sketch was distributed to FBI agents, and although it did not directly lead to Bruno Richard Hauptmann's arrest, agents claimed it bore a strong resemblance to the kidnapper. In 1937 J. Edgar Hoover again asked Berryman, now a *Star* sports cartoonist, to use his talents to sketch a composite of the kidnapper of ten-year-old Charles Fletcher Mattson of Tacoma, Washington, who was later murdered. Berryman based his sketch on conversations he had with the young kidnapped boy's teenaged sister and brother in Tacoma, but his career in police sketches ended there. Nearing the end of the 1930s, crime news was no long dominating the news as the Great Depression subsided. The brutal push of Hitler's Third Reich across Europe and the threat of another world war dominated the headlines.[12]

Jerry O'Leary returned to the *Star* after serving overseas during World War II as a reporter who used his Irish wit and charm to befriend many law enforcement officials even among the higher echelons of the FBI. O'Leary had the instinctive qualities needed to be a good crime reporter when he came to the *Star* as a copy boy in 1937 with the help of his father Jeremiah O'Leary Sr., the *Star*'s congressional reporter. O'Leary's contacts combined with his tireless gumshoe reporting meant covering crime stories was a natural for him. It is also equally true that O'Leary's alcoholism, according to his own family, kept him tethered to general assignment stories and crime reporting until he chose to stop drinking in 1963. In 1963, *Star* editors sent O'Leary to Dallas when President Kennedy was shot because of O'Leary's experience and skills in dealing with law enforcement and unraveling crime stories. In sobriety, O'Leary would use his talents even more broadly by covering Latin American and military affairs. O'Leary was always on the lookout for a good story, however, wherever it led. One day in 1949 O'Leary, as a good Irish Catholic, was looking through the Washington Archdiocesan newspaper *The Catholic Review*, when he noticed a paragraph about a fourteen-year-old Mt. Ranier, Maryland, boy who had been successfully exorcised of demons, which he later said "electrified me." Jerry immediately ripped out the article and pasted it onto one of the *Star*'s pink assignment sheets and gave it to Dan O'Connell, who was puffing away on his "foul pipe." Dan had been city editor to O'Leary's father through World War I but left to become the old *Washington Times* city editor. In 1930 Dan returned to the *Star* as assistant city editor. O'Leary showed O'Connell the pink slip and asked him what reporter he thought should be assigned the story, to which Dan replied, "Junior, I think that's one we'd better leave alone," and returned the slip to O'Leary. O'Leary persisted, and O'Connell told him to take it up with Chuck (Charles) Egan, the *Star*'s national news editor, who was a devout Catholic himself but a no-nonsense newsman. Egan was working on deadline when O'Leary approached him with the idea and shouted, "I won't touch it with a 10 foot pole, but if you want it done, do it yourself." O'Leary was hesitant because the story most likely would bring him a heavy dose of ridicule in the *Star*'s newsroom, but even more he was squeamish about "tampering with the supernatural," he would later write. O'Leary talked to the priests, the author of the *Catholic News Service* article, the Georgetown University Hospital that studied the boy, a parapsychological society, and others to write the story. O'Connell and Egan still refused to have anything to do with the story, so he went to the *Star*'s managing editor, Herb Corn, who delegated it to the back pages inside the B section of the August 19, 1949, edition. The lead sentence made the provocative claim that "a Catholic priest has successfully freed a 14-year-old . . . boy of possession by the devil here early this year" according to Catholic authorities. The next day the story was on page one of the *Washington Post*. A book loosely based on the story was published nearly two decades later, which was made into the extremely popular movie *The Exorcist*. O'Leary had been on to something after all.[13]

Miriam Ottenberg was hired as the *Star*'s first woman police reporter in 1937—the same year Jerry O'Leary started as a copy boy. Ottenberg came with a bachelor's degree in journalism from the University of Wisconsin and did a short stint as a society reporter at the *Akron, Ohio Times*. Through the 1930s, hard news and crime reporting had exclusively been done at the *Star* by men until Ottenberg came. Women reporters were usually found in the Women's Department covering society news on the fourth floor of the old *Star* building—not the newsroom on the seventh floor. World War II significantly changed the makeup of the newsroom when male staff left to fight overseas and editors chose female staff to fill in. Women like Ottenberg, Betty Miles (James), and Mary Lou Werner (Forbes), who showed they could write well and on deadline, stayed on in the newsroom after the men returned. Ottenberg was tough-minded, fair, talented, and competitive, and over time she earned the admiration of her colleagues for her investigative skills, tenacity, and crafting an absorbing narrative. Ottenberg was also known for her forceful and occasionally combative personality among those in the *Star* newsroom. Haynes Johnson recalled the day Ottenberg came to the newsroom after hearing about a brutal murder in the city during her lunch. Ottenberg told the city editor Edwin Tribble in a very loud voice so that everyone in the newsroom could hear, "Okay, do you want me to solve it, or do you just want color?" and Johnson recalled, "She meant it." When *Star* staffers reminisce about the old days, they inevitably recount another famous story about Ottenberg, who took the cloth belt from her dress and wacked an editor for not putting one of her stories on the front page. Ottenberg was self-confident and never shy about promoting herself or the stories she deemed important. Ottenberg's goal as a reporter in her own words was to "expose the bad and campaign for the good. That's the way I was brought up." Ottenberg's father, Louis Ottenberg, was a well-respected attorney and a founder of the Anti-Defamation League, and her mother, Nettie Podell Ottenberg, was a Russian immigrant, suffragist, social worker, and longtime advocate for public day care centers for working mothers. Ottenberg dedicated her 1962 book *The Federal Investigators* to "my father, who gave me faith in justice, and to my mother, who taught me to fight for it." Ottenberg's parents provided strong role models for the crusading and feisty woman she became.[14]

On the morning of January 15, 1953, Ottenberg was part of the crack team City Editor Edwin Tribble oversaw as they reported in breakneck speed on a train disaster occurring at Union Station. Tribble came to the *Star* in 1933 as a copy editor with experience already as a small-town city editor in his hometown of Macon, Georgia. In the late 1930s he became assistant city editor and then city editor in 1949. At 8:41 am Tribble got word over the police radio that a train wreck had just occurred at Union Station. Passengers on the Pennsylvania Railroad's Federal Express from Boston, many of whom were headed for Dwight Eisenhower's inaugural festivities, were unaware of the impending disaster until the very last minutes. As one passenger told a *Star* reporter, when the 150-ton locomotive continued to speed through curves and began rocking as they neared the station, she knew something was amiss. Train engineer Henry Brower discovered he had no air for the train's brakes three miles from the station and used the only warning he had—the train's horn. Tribble didn't know the extent of the damage, so he sent a reporter and cameraman to the station while another reporter was told to call the Pennsylvania Railroad offices in Philadelphia. An announcement had blared over the loudspeaker at Union Station announcing, "Runaway train coming at you—Track 16!" which saved many waiting on the platform just before the train crashed through the bumper block and "crossed the concrete platform and plowed into the concourse," wrote the *Star*. After news reached the city desk from reporters at the scene that the train wreck was truly serious, Tribble sent two more reporters and another photographer to the station and assigned Chic (Charles) Yarbrough to begin rewriting copy sent from the field for the first edition's lead story. Harry Bacus, a young reporter at the time, remembered Chic Yarbrough as a "diminutive, debonair rewrite man, devotee of classy women, sporty cars, and the well told-tale" and being "a little flushed, yet clean and creased, rattling out new leads, ads, and inserts" that day. When word came that the train had collapsed a portion of the terminal's floor before stopping and many people were injured as a result, four reporters were sent to the four city hospitals while another reporter in the newsroom compiled a list of the hurt and injured he received from reporters. With editors and reporters yelling, telephones ringing off the hook, copy running back and forth, dictationists typing frantically, barely controlled confusion and excitement reigned that morning in the newsroom. Thirty minutes after receiving word of the accident, Yarbrough had written a lead of about five paragraphs, but it had little detail. Tribble cleared the lead but was unsure about whether to run with the story when four or five reporters at Union Station called in with descriptive detail to add to the lead. The newsroom was still reeling when Tribble was granted permission to violate the deadline and stop the presses since reporters were still calling in stories from Union Station and local hospitals. The lead story on the accident in the first edition closed around 10 am with contributions from at least eight authors and the bold headline "RUNAWAY TRAIN RAMS STATION, 40 HURT." The *Star* hit the streets first with news and a full page of photographs from the accident. Reporters began compiling and updating details for the second edition with the composing room scheduled to close at 12:15 pm. A reporter assigned to the Capitol went down to the station with a congressional inspection party, and another at the District Building accompanied the District Commissioners on their inspection trip to get official reaction. The train wreck was followed that day by an even deadlier accident. Reporters then raced to the site of a battery store explosion in northeast Washington, which killed more people and got the largest banner headline in the final edition. The *Star* ran an editorial on January 16 calling for a full investigation of the train accident by federal and railroad inspectors and to especially look at "the human factor," based on comments from passengers about excessive speed just before the crash. The day after the wreck, *Star* photographer Paul Schmick shot an image from the floor above of the wrecked runaway train still vertically askew and corkscrewing through a huge section of the smashed passenger concourse that left steel girders and concrete flooring exposed and scattered. Tribble and his staff's coverage of the Union Station train wreck received the Washington Newspaper Guild's Front Page honors in 1953. Ed Tribble moved to Sunday editor in 1958, where as one reporter quipped his wit remained "wry, barbed, and lethal." Devoted city room reporters in the 1950s gave their editor a modern phonograph so he could listen to his ancient opera recordings, but he remained the "last holdout" on the modern television. After retiring in 1972, Tribble edited the Woodrow Wilson papers and became a successful author, even writing a book that ironically was sold to television, which he shunned.[15]

By the 1950s Miriam Ottenberg was respected and liked by many in the Washington Metropolitan Police force for her fairness and investigative skills in covering major murder cases in the city since the late 1940s. To attract readers, Ottenberg sometimes worked directly with police to bring attention to the investigation of an otherwise ordinary crime story. One such crime was the unsolved murder of an unassuming milkman named Sam Leo Hoyle in February 1953. Hoyle was shot for no apparent reason in his car late one winter night in a dark, cavernous parking lot sandwiched between two apartment buildings at 6th and Gallatin Streets. The Metropolitan Police had few, if any, leads in the murder. A week after Hoyle's dead body was reported to police, Ottenberg wrote an enticing account of the people and events surrounding his murder culled from police records and interviews and encouraged the public to come forward with any clues to solve the murder. Ottenberg's prime competition was usually *Washington Post* reporter Alfred E. Lewis, who was always one step ahead or behind her on a crime story but was late to the investigation of Hoyle's murder and could only report in April that homicide detectives were dismantling the separate command post setup to solve the murder. The police never solved the Hoyle murder, but Ottenberg got lots of good publicity. Similar stories she wrote contributed to her persona as a crime reporter willing to do her part in helping police and law-abiding citizens bring criminals to justice.[16]

Ottenberg covered a number of criminal justice policy issues in the 1950s. In January 1954, Ottenberg wrote a four-part series about the controversy surrounding Juvenile Court Judge Edith Cockrill's central authority in administering juvenile justice. The Council on Law Enforcement asked Congress to pass a statute giving the US Attorney Leo Rover rather than Judge Cockrill the ultimate power to determine whether certain juvenile offenders should be tried as adults. Of particular concern to Ottenberg was "hardened offenders who are juvenile only in age don't belong in Juvenile Court." Ottenberg won a Washington Newspaper Guild's Public Service Award for her coverage of the issue. A year later, Ottenberg revealed the district's corporation counsel had determined current law prevented the District General Hospital's psychiatric ward from treating mental patients involuntarily committed. Five months after Ottenberg's initial public revelation, District Commissioners reevaluated and reversed the corporation counsel's decision. Ottenberg in 1955 reported on the conflicting court decisions involving the use of the criminal insanity defense. In August, the *Star* claimed that President Eisenhower signed a recent bill to clarify the insanity defense when "the bill was pushed by the *Star* after prosecutors reported their hands were tied by a series of court decisions" and that psychiatrists, too, found the courts' decisions confusing. In 1958 Ottenberg reported on abuses by a chain of abortion rings in the D.C.

metropolitan area and the ramifications of the *Mallory* Supreme Court decision in which Andrew Mallory was convicted of rape in the district and sentenced to death but the Supreme Court had ruled his confession invalid because he was held too long between arrest and arraignment. In the wake of the *Mallory* decision, Ottenberg analyzed the decision's legal arguments and concluded that certain criminal suspects were going free in the district as a result of the *Mallory* ruling. The *Star* editorially opposed the *Mallory* decision because "it is utterly confusing," and until the court can define unnecessary delay then "the judicial scales of this city have become overbalanced in favor of the criminal." Under the leadership of Phil Graham and his city editor Ben Gilbert in the 1950s, the *Washington Post*'s stand on criminal justice was more liberal than the *Star*'s. The *Post* editorialized that to ignore "technicalities" that may free even "the most vicious of criminals" is to undo the "rights which lie at the very heart of a free society." The *Star* editorially was inclined to see law and order and the safety of law-abiding citizens as more important.[17]

Members of the Noyes and Kauffmann families and its city editors had perennially maintained close ties with top leadership in the Washington Metropolitan Police, judges, and law enforcement officials in the city. The *Star*'s editorial page took strong law-and-order stands as well, but it never got in the way of reporters following the facts of a story even if it led to corruption and abuse in police ranks. In August 1931, *Star* reporter Phil Love interviewed a number of district jail inmates who accused police detectives of beating confessions from them. To back up their stories, Love got signed statements from the inmates witnessed by a prison guard, which the *Star* printed with Love's story. A month after Love's story the US Justice Department conducted a probe into the charges and eventually indicted eighteen police officers on charges of "third degree practices" and fired many of the Metropolitan Police force's top leadership. More than twenty years after Love's story, Ottenberg with the help of the Metropolitan Police's internal investigation division brought to light police corruption. Washington Metropolitan Police investigated gambler payoffs to the captain of the 12th Precinct and the former head of the district's gambling unit, which led to their arrests. Four days after the arrests, Ottenberg implied her story headlined, "How the 'Secret Seven' Laid Trap for Police in Gamblers' Payoff Case" was a "behind the headlines" exclusive granted to the "*Star* by police and prosecuting officials" and released for publication because, as Ottenberg wrote, "The *Star* had agreed to cloak the identities of the gamblers in this account up to final planning for their arrest to guard against revealing secret evidence in the Government's case." By 1958, Ottenberg was so well liked and respected for her work by local and federal government law enforcement officials, they hosted a party in her honor to recognize her efforts in reporting crime.[18]

Miriam Ottenberg meeting with Attorney General Robert Kennedy, August 1962. Reprinted with permission of the DC Public Library, *Star* Collection, © *Washington Post*.

By the 1960s, Ottenberg had turned her attention to uncovering not just strictly illegal activity but also fraud, unethical behavior, and corruption that harmed law-abiding citizens. In 1960 Ottenberg won a Pulitzer for her series, "Buyer Beware," about the unethical practices of used car dealerships in the District of Columbia. One year later she continued in the same vein writing a "Home Owner Beware Series" and in 1962 "Investors Beware," which won her the Washington Newspaper Guild's Front Page grand award for exposing irregularities and abuses in local stock market and brokerage firms. After years of investigating crime, the criminal justice system, consumer fraud, and those who administer justice, Ottenberg was a solid investigative reporter. President Kennedy appointed his brother, Robert Kennedy, attorney general in 1961, and Ottenberg developed a close working relationship with Kennedy and his staff as the department enforced civil rights in the South and vigorously pursued organized crime bosses. In August 1963, Ottenberg's access resulted in her obtaining an exclusive on recent revelations to the FBI by one of the biggest bosses in organized crime. Joseph Valachi, once a foot soldier in the Cosa Nostra, decided to cooperate with federal authorities in exchange for federal protection from former mob associates intent on murdering him in an Atlanta federal prison. In a front-page story in the Sunday *Star*'s August 4, 1963, edition, Ottenberg wrote, "For the first time in the Federal war on organized crime, a figure once fairly high in the mob hierarchy is telling all he knows about crime in America." Ottenberg had sent a memorandum with a draft of the Cosa Nostra story to the *Star*'s managing editor Bill Hill before it was published to notify Hill that Kennedy's press secretary Edwin O. Guthman "will call you after he has shown the attached to Kennedy" and "if we get the go-ahead, please call Deke DeLoach at the FBI" to let him know. Ottenberg was in New York for the weekend but left Hill her contact information in hopes that the report would come out Monday. Ottenberg's revised story was published instead on Sunday and stated that the story had "been shrouded in a blanket of secrecy until now," but now it can be told. Joseph Valachi, who "late of Atlanta Penitentiary, whose present address is a closely guarded secret," in exchange for government protection, "has put the finger on the top racketeers already under investigation," and revealed a previously unknown secret society called the "Cosa Nostra" at the "hub of organized crime." Ottenberg would continue to write about the Cosa Nostra over the next two years, but as she explained to her literary agent in 1964, "it's impossible to be any more specific than I have been" about the story because the FBI "with some justification" after months of "cultivating these informants . . . wouldn't want to lose any of them by revealing the kind of job they're doing." Robert Kennedy wrote the foreword to Ottenberg's book, *The Federal Investigators*, published a year before the Valachi story broke. Kennedy described Ottenberg's investigative reporting as a "sometimes plodding, sometimes dangerous search for the truth [but] one of the highest aspects both of the newspaper profession and of the Federal investigator." Kennedy specifically praised Ottenberg for "winning the respect of the investigators about whom she writes—and whom she often assists with the result of her own digging for the facts." In 1964 Robert Kennedy delivered an inaugural address for Ms. Ottenberg's swearing-in as president of the Women's National Press Club. From 1966 to 1968, Ottenberg served as editor of "Action Line," one of the first news columns of its kind to investigate consumer complaints. Phil Love, a fine crime reporter in his day too, was features editor and oversaw the work of "Action Line" staff. Love and Ottenberg's skills uncovering crime helped make the column successful and popular with the public. One year into editing "Action Line," Ottenberg was diagnosed with multiple sclerosis, and as her health slowly declined and her work at the *Star* decreased, she retired in 1974. Ottenberg devoted the rest of her life to writing, investigating and lecturing about the disease that would eventually take her life.[19]

By the late 1960s, mob violence by crime bosses was still around, but political violence by extremists on the far left and far right increasingly eclipsed perennial vice and crime in the headlines. In 1965 in a special report titled "The Haters," Ottenberg wrote extensively about her investigation into a recent precipitous rise in right-wing militia and survivalist organizations like the Minutemen and the Christian Youth Corps with anti-Semitic and racists views who were amassing "caches of guns," operating in secrecy, and training recruits to arm themselves "in the paranoiac conviction that Communist invaders will take over the country." President Johnson and Congress at the time considered passing new gun laws to stop the flow of guns to political radicals. In February before "The Haters," article was published, Malcolm X was shot and killed by Black Muslims after he and his followers broke with the sect the previous year. The violent feud between the two sects would simmer for years after and eventually find its way to Washington.[20]

On January 18, 1973, five children and two adults, who were members of the orthodox Hanafi Muslim sect, were murdered in a three-story stone mansion owned by basketball star and Hanafi sect member Kareem Abdul-Jabbar in an upscale neighborhood on 16th Street in northwest Washington. The house was occupied by Hanafi sect leader Hamaas Abdul Khaalis and his extended family. Mr. Khaalis was not home the night of the murders. The Metropolitan Washington Police claimed the murder was the largest mass murder in Washington history. During a six-month investigation, the police used forensic evidence to link the mass murders to seven Black Muslims living in North Philadelphia. Indictments were brought by the grand jury in August 1973, and Khaalis's daughter, Almina, who had survived the attack by feigning death, became the prosecution's star witness. The first of a succession of trials was scheduled to begin in February 1974 for six of the seven accused of the murders. A month after the Hanafi murders, Paul Delaney, a former *Star* reporter, who was now with the Washington Bureau of the *New York Times*, interviewed Almina Khaalis, who told Delaney the men wanted to kill her father "because he had accused Elijah Muhammad . . . of teaching false doctrine about Islam" and "had written to all Black Muslim ministers urging them to reject their leader." Almina also told Delaney that before her attackers shot her in the head, they asked, "Why did your father write those letters . . . Why didn't you try and stop him? . . . You should have expected this." The Black Muslims repeatedly denied to the press and law enforcement that they had any connection to the murders. Delaney, like most reporters, never suspected the brutality he uncovered might find its way to his own doorstep. *Star* reporter Winston Groom was assigned to cover the Hanafi trial among a host of other trials taking place in Superior Court in 1973 to

1974, including those of the Watergate defendants. Groom, who was the *Star*'s reporter at Superior Court in those years, remembers, "I was doing so damn much, I remember sometimes I would have three to four front page stories a day. . . . two to three trials at the same time . . . I'd duck into and duck out of a trial, then go dictate a story on deadline and then come back and get the gist of it from a Judge's Clerk or talk to a defense lawyer." Robert Shuker, who was the prosecutor in the Hanafi trial, revealed to Groom that intelligence gathered during the criminal investigation had unearthed a credible threat by the Nation of Islam against Delaney's life. Shuker knew Groom kept in contact with his friend Delaney after he left the *Star*, so he asked Groom to warn Delaney to stay away from the upcoming Hanafi trial, avoid contact with Black Muslims, and contact the local police. When Groom told Delaney about the threat, he took it seriously and spoke with Sam Eastman, former Mayor Walter Washington's press secretary, whom he knew from covering city hall in the 1960s. Eastman referred Delaney to D.C. Police Chief Jerry Wilson, but Wilson said he knew of no such threats. Delaney suspected police informants inside the Nation of Islam would have known if there were any, but still Wilson sent police cruisers to provide surveillance for Delaney's home in the district for a time. Delaney avoided all contact and took no phone calls from anyone he suspected was connected to the Nation of Islam; he even began putting a snub-nose pistol under his pillow until he felt safe. Groom, who covered the first two Hanafi trials of the five Black Muslim defendants, later said, "The black Muslims did not much screw with white reporters who wrote bad things about them, but apparently they would kill any black reporter who did." Years later Groom couldn't recall for certain who shared that bit of wisdom with him, "but I think it was one of the U.S. Attorneys" he guessed. "That's why they were worried about Paul but not such much about me," said Groom, although he had written plenty of articles critical of Black Muslims too.[21]

The day before the Hanafi murder trial began on February 11, 1974, Groom wrote, "The trial will be conducted in an almost fortress like atmosphere with dozens of U.S. Marshals" at Superior Court to protect the jury, the judge, the attorneys, and others in the courtroom. Anyone entering the floor where the Hanafi trial was to be held was required to pass through a weapons detection device—rarely used in courtrooms at the time. Tension was high in the courtroom as Almina Khaalis began the most damning and emotional testimony of the trial. Groom described Almina "calmly but with a slight quaver in her voice" on her first day of testimony to identify John Clark and John Griffin sitting at the defendants' table as being in the house when the murders took place. After three days of prosecution questions and defense cross-examination, however, Groom saw Almina lose her composure and lash out at Black Muslims and their leader, Elijah Muhammad. After Almina's father, Hamaas, made a violent outburst in court directed toward the defendants, he was removed from the court. Defense attorneys called for a mistrial, but Judge Braman refused to find Hamaas in contempt or call a mistrial "because of the nature of the pressure on him," wrote Groom. After a three-month trial, an all-black jury found John Clark, Theodore Moody, William Christian, and John Griffin guilty of twenty-two counts of murder after two days of deliberation. Judge Braman sentenced three of the convicted men to life in imprisonment but called a new trial for John Griffin. The ruling meant Almina and Hamas Khaalis would face three additional trials: one for Griffin, and one for Ronald Harvey, who had recently been apprehended by police. The judge's rulings and the call for new trials created a festering anger and mistrust in Amina Khaalis and her father about ever obtaining justice in the courts. Jim Price agreed to testify in exchange for reduced charges but later reneged on the deal, and federal authorities stopped protecting him.[22]

In late December Jim Price's mutilated body was found hanging by his shoelaces from the ventilation shaft in his cell at Holmesburg Prison in Philadelphia in a cell block he shared with his codefendants. Days after Price was found dead, Groom and Brad Holt talked with Louis Aytch, superintendent of Holmesburg Prison, who claimed he didn't know Price was an informant or he would have housed him in a separate cellblock for his own protection. The reporters discovered that court transcripts showed Holmesburg Prison officials should have known Price was an informant because they were, in fact, present at Price's April 8, 1974, hearing. *Star* reporter Ned Scharff reported that a "knowledgeable source" told him "for some reason, there were no guards to prevent the killing" of Price late Sunday evening, and "it seems possible that the guards just found it easier to go along with the kingpins." Ronald Harvey was sentenced to seven life sentences for the Hanafi murders in a separate trial, and in August, Theodore Moody and John Griffin were sentenced to forty years for Price's murder. Amini Khaalis became emotionally exhausted and was unable to give further testimony against Griffin in his second trial. Griffin was never convicted of the Hanafi murders. Groom stopped reporting in 1976 to devote full time to writing fiction, and other young reporters took over covering the slow progress of the Hanafi case in the courts. They included Kenneth Walker, an African American and D.C. resident who became a *Star* reporter in 1972; court reporter David Pike; and crime/court reporter Toni House, who both had been with the *Star* since the late 1960s. Mary Ann Kuhn, who came to the *Star* from the *Washington Daily News* in 1972 when the *Star* bought the paper, also covered the superior and district courts as well as health and medicine. Younger reporters of all races and genders increasingly filled up the *Star*'s newsroom and brought with them a fresher and wider understanding of the world in which they came of age than their elders in the newsroom. They also came with a youthful competitiveness to beat the *Post* on a breaking story. In 1977 when the Hanafi's thirst for revenge could no longer be tamed by seeking justice in the courts, these young men and women reporters used their insights and knowledge of political violence and its causes to report on an important breaking story in the city.[23]

Barely five months after Griffin's mistrial, Hamaas Khaalis, seething with anger because he felt the criminal justice system had failed to bring his family's murderers to justice, led a group of men armed with "rifles, shotguns, automatic weapons and even machetes in guitar cases," on March 9, 1977, in a takeover of first B'nai B'rith, then the Islamic Center, and the Municipal Center. While hostages were still being held, the *Star*'s March 10 edition reported that the Hanafis had shot and killed twenty-two-year-old radio reporter Maurice Williams, a security guard who later died, and wounded eight others, among them Councilman Marion Barry, during their attack on the Municipal Center. Khaalis and his men held more than one hundred hostages at the three locations as ransom for a demand that the five men in jail convicted of the murders be turned over to the Hanafis for execution. They also demanded the movie *Mohammad, Messenger of God* showing at a local theater be canceled. The front page of the *Star*'s March 10 edition was exclusively devoted to the breaking story of the Hanafi siege as well as another five pages inside the paper. The front page's "In Focus" column by Ken Walker gave context and background for the violent siege, which many readers did not know or understand. Walker explained that in the past decade "scores had died" after a violent feud erupted between followers of Malcolm X, a "black folk hero" as Walker described him, and the late Elijah Muhammed, who led the Black Muslims until he died in 1975. The conflict arose after Malcolm X turned away from the Nation of Islam to follow more orthodox Islamic teachings and then tragically was assassinated in 1965 not long after the break with his former leader. The *Star*'s writer-in-residence Jimmy Breslin wrote a profile of the husband of a hostage still held at B'nai B'rith, and Gloria Borger and Robert Pear in the "Q&A" section on the front page interviewed two women who were barricaded for many hours at B'nai B'rith until they escaped with police help. A detailed hour-by-hour account of events since the takeover through 2 pm on March 10 was also provided, and Jerry Oppenheimer reported on a recent federal study that "predicted that 'quasi-terrorists' like those occupying the three Washington buildings would copy the techniques and methods of 'true political terrorists' including the taking of hostages." Around 8 pm on the evening of March 10, Khaalis agreed to disarm and speak with Egypt's ambassador Ashraf Ghorbal, Pakistan's Sahabzada Yaqub-Khan, and Iran's Ardeshir Zahedi—the "The Big Three, the heavies"—as *Star* reporter

Mary Ann Kuhn described them. Kuhn wrote an account of the tense talks at B'Nai B'rith among Khaalis and the negotiators who sat around a table with "no water pitchers, no ashtrays, no name plaques . . . this was going to be a meeting of minds, a philosophical discussion of advantages and disadvantages of weighing patience and time against guns and knives" while 104 persons were held hostage. The ambassadors read from the teachings of the Quran that emphasized peace and nonviolence to persuade Khaalis to end the siege, which he eventually did. Reporter Walter Taylor told the story of the siege through the eyes of Ed Mason, a hostage and contract painter at B'nai B'rith, who showed reckless courage throughout the ordeal. Mason told Taylor at one point when a Hanafi wielding a machete ordered him to move furniture "or I'll chop off your head," Mason responded, "When you've got to die, you've got to die," for which he received a rifle butt to the head that left him unconscious; he woke up to find his hands bound but he never moved the furniture. Mason's captors chose him and another hostage to carry a wounded hostage down eight flights of stairs to police while a Hanafi gunman threatened "drop him and you're dead" wrote Taylor. Khaalis, Abdul Muzikir, and Abdul Nuh were found guilty of murdering Maurice Williams and sentenced to life in prison after eight weeks of trial.[24]

Crime stories at the *Star* were not always grim. Sometimes reporters saw the lighter side of reporting crime. *Star* photographers Ken Heinen and Geoffrey Gilbert were once arrested for disorderly conduct when Gilbert yelled at an officer for pushing him with his nightstick after he ran to the scene of a motorcyclist being arrested just outside the *Star*'s offices on Virginia Avenue, SE after a high-speed police chase. Heinen was arrested too when he interfered. When both cameramen were released with a small fine, they were more concerned about having their camera equipment returned than the arrest. In the late 1960s when drug crime was in its infancy, young *Star* reporters Mike Adams and Jim Sterba wrote a story about the drug scene in Georgetown, which read more like a human interest rather than a crime story. While Adams was covering a boring meeting of the Dupont Circle Citizens Association in 1967, he overheard a narcotics squad detective mention rumors of heroin use by the drug subculture on the M Street strip in Georgetown and went to city editor Sid Epstein and managing editor Charlie Seib with the idea for a story. Adams claimed he recruited Sterba because he looked younger, had longer hair, and actually knew who Jefferson Airplane was. The two reporters dressed like hippies to blend in with drug scene, but their efforts produced mostly a comedy of errors and dead ends as they tried to hide from old buddies and girlfriends they kept running into. The reporters never found any heroin but wrote a story about their escapades, with hippies smoking joints and dropping acid.[25]

The *Star* thoroughly covered crime, disasters, murder, and mayhem from its inception to its closing. Hard news stories about crime and politics are historically the backbone and mainstay of any newspaper, but readers come to the daily newspaper for more than hard news. All work and no play is a bad formula for life and newspapers. Readers want to read stories about the lighter side of life too—the fun and games—and the *Star* gave them that too.

5

The "Soft News"

A sketch of Miss Helena McCarthy with wide, penetrating eyes, dark hair pulled high and neatly tucked, a high, starched collar, and an unflinching gaze hung on the newsroom wall of the old Evening Star Building for years, with the caption "Just tell me the names; I know the rags." Miss McCarthy trained as a reporter with her journalist brother John and started freelancing for newspapers, including the *Star*, in the 1880s. In 1891 McCarthy became the first permanent female member of the *Star* staff and a few years later its first society editor. In the paper's earliest years, male reporters reluctantly covered weddings, parties, and social gossip until the 1870s when the paper started hiring freelance women writers to cover society news. Among them was the mother-and-daughter team of Fay and Augustine Snead, whom Gore Vidal in his novel *1876* portrayed as ridiculous southern belles, slightly corpulent, and concerned mostly with recipes for beauty and unappetizing dishes. Miss McCarthy mentioned the Sneads too and other female freelancers, including Emma Janes, K. E. Thomas, and a Miss Nimmo. Unlike society news, the *Star*'s male newsroom was always enthusiastic about covering sports. In the late 1860s the *Star* gave Harry Fry, an old-time telegrapher and amateur athlete, the job of retrieving sports stories off the wires and getting newsmen to cover sports when he needed them. In the 1890s Alexander Cowell took over from Fry and began writing a sporting column full time about popular sports in the era, including baseball, horse racing, cycling, boxing, golf, tennis, and rowing. The paper even created its own annual *Star* trophy awarded to the best high school rowing team for the year. Philander Johnson began in 1889 writing the *Star*'s humor column "The Shooting Star," and later slid into the role of the paper's first unofficial arts critic. In 1914 Johnson replaced "Art Notes" with "In the Realm of Literature and Art" for those interested in the so-called higher arts, with critiques of art exhibitions, new artists, painting, sculpture, classical music, literature, and drama. The *Star*, like any good newspaper, was devoted to attracting and keeping readers with so-called soft news about the latest social gossip, sports, drama, literature, food, wine, and fine arts in the city and beyond. Soft news would only continue to grow, fill up more columns, and attract new loyal readers to the *Star* in the years to come.[1]

Tom Noyes, Crosby Noyes's youngest son, was an enthusiastic baseball fan who often took his niece, Elizabeth Noyes, with him to watch the young Washington Senators play. Noyes played a critical role in transforming the Senators from a floundering team to a seriously competitive club in the American League. In 1904 Noyes, with a hefty personal financial investment, joined a dozen other wealthy Washingtonians, including *Washington Post*'s managing editor Scott Bone and District Commissioner Henry Litchfield West in purchasing a controlling interest in the Senators. The new owners changed the team's name to the Nationals when they took charge and emblazoned it on team jerseys, but it never quite stuck with fans. A year after the purchase, the partners choose Noyes as the team's president. After years of humiliating defeats and a succession of bad managers, Noyes saw his friend Clark Griffith as the man who might turn things around. Noyes was impressed with Griffith's sixteen-year career as a fire-brand pitcher and then manager of championship teams in the American League. Noyes urged Edward Walsh, a partner and friend, to approach Griffith about taking over as Washington's team manager. At a meeting with the team's stockholders in Washington, the partners also asked Griffith to risk some of his own money. Griffith agreed but asked for time to raise the money. Then some of the partners raised the stock price to $15 a share rather than the $12.50 they originally proposed. Noyes took Griffith aside with the offer, "Griff, you can have my 800 shares for what it cost and I can say the same thing for my friends Ben Minor and Ed Walsh." Noyes also offered to "buy 800 more from those pirates at $15" for a total of two thousand shares to give Griffith a 10 percent interest in the team. Griffith, with no real cash assets, mortgaged his Montana ranch and became the team's largest stockholder and manager in 1912. In August that year while still the team's president, Tom Noyes tragically died from pneumonia at age forty-four.[2]

At the end of a less than stellar season in 1914, news leaked that Washington's star pitcher Walter Johnson was threatening to leave and play for the new Federal League's Chicago team for more money. Johnson was nicknamed "The Big Train" for his amazing fastball pitch. Ty Cobb in his autobiography, *My Life in Baseball*, described his first encounter with Johnson's pitch: "I hardly saw the pitch. . . . The thing just hissed with danger," and he and ballplayers everywhere knew they were facing "the most powerful arm ever turned loose in a ballpark." Washington fans idolized Johnson soon after seeing the talented young ball player from Weiser, Idaho, pitch his first game after signing with the team in 1907. *Star* reporter J. Ed Grillo reported in the paper's December 2, 1914, edition that "if the speed marvel intends to play here, he will have to make overtures to get a contract" because as Griffith told Grillo and other reporters, last spring's original offer of $16,000 had been withdrawn. According to Grillo's sources, the new Federal League was sending an agent to Coffeyville, Kansas, to offer Johnson $48,000 for three years, a figure that proved later to be pure rumor. The *Star*'s large banner headline read "JOHNSON ALONE MUST DECIDE WHETHER HE WILL PLAY HERE." The truth is Griffith was furious at management for retracting the offer and determined at any cost to get his famed pitcher back. Eventually he was able to negotiate a deal with Johnson to remain for the original $16,000 annual salary with a $10,000 bonus, a sum Griffith obtained straight from the American League, not the owners. Griffith's management of the team resulted in one world championship and three American League pennants over the next two decades. Those were the golden years for sports writers and Washington baseball fans.[3]

As the city's population grew and became less transient, the *Star* naturally turned to chronicling the city's local history for residents. The *Star*'s veteran crime reporter James Croggon retired from reporting the more gruesome side of life in 1895 and used his talents to write nostalgic stories about the capital in simpler times. Croggon's "Old Washington" column became very popular with *Star* readers. Historian John Clagett Proctor, who authored *Washington Past and Present* as the first comprehensive history of Washington, also wrote occasional historical pieces for the *Star*. The most enduring and popular of the antiquarian columns was the *Star*'s "The Rambler," which first ran in the 1912 Sunday edition and continued as a weekly column with various authors through the 1970s. Harry Shannon was the *Star*'s first Rambler chronicler. "Rambler" columns were not the invention of the *Star* but a phenomenon that took root at many newspapers in the country around the turn of the nineteenth century. Shannon referred to himself in the third person and rambled by foot or horseback throughout the city or in the nearby Virginia and Maryland countryside. Shannon carried a camera in a box on his shoulders, a tripod under his arm, a backpack full of glass photograph plates and his lunch. Photographs and scenic descriptions were always an important part of the story. Harry tracked down every lead to confirm the story's veracity and sometimes took a streetcar or train to a rural country courthouse when land records important to the story needed checking. As a native Marylander, he once proudly boasted "male ancestors in this part of the country" were known to "drink apple and peach brandy, chew tobacco or use snuff . . . buy lottery tickets, bet on horse races and play seven-up," and if one didn't then "he usually finds he was regarded with suspicions by his neighbors and was most probably not considered respectable in those lawless, free-and-easy, good old times." Shannon wrote his last "The Rambler" column just two months before his death in 1928.[4]

In the months before February 1906, the women's department was busy ferreting out and reporting the news of the preliminaries to the most anticipated celebrity wedding of the year. President Theodore Roosevelt's daughter, Alice Roosevelt, was engaged to marry Nicholas S. Longworth on February 17 in Washington. At the time, society news was covered by only three women reporters—society editor Helena McCarthy, assistant society editor May Carnes, and Nannie Lancaster. A week before the wedding, the *Star* printed an authorized statement from President and Mrs. Roosevelt, who apologized for not issuing invitations to everyone but space in the White House was restricted, so guests had to be "limited to the closest kinsfolk, the personal friends of Miss Roosevelt and Mr. Longworth and certain classes of officials in Washington." The front-page headline the day of the Roosevelt–Longworth wedding read "Happy the Bride the Sun Shines On" with oval-shaped photographs of the bride and groom prominently displayed. In melodramatic flourish, the paper's society reporters wrote that in the White House East Room "a distinguished and brilliant company . . . looked on at the culminating scene in a love story, each chapter of which has entertained two continents and which in our own happy land has become a familiar fireside tale." Unfortunately, the couple's love was a façade, they were never really happy, the marriage was a disaster, and it ended in divorce.[5]

By the twentieth century, the *Star* had added a number of columns designed to attract women readers from all classes of society, like "A Page for the Children," "Things Heard and Seen," news of the latest fashions from special correspondents in Paris and New York, recipes, club news, and household hints for the homemaker. Newspapers increasingly competed for women readers, who were the dominant consumers in households. *Star* women society reporters were separated in quarters on the third floor away from the seventh-floor newsroom in the old *Evening Star* building. Cy Perkins, who came to work for the *Star* in 1912, recalled a total of ten women on the *Star* staff, which included three women society reporters, two secretaries who worked for top executives Frank and Theodore Noyes and Fleming Newbold, a copyholder in the composing room, and four more women scattered in offices around the building. All but one of the women was unmarried. Katharine M. Brooks, who worked as the *Star*'s assistant society editor for more than thirty years, never married but instead devoted herself to reporting social events that only presidents, diplomats, and high society attended. Miss Brooks's reporting career spanned from a trip down the Potomac with Calvin Coolidge in the 1920s to the grand reception to honor General Charles de Gaulle and Mme. Chiang Kai Shek's address to Congress after World War II. Katharine Brooks trained as a reporter when working as an assistant to her mother, Mrs. Kate Scott Brooks, who was the *Washington Post*'s society editor from 1915 until the 1930s. Katharine Brooks retired in 1954 but often returned for holiday parties in the women's department, where she was affectionately known as Kay Bee. Brooks's longtime editor and colleague was Sallie V. H. Pickett, who was the *Star*'s second society editor in the 1920s and 1930s. In 1932, *Star* society reporters Katharine Brooks and Margaret Hart (Canby) cofounded the American Newspaper Women's Club. Katharine's mother was its first president, and V. H. Pickett its first vice president.[6]

"It was a wild night that sneaked up on this staid metropolis last night. A night to try men's lungs and emotions," read the *Star*'s lead on the night after Washington won the 1924 World Series championship. Washingtonians, whose baseball team a decade before had been the laughingstock of the American League, went wild as "dignified men wept in joy . . . policemen assisted motorists to break all rules," and "Bucky Harris, the impossibly young big league manager who had done the impossible . . . and his crew of young upstarts" threw their hats in the air after batter "Earl McNeely crashed that high bounder to the outfield" ending the game and giving Washington its first and only baseball world championship. In the locker room, the *Star*'s baseball sports writer John Keller along with other newsmen watched Bucky, who was "nearly crazy with gladness" and so elated by the win, come straight from the showers, seemingly unaware he was completely naked as he talked to them and combed his black hair "into a careful part." Keller also saw an ebullient Clark Griffith nearly close to tears as he slapped the back of any team member he saw and thanked each one. Walter Johnson told Keller, "I'm the happiest man in the world for Bucky having confidence in me and . . . can never thank Bucky enough." Nine years later Clark Griffith would hire Joe (J. Edward) Cronin as the National's new manager for another winning season. Early in the 1933 season, rookie *Star* sportswriter Francis Stann spoke with Cronin, the "boy manager," as Stann called him. Cronin, "with a sweep of his hand," told Stann as they sat in "Prexy Griffith's office" and rain poured down outside in the park, "This Washington park is so big it is necessary to have a varied attack . . . We've got some long hitters . . . but no team can count socking home runs and triples in a park where outfielders have so much room to drag 'em down" so "we have some fast men" and "we'll turn this speed loose." The strategy may have helped Washington win the American League Pennant that year, even though they lost the World Series. *Star* cameramen, who shot images of that game and many other sporting events the paper covered, sometimes captured more of the moment than words ever could. Two of the paper's earliest and most talented sports photographers were the Routt brothers, whose careers started in the early 1930s. In 1930 Ranny was hired as a copy boy but soon was assigned to photograph high school, college, and then professional sports teams. Young Francis had originally wanted to be a jockey, but when his mother determined jockeying was too dangerous for him, she pushed him to follow in his brother's footsteps. Mrs. Routt may have had a change of heart later because the small, scrappy Francis Routt took many risks to get the most eye-catching photo, like climbing to the top of a 416-foot radio tower and the Washington Monument or hanging out of a plane. The Routts's photos would appear in every section of the *Star* for nearly forty years, but they especially loved and excelled in sports photography—Ranny in baseball, football, and basketball, and Francis in boxing and horse racing. In the early 1930s the sports staff was relatively small with four to five writers, among them sports editor Denman Thompson; John Keller, who covered major league baseball; and Stann and Burt Hawkins, who covered and wrote about everything from high school and college football to heavyweight boxing, horse racing, tennis, and golf. Years later Hawkins recalled that weekends were particularly grueling for Stann and him as rookie sportswriters. Saturdays started at 6:30 am in order to finish that day's edition, and then the two newsmen would leave around noon to cover games at the University of Maryland and the Naval Academy and then back to college games at Georgetown, George Washington, and Catholic universities. By the time they finished writing copy for the Sunday edition, it was 3:30 am Sunday, just three hours short of a twenty-four-hour workday. Stann was a native Washingtonian who had played basketball at Central High and loved all sports, but his favorite was baseball. Stann would succeed Jack Keller as the *Star*'s baseball writer, and in 1935 he began writing the "Popping Off" column and later the daily sports column "Win, Lose, or Draw." In the 1930s the *Star*'s sports coverage lagged behind the *Washington Post* with excellent sports writers like Shirley Povich and wider coverage, as the *Star*'s managing editor Oliver Owen Kuhn had to admit to executive editor Theodore Noyes in a 1934 memorandum. Kuhn made suggestions on how to beat the paper's local competition, and over the next decades many of his suggestions were implemented. The paper hired more sports writers, added columns, and changed leadership to better compete with local newspapers.[7]

Francis Stann inaugurated his annual trek to Stuart, Florida, in the 1940s to cover the Senators' spring training camp, where he wrote thumbnail sketches of the twenty or so major league baseball teams and their prospects for the upcoming season. Stann did a little fishing in the St. Lucie River, too. Stann's favorites were baseball and golf, but he rarely missed covering most heavyweight fights and the Kentucky Derby. By 1937 Burt Hawkins joined Stann in the daily coverage of baseball as well as writing Stann's columns when necessary. Morrie Siegel, who was a sportswriter for the *Post* in the late 1940s before coming to the *Star* in 1962, never forgot the time Hawkins's response to having his journalistic integrity questioned made the headlines. With the alcohol flowing at a team party after Washington lost to the Cleveland Indians, Hawkins began hearing complaints from players about Ossie Bluege, Washington's manager. One player even threatened, "If Bluege is managing next year, I don't want to play with Washington." Hawkins revealed the players' dissatisfaction with Bluege in his column the next day, headlined "Dissension Over Bluege Blamed for Nats' Flop." Bluege, fighting mad, called a meeting at the clubhouse at Briggs Stadium the next morning, where he accused Hawkins of snooping around in his wastebasket to get the story rather than from anything his players said. Hawkins, sporting his usual jacket and tie even in the sweltering heat, responded, "You're a liar . . . and if there's anybody on this club who told you that I'd like them to stand." Fearing Bluege's retribution, none of the players admitted making the statements, and the official press release from club officials given to the gathered newsmen said so. Accusations continued to fly between the two men until Ossie lost control, and he "proceeded to give me the windmill treatment," wrote Burt, but his "six or eight punches . . . sho'nuff missed" and "succeeded only in disturbing my neat hair-do." Hawkins used humor to get even rather than his fists in reporting the dust up, writing, "honestly, I couldn't have hit this guy," which would be "akin to trying to stick your finger in a windmill during a tornado." Siegel claims *Star* management threatened to stop publishing news about the team until Bluege apologized for impugning Hawkins's integrity. Within two days after the incident, the *Star* reported that Bluege apologized to Hawkins in a hotel suite in Detroit, shook hands, and both men agreed that the "incident was closed and their relations were friendly."[8]

In 1937 George Preston Marshall moved his fledgling football team, the Boston Redskins, to Washington. The *Star* continued to devote most of its sports columns to baseball, but when professional football arrived in September, the *Star* sent reporter Bill Dismer to cover Washington's first professional football game in Frederick. Bill Dismer Jr. arrived at the *Star* in the fall of 1935 and was assigned to cover mostly high school and some college football, so when professional football arrived in Washington, he moved naturally into the new beat at the *Star*. Dismer explained to readers that despite the Redskin's 50–0 decisive win in Frederick, Coach Ray

Flaherty was stingy with his praise for the win against the "weak and so ill-organized" Frederick All-Stars. In 1940 Lewis Atchison came to the *Star* to write about college football after nine years at the *Post*, where he started as a police reporter and then moved on to cover sports under the tutelage of Shirley Povich. In the 1940s Atchison started a tradition of not only reporting on the Redskins' training camp but also living, eating, and sitting in on conferences among coaches and team members in order to write in-depth human interest stories about the players, the coaches, and prospects for the season. At the 1948 camp, Atchison speculated, "Can Harry Gilmer oust Sammy Baugh as the team's No. 1 quarterback?" Baugh hung in for few more years until his retirement in 1952 after serving as Washington's first quarterback. Baugh was inducted into the Football Hall of Fame in 1963, and a decade later Lew Atchison, who had known and written about Baugh's remarkable career, received the Dick McCann Memorial Award from the Professional Football Writers Association for his "long and distinguished reporting of professional football." Among fellow sports writers Atchison earned the moniker "Mr. Pro Football."[9]

Until the early 1950s the *Star* competed with three other Washington daily newspapers, and "soft news" played a crucial role in attracting readers. In early 1934, Sunday editor Hudson Grunewald concluded making changes to the paper's soft news was the best way to improve the *Star*'s columns after comparing them to those of other local newspapers. Grunewald passed on his suggestions to managing editor Oliver Owen Kuhn, who prepared a memorandum with the proposed changes for Theodore Noyes to consider. Grunewald saw the *Star* as "best in radio, aviation, auto news, best Garden editor, arts," and its extensive society news balanced out the *Post*'s better sports coverage. Grunewald also found the *Star* carried "superior" rotogravure images in its Sunday magazine, but it contained "no really good fiction" compared to other papers. Grunewald as Sunday editor recommended that the Sunday magazine devote a single page to book reviews, music, and the arts, plus expand its comics. Over the next two decades the *Star* experimented with home grown and nationally syndicated columns, magazine styles, and published a range of feature articles to attract readers. Philip Love was editor of the old Sunday magazine during its run from 1945 to 1963 after Grunewald left and was features editor and a columnist until his retirement in 1970. Love wrote the nationally syndicated column "Love on Life," which he continued in retirement, and in 1963 began the humorous column "On the Side" about life's foibles. As a trained cartoonist he also wrote a monthly column discussing the creators of comic strips. Alice Eversman, who was an opera and concert singer as a young woman with the Metropolitan Opera and Chicago Opera company, was the *Star*'s music critic from 1932 to 1954 and covered the historic Marian Anderson concert at the Lincoln Memorial as a young reporter. Marjorie Holmes, a Virginia housewife, wrote the twice-weekly syndicated column "Love and Laughter" from 1959 to 1973 about family life directed at wives and mothers. Readers and advertisers seemed pleased with the results since the *Star* remained until the late 1950s the most financially successful newspaper in the city. Grace Smith was among the many admirers of the paper's "soft news." Smith's letter to the editor sent in 1958 gushed with appreciation "for the most wonderful newspaper in the whole world," based on her thirty years of reading "wonderful features" like Frederick J. Haskin's "Answers to Questions" column, "Readers Clearing House," "our wonderful 'Features Page,'" "a small but very interesting mystery" in the Sunday magazine, and comics on Sunday and every day. Features and columns until well into the 1960s were mostly light hearted, humorous, tied to traditional values, and non-controversial. They served the *Star* well, but not all writers of soft news who came in the era fit this conventional mold.[10]

Jay Carmody, as the *Star's* drama critic from 1937 until 1964, brought style and modernity to the paper's coverage of drama. Carmody would achieve fame, cultivate many famous friends in the drama and film world, and develop loyal fans and critics alike during his nearly thirty-year career at the *Star*. Carmody first worked on the *Star's* copy desk in 1923 but then left to work as a columnist for a news syndicate. In 1933 he returned to the *Star* and moved to its drama department in 1937. By 1947 Carmody had a daily and Sunday column and did a weekly radio show at WTOP. Later he added "The Passing Show" column, which reviewed stage and screen favorites, and in 1952 he started the "Glamour Parade," a gossipy column about show business celebrities. Playwrights Carmody said he "most admired and felt closest to" were Thornton Wilder, Elia Kazan, and Moss Hart, and among actors, Audrey Hepburn, Eli Wallach, and Helen Hayes. One of Carmody's favorite directors was the "Rotund Alfred Hitchcock," as he described him, who he visited on the set in Quebec, Canada, in 1952 while Hitchcock was filming *The Lady Vanishes*. Carmody offered readers his own insightful assessment of Montgomery Clift, who was starring in the film, as "the most aloof and independent young man on Hollywood's acting roster . . . quiet, thoughtful, intelligent, and obviously deadly serious about the art of acting." Besides Clift, who played a Canadian priest accused of murder, the cast included Anne Baxter and Karl Malden, whom Carmody described "as serene a group of actors as ever put together a story calculated to frappe the blood of millions of moviegoers." In 1956 the Screen Actors Guild honored Carmody with its Critic of the Year award. In Carmody's acceptance speech, he pointed to the irony of "1200 natural enemies of the critic" seated in the audience giving him this award. With humility Carmody also wrote in a column just before receiving the award that he often stayed awake

at night wondering whether he had done "justice to everyone" after finishing a review. Carmody, however, occasionally displayed little public
remorse when his words tarnished an actor's career or ended a show. In
1960 Arthur Miller's *A View from the Bridge* at the National Theater was
closed a week early after sluggish box offices sales followed Carmody's
scathing review, calling the play "incinerated sludge." Luther Adler, the
director-actor who played an angry Brooklyn dock worker in the play, in
an emotional postcurtain soliloquy raised a "fistful" of Carmody's clippings and called the review "arrogant, insolent and insulting," which he
said had given no thought to "the kids in the show." According to the *Post*
reporter who covered the speech, the audience responded to Adler with
rousing applause. Adler asked Carmody to come to the theater to "get a
lesson in free speech," but Carmody curtly replied, "Busy. Where will you
be next week?" Adler told the *Post* reporter that the show had toured for
three years and received "rave reviews." Carmody never apologized but
instead told a *Daily News* reporter that Adler was "crass . . . crude [and]
insolent." When Carmody retired in 1964, fellow critics Dick (Richard)
Coe at the *Post*, Tom Connelly at the *Daily News*, and Harry MacArthur,
Carmody's longtime assistant and art critic at the *Star*, hosted a party at
the National Press Club. Carmody joked to the audience, "It just shows
what I've always said—any Tom, Dick and Harry can be a drama critic."
MacArthur and Carmody became friends in the *Star*'s art department.
When Carmody moved to the drama department, he brought MacArthur
along as his assistant, who often filled in as critic when Carmody was
away. MacArthur wrote the column "After Dark: Smart People, Smart
Things, Smart Places" for nearly thirty years that included interviews
with chorus girls to ballerinas. MacArthur became the *Star*'s chief art
critic and drama editor when Carmody retired.[11]

In the 1940s the *Star*'s society editor was Miss Margaret Hart, who
married local builder William Canby in 1946 to become Margaret Hart
Canby. Mrs. Canby fit the mold of the classic society writer, a well-
coiffed and mannered matron, attired in a hat and gloves, and who
wrote about every laborious detail of dress and manners on the diplomatic party circuit in Washington. Fortunately, the society and fashion pages of the *Star* got an injection of new talent in the 1940s. Eleni
Sakes was among the young women hired as a copy girl to temporarily
replace male staff who left for military service during World War II.
Eleni would later marry *Star* editor Sid Epstein to become Eleni Sakes
Epstein. For more than three decades Eleni Sakes Epstein would perfect
her innate skill for writing intelligently about fashion for generations of
women readers from housewives to career woman. Eleni was a dark,
petite, Greek beauty who had an eye and passion for couture fashion,
and from an early age she easily befriended and hobnobbed with de-

signers, buyers, and the wealthy from New York to Paris in the rarified world of high fashion. Sakes was eighteen and a recent graduate of Eastern High School when she started at the *Star* in 1943. Eleni's father emigrated from Greece to the United States in the 1920s where he settled in Washington and became a successful restaurateur. At age twenty-one Sakes was promoted to fashion editor, the youngest ever in newspaper history. In the post–World War II era, the *Star*'s insipid society pages also got a transfusion of political gossip when Betty Beale arrived. Socialite and society columnist Betty Beale came to the *Star* in 1945 in the same era as Eleni after writing the column "Top Hats and Tiaras" for the *Post*. Betty was rarely seen working in the *Star*'s offices but instead preferred writing her daily column in the comfort of the large upstairs den of the elegant family home on Tracy Place. Beale's philosophy was to never take notes, never drink, and never smoke at parties because you might miss something. By sticking to these rules, she boasted that she could hop from party to party and speak to nearly one hundred people every fifteen minutes. Beale would then come home to write her story until the wee hours of the morning and deliver copy to her editor still dressed in her evening gown. Not long after arriving, managing editor Herbert Corn called Beale to the seventh floor and told her to moderate the politics in her column. Instead of acquiescing, the headstrong Beale protested to Corn that political gossip was probably more interesting to her readers than the fashions guests wore or the food they ate. Betty always believed editor Ben McKelway was behind Corn's request, but neither McKelway, Corn, nor Canby could have kept Betty from writing about politicians and political gossip. In 1952 McKelway sent Beale to the first political convention a *Star* society reporter ever covered. In 1953 Beale began writing "Exclusively Yours" as a weekly column for the Post-Hall Syndicate and four times a week for the *Star*. Beale was known for being candid and unapologetic about her inbred snobbery. In the 1950s she told a reporter, "Men make money but they cannot create background for themselves if they were not born with them." Beale also wrote, "Society should be made up of only the finest and best . . . But it never is." Betty Beale was exposed from an early age to the foibles and manners of Washington's elite society. As a young girl she often visited her "Aunt Bep" and "Uncle Brownie." Her mother's sister, Elizabeth Sims Brownlow, was married to Louis Brownlow, district commissioner during Woodrow Wilson's two terms. Her maternal grandfather was a congressman for twenty-four years, her father was vice president of American Security and Trust Bank, her brother William Beale was chief of the Associated Press' news bureau in Washington, and her brother-in-law William Lowe was editor of *House and Garden*. Betty graduated from Holton-Arms High School and then Smith College. Raised with

Society Department staff (L–R): society editor Katharine M. Brooks, columnist Betty Beale, and reporters Margaret Germond and Ann Cline wish Ms. Germond well as she retires, August 1950. Reprinted with permission of the D.C. Public Library, *Star* Collection, © *Washington Post*.

privilege in the world of early twentieth-century elite Washington society, Beale retained her prejudices about society, politics, and power throughout her career.[12]

In 1957 George Kennedy became the "The Rambler" for the *Star* and was a very different and far more modern version of the rambler than his predecessors had been. Kennedy had a full head of wavy gray hair, a long gray beard to match, often wore snow-white suits with a bow tie, and traveled around the city and countryside in a flashy sports car attracting attention wherever he went. Kennedy came to the *Star* relatively late in his career, having worked at a series of jobs as a reporter, advertising agent, and federal information officer in New York and Washington. Until Kennedy became "The Rambler," he was a general assignment reporter whose broad interests led him to write a hodgepodge of stories ranging from World War II wounded soldiers, D.C. neighborhoods, a delicious omelet in Mont St. Michel, France, and reports from Harry Truman's road trip to Missouri after leaving office. Kennedy began writing "The Rambler" column on a trial basis after another writer had tried with minimal success. Kennedy's version of "The Rambler" was popular and his permanent and most enduring beat during his last seven years at the paper. Harry Shannon as the rambler before him had faded into the background, but Kennedy created the persona of "an old geezer—born in the last century" as the main character in his stories because "if there is anything a columnist likes to write about, especially this columnist, it's himself." Shannon traveled by horseback or train, but Kennedy admitted he preferred traveling as fast as twentieth-century transportation took him. Kennedy loved speed and bragged about his adventures "in a Navy jet plane that goes through the sound barrier at 732 miles an hour" or "a souped-up hot rod at 115 miles per hour on a quarter mile drag strip." One *Star* staffer claimed Kennedy was the "master of the adjusted expense account" too and a "four hour lunch," where he invited loads of staff to his table at Hammel's, drank goblet-sized martinis, and then excused himself loudly without paying the bill. Kennedy wrote the popular Rambler column every weekday until 1964 when he retired. John McKelway then wrote "The Rambler" until the column disappeared from the paper around 1975.[13]

Margaret Hart Canby retired as the *Star*'s society editor in the early 1950s, and Ann Cline was picked as her temporary replacement. Ann was the younger sister of *Star* editorial writer John Cline and came to work as a copy girl during World War II. During the war years Ann reported on sporting news despite having little knowledge of the topic and did it well, but when the men returned from war, she was sent to the women's department. Ann Cline would end her career when the paper closed in 1981 as deputy director of the *Sunday Home/Life Magazine* launched in 1976. Lee Walsh was hired as the permanent society editor in 1954 and renamed the society pages "Today in the Women's World," which became slightly more relevant to the modern woman. Walsh was already an experienced editor who had written society news for other newspapers since the 1930s and came to Washington in 1944 to be the *Washington Daily News*'s society editor. Walsh showed more interest in political talk on the Washington party circuit than her predecessor, and like Betty Beale, she was friendly with Perle Mesta, Washington society maven in the 1940s and 1950s, and her circle of friends. In 1958 Walsh was named president of the Women's Press Club, and when she left that office a year later, Mesta hosted a cruise on the Potomac in honor of Walsh with a full dance band to entertain fifty invited guests, including eight ambassadors. Still, "Women's World" diverged little under Walsh from the subjects perennially found in the society pages of Washington's daily newspapers.[14]

Lee Walsh was in bed reading in her Georgetown home when she got a call from Isabelle Shelton at 11 pm on November 24, 1960, that Jackie Kennedy was about to give birth. Shelton was at the Georgetown Hospital and did the lion's share of preparing the story of John Jr.'s birth, although Walsh's byline appeared in the November 25 front-page story. In 1950 Isabelle Shelton at thirty-three had joined the *Star*'s women's department after working at the *Chicago Sun*. Shelton, like other *Star* female colleagues of her generation, got her start in journalism during World War II filling in for the men overseas and never left. Typical of young, professional women in postwar America, Shelton carefully balanced between a foot in a traditional women's role at home and another in her newspaper career. From the start, Shelton brought humor and irony to her writing. One of Shelton's earliest articles inadvertently would go into the *Star*'s treasure trove of humorous anecdotes often recounted at parties or in the newsroom. Shelton was covering the preparations for "two inaugural balls" that president-elect Dwight Eisenhower was having instead of the traditional single inaugural ball. Shelton was very careful to always write "two inaugural balls" whenever it appeared in her copy. When her husband returned home from a National Press Club lunch one Saturday, he told her, "Well, kid, you stopped the presses today." An unknown *Star* editor had changed her careful phrasing to "two identical balls," which ran on the front page under her byline. The press room caught it and stopped the presses, but some editions did get out. Despite the embarrassment, Shelton couldn't help but roar with laughter every time someone retold the story. By the 1960s Shelton was covering the White House and politics for the women's page, had authored a book, and wrote the syndicated column "Capital Footnotes" for the North American Newspaper Alliance. So when President Johnson wanted a reporter to write a piece about his efforts to upgrade women into top jobs in both government and private industry in 1964, he handpicked Shelton. Shelton's account was titled "A Mad Day with LBJ," written from her perspective as a working mother trying to put together an important story on the same day she was giving her teenage daughter a birthday party. Shelton's article was so well received, it was republished in *US News and World Report* a month later. Shelton's reporting continued to intrigue and attract readers with its modern and ironic take on society news in Washington. Typical is a comment from a reader congratulating Shelton's "comical coverage" of the Luci Baines Johnson–Patrick Nugent wedding as compared to the "maudlin and sticky-sweet" stories elsewhere. In 1964 Lee Walsh left the newspaper business when President Johnson appointed her to a high-level position in the State Department. Gwen Dobson, who had been the *Star*'s Women's Sunday editor since 1961, was named its new society editor.[15]

Chuck Egan gladly moved to sports editor after ruthlessly serving as the paper's wartime news editor where he had pulled together a rag-tag team staff of young women and veteran male reporters. Egan, a husky ex-Notre Dame football player, equally loved fast horses and Irish whiskey and was well known by his colleagues for singing Irish melodies or show tunes after hours at Harrigan's and occasionally settling scores with his fists. Those who knew him judged Egan as one of the finest newsmen and toughest editors at the *Star* from the 1930s until he retired in 1961. Egan was also famous for shouting matches and red-faced, sharp-tongued exchanges when a deadline was close, but few took it personally—that was just the newspaper business. Carl Sell as a copy boy in the 1950s remembered Vice President Nixon liked to drop by the *Star*'s sports desk to discuss the latest sports news in the old Evening Star Building. Sell thought Nixon didn't have much else to do but, of course, the reporters had lots to do. Merrell Whittlesey covered mostly college and professional basketball with George Huber and Bill Fuchs. Dick O'Brien began "The Bowling Line," Joe Kelly covered racing, and Steve Guback, Dick Slay, Bob Hanson, and Steve Hershey wrote about local college and high school games in the columns "With the High Schools" and "Sports Spotlight." Egan retired as the sports editor in 1961 after a long career, and Bill Peeler became the new sports editor. Like Egan before him, sportswriters were sometimes the target of Peeler's explosive temper when a deadline was approaching. Peeler was a meticulous, old-school editor who figured bruising an ego was just part of an editor's job if you wanted consistently good copy. In the 1960s when Dick Heller was the *Star*'s new golf writer near the bottom of the career ladder, Carl Sell heard Peeler yell one night, "Heller, goddammit, get over here! Look at this caption you wrote—you've got somebody falling off of a horse. Off of, for God's sake. A man ought to be fired for writing that." As Sell told Heller jokingly, he thought "Goddamit"—not "Dick"—was Heller's first name for some time. Peeler was tough, but young reporters like Heller and Sell learned a lot from his tough lessons. Charlie (Charles) Barbour, who was the *Star*'s assistant sports editor at the time, was a "crusty old newspaperman," as one colleague described him, with many intriguing stories from years as sports editor at the old *Times Herald* and a soldier fighting in Patton's army across Europe. Among the more interesting stories Barbour told was his friendly teasing of the young *Times Herald* photographer Jackie Bouvier, who worked down the hall from him when he was night sports editor in the early 1950s. When Jackie began dating the junior senator Jack Kennedy from Massachusetts, Barbour kidded her that her new boyfriend would never amount to anything. Jackie called Barbour after Jack Kennedy was elected president to remind him of his prediction.[16]

Flamboyant Redskins owner George Preston Marshall was more interested in entertainment than spending money to field a winning team in
the 1950s and 1960s. Marshall's stubborn southern prejudices against using the talents of African American players may have contributed to the
team's decades of losses as well. The black press had challenged racial
discrimination in sports for years. The *Post*'s Shirley Povich, however, was
the only white reporter among Washington's dailies to candidly express
his dislike for Marshall's racial bigotry. The catalyst for change in Washington occurred when the seventy-year-old Griffith Stadium shuttered its
gates in 1961 and the new D.C. Stadium was slated to open on grounds
owned by the Interior Department in the fall for football season. President
Kennedy's Interior Secretary Stewart Udall told the press at a March 24,
1961, press conference that he had submitted a letter to Redskins management informing them of the team's violations of antidiscrimination
laws. *Star* sportswriter Lew Atchison reported that Udall threatened to
charge the team with a misdemeanor and could take "action . . . against
the team's right to use the stadium" if racial discrimination on the team
continued. Marshall's response, as Atchison wrote, was "I am surprised
that with the world on the brink of another war they are worried about
whether or not a Negro is going to play for the Redskins . . . I would think
they had more important problems." In August Pete Rozell, the NFL's
new young commissioner, negotiated a compromise between Marshall
and Udall to give the Redskins until the 1962 season to sign black players.
The *Star* editorialized, "Mr. Marshall . . . must know by now that he was
inviting increasing public ridicule . . . by a tacit policy of excluding from
his squad Negro players," and although the compromise is temporary, it
should become permanent because "without the Redskins, the stadium financing will flop. Without good football players, regardless of their color,
the Redskins will flop." Walter Tobriner, president of the District Board
of Commissioners, refused to attend Redskins games at D.C. Stadium in
1961, and the NAACP picketed the stadium regularly. In December the
Redskins picked Ernie Davis from the 1962 draft but quickly traded him
to Cleveland for Bobby Mitchell. On December 10, 1961, Atchison wrote
the Washington Redskins "broke the traditional color line" when they
signed "Ron Hatcher, broad-shouldered Michigan State fullback" as their
"First Negro" player. Marshall refused to pose for pictures with Hatcher.
Hatcher played the 1962 exhibition season but was cut before Washington's opening game, so Atchison's statement in hindsight was incorrect.
Bobby Mitchell was the first black player to ever play for the Redskins in
the regular season and was joined by two other black players in the opening game of 1962 against the Dallas Cowboys. Hatcher returned to play
with Washington later in the 1962 season.[17]

Lew Atchison began the column "Atchison's Angle" in the 1960s, which included a range of topics from accolades for fellow sportswriters, poetry, or praise for Redskins coach and general manager Vince Lombardi in 1969. On Christmas Eve 1964, Atchison composed an eighteen-stanza poem titled "Crystal Ball Is Cloudy, Game Will Be Rowdy" to the rhythms of "Twas the Night Before Christmas" for the 1964 playoffs. Some of Atchison's critics and fellow sports writers thought he was a little too fond of the Redskins to be entirely objective about the team after covering them for more than twenty-five years. In 1966 Atchison admitted he "dies a little bit" after every disappointing game, especially during the 1950s and 1960s when the team never made it to an NFL playoff and had one of the worse records in the League. Fortunately, football was not the only game in town for Washingtonians in the 1960s. They also wanted to read news about baseball, basketball, boxing, horse racing, golf, and local college and high school sports teams. Whittlesey wrote the "Baseball Beat," Dick Heller covered golf, and Francis Stann and Burt Hawkins were still writing the "Win, Lose, or Draw" column. The *Star*, however, was looking for some bite and controversy on its sports pages to attract new readers from the competition, so in 1962 the paper hired veteran sports columnist Morrie Siegel. Before coming to the *Star*, Siegel's writing at the *Atlanta Constitution*, the *Daily News*, and the *Washington Post* had earned him a reputation for stirring up controversy. Siegel launched the "Siegel at Large" column when he joined the *Star*. Famed sports writer Red Barber judged Siegel's story, "Born Loser," which was based on an interview with boxer Joe Louis, as one of the top five best sports stories that he and other sports writers picked for the book *Best Sports Stories of 1966*. By the early 1970s Siegel had added sports announcing at WRC radio-TV and celebrity prize fight coverage like the Muhammad Ali–Joe Frazier fight in 1971 to his repertoire. Fellow sportscaster Nat Allbright of WAVE and WEAM radio in a 1972 *Star* profile of local radio and TV announcers sardonically told *Star* reporter Russ White, "Mo is a writer, not a broadcaster . . . he belches too much on the air. He hasn't got a name straight in years, including his own." In the same article most of Siegel's peers viewed him as controversial, but as White wrote, "Siegel, his peers say, sticks more to the staples and relies on his vast knowledge of sports in tandem with a rapier wit and strong opinions." Morrie came to love the *Star*, and three years after it closed he wrote, "There was a feeling almost like brotherhood there. We had our fights and whatnot, like employees everywhere, but in the nitty-gritty everybody got along better than the people at any other paper I've worked at." With typical self-deprecation in moments of clarity, Siegel wrote, "It was a highly moral paper. I don't know why a guy like me was working there. Obviously, I was outvoted."

After two years at the paper, the forty-six-year-old bachelor Siegel married young *Star* reporter Myra MacPherson.[18]

Around the same time the veteran Mo Siegel was making his start at the *Star*, a young Fifi Gorska got her break. Fifi was "doing the deaths," a common phrase for writing newspaper obituaries, when she was picked to start a "Teen" section. Carter Warren Dawson was hired as a teenage copy girl during World War II when the men went off to war. In 1951 Carter married Julian Gorska, the only Polish count in the area, and was forever known as Fifi Gorska. When rock 'n' roll music, teen movies, teen celebrities, and youth culture became an economic and social force in America, the *Star* saw a market and asked Gorska to put together a weekly teen section. Gorska was barely a decade older than the teens for whom she wrote, but as a perennially lighthearted, youthful soul, she was perfect for the job. Charles Tracewell captured Fifi's spirit in his "This and That" column, writing, "Every office has a Fifi. She is always one of these happy, irrepressible people who bounce through life with the aplomb of a bulldozer or something. She makes everybody feel good just to see her." During the 1950s, the teen section included reviews of pop music and teen books, profiles of rock and roll stars and teen idols, letters from local teens, a "School-of-the-Week" article, short stories, and more. By the late 1960s Fifi was soliciting teen opinions on the Vietnam War and the Jefferson Airplane to reporting on the first annual Wildcat Twirlathon. Beginning in 1965, Ronnie Oberman wrote articles about everything from the local rock scene to national bands like Frank Zappa to The Mamas & the Papas for the *Star*'s "Top Tunes" column. Ronnie's brother Mike took over the column in 1967 as a twenty-year-old electrified by the music of his generation. Mike's interviews and reviews of some of the best-known rock, country, and rhythm and blues artists were extremely popular with the students and young professionals flocking to Washington in the 1970s.[19]

Through the 1960s Betty Beale was a popular, nationally syndicated society columnist and still the *Star*'s best asset for news on the society pages. Betty's well-placed society friends included Emily Post, and her best friend was political socialite Perle Mesta, who along with Lady Bird Johnson's press secretary Liz Carpenter threw Beale a party in 1969 to celebrate her engagement to George Graeber. Beale preferred the company of powerful political families, the wealthy, diplomats, and their wives to journalists. When Queen Elizabeth and Prince Philip visited the United States during Truman's term, Beale was one among a few society reporters that received a crested invitation to a royal reception for 1,800 guests at the White House. The remainder of a much larger press corps was relegated to a "raised platform behind a rope," gloated Beale when she wrote about it much later. Betty Beale could be ruthless and pushy when she wanted a good story. "If you want someone to talk, never ask him directly," but instead "say 'I think it's just awful what they are saying about you.' Right away you get him to tell all." Washington elites sometimes bristled at her words and other times basked in her praise, but they always read what she said about them and respected her formidable personality and influence. Beale interviewed Jackie Bouvier when she became engaged to Jack Kennedy and was invited to their wedding in 1953 along with one thousand other guests. When Press Secretary Pierre Salinger limited coverage of embassy functions to only six men and six women, Beale complained directly to President Kennedy at a party and the policy changed. Beale never hung out with other society writers because she viewed them as competition, and the antagonism was reciprocated. "I don't want everybody else benefiting from" my contacts, said Beale about other society reporters. When an unattributed *Star* reporter made a snarky remark about Betty's dancing at an LBJ inaugural ball, she seemed genuinely hurt, responding, "They don't think I have any feelings," said Beale, and "I think a lot of them don't like me and I don't know why."[20]

By the late 1960s, society, gender roles, race relations, and politics were changing in the capital, but stodginess and old Washington establishment values still dominated the *Star*'s society pages. Betty Beale had been a trailblazer when she challenged the *Star*'s status quo in 1954 as its first society reporter to attend a presidential nominating convention, but by the late 1960s she spoke for a previous generation. In 1968 when Beale attended the Democratic convention in Chicago, she was scathingly critical of the press. Beale wrote, "It is time one member of the media gave the other side of the picture" and stop "overreacting" to any effort made by law enforcement "whatsoever to stop the hippies from the flagrant civil disorders and their disgusting disturbances of the peace . . . I used to think that insulting an officer was against the law!" Gwen Dobson, the *Star*'s society editor since 1964, according to *Star* reporter Joe Volz, ran "a bland society section" where "readers heard cliché after cliché . . . and the blandest item of all was her prominently displayed column titled 'Luncheon with . . .'" In the that mold, Ymelda Chavez Dixon, with her extensive social connections as the daughter of the late New Mexico senator Dennis Chavez, joined the *Star* to write the column "Your Date with Ymelda" about Washington's political and diplomatic party circuit in 1969. Still, the society pages had veteran and younger writers in its ranks that were independent, modern, and witty. Anne Christmas, who had been a general assignment reporter for nearly twenty years at the *Star* and other newspapers, was sent to write for the society pages in 1969, which she sarcastically called "Needlepoint." Christmas wrote witty and contemporary stories to engage readers, like a full-page article titled "Hangover-Anyone" on New Year's Day 1969 with homemade remedies for a night of hard drinking, and an interview with Lionel Hampton, who was scheduled to play an "Inaugural Groove-In" at Nixon's 1969 inaugural ball. British native Anne Willan as food editor brought a global flair to the *Star*'s food columns, and Eleni Epstein continued to write about modern fashion that attracted both new and longtime loyal readers. As the Watergate scandal heated up, Isabelle Shelton would take a small stand for press freedom when the Nixon press office banned the *Post*'s respected and well-liked senior society reporter Dorothy McCardle from social events. Shelton joined McCardle in the press office until the ban was lifted, and the *Star*'s generally conservative editorial page, often friendly with President Nixon and his policies, supported her stand. A *Star* editorial protested Mrs. McCardle's exclusion from social events "has been widely interpreted" by the public as a "way of punishing the *Post* for its vigorous attention to the Watergate affair," so if Press Secretary Ron Ziegler's denial of the rumor that he intends to "spread around" the exclusions is correct, then until Mrs. McCardle is invited back "we should take our fair turn in the cold" too because as Zeigler said himself, the *Star* "is not an administration newspaper." Kay Graham wrote *Star* editor Newby Noyes thanking him "for the nicest, most generous minded statement I can imagine on behalf of the competition . . . in light of all that's going on for the powers that be to know that we care about the ethics of our profession, and will stick together." Shelton would move out of the women's department later in the 1970s to the transportation beat for the paper.[21]

Young female staffers like Joy Billington, Judy Flander, and Mary Anne Dolan wrote features and stories geared to attract a newer generation of women readers to the paper by the 1970s. Kay Elliot inaugurated a weekly "HOME Indoors and Out" section in 1969 with articles about gardening, home decorating, wine, leisure activities, and even pets. Elliot asked Diana McLellan, a copywriter in the *Star*'s promotions department, to write for the section. Editors in the coming years would give Diana and other talented women at the paper a platform beyond the traditional society columns to shine. Editor Newby Noyes brought in David Kraslow, *Los Angeles Times* Washington bureau chief, as assistant managing editor in the last two years before the Noyes, Kauffmann, and Adams families sold the paper to Joe Allbritton in 1974. Kraslow tried to make the paper's columns about society, culture, the arts, and sports more current and lively, and his most noticeable change was to collapse the disparate subjects under a single and new "Portfolio" banner. Kraslow also wanted to bring new and younger talents to the *Star*, but Dobson had a way of sabotaging Kraslow's efforts when they impinged on her tastes. Gwen Dobson's last actual "Luncheon with . . . " for the *Star* was not with a social celebrity but with Judy Bachrach, who Kraslow wanted to hire as a feature writer. After Bachrach graduated from Columbia University School of Journalism, she took a job as the *Baltimore Sun*'s TV critic. She thought at the time it was a pretty good job since she concluded all they did in Baltimore was watch TV. Still, Bachrach was one of only two women on staff, and "the *Sun* didn't know what to make of me . . . Baltimore was a town where women got married at 21 and divorced at 41," she said years later. Bachrach thought "D.C. was the place to be" and would have done anything to get out of Baltimore. The *Star* was not her first choice, but after the *Post* offered her a job in the Metro section, she turned it down and talked with Kraslow, who offered her a feature writer job in Portfolio. Kraslow, however, wanted Judy to first meet with Gwen Dobson over lunch. Bachrach knew Dobson "was of a different age and a different attitude," but when she asked her about her plans for marriage, she was amazed that "anyone even in that day and age" would ask such a question during a job interview. Bachrach told Dobson that she didn't think she would ever get married, to which Dobson responded, "Well what about kids . . . don't you want kids?" By this time Bachrach was pretty irritated by the intrusion into her personal life and retorted, "I'd have a kid but probably without being married." Dobson scolded, "That's awful; you're going to the level of the Negro instead of bringing him up to your level." Bachrach ended the interview as soon as she could and left knowing she wouldn't take the job. Judy called Gene Roberts at the *Philadelphia Inquirer* to see if the job offer as feature writer was still open, to which he replied, "You bet" and she accepted. When Kraslow learned Bachrach was not coming to the *Star*, he called and asked, "Judy, how could you have done this? Why didn't you come to me?" to which she replied, "I don't want to get involved . . . I can't believe there is such racism on your paper and someone you wanted me to work for." Kraslow claimed Dobson had said such things to discourage Bachrach from taking the job. There was a long silence on the other end of the phone until Kraslow blurted out, "Well, what if we fire her?" which didn't help. Judy told him bluntly, "If you think I'm coming to a place after being responsible for the firing of a superior—I'm not going to do that." Editor Newby Noyes fired Dobson after the incident anyway. Bachrach viewed the *Star* at the time as "an old fashioned newspaper with old fashioned people. I'm putting that nicely," where she felt she wouldn't have fit in. Bachrach would finally return to the *Star* as a feature writer in 1979 when Time, Inc. took charge.[22]

When Joe Allbritton bought a controlling share of the *Star* from the three families in 1974, he hired Jim Bellows as the new editor. Bellows's reputation as editor at the *New York Herald Tribune* and more recently at the *L.A. Times* guaranteed he would shake up the *Star*'s staid reputation. Bellows knew the *Star* had to be a sassier and more entertaining alternative to the *Post*, and spicing up soft news was a big part of his strategy. David Burgin was a sports writer at the *Herald Tribune* when Bellows was editor and came to the *Star* in 1971 as its sports editor to replace Bill Peeler. The thirty-two-year old Burgin brought his youth, new people, and bold ideas to the sports pages and as its features editor. By the 1970s the *Star*'s sports pages were much improved since the 1930s when it had lagged behind the *Washington Post*. Still the *Post* was a huge competitor for the *Star*, and Burgin wanted to get the attention of readers beyond traditional sports news covered by the other paper. The Senators left in 1971, but the *Star* attracted loyal baseball fans by switching their coverage to the Baltimore Orioles when the *Post* did not. Fortuitously after the Senators left, the Washington Redskins under Coach George Allen started winning again after decades of losing. Veteran sportswriter Steve Guback, who started at the *Star* in 1961, was thrilled to cover the Redskins as a winning team. Guback claims he was the first to use the phrase the "Over the Hill Gang" for the Redskins when a fan called him near deadline and used the term after the veteran Redskins team opened with two straight wins on the road led by second-string quarterback Billy Kilmer. On the other hand, Tom Dowling and David Israel, who Burgin brought to the *Star*, were of a somewhat different breed than traditional sportswriters. Readers either loved or loved to hate them but rarely ignored them. Dowling came to the sports desk when Burgin arrived, and Israel in early 1975 not long after Bellows came. Dowling was a graduate of Harvard University and majored in English and history, spoke two languages, and had traveled widely for the US Foreign Service before becoming a reporter. The twenty-four-year-old Israel was a graduate of Northwestern's Medill School of Journalism and came to the *Star* after working briefly as a sportswriter at the *Chicago Daily News*. Dowling's commentary included controversial topics like the the "Phoenix Nine"—a group of Washington businessmen who unsuccessfully attempted to revive major league baseball in 1972—and George Allen's coaching. Dowling and Israel both generated a lot of letters to the editors over their criticism of George Allen's coaching. When Allen was fired in 1978, the *Star* printed an almost entire page of letters to the editors responding to Israel's long criticism of Allen. Comments from readers included "my stomach was turned" by Israel's "disgusting article," and an Allen associate who wrote "Israel had no notion of the dedication and sacrifice" the coach made to give "us the greatest football years" in Redskins' history. Yet other readers called Israel's reporting "excellent," and another agreed with Israel's assessment of Allen's poor coaching. The *Star*'s ombudsman, George Beveridge, explained to readers that "rah-rah sports writing is over," but to be fair, he had to admit that Israel had "lost his cool" and his essays often "read merely as mean-spirited and vindictive" with little balance.[23]

Burgin and Bellows had been colleagues at the *New York Herald Tribune.* When Bellows arrived in 1974, he immediately liked the "hot-blooded" Burgin, whose "ideas were irrevant and he had a million of them." Burgin asked Bellows on his first day at the paper to join him and feature writer Mary Anne Dolan for lunch. Dolan later recalled Bellows showed up wearing "bellbottom pants, brass-buckled patent leather loafers and an Elvis-collared polyester disco shirt . . . open to chest hair—well it was a shock." Mary Anne impressed Bellows when they met over lunch as "smart, tough, modern, and imaginative," he said later. What really sealed his faith in her was her deft handling of a dinner party for twelve, which Bellows attended at her Old Town Alexandria home. Soon after the party, Bellows asked her to edit the *Star*'s Portfolio section. Burgin and Dolan played a key role in tapping talent and shepherding Bellows's sassy ideas, and even created a few of their own. Lynn Rosellini was working in the Washington Bureau of *Newsday* when she heard Bellows would be the *Star*'s new editor. Rosellini admired Bellows and wanted to work for him. A former editor offered to recommend her to Bellows, and she sent her resume to the *Star* but was a bit perturbed when all she received was a form letter from Jack Germond, head of the national news desk, politely saying, "We're not hiring right now." Rosellini impetuously called Bellows with the "sense of entitlement" of youth, she later admitted, and to her complete surprise Bellows answered the phone. It was an auspicious day since sports writer Joan Ryan had just quit to write for the *Post* and Bellows wanted someone to replace her. Kathleen Maxa was the only other woman writing sports columns for the *Star* and would remain with the paper until it closed. In the late 1970s Kathleen earned the first Mary Garber Female Sportswriter of the Year Award at age twenty-eight. In 1973 Maxa covered the famous tennis match between Billie Jean King and Bobby Riggs as Rosellini did for *Newsday*. Lynn had written few other sports stories in her career when Bellows offered her the job. To Rosellini's surprise, Bellows added a signing bonus because he feared she might refuse his offer due to a recent four-day workweek negotiated between the unions and management. Lynn gratefully accepted the offer, "but he could of paid me nothing . . . it was never about the money, it was the chance to work for a really great editor," she said later. Lynn, a slim, soft-spoken woman, was often the only writer in the newsroom during the day since most traditional male sports writers were out covering games. Rosellini never felt any gender bias and got along with all the male sports writers. Lynn saw Burgin as "atypical of sports editors" who was more "interested in the unusual angle, the controversial . . . in depth profiles" and thought she could do such things well.[24]

One of Lynn's first stories that got attention was a feature she wrote about a down-on-her-luck gymnast who was a stripper at the Silver Slipper, a local strip club, frequented by, among others, Wilbur Mills. Lynn even got a handwritten note of praise from Mary McGrory for it. Burgin loved the story too and picked her for what would become a groundbreaking feature series on gay athletes. Burgin came up with the idea after seeing the Cincinnati Reds' scathing response to an appeal to major athletic teams for interviews with athletes who lived a gay lifestyle from the *Advocate*, a national newspaper devoted to gay issues. Burgin jumped at the chance to take on the controversial subject in print and besides, as he told Rosellini, "There was something unfair and kind of dishonest going on here with this macho image of sports where people were so threatened with the idea that you could be gay and still be an athlete." At first, the two envisioned it as a single feature story, but it naturally grew into a series when Lynn with luck and persistence talked to more than sixty athletes, coaches, sports officials, psychologists, and gay athletes around the country. Lynn found the broader gay community to be the most responsive even if most gay athletes preferred to remain anonymous. Still, some like Billie Jean King hung up on her. Others in the sports world were either "standoffish or downright hostile," she recalled. Burgin then suggested she try to interview Jerry Smith, tight end for the Redskins, who was rumored to be bisexual.[25]

Rosellini called the Redskins' public relations office to ask for an interview with Jerry Smith without mentioning the subject of her story. Smith probably thought she was interviewing him to write a piece about the new season. When Smith arrived at a coffee shop in suburban Maryland for the interview and sat down across from her, Rosellini began shaking as she saw this "huge" man with hands so "massive and scarred, a football player's hands" on the table who had no idea of the very personal questions she was about to ask him. When she told him she was doing a series on gay athletes, "for a moment all the expression washed out of his face and went blank," she recalled. Lynn then gently approached the rumor that he might be gay. They both waited in silence until Smith finally said to her, "Okay but you can't use my name or any identifying information but I'll talk to you." Years later Lynn felt released from her promise not to reveal Smith's identity after a documentary on his life as a gay athlete was released. Rosellini was humbled by Smith's trust in her in that moment, saying later, "Why should he trust me . . . a reporter can destroy you, and yet he was telling me intensely personal stories that could ruin his career and possibly his life." Smith talked candidly about his relationships, his self-loathing, his inability to trust, and the realization that despite being "a pro football player, with a lot of money and fame . . . I decided if I have all these things and I have no love, what does that mean to me. It's not something I've chosen. It's a lifestyle I've accepted." Rosellini thought it was "a powerful story" and wanted to do it justice but got lots of criticism for her heavy reliance on anonymous sources. Then Rosellini got a real break when David Kopay, former running back for the Redskins, agreed to talk to her on the record about his homosexuality. Kopay arranged to meet Lynn at a fast food restaurant inside a rundown indoor shopping mall in Southwest Washington near her apartment, where they talked and then moved on to her apartment. *Star* photographer Walter Oates came to the apartment later and photographed the 6-foot-1, 205 pound athlete with wavy long blond locks framing a handsome face with eyes that stared pensively at the camera. Now retired from football, Kopay told Rosellini, "It seemed like the right time and the right place to discuss my feelings" if the disclosure "might help some people . . . especially younger people who are going through similar experiences and haven't had anyone to talk to about it." Lynn was thrilled with the series because it was "exciting, controversial, explosive and exclusive scoop for her and the *Star.*" *Star* writer Jane O'Reilly, who wrote about the public reaction to Rosellini's series, found that few professional athletes "seemed to care little about what anyone else did sexually" as long as it didn't affect winning and the business. The vast majority of readers, though, felt much like the one who wrote, "it's stupid to print those things in the paper on the sports pages—it's a sacred page," or as University of Maryland basketball coach Lefty Dreisell bluntly told Portfolio editor David Burgin, "It is beyond my comprehension that a responsible sports editor could stoop to such trash" and if kids read the series, they "might think that to get publicity for playing sports you have to be queer?" O'Reilly scorned those who were unwilling to question the absolute pure macho mystique of "aggressiveness, winning, hard living—all that junk" of the male athlete. Lynn was disappointed that the topic disappeared from news columns for so many years after her groundbreaking series.[26]

Jim Bellows had a real genius for imagining bold ideas and then finding talent to make them a reality. One of Bellows's most daring and successful inventions was publishing a gossip column. When Bellows told Mary Anne Dolan he wanted to start a gossip column, she recommended Diana McLellan to write it. By the time Bellows came Diana had been at the *Star* off again and on again for more than a decade. In 1963 McLellan applied for a job in the art department, but as she later recalled, "I think I looked a bit funny that day . . . I was wearing a very hip little dress if I do say so" in a "very flannel" place, so she didn't get the job. McLellan returned a few days later "dressed very proper," she recalled, and landed a job writing and selling advertisements on the business desk. Diana, a petite blonde with short, bouncy curls, a trendy wardrobe, pretty face with hazel eyes, painted nails, a fetching British accent, and irreverent attitude, made friends, had fun, and wrote an occasional article for the *Star* magazine. When Diana returned a few years later after a personal hiatus, she was offered a job writing promotions for direct mail, TV, and radio. McLellan lacked any formal journalistic training, but as she once told a reporter, "I mean who have you ever met from journalism school who could write?" Diana credits her crisp writing style to her boss, Paul Martin, in the *Star*'s promotions department, who taught her, in her own words, to "use of a lot of verbs and not mess about." In 1969, McLellan wrote for the new Home Section for about a year and then wrote features for Woman's World and later Portfolio. Diana remembered in the years when Gwen Dobson was editor, she went to three parties a night in her little black dress, sometimes in the back of a friend's jeep, which "was a lot of fun but five years was enough, I guess." McLellan was excited when Joseph Allbritton bought the *Star* but also apprehensive that changes would come too. Diana had been fond of the families and found the paper a fun place to work. Still, she had to admit when Bellows came to the *Star* "he changed it totally" for the better, including her career.[27]

When Bellows asked McLellan to write the new gossip column, her first reaction was she didn't want to do it because it was tacky, and besides nobody in Washington would read it. Bellows ignored her fears and just mumbled the column was starting Monday. At a British embassy soiree right after the offer, Diana asked the advice of her husband and friends. Jerry Campbell, a former gossip columnist for the *London Evening Standard*, told her not to do it under any circumstances because in England they are called "the friendless ones," and her husband, Dick, said the idea "gave him the heebie jeebies" but if she got an assistant and remained anonymous, he thought it might work. Diana told Bellows if she did it, she needed help and wanted Louise Lague, a *Star* feature writer in Portfolio, to share the writing. Diana and Louise were not close, but she thought Louise "was a very good writer with a light touch." Lague, a writer of celebrity features at the *Daily News* when the *Star* bought it, had grudgingly worked on the *Star*'s city desk at first but then managed a transfer to Portfolio, where she wrote features about celebrities. Louise was ten years younger and taller at 5 foot 8 inches than Diana, and she was of French Canadian descent with a gift for foreign languages. McLellan met with Lague to discuss Bellows's proposal, and they both concluded that "Washington was too sophisticated for gossip" and marched to Bellows's office to tell him to forget it, but, said Diana, "he had the good sense not to be there." On Sunday, June 22, 1975, Diana and Louise wrote their first column and called it "The Ear," which according to Diana was "a small-scale disaster." *Star* insiders thought it "was a bunch of crap," Diana remembered later, and hard news reporters everywhere were contemptuous. Diana and Louise at first roamed through the *Star*'s newsroom for the latest gossip, but as "The Ear"'s popularity surprisingly grew with readers, the phone started ringing off the hook constantly with tidbits of gossip from callers. As a quirky promotion, the *Star* sent tiny pins resembling an ear, dubbed "Earwigs," to anyone ever mentioned in "The Ear." After a year of "The Ear," Maria Fisher, an elderly socialite, admirer of "The Ear," and a favorite among fundraisers, initiated an annual fundraising Ear Ball for district charities with Earwig recipients as guests. Diana and Louise were there, too, after having long lost their anonymity as the column's authors. The first Ear Ball was held at the Hyatt Regency for a $20 a head to benefit Gallaudet College and included "cops and diplomats, Beautiful People and television personalities, . . . Pisces people and Tune Inn types," among others, wrote the *Star*'s David Braaten.[28]

"The Ear" was a satire of a gossip column written to puncture the egos of self-important people with mock flattery. Louise later said she thought it worked because "we didn't point fingers at anybody. It was always very approving." Diana said she didn't want to "make the mistake of getting sucked into the social thing and start promoting your own people," which to her just wasn't funny, and Louise never felt comfortable "hanging out with society, embassy crowds, and congress people." When they got suckered into passing on falsehoods, each would take her turn at writing the "Grovel," a flippant apology written to mock the offended. They both agreed on certain standards for gossip too, like no gays out of the closet, only covert references to infidelity, and no sour grapes, which "is not a fun thing—sour grapes is a sad thing," said Lague. Diana's primary philosophy was "if you can't make people laugh it doesn't work." One of the funniest inventions of "The Ear" was the O.P. (Other Paper, i.e., *Washington Post*) and the Fun Couple—the illicit romance between *Post* editor Ben Bradlee and *Post* style feature writer Sally Quinn. Repeated sightings of the Fun Couple in "The Ear" was a particular thorn in the side of Bradlee but wildly popular inside the *Star*. Bellows said of Bradlee, "Ben was the perfect target for us, and I took delight in tweaking him," not because Bellows didn't like or admire Bradlee "but because it worked wonders for the *Star*." The Ear's mentions of the Fun Couple stopped for a short time in early 1976 when Bellows asked Bradlee for permission to reprint Chicago columnist Mike Royko's article headlined "Football on TV Just Isn't the Same," in which Royko complained that revelations about gay athletes on the football field in Rosellini's series ruined the game for him. The *Washington Post* owned the rights to Royko's column, so Bradlee told Bellows he would give permission if the *Star* stopped publishing gossip about him and Sally Quinn for a month. Bellows agreed, but as a joke he posted Bradlee's written confirmation of their agreement on the *Star* staff bulletin board, which elicited roars of laughter. In the fall of 1977 Louise left the *Star* and "The Ear" because she wanted to return to feature writing. Lague later said of the seventeen months she wrote "The Ear" with Diana, "I loved it, but it just wasn't enough," even though it was an immensely successful and syndicated in nearly forty newspapers by the time she left. When Time, Inc. bought the *Star* in 1978, "The Ear" was a treasured commodity, just like Bellows foresaw despite the naysayers.[29]

Jim Bellows tried a number of other innovative ideas to make the *Star* an entertaining alternative to the *Post*. Bellows asked Mary Anne Dolan to pick staff and be the editor for what would become the "Federal Triangle," a daily satiric soap opera of the Washington political scene. Along with Diana and Louise, Dolan chose the *Star*'s theater critic Dave Richards, national reporter Michael Satchell, local reporter Gloria Borger, The Rambler John McKelway, and obit writer Richard Slusser. Among the Portfolio writers already there when Bellows came were Ben Forgey, who had covered visual arts since 1965; Anne Crutcher, who wrote features about art and life; Dave Richards, who covered theater; Donia Mills, who reviewed movies; and Boris Weintraub, who commented on popular music. George Gelles wrote about classical music and dance, Judy Flander and Bernie Harrison informed readers about the best, worst, and newest shows on TV, and Dennis John Lewis did the same for radio. In 1978 Mills would move to the Metro section and Gelles would leave. Except for Bernie Harrison who died at age sixty-four in 1980, the rest continued to write about arts and entertainment until the *Star* closed.

Two years after Lynn Rosellini wrote her groundbreaking but controversial series on gays in sports, Jim Bellows and Dave Burgin suggested she tackle another controversial subject—the life and work of *Washington Post* publisher Katharine Graham. Lynn was not keen to do the Kay Graham series because it was "a no-win situation." Lynn would either be accused of "sucking up to Kay Graham like everyone else in town" with a fawning piece of journalism, or if she wrote a really hard-hitting piece of journalism, critics would accuse her of "a hatchet job," especially for a reporter at the competing newspaper. Bellows, however, believed in Rosellini's talents and nudged her to do the series as he had with Diana McLellan to write a gossip column. For weeks Rosellini's calls to Graham and her friends for interviews went unanswered. Years later Lynn remembered one especially hot summer afternoon in August after making more than a dozen calls with no luck, she gave up and drove in the sweltering heat to watch an afternoon matinee of the *The Rose*. The morose movie only depressed her more. Finally, after Mrs. Graham's personal secretary had repeatedly blocked Rosellini's calls, she asked her to let her boss know that she was going ahead with the article with or without an interview but to tell her, wouldn't it be better "to have your voice heard?"

It worked. Katharine Graham agreed to two one-on-one interviews with Rosellini in her office. Rosellini later remembered that despite Graham's reputation for being arrogant and a bit of a tyrant when crossed, during their private conversations she exhibited a "kind of vulnerability," and "I remember kind of liking her." Lynn was amused by her sort of "clench-jawed," upper-crust speech, reminiscent of famous women like Katharine Hepburn, who said things like "No, no, Darr-lingh." After Mrs. Graham opened the door to Rosellini, friends, family, and colleagues were more willing to talk over the phone with the reporter on and off the record. One anonymous source who knew Kay Graham well gave her the idea for the "Katharine the Great" label and provided her with lots of behind-the-scenes stories of Kay's volatile personality and catty attacks on people she disliked. Lynn also talked with a few people at the *Post* openly, like Bob Woodward at a Hot Diggity Dog stand, but he wasn't very helpful, and neither was Ben Bradlee. Most of Graham's friends and acquaintances were reticent to say anything too critical since as Polly Fritchey, one of Kay's best friends, told Rosellini, "People never wanted to say anything to offend Kay . . . because she could be pretty vicious." Although those who spoke off the record claimed they were afraid of Kay Graham, Lynn later said, "I didn't get that" from her. Rosellini found Kay Graham, however, reluctant to talk about the suicide of her late husband, Phil Graham. Graham also showed no hint of regret or self-reflection on the tough tactics she used during the contentious 1975 strike at the *Post*, but saw her actions as her only alternative.[30]

Lynn worked hard on the piece all through the summer of 1977. Then Allbritton balked and refused to run it, most likely because he didn't want to make waves. In fact, Allbritton went so far as to have Bellows and managing editor Sid Epstein, sign a written agreement pledging not to publish Lynn's series without Allbritton's personal approval. In Bellows's book *The Last Editor*, Mary Anne Dolan said of Allbritton, "He was frantic and paranoid, simply overwhelmed in a world he didn't know where Mrs. Graham made all the rules." Lynn tried repeatedly to contact Allbritton to plead her case for publishing the series, but to no avail. She then took a leave of absence upon receiving a publishing contract to expand her series into a book, but Kay Graham "closed down all sources," so she returned to the *Star* when Time, Inc. bought the paper and Murray Gart was named editor. Gart decided to make a splash and publish the Graham series. Charles Seib, who had been managing editor at the *Star*, by 1977 was the *Post*'s ombudsman. Seib bluntly called Rosellini's series "A Bid for Washington's Attention," and "less than great journalism" because it "read like five long gossip columns about one person" that heavily relied on unnamed sources. On the other hand, William Safire of the *New York Times* thought Kay Graham "a newsworthy subject" and welcomed the "lively five-part series." When Bellows left in December 1977, Lynn never comfortably adjusted to Gart or Time, Inc.'s brand of journalism and left for a job with the Washington Bureau of the *New York Times*. A few years after Lynn left the *Star*, she and her husband, Graham Wisner, the son of Kay's friend Polly Fritchey, were at a Boxing Day event after Christmas when they ran into Kay Graham. The next morning Kay called Graham to invite the couple to lunch at her Georgetown home. As the three sat together awkwardly at the end of a long dining table and servants in perfect quiet served the food, Mrs. Graham suddenly began talking about how she was so embarrassed when Lynn's series was published that she didn't go out of the house for weeks. After Mrs. Graham's long tirade ended, she escorted them to the door and blurted out a kind of dispensation, saying, "You are forgiven," as they exited. Outside the couple quizzically looked at each other and simultaneously said "what was that all about" and walked away chuckling. Lynn believed Mrs. Graham never forgave her for the series.[31]

Murray Gart hired Jonathan Yardley in 1978 as the *Star*'s book reviewer from the *Miami Herald*, where he had been book editor for four years, and in 1980 Pat Dowell as the *Star*'s music critic. Editorial page editor Edwin Yoder, who had worked with Yardley at the *Greensboro Daily News*, championed his old colleague when Gart opened up a new slot for an editorial writer. Yardley was eager to come to the *Star* as book editor but agreed to use his erudite talent to write both book reviews and editorials for a time to secure the job. Murray Gart lured feature writers Judy Bachrach and Nancy Collins from the *Post*, magazine feature writer Sandra McElwaine, and Jurate Kazickas, a young Associated Press reporter, to write for the Lifestyle pages. They were sometimes referred to as "Murray's Angels." Gart told Judy Bachrach in her initial interview, "I want to spoil you. I want you to do whatever you want at the *Star*." Bachrach was unhappy working at the *Post* and later admitted her time there was "a disaster . . . a very stupid career move," where she had few opportunities to excel and little freedom to write what she wanted. After the contentious *Post* strike ended, Bachrach realized, "Katharine Graham was going to ride us with a tough whip and she did. She gave none of us raises . . . none of what we needed," and Judy wanted out. Murray provided Bachrach with an almost unlimited expense account to travel and interview celebrities, a respectable salary, and freedom—a long tradition at the *Star* that allowed reporters to write "pretty much anything" as long as they didn't lie or libel someone. Sandra McElwaine, who Gart hired around the same time, was equally thrilled by the freedom. McElwaine explained, "I rarely got a direct assignment because I always had hundreds of things I wanted to do," and editors were happy she was willing to stay late and go the extra mile to get the story. McElwaine interviewed a score of celebrities, politi-

cians, and businessmen in Washington and New York like Ingrid Berg-
man, the shah of Iran's sister Ashraf Pahlavi, Duke Ziebert, New York
City mayor Ed Koch, and many others. Judy said of Murray, "I loved
him," and McElwaine called him a friend, but both knew he was unpopular with *Star* reporters he had not hired. Their editor, Denis Horgan,
was no fan of Gart's. Horgan had been intrigued and pleased when Gart
anointed him with the title of "director of editorial features" to rebuild
the lifestyle pages. The Portfolio section was redesigned and renamed
"Washington Life" in November 1979. However, Horgan over time
grew to deeply dislike Gart because, as he said later, he was "a horrid
individual to work for; he was mean and vindictive and he would play
favorites in ways that hurt the paper." Horgan had been with the *Star*
since 1971 starting on the copy desk and then working his way through
jobs as foreign editor and as assistant national news editor in charge of
special projects for Bellows. Denis admired Bellows as "a genius" and
"the best editor I have ever worked for in a 45-year career." Although
Horgan and other veteran staff did not share the same high opinion of
Gart that Bachrach and McElwaine did, Horgan never saw new and old
hires separate into two warring camps in the newsroom. To Horgan,
the staff were all "*Star* guys" working hard to beat the competition, and
besides, Gart "didn't bring in a bunch of chumps but neither were we a
bunch of chumps either." McElwaine adored Denis, and Judy and Sandra
both appreciated his light touch. Bachrach, however, realized that veteran
staff were understandably resentful at the perks she and new hires like
her friend Sandra were receiving. Still, she claimed, they "were all very
nice to me." Horgan often mediated between Gart and a reporter on his
staff who had violated some rule or unanticipated grievance of Gart's and
was threatened with dismissal. One of those was Tom Dowling, who was
now the *Star*'s film critic. Dowling had flourished under Bellows but was
the quintessential brash and independent reporter Gart could not abide.
In 1980 after Dowling saw the anticipated sequel to the Star Wars movie
The Empire Strikes Back, he wrote, "Never had such unlimited resources,
unparalleled good will and guaranteed formula of success been frittered
away," and continued unmercifully expressing his disappointment with
the film. Unfortunately, Dowling's full-throated pan of *The Empire* coincided with *Time*'s cover story glorifying the movie and director George
Lucas. In addition, the paper received a number of letters from readers
who were displeased with Dowling's critique. Horgan explained to Gart
that Dowling was paid to be an independent critic and did not deserve to
be fired for doing his job. As a result, Dowling was not fired but instead
was reassigned to write the boring column "Federal Cases" until the paper closed. Gart was the antithesis of his predecessor Bellows in so many
ways. Not only was Gart not universally beloved by staff like Bellows,

but he also jealously sought out Washington society's attention and favor by attending every party he could and expecting the lifestyle pages to cover them all. In contrast, Bellows had assiduously avoided Washington society to remain impartial. One *Star* veteran, however, that welcomed Murray's arrival was Betty Beale, who found getting space for society news under Bellows had been "hellish." Finally, in 1981, just weeks before Time, Inc. announced it was closing the *Star*, Denis left the *Star* because, he later said, Gart "just ground me down," and although he hated to leave, "my best pals ever . . . I dreaded going to work" every day, so to retain "some dignity, some pride," he left the paper.[32]

A year after starting at the *Star*, Bachrach's British boyfriend told her she should cover the upcoming trial of former Britain's Liberal Party leader Jeremy Thorpe. Bachrach did not even know who Thorpe was. The erudite and popular Thorpe was stripped of his leadership in 1979 after nearly two decades of titillating rumors about his homosexual affairs finally became front-page news. Norman Scott, a former gay lover, accused Thorpe of attempted murder to keep him quiet about their affair. Gart agreed to Bachrach's request, suggested she read the trial of Oscar Wilde to prepare, and file every day. Judy stayed with her boyfriend's sister in London for two months to save money but never read Oscar Wilde's trial. Bachrach arranged an interview with Scott at his home soon after she arrived in England. Scott was tall and slender, "with startling blue eyes set in a ruined and dissolute face," Judy wrote, who claimed about eighteen years ago Thorpe seduced him when he was twenty and had no money. The tale of Scott and Thorpe was to Bachrach "a thoroughly English story . . . farcical to the extreme and tragic as well" that has "ripped the entire fabric of British complacency with its long, ragged fingernail." On the first day of the trial on May 9, 1979, Bachrach told readers the "Trial of the Century is either the biggest hoax ever perpetrated on an innocent political figure and a gullible public or it's the most stunning example of crazed malice on the part of a man who so feared his homosexual past that he was willing to murder a man to hide it." Jeremy Thorpe and his three codefendants eventually were cleared of all charges. Americans and Brits read her stories about Thorpe religiously, even though they often complained bitterly about the reporting. When Bachrach returned home, Denis Horgan gave her a welcome-home party to celebrate the story's success.[33]

Bachrach was in England covering Prince Charles and Diana's wedding in July 1981 when she got the news the *Star* was closing. She remembered, "I was crying every day . . . it affected me very strongly and I don't think I've every totally gotten over it . . . I felt an affection for the *Star* . . . because it had a heart . . . a feistyness . . . a million weaknesses, many lovable," but she never loved a newspaper more in her long career. Sportswriters Betty

Cuniberti and Tim Kurkjian, who were also hired during Time, Inc.'s ownership, had much the same reaction to the *Star's* closing. In the *Star's* last edition on August 7, 1981, Cuniberti wrote during her short time she found "greatness, generously sprinkled with frailty," at a paper that still was "haunted by failure." Kurkjian told "grizzled veterans" on the sports desk that if they thought "a little 24-year-old kid with bowed legs and the voice of a 10-year old" wouldn't have lots of stories from his two short years, they were wrong. "The *Star* has given a lot" and "it stinks" that it's closing, wrote Tim.[34]

Gart told Bachrach, soon after she arrived, that he saw a political column in her future at the *Star*. When Judy began the column, however, she felt it was not taken seriously and even resented by some of her "hard news" colleagues after her career as mostly a feature writer. The split between the lighter and serious sides of news gathering at the *Star* was there from its beginning, although romance and friendship between individuals across those lines took place for years. Reporters, editors, and even advertising executives at the *Star* understood the importance of both sides of the news, but for most of the *Star's* history, they rarely overlapped. Covering the "hard news" of politics, wars, assasinations, foreign affairs, and US presidents is the lifeblood of any major daily American newspaper. The hard news stories in the headlines and the stories of reporters who gathered and wrote those stories at the *Star*, a major daily published in the nation's capital, provide the reader with a singularly distinct view of more than a century of American history.

6

✝

Reporting on Presidents, Politics, and War, 1868–1945

On May 16, 1868, Congress voted down the eleventh article of impeachment to remove President Andrew Johnson from office. Noyes had predicted a "Virtual Acquittal" in the early edition, and all afternoon crowds packed the *Star*'s business office as they waited for news of the impeachment in later editions. After the acquittal was announced, Noyes wrote, "There was instantly a great rush for the different exits from the Capitol . . . the pressure was great, the wreck of crinoline immense," with many in a "taunting mood" and "sweating mad," but they were unable to move, much less "strike a blow" at their political enemies. A Radical Republican Congress tried in vain to impeach Andrew Johnson, a southern Democrat and a foe of their ideas on how to remake the country in the wake of the Civil War. The *Star*'s prescient editorial saw Johnson's acquittal as a catalyst for reuniting moderate and radical Republican factions squarely behind a single Republican candidate in the 1868 election. Ulysses S. Grant was elected president on the Republican ticket in November. Noyes, Samuel Kauffmann, and associates, who had recently bought the *Star* from the Democrat William Wallach, endorsed Grant. The new owners and their descendants from 1867 to 1974 endorsed eight Republicans, were uncommitted in eight presidential elections, and supported only three Democratic candidates—Winfield Scott Hancock in 1880, who lost the election; Franklin Delano Roosevelt; and Lyndon Johnson in 1964. Crosby Noyes and Samuel Kauffmann were moderate Republicans, and the paper's editorial pages usually reflected those views. Noyes and Kauffmann, however, promised readers upon purchasing the *Star* that the paper would remain staunchly independent and free of political influ-

140

ences. Samuel Kauffmann's grandson and namesake, Sam Kauffmann, in 1952 during the commemoration of the *Star*'s one hundredth anniversary agreed that the nineteenth-century *Star* was a politically independent and fair paper by the standards of the time, but he also found news stories in its columns "so atrociously slanted that the toughest editor of the modern partisan press would have to confess himself outdone." Crosby's son and successor Theodore managed to reverse that practice, and by 1923 progressive journalist and media critic Oswald Garrison Villard wrote, "Mr. Theodore Noyes's editorial page, such as it is, is entirely free and is independent of the news policy of the paper." The *Star*'s newsroom from its earliest years was a "reporters' paper" because the man or woman on the beat drove the news published in the paper—not editors.[1]

Veteran *Star* reporter James Croggon was on a routine assignment to cover the departure of President James A. Garfield from the Baltimore and Potomac railroad station in Washington on the morning of July 2, 1881. Charles Guiteau, a deranged and thwarted office seeker, shot President Garfield twice with a revolver as he walked through the station's nearly deserted ladies' parlor with Secretary of State James Blaine. The police quickly cordoned off the station and apprehended Guiteau in seconds. Croggon was unable to leave the station and later claimed he scribbled notes on scraps of paper, ran up the stairway to an open window, and called below "Get this to the *Star*! Hey, take this to the *Star* office." An unknown passerby heard Croggon's shouts and took his notes to the *Star*'s newsroom immediately. In an hour the *Star* was off the presses and on the street and sold more than sixty thousand copies that day compared to a normal daily run of eighteen thousand. By 4 pm the *Star*'s fourth edition reported there was "not one chance in Hundred of his recovery." Although Garfield suffered only minor injuries, he wasted away for twelve weeks until he died from severe infections caused by physicians using unsterilized instruments to probe his wounds. In the four decades following the Civil War, there were three US presidential assassinations, severe economic depressions, a major industrial revolution, labor unrest, the first US war on foreign soil, and mass migration of non-Anglo peoples from southern and eastern Europe. Issues in the era generated high rates of political involvement and made newspapers popular, indispensable, and profitable. As a consequence, the *Star*, like other major city dailies, prospered and expanded its staff of reporters to thoroughly cover political news. In the early 1890s, Gideon Lyon covered the Senate and Jack Messenger the House; John Miller reported on national political conventions; special correspondent and Welshman George Harries covered the Homestead Strike and the Massacre at Wounded Knee in the Dakota Territory; and ace reporter Victor Kauffmann covered breaking national political news. An 1894 profile of the *Star* as a successful business enterprise shows a staff of mostly young men, but whether young or old, almost all the men sported fashionable walrus mustaches and bow ties or cravats popular with men in that era. Only one woman, the young and prim society editor Helena McCarthy, is pictured. The clean-shaven, three-hundred-pound Fatty (William W.) Price's photograph does not appear in the article, although he would later become famous for opening the doors of the White House to reporters while a *Star* reporter. No reporter had ever covered the White House full time until Price pursued the beat seriously. Price left his reporting job in South Carolina in 1896 and moved to Washington, hoping to get a job at the *Star*. City editor and chief reporter Harry Godwin sent Price to the White House to dig up a story in hope of ridding himself of the pesky job seeker. Godwin knew President Grover Cleveland was hostile to the press, and Price never made it inside the

Star newsroom in 1897. (R–L): Tom Noyes, who covered Coxey's Army and was city editor seated at desk at center right; reporter John P. Miller with beard and bowler hat is seated at first flat desk in right back; Fred C. Cook, who was later city editor and then news editor, is hatless and seated cross-legged at center back; large, hatless man standing left rear is Fatty (William) Price, who later was the *Star*'s first White House Correspondent and founding member of the White House Correspondents' Association; standing on chair behind Price and wearing a bowler hat is sports reporter Harry Fry; other unidentified men are reporters, messengers, and a stenographer. D.C. Community Archives, *Washington Star* Papers, D.C. Public Library, Neg. #154971.

White House on that first visit. Price, however, returned repeatedly and stood outside the White House gates peppering visitors with questions as they left or entered the gates. Price's persistence worked, and he eventually was admitted to the White House, which he thereafter regularly visited to pursue news stories. In 1896 large crowds gathered across from the Evening Star Building on Pennsylvania Avenue to watch election returns for the presidential race between William McKinley and William Jennings Bryan projected onto the building by a stereopticon. Of course, the *Star* offered late editions to the eager crowds too. McKinley would win a second term in 1900 but served only nine months in office when an unemployed factory worker turned political anarchist Leon Czolgosz shot him at the Pan American Exposition in Buffalo, New York, in 1901. Czolgosz's anger was fueled in part by the stark economic inequities spawned during the nineteenth-century's Industrial Revolution.[2]

In 1893 an economic depression swept across the country under President Grover Cleveland. Wealthy Ohio businessman Jacob Coxey and the flamboyant Carl Browne organized an industrial army of unemployed men in 1894 to march from Ohio to Washington to petition the federal government for jobs. Coxey believed that if Congress passed legislation to hire unemployed men to build badly needed roads and fund it with noninterest-bearing bonds, the country's economy would improve. Coxey's scheme probably would never have attracted the press and Congress's attention if it hadn't been for the colorful Browne, a self-promoter who dressed in buckskin and a big white sombrero, believed in reincarnation, and had been a cartoonist, political activist, journalist, and rancher. Coxey met Browne at the Columbia Exhibition and persuaded the charismatic Browne to join him in promoting his campaign. The two concocted the idea for the march and publicized it in labor newspapers and circulars. An editor at the *Masillon Independent* took an interest, and a handful of correspondents began sending out news of the march on the wire services, which attracted major newspapers to the story. The marchers set out in late March, with reporters covering them daily as they journeyed east. City editor Harry Godwin suggested that the twenty-six-year-old Tom Noyes, the youngest son of Crosby Noyes, make the strenuous trek with the marchers and report the story. Tom Noyes was a natural choice as an energetic young reporter with an adventurous spirit and innate gift for prose writing and hard news gathering since coming to work at the paper in 1889 immediately after graduation from Princeton. Noyes joined Coxey's Army sometime in early April near Pittsburgh in the Monongahela Valley on its way to Uniontown, Pennsylvania, at the foot of the Allegheny Mountains. Noyes painted a grim picture of men in a foul mood at the camp, who were preparing to make an "eight-mile tramp" over the mountains today "with snow coming down in a regular blizzard and with a bitterly cold wind blowing" fortified with rations of only coffee, bread, and "a microscopic piece of pork" for breakfast. Noyes often spoke with both Coxey and Browne on the trip and viewed the Masillon conservative businessmen's views as "well defined" and reasonable, but he was amused by the bizarre Carl Browne, who created a carnival atmosphere at the camp. Noyes, however, distinctly refrained from calling the unemployed marchers "tramps," like much of the press. In a Cumberland, Maryland, camp he observed, "Professional tramps are not given to playing baseball or getting shaved, neither have a passionate fondness for washing themselves or their clothes." An unemployed machinist told Noyes, "I have seen plenty of tramps in my day . . . and men of that character would no more have come with us, through the weather and over these roads that we have endured with nothing to eat but hard tack and coffee . . . We are not tramps." Noyes saw a few young men among the marchers who were only along for the adventure, but "a majority were honest men, workmen, and anxious to work."[3]

The press began referring to the unemployed marchers as "Coxey's Army," as they neared the nation's capital. They reached Washington on Sunday, April 29, 1894, and camped just inside the city's limits at Brightwood Riding Park. Coxey visited Capitol Hill and the District Building on Monday seeking support for his Good Roads Bill in Congress, permission to deliver his speech on the Capitol grounds, and more permanent quarters for the marchers. Washington Metropolitan Police Commissioner William Moore informed Coxey that if he tried to make a speech or gather marchers on the Capitol grounds the next day, he would be arrested. Browne persuaded Coxey to accompany him to the *Washington Times* office to give the paper an exclusive "scoop" on tomorrow's May Day march for the morning edition. Browne considered the *Times* a "workingmen's paper" because unemployed printers of the Columbia Typographical Union began publishing it that same year in response to the economic depression. *Star* reporter Gideon A. Lyon Jr. covered the May 1 parade. Lyon was a slim, tall, and wiry twenty-six-year old with fine, chiseled features who dressed conservatively and kept a neatly trimmed mustache. Lyon had no formal journalistic training, but with raw talent, he landed a job covering the White House and other executive departments for the *Star* at age nineteen and was an experienced newsman by the time the March occurred. Lyon described the marchers at the start of the parade as "the most motley procession that ever was conceived of outside of a carnival masquerade." Coxey lead the parade with his wife and infant child in an open carriage followed by his beautiful seventeen-year-old daughter, Mamie, riding a grand, white Arabian stallion dressed in a "white riding habit . . . red silk necktie . . . tied in a bowknot at the collar and a wealth of blond hair that the sun's rays lighted into gold flowed loosely from beneath a jaunty blue cap," wrote Lyon. Lyon asked Browne, "Suppose the authorities carry out their present intention and prevent Mr. Coxey and yourself from going on with the program at the Capitol?" to which Browne responded by "swelling out his leather coat with a puff of importance 'Such action would still further inspire the sympathies of the great masses . . . and accentuate in their minds . . . that the plutocrats will not brook interference, no matter how peaceful.'" A huge crowd of bystanders watched the marchers as mounted police controlled their advance with billy clubs. Coxey escaped the crowd and police with Browne's help, leaped shrubbery surrounding the Capitol grounds, and mounted the Capitol steps. The police, however, quickly spotted Coxey and denied his request to read his protest. As they escorted him away amid a surging crowd, Coxey handed his printed protest to Lyon and other reporters. Coxey's protest was printed in the May 1, 1894, *Star*. Browne resisted his removal from the Capitol steps, and violence erupted among the marchers. Lyon observed that policemen were using their "billies with vigor, hitting the men over the heads . . . and pounding Browne, who was still fighting at full bent" until many of the men were "probably pretty badly bruised up . . . but the fight was over in a very few minutes." In 1908 when Theodore Noyes became editor after the death of his father, Lyon replaced Noyes as associate editor and had a long and illustrious career at the *Star* until he retired in 1948 at the age of eighty. On May 1, 1944, Coxey at age ninety returned to Washington and spoke to a crowd of about three hundred curious onlookers from the Capitol steps. According to *Star* reporter George Kennedy, Coxey said, "I was denied permission to speak here 50 years ago, but a reporter from the *Washington Star* took my proclamation and gave it to the press and to the Nation." Kennedy shouted, "Here he is, General," and prodded Lyon to step forward. Coxey again gave Lyon his proclamation, but it was not printed a second time.[4]

As the twentieth century dawned, the first signs of war heated up just off the shores of Florida on the Island of Cuba as rebel insurgents fought a war for independence in the late 1890s. *Evening Star* editors depended on intrepid and sometimes foolhardy freelance correspondents to report on the rebellion. Cuban rebels secretly escorted Captain William Mannix, a stringer for the *Evening Star* and the *Army and Navy Journal*, into the island's interior to interview Salvador Cisneros, president of the rebel Cuban Republic. Mannix left Havana by steamer dressed as a typical Cuban to disguise his American identity and then traveled by train to rendezvous with agents who led him into the interior on horseback. They traveled through cane fields charred by war, a series of picturesque safe havens, and finally by foot up the Cubitas Mountains. In early January, Mannix arrived at a "fertile plateau of 8,000 acres," impregnable to attack, where Cisneros boasted to Mannix, "You may tell the American people . . . through the *Evening Star*, that the cause of the republican Cuba will win" and that the rebel movement is "blessed by heaven . . . and praised by all lovers of liberty." Eight days after meeting with Cisneros, Mannix arrived by foot at an outpost sixty miles from Havana to meet with the insurgent's military leader General Máximo Gómez. Gómez told Mannix upon his arrival as he dismounted his horse, "I am pleased to welcome an American newspaper man," then laughed heartily and told Mannix, "but I don't know what I would do to an American Congressman who would come to my camp." When General Gómez learned from Mannix that General Arsenio Martínez-Campos, commander of Cuba's Spanish forces, had been relieved of his command, the general feared the worse because only Campos's hand had "stayed the bloodthirstiness of Spain," said Gómez. Campos's replacement, General Valeriano Weyler, harshly treated the Cubans, which precipitated even more impassioned rhetoric in the American press.[5]

On January 29, 1896, William Mannix cabled the *Star* about being black-listed and expected his expulsion from Cuba within two to three weeks. When Spain's US ambassador Enrique Dupuy de Lôme was questioned about the expulsion, he told a *Star* reporter that Mannix had approached Spain's consul general in New York suggesting that Spain would be well served by an American correspondent like him in Cuba, "who would tell the truth about the conditions as he found them, unbiased by sentiment or partiality." Mannix also told the minister "he was very poor" and needed financial assistance to travel to Cuba. De Lôme approved the funds and insisted "no bribery was intended." Spain expelled Mannix, according to Dupuy, when he "began to write letters absolutely untruthful and alto-gether false . . . undoubtedly furnished to him by insurgent sources." Reporters who managed to cable reports without the imprimatur of Spanish censors were often expelled or imprisoned. Mannix was among them, as was Sylvester Scovel of the *New York Herald* and William Harding Davis of the *New York Journal*. Scovel's reporting for the *New York Herald* would earn him a job at Joseph Pulitzer's *New York World*. By March Mannix was back in Washington, but Scovel returned to Cuba with a false passport and was later imprisoned. James Gordon Bennett's *New York Herald* and William Randolph Hearst's *New York Journal* competed zealously to publish the next most provocative stories from Cuba. Crosby Noyes and his son Theodore held in contempt the yellow journalism practiced by Hearst and Bennett in the run-up to the Spanish–American War. The *Star*, like other newspapers, however, had no reservations in repeatedly calling General Weyler the "butcher" after correspondents learned he was ordering troops to round up civilians in the countryside and house them in reconcentration camps where many were dying from starvation and disease. President McKinley, as a Civil War veteran, preferred diplomacy over war with Spain, so he awaited the results of negotiations between Cuban insurgents and Spanish diplomats for partial Cuban autonomy. Then on the morning of February 9, 1898, Hearst published a private letter in the *New York Journal* sent by de Lôme to his friend, Señor Don José Canalejas, foreign minister of Spain. In ordinary times, the letter's contents would have been a major diplomatic faux pas and cause for de Lôme's dismissal, but nothing more. The letter was printed in many newspapers, including the *Star*, and described President William McKinley as "weak and catering to the rabble, and besides, a low politician." McKinley's aversion to war would be soon challenged by a much more provocative and deadly incident.[6]

The USS *Maine* left Key West, Florida, for Havana, Cuba, on the morning of January 25, 1898, under the command of Captain Charles Sigsbee on what was publicized as a friendly visit to protect American interests. Soon after the *Maine*'s arrival, the American consul gave a banquet at the Havana Yacht Club for military and diplomatic officials to meet Captain Sigsbee. Among reporters invited to the banquet were Charles Pepper of the *Star*, F. J. Hilgert of the Associated Press, Honore Laney of the *Journal*, Freeman Halstead of the *New York Herald*, and Scovel of the *New York World*. Less than a month later on a balmy, calm night in Havana Harbor just thirty minutes after taps aboard the *Maine*, a deafening explosion from the harbor broke the night's peace. The *Star* reported in its February 16, 1898, edition that Sigsbee had cabled Commander Forsythe at the Key West Naval Station to "tell admiral the *Maine* blown up and destroyed . . . Many killed and wounded . . . send light house tenders." The *Star*'s Cuban correspondent, Charles Pepper, was not in Havana but in the Cuban interior the night of the explosion. After finally receiving word from Pepper two days after the explosion, the *Star* in a front-page article apologized profusely to its readers for his absence. In the meantime, *Star* reporters focused their coverage on reactions from officials in Washington. *Star* newsman Fatty Price found Secretary of the Navy John D. Long as he entered the White House around 9 am the day after the explosion, and Long, hoping to dispel rumors of foul play, told Price, "I do not see cause for alarm. . . . Of course the catastrophe is a terrible one and excites suspicions," but to wait until a full investigation before reaching any conclusions. Victor Kauffmann and other reporters spoke with naval officers and found "perhaps a majority" of them were inclined to believe the explosion was an accident, but some speculated it might have been caused by a torpedo and other "some infernal machine . . . smuggled aboard the ship." The *Star* questioned the motives of the president and the naval secretary, who were advancing the accidental theory because for them to say otherwise would be "equivalent to charging treachery upon Spain" and lead to "war at once." Price and Victor Kauffmann attempted to track down information about a naval dispatch the *Star* had obtained describing an "8-inch percussion hole in the plate of the ship," but President McKinley told Price at the White House that he had not seen the dispatch and had no comment to make. In the days to follow, the initial rumors of a torpedo attack were disputed by US naval experts, but it made little difference. Public sentiment in favor of intervention in Cuba spurred on by newspapers coupled with Spain's own ineptitude finally led McKinley to ask Spain to grant full independence to Cuba. Spain refused, and on April 19, 1898, the United States passed a resolution declaring war with Spain.[7]

Over 150 correspondents were at the siege of Santiago. The *Star* had two correspondents with the District Regiment who reported from the front lines, and six or seven freelance correspondents who landed with General William Shafter's army in Cuba. Major dailies like the *Star* hired boats that constantly traversed the waters between Key West to within eighty miles of the blockade of Cuba at locations in Haiti and Jamaica. Lieutenant Colonel Allen of the Signal Corps was in charge of censoring cable transmissions by the press from Key West. At first Allen opened lines only once in the morning and in the afternoon for two-to-three-hour intervals, but by the end of the war with so many reporters representing major newspapers, the lines were opened all day. The conflict in Cuba only lasted from April to August 1898, but as a result the United States added the Philippines, Puerto Rico, and Guam as territories at the end of the war with Spain. From 1899 to 1902, US forces fought a Philippine insurgency that waged a fight for its independence against American forces. Crosby's son Theodore in 1900 traveled to Hawaii, the Philippines, and Samoa and sent back numerous travel logs for publication in the *Star*, which expressed his approval of American imperialism. Noyes wrote the Filipinos were not "fit for independent self-government," and US development will turn the island into "a valuable national asset in our commercial and business relations with the world," which can only be accomplished "through an exploitation which applies to people as well as to soil, and which brings prosperity to both."[8]

The *Star* editorially opposed William Jennings Bryan's successive runs for president as well as other populist leaders. It also supported the gold standard, and with reservations recognized labor's right to organize and bargain. Theodore Roosevelt ascended to the presidency after McKinley's assassination in 1901 and was popularly reelected in 1904. Crosby Noyes and the *Star* did not endorse Roosevelt or his opponent in 1904, and after Noyes's death, Noyes's son Theodore as editor again withheld the *Star*'s endorsement of any candidate when Roosevelt ran in the Bull Moose Party ticket in 1912. Crosby Noyes maintained a friendly working relationship with Teddy Roosevelt and admired TR for his "energy and tenacity," but he was not reticent about criticizing what he considered the sometimes harmful consequences of Roosevelt's forceful personality. In a 1907 speech Noyes described Roosevelt as "a law unto himself" who goes to great lengths to keep reporters out of the White House, doesn't like their criticism, and "nowhere has a word urging the practice of the rules of equity, even handed justice, the spirit of toleration, and the exercise of reasoning." In January 1907 near the end of Crosby Noyes's life, the *Star* enticed the talented political cartoonist Clifford Berryman from the *Washington Post*, whose success was closely linked to Teddy Roosevelt folklore. In 1902 while at the *Post*, Berryman drew the "Berryman Bear," a caricature of a defenseless bear cub TR refused to shoot on a bear hunt. The adorable, small, fuzzy bear cub became Berryman's lifelong trademark and the model for the popular Teddy bear. Berryman, a self-taught artist, grew up in rural Kentucky and came to Washington in 1886 at age nineteen at the behest of his benefactor, Kentucky senator Joseph Blackburn, who recommended him for an illustrator's job at the US Patent Office. Eventually Berryman became enamored with political cartoons and started freelancing. In 1896 the *Post* hired him full time. Not long after Berryman arrived at the *Star* he noticed Crosby was feuding with Roosevelt on the *Star*'s editorial page, and Berryman decided to join the fray. Berryman substituted Charles Dickens's character Bill Sykes for Roosevelt, who threatened his dog, "the G.O.P." with his club. When "Old Crosby Noyes" saw the cartoon, recalled Berryman, he commented, "This is much the strongest thing you've done for us. It is wonderful, wonderful . . . and don't you ever draw another picture like it as long as you're here. It isn't your style at all." Berryman followed Noyes's advice and credited the gentle humor in his cartoons in some measure to it. Berryman's career is known for caricatures that capture the likenesses and personalities of famous people with a humor that is largely devoid of invective or sarcasm. Teddy Roosevelt was the first president the young *Star* reporter G. Gould Lincoln ever personally interviewed. One quiet summer afternoon in 1907 Lincoln walked unobstructed into the White House's west wing offices to speak with the president's secretary about a local district matter he was covering. Finding no one around, Lincoln wandered further inside, and to his surprise encountered Roosevelt, who greeted him with a broad, toothy smile as the president ascended from the basement stairs. As Lincoln said sixty years later, "If you tried that today you would have the Army, the Marine Corps and everybody else on your neck before you could get inside." Like his predecessors, Roosevelt favored a few select reporters. Still when TR saw the gaggle of less-favored newsmen who hung around outside the White House gate in rain or snow, he took pity on them and provided at least an anteroom inside.[9]

In 1912 Woodrow Wilson claimed the mantle of progressivism and won the presidency. Gould Lincoln judged Wilson, as the "first man who really had a press conference as of today" with the whole press attending, rather than inviting only certain favored newsmen or small groups. Lincoln remembered "very well when we were all invited down to the White House" for the first time by Wilson to ask him questions. Newspapers had smaller staffs then, and Lincoln recalled "everybody" was there and were pretty excited. During the Wilson administration, the White House Correspondents' Association, which screened reporters for White House press conferences, was founded with *Star* reporter Fatty Price as its founding chair. But "then the War came along and of course, that was the end of the press conferences," recalled Lincoln. Lincoln covered his first national political convention in 1920, and five years later the *Star* considered him experienced enough to become its chief political reporter at age forty.[10]

Two years into Wilson's first term, war erupted in Europe after Archduke Ferdinand, heir to the Austro-Hungarian Empire, and his wife were assassinated in the city of Sarajevo. Despite Wilson's 1916 ubiquitous second-term campaign slogan "He kept us out of war," the nation's capital steadily began preparing for war. Before the election in November, the *Star* became a key organizer and supporter of a War Preparedness Parade in Washington scheduled for Flag Day on June 14, 1916. Rudolph Kauffmann, the *Star*'s managing editor, was the parade committee's treasurer. The *Star* actively promoted the parade by printing names of sponsors, writing supportive editorials, and devoting news coverage to it weeks in advance. The day of the parade was declared a holiday to give as many Washingtonians as possible a chance to attend. The *Star* carried a photo of President Wilson leading the parade, with Rudolph Kauffmann on his left and William Gude, chair of the parade committee and local entrepreneur, on the president's right. The *Post*, a Democratic Party paper, was lukewarm in its support of preparedness, carried little news about the parade, and cut out the image of Kauffmann in its coverage. The *Star* praised the parade's success in an editorial and called for Congress to enact legislation to prepare the country in the remote chance of attack by a foreign enemy. Since 1915 when a German U-boat sank the British RMS *Lusitania* with Americans aboard, US leaders became increasingly alarmed by German submarine attacks on neutral US ships carrying armaments to Britain. Finally, in April 1917, Congress declared war on the Central Powers of Europe. The Wilson administration used the Espionage and the Sedition Acts of 1917 and 1918 to jail or deport hundreds of conscientious objectors and silence those who spoke or wrote against the war. The original legislation contained a press censorship provision that US newspapers strongly opposed. The "press will do its duty," said a *Star* editorial in late April 1917 as part of the "best organized and most progressive press in the world" and report the news to an educated public who "demand a full and free chronicle of passing events and editorial observations" without regulations from the federal government. The American Publishers Association of New York was more provocative in its assessment, calling the provision "an assault upon the very foundation of our free institutions, freedom of thought and . . . speech." In May Congress struck the provision. By November, however, Wilson was still complaining about the press when he responded to Breckinridge Long, an assistant Secretary of State, about the "glaring breaches of patriotic procedure" in newspapers like the *"Washington Post*, which apparently nobody can control." In the spring Wilson established the Committee on Public Information (CPI), headed by George Creel, a muckraking journalist, to develop propaganda tools and asked Long to look into the effectiveness of voluntary press censorship. Creel assured Wilson that despite some breaches of the CPI's voluntary guidelines, the Committee's efforts were working well, since much of "our matter goes into the papers by thousands of columns." Except for the *Star*'s initial opposition to press censorship, the paper remained largely uncritical of the CPI's efforts to suppress public criticism of the war. Editorially the *Star* tended to call any opposition to the war as "unpatriotic" or "seditious." "It is part of the German political creed," wrote the *Star* in response to the leaking of naval secrets in May 1917, "that any work for the fatherland is meritorious. Every German citizen . . . wherever he may be domiciled is potentially a spy for his government," and although exemptions from conscription for disability or family hardship are valid, those involved in "anti-registration and anti-conscription agitation . . . need the most severe treatment prescribed by the law for seditious enemies of the state."[11]

On June 20, 1917, a delegation from the new Russian Republic on their way to discuss with Wilson the Republic's part in the European war passed through a picket line of suffragists. The suffragists unfurled a provocative banner before the Russian delegation, whose new country gave women the right to vote. It read, in part, "They say we are a democracy. . . . We the women of America tell you that America is not a democracy when 10,000,000 American women are denied the right to vote." The *Star* reporter covering the event witnessed shouts of "sedition, shame, outrage" coming from an "angry mob" of nearly one hundred people who "smashed their fists through the banner." The *Star*'s editorial the next day described the "Seditious Suffrage Picketing" as "nagging and annoying," "unpatriotic . . . . an outrage upon American Citizenship," and dangerous in a time of war. The daily picket lines, which began in January 1917, were organized by the

National Women's Party (NWP), a splinter organization formed in 1915 by Alice Paul as a more radical alternative to the National American Women's Suffrage Party. Paul welcomed any press attention—good and bad—and produced her own press release about the incident. On June 22, the *Star* reported the arrest of Lucy Burns and Katharine Morey for obstructing traffic as "one of the mildest occurrences of the kind," with only the shutter of cameras and "clicking" of "movie reels" in the background in the early morning hours. Lucy Burns planted "her left foot forward . . . and began to recite her lines . . . Joan of Arc could not have been milder or more righteous as she said in a low tone . . . this is private property and you have no right to touch our banner." The Metropolitan Washington police at the direction of the three commissioners arrested and jailed nearly one hundred picketers in June and July. The women were imprisoned in Virginia's Occoquan Work House when they refused to pay the $25 fine. In July Arthur Brisbane, who had just purchased the *Washington Times*, told Wilson's secretary, Joseph Tumulty, that Theodore Noyes had suggested to him "having a bare statement of fact, but no publicity" about the suffragists in their respective newspapers so as not to "feed their vanity." Although Noyes supported women's suffrage, he had little tolerance for public protest, especially in Washington, which he felt tarnished the city's reputation. Brisbane agreed but feared that a "conspiracy of silence" in their newspapers about the suffragists' protests would push the women to more violent action to get attention. Brisbane instead recommended they print only a "colorless chronicle," no "interesting reading," or front-page headlines about the pickets. Brisbane also tried but failed to convince Paul to stop criticizing Wilson by offering her daily back-page coverage. Paul was only amused by the offer. The *Star* and the *Times* stuck to the scheme for a while, but *Washington Post* editor Ned McLean was not part of the bargain and so the arrests and picketing continued to make front-page headlines at the *Post*. In any case, the story proved too compelling for reporters and editors of any paper to push to the back pages. The suffragists imprisoned at Occoquan were fed bug-infested food, tied to their cell doors, and denied visitors, including meetings with their attorneys. In October nearly thirty suffragists went on a hunger strike at Occoquan, and NWP leaders, including Alice Paul, endured forced feedings. Suffragists were eventually released on a writ of habeas corpus with no explanation after influential friends pleaded their case to Wilson and other high-ranking officials. The NWP's strategy was a key factor in pushing Congress to act on the eventual ratification of the Nineteenth Amendment giving women the right to vote in 1920. A report by the District of Columbia Board of Charities into accusations of prisoner mistreatment at Occoquan concluded that the women's conduct warranted their harsh treatment, and no misconduct by prison officials had occurred.[12]

Dan (Daniel E.) O'Connell was the *Star*'s city editor during World War I. Dan O'Connell came to the *Star* in 1913 as its city editor after working as a reporter and editor at the city's three other dailies. One colleague remembered Dan as a "man with a routine," who constantly puffed on a pipe or cigar, "was rotund, wore a homburg in the winter and a panama in the summer," always vacationed in Colonial Beach, drove the same route to work every day, and was usually good for a loan. Dan's steadiness, generosity, but most of all his encyclopedic knowledge of the city and its people served him especially well while novice reporters were filling in for veteran reporters fighting in Europe. The city was overcrowded with war workers, prices were inflated, and housing and fuel were in short supply. Then in the fall of 1918, the Spanish influenza epidemic hit Washington. The epidemic would take more American lives than those lost on the battlefields of Europe, and an estimated 1,500 died in Washington, D.C. During the Great War, nearly eighty thousand new residents crowded into Washington to work in the War Industries Board and other agencies, many of which were housed in temporary buildings on the mall. Another 130,000 soldiers were stationed in nearby camps. The *Star*'s October 6, 1918, headlines read, "Huns Burn Villages in North Preparatory to Retreat to French Frontier" while "talk of peace" hung in the air, alongside the headline, "Thirty-One Die from Influenza Here in 11 Hours." The flu outbreak closed churches, libraries, schools, and "recreational entertainments." Washingtonians had been reading since August about the epidemic's devastating death toll in the East Coast cities of Boston and Philadelphia. A few cases were reported in military camps outside the city in September, but by October the epidemic was spreading among city residents. O'Connell sent reporters to boardinghouses where war workers lived and many of the cases were first reported. One reporter found that some landlords were not allowing tenants, who had moved to D.C. from other cities to work in war industries, to return to their rented rooms from a fear such tenants might spread the flu. The paper also reported that landlords were saving money by cutting back on heat despite the sickness all around them. Commissioner Brownlow forcefully condemned the landlords' actions and threatened large fines for such "cold landlords" in the local press. On October 12 the *Star* announced there was an "acute shortage of grave diggers" and printed a half page of the individuals who had died from the epidemic. The city's mounting death toll was printed for every twenty-four-hour period for almost two weeks in the *Star*. The paper reported a total of forty-seven deaths on October 8, fifty-seven on October 10, seventy-three on October 11, and at its crest on October 18, ninety-one deaths. By October 21 the number of deaths appeared to be diminishing. By November 1918 an armistice was called, the fighting ended in Europe, and American soldiers still in Europe began returning home from the battlefields. Dan O'Connell left the *Star* after World War I ended to be editor at the *Washington Times*, but he would return later.[13]

The *Star* sent Oliver Owen Kuhn to report on negotiations at the Paris Peace Conference among diplomats from more than thirty-two countries held in Versailles just outside Paris in early 1919. Kuhn had analyzed European politics and diplomacy during the Great War and also wrote a lighter column titled "Shrapnel" with tidbits of trivia from the war, like revealing British Field Marshal Haig was color blind or "Tommies" (British soldiers) didn't like German music. In 1912 at age twenty-six, Kuhn started at the *Star* as a copy reader after working as a reporter and then managing editor at papers in his home state of Indiana and then the *Washington Post* and *Washington Times*. In late March, Kuhn left the peace conference to visit war-torn northern France and wrote in an article for the Paris newspaper *Le Matin*, "If anyone dare . . . doubt the justness of the demand by France that raparation should be fairly made, put to him . . . that which was the old and splendid little city of Arras." Kuhn saw "the poisoned breath of the German beast," as he characterized it, everywhere he went in France. The Europeans felt similarly aggrieved and rejected some of Wilson's more liberal Fourteen Points, especially the amount of territory and war reparations allotted to Germany. Despite the rejection of some of Wilson's principles in the treaty, the League of Nations was established and the president returned home in August asking Congress to ratify the treaty. Wilson suffered a stroke in September, and whatever influence he might have had waned. Congress balked at ratifying the treaty, argued it was too harsh, and opposed US membership in the League of Nations. The *Star* editorialized that "Uncle Sam should sign the Paris treaty in order not to be a quitter" because negotiating a separate treaty would be "a shameful course of utter selfishness," and with less stringent terms might "lead to the encouragement of the enemy and eventually his emergence from defeat." Then the campaign for a new president began in 1920 and the *Star*'s endorsement of Republican candidate Warren Harding, who opposed ratifying the Treaty and the League of Nations, meant the *Star*'s editorial board had to carefully choose its words. The *Star* argued that a Republican Party victory on November 2 should not necessarily mean support for "isolation and for repudiation" of all responsibility to cooperate with the allies in ending the war. The editorial argued that favoring a Republican in the White House only means the United States will not become part of a "Federation of the World" because "to do so would give too much power to the supergovernment." Harding's election in 1920 resulted in the United States signing separate treaties with Germany, Austria, and Hungary and never joining the League of Nations. Harding would die in office and be tainted by the Teapot Scandal, which swirled around but never touched him. The cost of reparations and loss of large tracts of land led to humiliation and economic hardships among Germans, which many historians have speculated contributed to the rise of Hitler and fascism. After returning from Paris and at the end of World War I, Kuhn asked for a leave of absence to assist in writing a book on Italy's involvement in the war. When Kuhn returned to the *Star*, he began hosting the "National Radio Forum" sponsored by the *Star*, where well-known government officials and experts discussed important national and international issues. Oliver Owen Kuhn died unexpectantly in 1937 at age fifty-one, while still the *Star*'s managing editor.[14]

Congress passed legislation in 1924 to give a $1,000 bonus to World War I veterans for their war-time service. Veterans could borrow money with interest from their bonus, but Congress delayed the payment of the entire amount until 1945. The American Legion with the help of congressional supporters like World War I veteran and Texas congressman Wright Patman pushed for an immediate payment in the 1920s, but Republican presidents Warren G. Harding and Calvin Coolidge blocked their efforts citing concern over the federal budget and what they saw as preferential treatment of veterans versus the needs of all Americans. The *Star*'s editorial board was pleased with the string of Republican presidents elected in the 1920s, and the paper prospered, as did most of the nation during their terms. *Star* executives planned and built a new annex and substantially expanded employee benefits. The nation was at peace, and except for the Teapot Dome scandal, national political news was pretty bland. A crime wave instigated by Prohibition plus the personal triumphs of Charles Lindbergh and Amelia Earhart making long-distance solo flights were some of the biggest stories of the decade. The seeds of the Great Depression to come were planted in those boom years, however. The excesses of Wall Street and the fragile boom ended just months after President Herbert Hoover took office in March 1929. On October 29, 1929, the stock market crashed and the longest economic depression in American history began. Millionaires were reduced to poverty, banks failed, farms and homes foreclosed, and scores of people couldn't find jobs, including World War I doughboys. The thousands of unemployed World War I veterans who came to Washington in 1932 asking for the immediate payment of their bonuses became one of the biggest news stories in Washington, D.C. Thomas Henry, a veteran of the "Great War" himself and a *Star* reporter, was the primary newsman on staff covering the story of the Bonus Army, or the Bonus Expeditionary Force (BEF), as the veterans called it. Henry came to the *Star* in 1922 as a reporter after a career first at the *Washington Herald* as news editor and then city editor at the *Washington Daily News*. Henry's writing provides some of the most vivid and intimate accounts of the veterans' fight to receive their bonuses.[15]

Without homes and livelihoods, thousands of unemployed veterans, the main contingent of which was led by Portland, Oregon, veteran Walter W. Waters, began arriving in Washington with their families in the spring of 1932. The *Star*'s April 8, 1932, front page carried a photograph of approximately one thousand veterans, who gathered on the steps of the Capitol to present a petition asking for the bonus to congressmen Wright Patman, Democrat of Texas, and Democratic Party leader Henry R. Rainey containing more than two million veterans' signatures. The article also reported President Hoover had vetoed the bonus bill a year ago and was still opposed because the federal government needed to decrease government expenditures in order to balance the budget. When Henry interviewed bonus marchers two months later, he found the "bonus excuse is merely something tangible, something they can understand . . . and talk about" since nothing else has worked. These unemployed men, wrote Henry, represent "a beginning crystallization of the great, growing bewilderment of people" who were grasping for answers and relief from the huge economic hardships they faced. Henry spoke with cowboys, truck drivers, blacksmiths, bootblacks, steel workers, coal miners, stenographers, and common laborers. He found black and white, illiterate, and well-educated men and those fluent and barely able to speak English. Yet despite their differences, he found they share "one thing in common—a curious melancholy, a sense of the futility of individual struggle . . . of being in the grip of cruel, incomprehensible forces." Henry sympathized with the Bonus Army's plight but saw the veterans' demand for an immediate bonus a "flight from reality," to expect the current government to provide for them as it once did during wartime while an economic depression gripped the nation. Pelhem D. Glassford, superintendent of the Washington Metropolitan Police, had commanded troops in France during World War I and was sympathetic to the veterans' cause. Glassford fed and sheltered them as best he could with the help of beneficent donors like Evalyn Walsh McLean, wealthy socialite and wife of *Washington Post*'s publisher Ned McLean. In June Glassford got permission from the Office of Federal Buildings and Federal Parks to set up a makeshift camp on federal land on the Anacostia flats overlooking the city the veterans dubbed Camp Marks. Although some BEF members continued to stay in various abandoned buildings in downtown Washington, most veterans and their families made their homes at Camp Marks. The House of Representatives passed Patman's bill to pay the bonus on June 15, but two days later the Senate killed it temporarily by tabling it for the next session in hopes the marchers would go home. Congress adopted a joint resolution in early July to appropriate $100,000 to a fund to pay marchers for travel expenses home if the veterans left the city by July 15 when Congress adjourned. All five Washington dailies urged veterans to take the money and return home. The *Post* urged them to seek relief work at home, and the *Star* asked BEF leaders to tell their ranks to take the money before the offer expired because staying would put them "in deeper and deeper distress" and encourage the radical element among them. Some bonus marchers did take the offer, but many stayed.[16]

On July 12, Royal Robertson led his new California contingent of bonus marchers to the Capitol, where they were joined by other marchers who threatened to camp on the Capitol's grounds until Congress passed the bonus bill. Superintendent Glassford informed the veterans the next day the only way they could stay was to march without stopping. The men began a slow, quiet shuffle around the Capitol, which became known as the "Death March." The *Star*'s July 15, 1932, edition ran a photo of the sweaty, tired, disheveled men of all races and nationalities in loosened ties, white shirts, and fedoras or caps pacing in an unending corkscrew line enveloped by a dark night lit only by street lamps. Henry expressed admiration for their determination, but also found "the mind of the B.E.F." ranged from "the highly original economic philosopher to the purely parrot-like creature of mass suggestion." A former hotel business owner in the march explained to Henry, "I joined this movement because I realized it is the only constructive movement in the country toward a return to real values," while another waxed on endlessly about his reasons but finally admitted, "he hasn't got the words to bring it out," and a Negro bootblack from California who had lost his business expressed his reason plainly, "Do I think the Government can afford to pay the bonus? Yes sir . . . I can't see no reason they can't pay it." Throughout July the *Star* and other local dailies reported on the illnesses and unsanitary conditions at BEF camp sites, power struggles, escalating violence between police and veterans, and a subversive communist contingent. Police estimated around twenty-one thousand veterans were in D.C. in early July. After Congress left with no bonus bill passed and the offer of travel money for veterans to return home expired, approximately twelve thousand homeless, destitute, and angry veterans and their families remained.[17]

General Douglas MacArthur was strongly opposed to the BEF presence in Washington. MacArthur thought its members were mostly imposters and communists who posed a violent threat to the country. President Hoover hesitated in declaring martial law to rid the city of destitute veterans who had fought for the country despite their presence being a visible sign of his failure. Hoover framed the problem in the press as a local issue for the D.C. Commissioners and Washington Metropolitan police to handle. Then on July 20 Glassford received orders from US Attorney General William D. Mitchell to evict veterans housed in abandoned federal buildings and scattered public sites in downtown Washington by July 25. Glassford kept negotiating with the D.C. Commissioners and various federal officials to delay the evictions. Despite Glassford's best efforts, a "riot" erupted between the police and the bonus marchers on July 28. The *Star*'s afternoon edition reported two injured policemen and twelve veterans had been taken to Providence Hospital, including an "unidentified bonus marcher" who was shot by policeman George Shinault. The unidentified veteran was William Hushka, a World War I Chicago veteran who would die soon, and a second veteran would die a few days later. The *Star* also printed a front-page special bulletin signed by Secretary of War Patrick J. Hurley with instructions to Gen. Douglas MacArthur, which read, in part, "The President has just informed me that the civil government of the District of Columbia . . . is unable to maintain law and order in the District. You will have United States troops . . . co-operate with the (D.C.) police force [and] surround the affected area and clear it without delay." According to the *Star*, early that afternoon "two troops of cavalryman from Fort Myer crossed the Arlington Bridge and came up Seventeenth street" to take "position on the Ellipse, south of the White House," with "five tanks and machine gun equipment" arriving a little later. MacArthur with the aid of his lieutenants Dwight Eisenhower and George Patton led the troops to the encampment at Camp Marks that evening. Henry and other reporters were there to witness the confrontation. The newsmen moved up the hill where Henry found "ragged women" waiting anxiously for their husbands and the anticipated destruction of the "filthy hovels" to which they had added "touches of domesticity" brought with them to make a home. Henry saw the infantry cross the drawbridge to the camp with "glistening bayonets fixed to their rifles" and push a "mass of citizens" to the east side of the bridge as they attempted to leave the camp. The soldiers then threw tear-gas grenades into the crowd nearby, and as the fumes reached the eyes of the women and children Henry saw through the haze "a wild scramble to escape from the bridge" to the park below. The calvary rode with "little relish for the job ahead of them," judged Henry, to "the first deserted row of tents" and halted. Veterans moved forward and exchanged cigarettes with the cavalrymen, and then MacArthur entered the field with "the breast of his uniform covered with brilliantly colored campaign ribbons and with medals." "He alone," wrote Henry, "has authority to make terms." According to Henry's account, General MacArthur negotiated with the veterans, who agreed to leave the camp if a sufficient number of their own were allowed to remain behind to protect their property. Henry then moved with a group of newsmen "back into the darkness" where he heard a contingent of belligerent men armed with rifles cursing, and "swearing they would stick to the death." These veterans were in no mood to speak with reporters and told them to leave or "they would be lynched." As Henry left, he saw defiant men and a "huddle of women" waiting on the hillside for the "sound of shots which would be the signal for battle." At the bottom of the hill Henry and other reporters saw the camp above rise in a "tower of flame," and then he witnessed a veteran who, after finding a box of matches, shouted "we're going to burn them—every damn one of them," while the veterans marched up the hill into the darkness as more tents and hovels burst into flames. Henry wrote melodramatically that in the end the "wounded beast of poverty and despair, who came out of the black jungles of city slums and desolate abandoned farms" was "valiant in its passing," and although destroyed, "did not surrender" but instead made a "dramatic show of defiance" in the "burning of its ramshackle, junk-pile city to keep it from destruction by the 'enemy.'" In 1933 the Pulitzer jury awarded Henry honorable mention for his "vivid descriptions of the rise and fall of the bonus army . . . and his gripping account of the battle of Camp Marks." Henry would have a long and distinguished thirty-five-year career at the *Star* as a decorated World War II war correspondent, science writer, and columnist. He remained with the *Star* until his retirement in 1958. Democratic Party candidate Franklin Delano Roosevelt (FDR) read about the military force used to evict the Bonus Army in the *New York Times* the morning after it occurred. FDR told an aide it was no longer necessary to continue his campaign against Hoover because it appeared his opponent had fallen on his own sword. Roosevelt would continue to oppose the bonus bill until it was finally passed over his veto in 1936.[18]

In November 1932, Americans elected Franklin Roosevelt president because he offered to make fearless and revolutionary change to get Americans back to work and the economy growing. Roosevelt understood he needed the press to publicize his progressive agenda to the public, so he began twice-weekly press conferences with reporters in a packed oval office. There Roosevelt wooed their favor with charm, humor, and an abundance of information, even if he carefully orchestrated the facts to his advantage. Russell Young, who was the *Star*'s White House correspondent when Roosevelt took office, was assisted by political reporter Gould Lincoln, who had covered Capitol Hill, presidential campaigns, and conventions for more than a decade. Lincoln also started writing the column "The Political Mill" in 1930, which he would continue until his retirement in 1964. In 1932 Lincoln correctly predicted Roosevelt's win, which he said later "damn near cost me my job," and again in 1940 when FDR was reelected. Lincoln had accurately picked the presidential winner and many other political contests since 1920 by conducting his own unofficial poll while crisscrossing the country to cover campaigns. Although Lincoln was an avowed Republican, he admired FDR and later told an interviewer, "it was an amazing thing" how Roosevelt used his "personal magnetism and voice" to win over reporters during press conferences.

When FDR addressed reporters with his usual engaging "'my friends,' everybody just moved up a little closer to him." Lincoln was also well aware that President Roosevelt carefully controlled the message by allowing reporters to publish only what he "permitted." Occasionally FDR would jokingly tell a reporter to "stand in a corner with a dunce cap on," remembered Lincoln, when the president took umbrage with a newsman's comments or questions. Franklin and Eleanor Roosevelt hosted annual receptions for the White House press corps and invited individual reporters to private social gatherings at the White House and picnics at Hyde Park to win them over.[19]

On the anniversary of President Roosevelt's busy first year in office, the *Star*'s March 4, 1934, front page contained a long news article written by Lincoln detailing "governmental and economic experiments" of FDR's New Deal. Lincoln viewed taxes and the deficit as looming problems for FDR to carry out his aggressive agenda, but saw President Roosevelt as "the dominating figure in both matters of legislation and politics," and the last year as "one of great effort and unusual achievement." The *Star*'s editorial that day expressed some ambivalence about FDR's bold policies but had no doubt that the president has won the "unquestioning confidence and respect of the people," and his "personality has gripped the imagination of his countrymen, restored faith and confidence that were all but shattered and offered leadership that even those who doubt do follow." Still the *Star* hopes that as Roosevelt's "first year lengthens into the second, that there will be a renewal of the once inherent tendency of Americans to rest faith in and derive courage and inspiration from institutions and principles" and a lessening of "idolatry" for "one man or group," because the challenges the country faces are "too great for any one man to shoulder alone."[20]

In the summer of 1936, *Star* executive editor Theodore Noyes sent a scolding memorandum to the paper's editorial page staff while he was away at the Noyes's family summer home in Maine. Noyes admonished them for printing an editorial expressing "to a cocksure certainty what the President and his expert advisors do not, or may not know concerning conditions in American industry," about which "he has made up his own mind and which is now testing out." Noyes pointed out that the *Star* had freely criticized New Deal policies in the past, like FDR's unwise monetary policy or "oppression of American industry." On the other hand, the paper had agreed in editorials with New Deal efforts to eliminate child labor, shorten work hours, and create equity between labor and business. Noyes, however, thought the *Star*'s editorial writers in this instance had yielded "to the temptation to gain literary distinction as a witty, satirical assailant in partisan propaganda." The dignified Noyes had little tolerance for self-important writing intent on pushing a political agenda that lacked objectivity and balance. From the historical record, we cannot know with any certainty what editorial Noyes criticized, but it is clear his main objection was to the paper forgetting its duty to D.C. residents, over which the national government has, he wrote, "absolute executive and legislative control," and "the *Star* as its representative and defender" should not "intimately or conspicuously" identify with any political party. Liberal journalist Oswald Garrison Villard was highly critical of the cautious and balanced editorials Noyes fostered. In a critique of local Washington papers in 1944, Villard derisively wrote of the *Star*, "from the beginning editors and owners decided not to have either an interesting or an informative, or an able editorial page," and to "injure no one's feelings and, above all to avoid criticism of influential persons." Still Villard judged Noyes as an honorable man and the *Star* a respectable and certainly successful paper in the city. Noyes's cautious approach, Villard wrote, "Has not prevented generations of readers from believing in it thoroughly, in its honesty of purpose and devotion to their interests and those of the peculiar community" of the District of Columbia. Between the twentieth century's two world wars, the *Star*'s range of columns on its editorial pages range from the erudite and intellectually challenging to the boring and equivocal. Gould Lincoln began writing the savvy "Political Mill" for the paper in the 1930s, and it carried the nationally syndicated columns of conservatives David Lawrence, Mark Sullivan, Paul Mallon, and its own foreign affairs editor Constantine Brown. The *Star* also ran the syndicated column of liberal commentator Dorothy Thompson, but never carried the more liberal column "The Washington Merry-Go-Round," written by Drew Pearson and Robert S. Allen. When Theodore Noyes was the paper's editor, the page of syndicated columns always had the disclaimer "the opinion of the writers on this page are their own" and are presented to give readers different points of view that "may be contradictory among themselves and directly opposed to *The Star*'s," which generally leaned toward moderate conservative Republican Party politics. In the 1930s the *Star*'s balanced but unimpressive editorial page would be overshadowed by the *Washington Post*'s when Eugene Meyer, a Republican in the Hoover administration, bought the *Post* in 1933. Meyer devoted much of his money and energy to hiring writers to create a nationally significant editorial page. In 1938, *Post* editorial writer Felix Morley won a Pulitzer. Meyer, however, never slowed the bleeding of red ink at the *Post* in the 1930s while the *Star* continued to make a hefty profit.[21]

On May 28, 1935, the Supreme Court in three separate unanimous opinions found the National Industrial Recovery Act, other New Deal legislation, and certain executive actions unconstitutional. The justices ruled that the president had assumed powers far beyond his executive authority over American industry and government. A day after the

decisions were announced, a *Star* editorial praised the Supreme Court
for restoring the Constitution "in the twinkling of an eye" and turning "back those who have sought to set Federal power above law" by
granting to the president power that "bordered on a dictatorship." By
1937 Roosevelt repeatedly had been stymied by the Supreme Court,
which ruled against many of his New Deal programs. In the wake of
Roosevelt's landslide victory in 1936, he concocted a scheme to pack
the Supreme Court with justices who would rule in his favor. Lincoln
recalled that Roosevelt kept the reporters "shut in" at the White House
on February 5, 1937, when he announced his "court packing" bill, until
"he said everything he had on his mind about the Court" ad finitum
when all reporters wanted to do was get to the nearest telephone as soon
as possible to call in their stories. After a few months of controversy
in the press, the *Star* found opposition to the court-packing plan was
"no partisan political fight," but one in which "the men whose names
have been synonymous for years with liberal principles and progressive government are found in opposition." The *Star* named, among
others, progressive Republican senator William Borah, Farm-Labor
Party senator of Minnesota Henrik Shipstead, and Nevada Democratic
senator Pat McCarran, who were critical of the plan. Even FDR's vice
president, John Nance Garner, gave it a visible thumbs-down in the
Senate chambers when it was introduced. The court-packing plan faded
from importance when the Court began to rule more often in the president's favor. In 1940 Roosevelt nominated *Star* White House reporter
John Russell Young as a District of Columbia Commissioner, to the
complete surprise of the White House press corps, the *Star* newspaper,
and city government. Reporters who gathered for their regular press
conference were flabbergasted when they heard the president announce
Young's appointment. Then FDR asked Young to say a few words, to
which the usually loquacious Young muttered "do the best I can" and
then continued that "he hoped there was no political significance involved . . . and no rigidity about the terms of service." Longtime *Star*
reporter Jerry O'Leary, who was a young copy boy in the late 1930s, said
Young "wrote incomprehensibly," and rewrite men and deskmen were
charged with converting his convoluted prose to English. Jerry's father
Jeremiah O'Leary Sr. began at the *Star* in 1917 and by the 1930s was
the paper's respected and well-connected congressional reporter who
covered Capitol Hill, political campaigns. and conventions. When Jeremiah O'Leary Sr. died in 1969, Senate Majority Leader Mike Mansfield
said, "Jerry was one of those old-fashioned newsmen who kept his feet
on the track and his nose on the scent until he got the story." A young
Jerry O'Leary recalled that a number of the senior reporters and editors
in the 1930s were veterans of World War I, including Young, associ-

ate editor Newbold Noyes Sr., and court reporters William G. Pollard, Benjamin McKelway, and Herbert Corn. Men who served in the "Great War" dominated the *Star* newsroom then, kept their beats for years, or rose through the ranks to top editorships. News and opinions about the dynamic Roosevelt administration often appeared on the same page with the dreaded news of Adolf Hitler's rise to power, his aggressions, and alliance with other fascist regimes in Europe throughout the 1930s. Americans could never have imagined how much the world and their nation would change after fighting and winning the next world war. The *Star* changed too as a new crop of newsmen and women whose experiences fighting, reporting, and living through the Nazi horrors of World War II at home and abroad would forever shape their personal and professional lives.[22]

"Long-awaited war came with stunning suddenness yesterday," wrote Thomas R. Henry, in the *Star*'s afternoon edition the day after Japan's attack on Pearl Harbor on Sunday, December 7, 1941. Thomas Henry, who had written so eloquently about the World War I veterans of the Bonus Army, now tried to capture that "afternoon of suspense—but of calm

Horseshoe copy editor's desk in the old Evening Star Building, ca. late 1930s. D.C. Community Archives, *Washington Star* Papers, D.C. Public Library.

suspense" when no details were available and "the diplomatic corps was taken completely by surprise." Henry describes a sleepy Sunday afternoon when much of the Roosevelt administration was out of town and most Washingtonians were absorbed in the final game of the Washington Redskins season against the Philadelphia Eagles at Griffith Stadium. As word of the attack reached sportscasters, the crowd of nearly 27,000 fans at the stadium couldn't help but notice the commotion in the press box above them. The stadium's management had decided not to announce the attack during the game, but as calls went over the PA system for pressmen and reporters to return to their newsrooms and navy personnel to their commanding officers, the crowds became increasingly suspicious. Rumors of war spread, and many seats became vacant. Henry describes a city that was "swelled by hundreds of soldiers on leave from nearby camps" who probably has just finished Sunday dinner and were tuning in their radios to hear the Redskins game broadcasted but instead heard "like so many bombs dropped in quick succession on Washington's roofs came the succession of radio announcements." The National Press Club was having its Sunday afternoon tea dance on the top floor of the National Press Club Building that afternoon, which was only a few blocks from the White House. Couples danced to the swing orchestra and reporters drank cocktails at the club's bar when they heard the news of the attack on the radio. Henry most likely was enjoying a drink at the club's bar when he heard the news. Henry walked a block to the White House, where he found a small crowd gathering near West Executive Avenue to watch and wait while a host of high-level officials arrived by car to meet with President Roosevelt. Later in the afternoon police officers gently pushed the swelling crowd of onlookers away from the gates to make way for the continuous line of cars still coming to the White House. By dusk Henry saw "a misty three-quarter moon that shone over the White House," and nearly a thousand people who stood in Lafayette Park across the street from the White House. "Folks wanted to be together," Henry observed. "Strangers spoke to strangers" and "a sense of comradeship of all the people was apparent" as the "shrill voices" of newsboys calling "war extras . . . broke the ordinary Sabbath evening calm." The *Star* issued an extra early the next morning after the Sunday attack. With biting anger Henry wrote, "The arrogant Nipponese had stepped on the Republic's toes with increasing impudence for four years" but "now there was hardly a shadow of doubt in the minds of any one in Washington—an inevitable war of blood and bombs."[23]

The *Star*'s White House Correspondent John C. Henry was in the press gallery on December 8, 1941, when President Roosevelt told a "hushed and expectant Congress" that "the date of the first Japanese attack, December 7, 1941, is one which 'will live in infamy.'" Congress's vote to declare war was quick and nearly unanimous, with only Jeannette Rankin of Montana voting no. "In the presence of a large congressional delegation," Henry wrote, Roosevelt signed the resolution of war at 4:10 pm in his executive office. The *Star*'s night final on December 8 reported men had crowded the National Guard Armory at 6th and Pennsylvania Avenue all day waiting to enlist. In barely six months John Henry would enlist to serve as a war correspondent in the European Division of the Airport Transport Command. Henry returned from overseas to the *Star* as a Sunday editor, later editorial writer and business editor. Sixteen *Star* copy boys went overseas, among them George Beveridge, who would win a Pulitzer a decade later for his analysis of metropolitan Washington, and Jerry O'Leary, who, among his many reporting adventures was arrested in Castro's Cuba and stood steps away from Jack Ruby when he shot Lee Harvey Oswald. O'Leary joined the marines, earning a Bronze Star and a Purple Heart for his service in the Pacific. World War I veteran Thomas Henry, whose Bonus Army coverage received acclaim, sent dispatches from overseas to the *Star* when he could and was among the first line of soldiers of the Ninth Armored Division who crossed the Remagen Bridge over the Rhine into Germany before it collapsed on March 7, 1945. State Department and White House correspondent E. Blair Bolles became a war correspondent for the *Star* based in neutral Stockholm, where he reported on the Axis powers. Many young men in the Noyes and Kauffmann families enlisted. Crosby Noyes, Frank Noyes's grandson, flew combat missions for the army air force, trained free French pilots, and earned the Distinguished Flying Cross and Air Medal for his bravery. Jack Kauffmann, the *Star*'s last president, flew bombing missions as a gunner staff sergeant on a B-24, and John W. Thompson, Theodore Noyes's grandson, fought in Normandy, France, and the Battle of the Bulge and won the Bronze Star for his service. Theodore Noyes McDowell and Rudolph Kauffmann II both served in the navy. Newby Noyes left his editorial job at the *Star* in November 1942 to drive an ambulance for the American Field Service in Damascus, Egypt, Africa, Tripoli, Italy, and then in Naples just before it was taken by the Germans. Noyes accompanied British forces into Albania and later Greece, writing about the liberation of Athens in October 1944. In November 1944 Newby Noyes was at a bomber base in Austria looking for his next news story when he learned that a "Washington boy" was scheduled to be part of the flight crew on a raid of Steyr, Austria. Judging the mission to be just a "milk run"—a relatively safe mission—Noyes asked to go along thinking it would be a good action story with a local angle. During the confusion and rush to make the mission, Noyes realized at the last minute while still in the middle of attaching his parachute harness that he would not be in the bomber plane the hometown boy was piloting. Noyes tried to switch planes, but it was too late. Noyes, however, remained in the assigned "box of six bombers," as he described it, which included the bomber pilot from the district. During the mission Noyes found himself not on a "milk run," but instead in the middle of "a terrific running battle" in which 157 enemy and 36 American planes were destroyed. Over Steyr, Austria, Noyes saw out of his window the engines knocked out of the plane the hometown pilot was flying, then the plane staggered for a moment and "disappeared earthward." "It made me superstitious I guess. Never again have I gone out of my way to cover the local angle," Noyes wrote. Near the end of World War II, Noyes covered the entry of Allied parachutists into southern France and found time to interview Gertrude Stein, where she hid in the South of France from the Nazis. Newby Noyes would become the *Star*'s last editor, and his brother Crosby Noyes would establish a European office in Paris for the *Star* after World War II ended. The *Star* honored more than 160 World War II veterans on its staff at a special event at the Willard Hotel in March 1946.[24]

On the home front, wartime Washington was a bustling, cramped, hard-driving city where every person, from school child to government office worker, was devoted to winning the war against fascism. The *Star* did its part. City editor Bill (William) Hill, national news editor Chuck Egan, and managing editor Herb Corn during the war years recruited a number of women to the newsroom after the men left. They included many who stayed at the paper and forged successful careers, including Mary Lou Werner, Carter Warner Dawson, Ann Cline, and Eleni Sakes. Miriam Ottenberg, who came to the *Star* in the late 1930s, covered the draft, civil defense, and mobilization as well as crime during the war years. Hundreds of images of wartime Washington were captured in the *Star*. Photographs appeared in daily editions, but especially in the Sunday *Star*'s photogravure section. The photos came from the AP and Wide World wire services, the local Harris & Ewing Studios, as well as *Star* cameramen who shot images of government girls, long ration lines, scrap drives, boarding houses, government offices, recruitment centers, and the many soldiers, sailors, and aviators who passed through Union Station. Photos of the War Wagon, floating barges for "Watergate concerts" on the Potomac River, the Stage Door Canteen, and Gold Star mothers honored at Griffith Stadium were unique Washington wartime scenes. Despite the rationing of newsprint, the *Star* missed only three days of publishing from 1941 to 1945. The paper also published a weekly overseas *Evening Star* edition for servicemen from September 6, 1944, to August 14, 1946, as a joint project with Lansburgh's department store. The *Star* supplied the content and makeup while Lansburgh's set up a war bond booth provided with newspapers, envelopes, and stamps for sale to mail the paper overseas.

The edition was an eight-page illustrated tabloid with a run of 10,000 copies for its first edition, a 35,000 average run, and 85,000 copies for its last edition. Six days before Pearl Harbor, the *Star* partnered with the PTA to begin the "*Evening Star*-PTA Salvage for Victory Campaign" and during the war organized "paper troopers" at D.C. schools to collect scrap paper. For local residents, the *Star* published "You and an Air Raid," a special supplement of maps of the European and Pacific fronts showing troop movements and the war's progress, and the somber "Roll of Honor," which paid tribute to local residents killed, missing, and wounded with a short description of each man's service. The Noyes school, named for *Star* founder Crosby Noyes, began a "Salvage the Orphan" drive just before the war began, which then caught on at other schools. The money earned was sent overseas to help war orphans.[25]

In April 1943 Joe (Joseph A.) Fox became the *Star's* White House Correspondent after John Henry went overseas. Fox, a World War I veteran, came to Washington in 1922 as a reporter for the Associated Press after working on newspapers in his home state of Missouri and later Texas. Fox covered Roosevelt's campaign in 1944 and especially remembered a sixty-mile trip through the rain in New York. Yet as bad as the weather got, Fox saw supporters who flocked to campaign events flashing their homemade signs for FDR because "people were crazy . . . the people worshipped Roosevelt, absolutely worshipped him." Fox remembered how "working with Roosevelt was just exactly like being part of a stage production" because "he was always the center figure" putting on a good show while the "spear carriers" surrounded the leader they worshipped. Roosevelt was easily elected in 1944, and normally the *Star* sent more than a dozen reporters to a presidential inauguration, but Fox and his wife were the only ones to represent the paper on a "cold gray day" when FDR spoke from the south portico of the White House with a only small audience to hear the president. In March 1945 President Roosevelt returned from the Yalta conference exhausted and ill after intense discussions with Winston Churchill and Joseph Stalin about the future of war-torn Europe as the war wound down. Not long after FDR's return, the president was guest of honor at the White House Correspondents' Association dinner. Fox, who was the Association's president that year, sat next to Roosevelt all night and remembers FDR appearing to be "in the finest shape," drinking his "usual two martinis before dinner," and telling jokes to a rapt audience. After dinner the president announced to rousing cheers from the press that he was canceling tomorrow's press conference to give them time to recuperate from the night's festivities. The next day President Roosevelt left for Warm Springs, and Fox never saw him again. After the last afternoon edition had gone out on April 12, 1945, the *Star's* newsroom was quiet and only a handful of reporters and editors remained. A news flash that read "FDR DEAD" came over the wires a little after 5:50 pm, and loud bells rang repeatedly to alert the newsroom of dire news. Assistant city editor Ed Tribble picked up the phone to hear "This is AP. The President is Dead." Associate editor Ben McKelway, who had been writing an editorial, took charge immediately. The *Star*'s telephone operator called reporters, editors, and heads of mechanical departments. Most were at home relaxing, eating dinner, or mowing lawns on an ordinary Thursday evening. Joe Fox had left the White House with AP reporter Douglas B. Cornell around 4:15 pm and was at home enjoying a cocktail with Cornell when he received a call from *Star* reporter Harold Rogers, who said, "Joe, the President has just died. Start dictating." Fox dictated to Rogers for about forty-five minutes all the things he had held back about FDR's failing health and his own personal remembrances of the president. One editor was notified as he stood in the shower at the Chevy Chase Club, and a reporter in the newsroom pulled a few newsmen out of downtown restaurants and bars. Another reporter raced upstairs to the composing room and stopped some compositors headed out the door when he shouted, "The President is dead." The third extra informed readers that Harry Truman had been sworn in as the thirty-second president, and the last extra of the day was an AP story from Warm Spring about Mrs. Roosevelt's reaction. The *Star* distributed more than 39,000 extra editions that day. The longest-serving president in American history who had led the nation through the Great Depression and a world war was dead, and the little-known new president Harry Truman would now have to lead the country out of war and beyond.[26]

As the nation both mourned its beloved president and read news about the Allies' final victories against the Nazis in Europe, news from foreign correspondents about atrocities in German concentration camps began appearing in US newspapers. *Star* reporter Thomas Henry was part of the American First Infantry Division in April 1945 when troops began to liberate Nazi concentration camps. "In Washington three months ago skeptics asked me," Henry wrote from Germany in April, "Did you ever see a Nazi atrocity. The answer is a double yes. I've seen Buchenwald." When American troops entered the prison a week before they found "21,000 starving, 3,000 at the point of death," Henry wrote, and despite efforts to save camp survivors, the death rate was one hundred per day during his first week at the camp. Henry especially wanted those back home to know about the unimaginable scientific experiments conducted at the camp, writing, "A personal message to my good friends in the District of Columbia Medical Society. Today . . . I visited the castration ward . . . the hanging chamber . . . I saw the typhus experimental clinic." Henry said he had intended to write a "cold scientific story on wholesale starvation" of human beings, but as he walked through the children's wards and looked into patients' eyes, it was "like looking into a puddle of muddy water" and "somehow science seems far away." The children he saw were mostly Polish Jews who had lost their parents in the gas chambers. Henry in August 1945 would send similar dispatches from Dachau prison camp. As American and British troops liberated the concentration camps on the western front, General Dwight D. Eisenhower, commander of Allied forces in Europe, cabled General George Marshall asking him to arrange for congressional leaders and newspaper editors and publishers to examine the camps and verify to the American people what some in the public have characterized as the "exaggerated dispatches of war correspondents" about atrocities at the camps. Representatives of the Office of the Chief of Staff met with the congressional leadership and selected seventeen editors and publishers to visit the camps. Among them were the *Star*'s associate editor Ben McKelway, Julius Ochs of the *New York Times*, editor and publisher of the *St. Louis Post Dispatch* Joseph Pulitzer, editor of the Scripps-Howard newspaper chain Walker Stone, and editor of the *Saturday Evening Post* Ben Hibbs. Six members of Congress on the Naval Affairs and Foreign Affairs Congressional Committees joined the editors. Since the camps needed to be dismantled as soon as possible, the group was quickly assembled and left within a matter of days from La-Guardia Airport on a transport plane headed for Paris.[27]

By May 4, McKelway was at Buchenwald prison camp witnessing what Henry had seen a month before. The editors met with Eisenhower and General Omar Bradley and then were escorted through the camp by an American doctor who had begun caring for the survivors a few days after liberation. The doctor described to the newsmen how medical staff took patients outside for fresh air and sun as the hospital was being cleaned but the patients instead crawled back inside to what was familiar and clung to each other in cramped beds like "human parasites in order to live," wrote McKelway. The editors were free to speak with the survivors, and when McKelway asked a "Hamburg Jew" if the German people on the outside were aware of what was happening in the camps, he told McKelway "he did not think so . . . the people of Weimar knew . . . but anybody on the outside who talked about the camps would be found out and punished by the Gestapo." Another camp survivor disagreed, telling McKelway, "How could they not help but know?" McKelway concluded, "whether the well-fed comfortable looking people of nearby Weimar knew what was going on I do not know," but it is a fact the mayor and his wife committed suicide and "regardless of what actually went on inside the camp . . . its mere existence is enough to indict the German people." McKelway's most poignant encounter was with a young boy, emblematic of the hundreds of orphan children left behind after the Holocaust. When soldiers and relief organizations handed out toys to the morose children in the camps, the children cried to receive them after being deprived for so long of any morsel of human kindness or pleasure. "With the new ball in one hand and the racquet in the other, trying to keep saddened tears away, occasionally brushing his eyes with his coat sleeves," observed McKelway, in the boy's face "was written all the tragedy and wrong that these camps stand for. Nobody knows what to do with these boys and what will become of them." The editors then visited the Dachau concentration camp and issued a report signed by every editor that reached "the inescapable conclusion" based on their direct observations that "convincing proof" existed to show the German camps operated under a "master plan . . . of calculated and organized brutality" and that "sadistic tortures too horrible and too perverted to be publicly described were embraced by the Nazi system." A month after returning from Europe, *St. Louis Post-Dispatch* editor Joseph Pulitzer and McKelway jointly organized an exhibition in Washington of life-sized photomurals of scenes of the concentration camps. Photos were gathered from the Associated Press, Army Signal Corps, and the British Information Service and displayed at the Library of Congress in an exhibit titled *Lest We Forget*, from June 25 to July 28, 1945. The day before the opening a small group of Washingtonians were guests of the *Star* at the Pentagon Building for a private showing. At the opening McKelway told the guests, "In the opinion of the *Star*, it is important that Americans see and know about the subject of these pictures" because they "contain a lesson, not merely in the pitiable condition of human beings subject to Nazi atrocities, but in the degradation of a nation which suffered such conditions to exist. The pictures show what our soldiers saw and if our people at home . . . see the same things . . . the danger of future wars would be remote." A film about the camps was also shown in eleven District of Columbia public high schools, six junior high schools, and the Barry Farms Community Center. Joseph Pulitzer then took the exhibition on to St. Louis when it closed in Washington. A year later McKelway was asked to tour military bases in the Pacific on an eighteen-thousand-mile trip with two other editors and wrote a seven-part series in March 1946 on his travels. During his trip he met with and interviewed Hirohito, General Douglas McArthur, General George Marshall, and Madame Chiang Kai-shek on the future of war-torn Japan, China, and other Asian countries in the Pacific.[28]

The final step to peace was already being constructed in secret military installations in New Mexico and Washington State when Harry Truman took the oath of office after FDR's death. The deadly serious news of the dropping the first atomic bomb on the city of Hiroshima ironically would collide with one of the most often told and strange fables in *Star* newsroom folklore. Midmorning on August 6, 1945, Joe Fox at the White House called the newsroom to inform them he would be calling back with an important announcement in about twenty minutes and to hold the presses. As Ludy Werner remembered years later, when Fox did call back either from the White House or the Pentagon with the news, Carter Dawson (aka Fifi Gorska), who had just started as a dictationist and was a poor speller, was on the dictation desk. The newsroom sensed the importance of the news, so rewrite men and desk men huddled around her typewriter waiting anxiously for her to finish so they could get the important news edited and onto the presses. National news editor Chuck Egan was giving instructions to prepare a banner column when someone shouted out what they saw in the typewriter: "We've dropped a bomb on Japan equivalent to 20,000 tons of TNT." Skeptical, Egan asked his dictationist to check with Fox to be sure; she did and Fox said he was sure but Egan shouted back "that can't be right" and she asked again. This time, Fox exploded at the other end of the telephone line while Fifi kept her calm and continued. One spelling error, however, got through in the confusion. An important line in the text was typed, "President Truman today announced that the United States has dropped an 'Adam' [not Atom] bomb on Japan." In the rush, no copy editor, rewrite man, editor, or typesetter caught the error until Ludy, who ironically had planned to study psychics in college, saw the error when the first few prints rolled off the presses. Werner, a copy girl and still a teenager then but tall and with a no-nonsense demeanor, quickly brought the error to the attention of her immediate boss, city editor Bill Hill, who told Egan to stop the presses. Fifi kept her job, but the story stuck to her ever after.[29]

Barely a week after the dropping of three atomic bombs, the mood in the *Star*'s newsroom turned from somber to jubilant as World War II officially ended. At 7 pm on August 14, 1945, President Truman surrounded by civilian and military members of his administration read to the newsmen gathered in the Oval Office the expected announcement of Japan's surrender. Joe Fox, along with the other reporters at the White House that night, grabbed the press release, and as soon the president finished, they walked out of the Oval Office, but once out the door they all sprinted to telephones to dictate their stories to newsrooms. Truman had also decreed a two-day holiday for a national celebration, and the city went wild. The crowds celebrated at full throttle below the *Star*'s newsroom on Pennsylvania Avenue. Metropolitan police estimated six thousand people crushed into the space between Lafayette Park and the White House grounds. At one point the crowds surged against the White House fence in excitement and then formed a conga line to dance on the lawn. A much larger crowd of more than one hundred thousand celebrated in streets, nightclubs, saloons, and restaurants in the heart of downtown Washington. The sounds were deafening with blowing horns and even "live ammunition . . . placed on trolley cars" that ignited and "pistols fired in the streets," reported the *Star*. The *Star* carried a full page of photographs showing revelers jamming traffic to a complete halt on F Street, dancing in the street, ticker-taped-covered people, and sailors standing atop streetcars. *Star* newsmen reported a Connecticut Avenue tavern keeper began mixing Tom Colinses when he heard the news and treated everyone who entered the door. At Union Station authorities stubbornly refused to publicly announce the surrender, but the *Star*'s extra was on newsstands within an hour of the announcement. "People rushed up to the trains waving headlines" and a *Star* reporter claimed "a veteran of three years overseas, grabbed" a *Star* extra and "kissed it." Lots of kissing between total strangers took place that night. The *Star* reported a British sailor, "more polite than most of the festive tipped his cap and asked a WAVE 'May I kiss you now the war's over?'" to which she responded "You sure can sailor." A "colored cab driver" said he was "the happiest man in the world" because his two brothers were coming home. The cabbie's elation was sadly softened though as he then told the reporter that another brother would not be returning because he "was killed in New Guinea."[30]

The decades after World War II brought dramatic political, economic, and cultural changes in Washington and the country. Washington was no more a sleepy southern city but the capital of the most powerful and respected nation in the free world. The fortunes and future of *Star* reporters and the paper itself would be made and at the same time undone by the *Star*'s response to changes in post–World War II America.

7

+

Covering Politics in Postwar America, 1946–1963

In August 1948 the Washington Newspaper Guild membership voted for the second time not to hear the grievance of *Star* reporter Thomas Gettings Buchanan. The *Star* fired Buchanan when it learned he was a Communist Party member. The national Newspaper Guild urged the local to prosecute Buchanan's grievance, but it refused. In the years immediately following World War II, the hunt to weed out communists on American soil extended from government to academia and industry to the media. Joseph Stalin, who was once an ally in the fight against fascism, advanced communism into Eastern Europe, and Mao Tse Tung brought communism to China. The Middle East and Southeast Asia became pawns in the struggle between communist and western capitalist democracies. The Soviet threat to western democracies was very real, but the response was not always proportional. At the *Star* the Cold War for decades shaped the national and political news the paper covered, its foreign correspondents and bureaus, its political opinions, its staff, and even its future prospects.[1]

In March 1947 President Truman issued Executive Order 9835 establishing the Federal Employee Loyalty and Security Program ostensibly to bar persons disloyal to the United States from holding federal jobs. Truman believed Republicans and the FBI exaggerated the threat of communists inside the federal government, but he issued the order not to appear soft on communism and to limit more extreme measures from the Republican-dominated House Un-American Activities Committee (HUAC). From 1947 to 1951 the Civil Service Commission (CSC) investigated three million federal employees and the FBI investigated fourteen thousand, but only 212 were dismissed for disloyalty, and no one was ever indicted for espionage. The loyalty program in Washington bred a particularly noxious atmosphere of suspicion and mistrust since many residents were federal employees. In 1949 Dorothy Bailey was among those federal employees who lost her civil service job in D.C. Newby Noyes saw Bailey's case as a perfect example of the loyalty program's unfairness and believed her dismissal was based on secret evidence and rumor after reviewing transcripts and interviews of those involved in her case. FBI informants provided sworn statements from Bailey's associates that she was a Communist Party member when she was president of Local 10 of the United Public Workers of America (UPWA) from 1943 to 1948. Bailey repeatedly denied she was a communist or knowingly associated with UPWA's communist leaders. The CSC judged Bailey disloyal, and she appealed the decision to the Federal Loyalty Review Board. Bailey's attorney told Noyes the allegations against her were the result of "malicious, irresponsible, reckless gossip" without foundation that stemmed from "an internecine union controversy." Noyes found union members in "the former right-wing camp of local 10" willing to speak with him, and although many criticized Bailey's tactics, none judged her a communist since as one member told him, "I am convinced that she has been completely objective and completely loyal" to the United States. The board denied Bailey's appeal and issued no published opinion. Noyes explained to readers that the *Star*'s main purpose was not "to prove that Miss Bailey is innocent, or to argue the point" since "neither the *Star* nor Miss Bailey knows, nor anyone else outside of the FBI and the loyalty boards knows or can find out what those reasons are." Instead, Noyes wanted to reveal the "dilemmas and possible dangers of the loyalty program" because it denies the basic rights of the accused "to know the particulars of the charge and confront his accusers." Noyes received the Front Page Award from the Washington Newspaper Guild for coverage of the Bailey story, which it characterized as "an example of fearless and intelligent coverage on a difficult and explosive subject . . . written in a detailed and dispassionate manner." Noyes would move up the ranks to be the *Star*'s last editor before the families sold the paper, and he was judged an excellent editor by most journalists who knew him well. As a young reporter Noyes had written memorable and important stories for the *Star* while serving overseas in World War II and covering the Nuremberg trials after the war. Marty (J. Montgomery) Curtis of Knight Newspapers fondly recalled once when writing to Noyes in retirement, "Whatever be your future trend in this profession, please do return to writing. Sure, you are a great editor and a great newspaperman but there are a lot of those around" but "there are so very, very few superb writers . . . I want you to get back to that typewriter." Pushed by family obligations, Noyes would leave reporting and move through the paper's ranks to become the *Star*'s editor in 1962, and he never returned to writing.[2]

Most of the press was betting against Harry Truman's chances of remaining president during the 1948 presidential campaign. Joe Fox, the *Star*'s White House correspondent and a self-identified Democrat, was not one of them. As Fox traveled, he estimated, almost "30,000 miles in 36 states" by car and train without a day off from covering Truman's campaign from June to November, he became increasingly confident of Truman's reelection chances. Fox saw voters warm to the president and crowds grow as the campaign progressed, like the unexpectedly large crowd he saw show up at 3 am at the Toledo, Ohio, train station to see Truman on his Whistle Stop Tour. Near the end of the 1948 campaign, Fox was so sure of Truman's reelection that he made a small bet with *Star* president Fleming Newbold that the Republican candidate Thomas E. Dewey would lose. *Star* staff waited in the newsroom through election night until the next morning when the final results came in and Dewey conceded. Fox was in Kansas City watching the ticker at the Muehlebach Hotel when the final electoral votes from Ohio put Truman over the top. Fox immediately sent a one-word telegram to the *Star*'s newsroom saying "Sorry" addressed to Newbold, who was crushed by Dewey's loss. A banner that read "Welcome Home Joe" greeted Fox when he returned to the newsroom a few days later. George Kennedy presented Fox with the "Idaho Oscar" award (a potato), which the silver-haired and slightly pudgy Fox, who stood just 5 foot 8 inches and often sported a bow tie, proudly accepted. *Star* political reporter Bob (Robert) Walsh, who substituted for Joe Fox when he was away, saw Truman as "quite amateurish" at White House press conferences just after Franklin Roosevelt died. Walsh found Truman, however, was a far more confident and relaxed president after his reelection in 1948. Walsh had worked as a reporter since 1924 at newspapers in St. Louis, Missouri, and Rhode Island and came to the *Star* in 1946 as a seasoned reporter of the courts and politics. Walsh would later cover the McCarthy censure hearings, civil rights legislation, and many historic Supreme Court cases in the 1950s.[3]

On August 3, 1948, Miriam Ottenberg reported that Whittaker Chambers, a senior editor at *Time* and "an avowed ex-Communist," testified before the HUAC that Alger Hiss, Nathan Witt, and Lee Pressman, among others, were leaders of a secret communist organization in the US federal government. Witt and Hiss had held top positions in FDR's administration, and Pressman was general counsel for the CIO and a recent Labor Party candidate for Congress. Ottenberg and Walsh covered the Hiss story. Walsh was skeptical of Chambers's accusations that communist spies had infiltrated the US government, although he did believe in the 1930s some people Chambers named had participated in "little circles, little cells" of communists but nothing more, and if it hadn't been for Nixon, the investigation "would have died overnight." At first Walsh viewed the hearings as an orchestrated "smear" by Republicans and Chambers as not being very impressive. When Hiss took the stand, however, Walsh saw a witness who "was very evasive, too legalistic" and "didn't deny everything but didn't admit much" either. Hiss claimed he knew Chambers as Crosley who had subleased his apartment. Walsh interviewed residents of the Woodley Manor Apartments where Hiss lived, but no one remembered Crosley or Chambers. The *Star's* August 22, 1948, edition contained excerpts from the Hiss hearing transcripts headlined "Somebody Is Lying—Who?" which succinctly captured the uncertainty and mystery that surrounded the Hiss case then and now.[4]

In May 1949, Newby Noyes traveled with Walsh to a New York City courtroom to cover Alger Hiss's espionage trial along with a phalanx of other reporters. After the August HUAC hearings, Chambers repeated his allegations against Hiss on *Meet the Press*, and Hiss sued Chambers for slander. In response, Chambers presented evidence to prosecutors that purportedly connected stolen government secrets to Hiss. The statute of limitations precluded the government from trying Hiss on espionage charges, but a grand jury indicted Hiss for lying to the HUAC. The first Hiss trial lasted little more than a month and ended with a hung jury, but the second trial found Hiss guilty of perjury in January 1950. Walsh covered both trials and told an interviewer much later, "If I had been on the jury, in all honesty, I would have to convict Hiss of perjury, because they had not only the 'Pumpkin Papers' but the FBI did a job." After the verdict, Noyes heard Hiss tell reporters, when they asked if he had any comment, "No, I have nothing at all to say," and then he embraced his "sickly-pale . . . gray-haired wife" as they silently exited the courtroom, crossed the street to a red Chevrolet where a driver waited to drive them away as photographers ran alongside the car clicking their cameras. Noyes wrote, "Alger Hiss, once a fair-haired boy of the State Department stands convicted of perjury tonight branded by a Federal Court jury as a liar and spy." Noyes closed his article with reactions from ordinary New Yorkers he interviewed after the trial. An elevator operator, who took the Hisses every day to the thirteenth floor of the skyscraper courthouse, told Noyes, "The verdict made her sick to her stomach . . . maybe it's because I'm a woman but they did seem like such lovely people." The bartender at the bar across the street from the courthouse saw it very differently, telling Noyes, "They ought to shoot him," while another man in the bar simply concluded that "a lot of people were Communists in 1938. It's the lies that matter, not that spy stuff . . . but no matter who you are this whole thing leaves a bad taste in your mouth." Hiss was sentenced to five years but only served three in Lewisburg Federal Prison. As an objective reporter, Noyes gave no hint of his own low opinion of Hiss but told President Nixon years later how he always admired "the way you blew the whistle on that guy."[5]

Republican senator Joseph McCarthy of Wisconsin first came to the attention of the national press on February 9, 1950, when he announced in Wheeling, West Virginia, that he had evidence that proved 205 communist spies were working in the federal government. Veteran political reporter Cecil Holland would be the primary *Star* reporter covering McCarthy for the next four years. *Star* editorials were critical of McCarthy's bullying demeanor and methods because they violated basic due process rights but also questioned the credibility of some witnesses the senator cross examined. In the 1950s the *Star*'s chief editorial writer and editor for the opinion pages was John H. Cline. Cline earned a law degree from George Washington University and worked for Midwest papers before coming to the *Star* in 1928. Cline started writing editorials in 1938. The *Star* received many letters from readers displeased with its criticism of McCarthy, like the "patriotic American" and longtime subscriber who was "surprised and shocked" that the *Star* in an editorial called McCarthy's tactics "A Shame and a Disgrace," and another reader who quipped, "The *Star* leans far to the left of right." But others thought the *Star* courageous for standing up to McCarthy when it wrote he shamefully "prospers politically on denunciation."[6]

Congress held the Army–McCarthy hearings to investigate contradictory accusations made by McCarthy and the US Army after the senator searched in vain for communists in the Signal Corps. Cecil Holland with the help of Allen Drury began reporting the news of the Army–McCarthy hearings starting in the fall of 1953. National news editor Newby Noyes made an unusual but astute decision to ask Mary McGrory, then a young and unknown voice in political commentary, to begin attending the hearings in the spring of 1954 and write a different kind of story. Mary, a native Bostonian, started as an assistant book reviewer at the *Star* in 1947. Mary had a bachelor's degree and secretarial training, which in those days landed her a job first as a secretary and then as editorial assistant at Houghton Mifflin Publishing. She then worked as an assistant to the *Boston Herald Traveler*'s book editor while also writing occasional book reviews for the *New York Times* book editor John K. Hutchens. When McGrory arrived at the *Star*'s "picturesque nineteenth-century" building, she recalled, "I loved it the minute I set foot in it," with its wrought iron and carved mahogany wood. Mary especially liked hanging out in the newsroom, which to her was the most "entertaining place I'd ever been in my entire life," with colorful characters like national news editor Chuck Egan, who "was built like a truck and had an enormous voice." After seven years as a book reviewer, Noyes spotted her wit, honesty, and keen observations in the occasional light editorials and political profiles she wrote. Newby clumsily broached the subject of her covering McCarthy by asking Mary a question a boss wouldn't dare ask a modern woman today, "Will you every marry?" Mary replied candidly, "Well, you know, I hope so, but I don't know." The young and brash Newby with his gray eyes gleaming behind thick, dark glasses looked directly at Mary and said in his loud, patrician voice, "Well, because if you're not, we just always figured that you'd get married and have a baby and leave us, so we haven't tried to do a great deal . . . we think you can do more . . . you should add humor and color and charm and flair to the news pages." McGrory later discovered that before Noyes asked her to cover the hearings, he and Jim (James Y.) Newton discussed the idea over drinks at the Chicken Hut, a popular downtown hangout for newsmen near the old Evening Star Building. Noyes asked Newton if he thought other staff would resent McGrory as a young female reporter without much reporting experience covering such a big story. Newton simply said no, and for Noyes "that was that." After McGrory returned from the second hearing, Noyes suggested she "write it like a letter to your favorite aunt," which she understood because she often did just that. From then on Newby would meet with her in his office to work on the lead and second paragraph because from his experience readers often drift off by the second paragraph if it "was deadly dull." After that he left her alone to write the rest of the story. Mary remembered once when she made a grammatical mistake, Newby removing the ever-present cigar hanging from his lips and saying in a loud voice so everyone in the newsroom could hear to her embarrassment, "Well, we expected to have a lot of trouble with you, but we didn't think there'd be any problem with your grammar." During the hearings McGrory wrote almost daily humorous and sardonic descriptions of what she saw and heard that poked fun at the increasingly explosive and bullying McCarthy. Mary was neither taken in nor intimidated by McCarthy, but instead "laughed at him . . . I just thought he was an Irish bully, I'd seen the type," as a young girl growing up in Boston. McGrory rarely directly attacked McCarthy but would use the words of others to capture his personality, like the woman who observed, "I don't know, but it seems kind of funny to me. If you're on trial, like you don't keep buttin' in all the time." Mary described Roy Cohn, the Senate Sub-Committee's chief counsel in the Army–McCarthy hearings, alternatively as "the smartest boy in the room" to "pale, wan, and a trifle aggrieved . . . like a boy who has had a letter sent home from school about him, and comes back with his elders to get the thing straightened out." Letters to the editors and phone calls poured in and ran the gamut from a reader who accused her of being in cahoots with Alger Hiss to another couple who thought she was wonderful and wanted to take her to dinner. A letter from "A Grateful reader" to the editor of May 14, titled

"Bouquets for McGrory," described her talent well, writing: "the unassuming, pertinent, talented Mary McGrory can pinpoint without pricking. She has humor without ridicule, and without saying one harmful word she can expose 'McCarthyshines' as well as any satirist." McGrory said Newby kept the critics away from her, told her just keep "doing what she was doing," and he would take care of the rest. Managing editor Herbert Corn, who was sensitive to negative publicity, was uncomfortable with McGrory's commentary. Noyes calmly reassured Corn and kept him away from Mary. McGrory understood the significance of the hearings and was humbled to sit every day next to "the best people" in journalism. Among those most generous to her were Walter Winchell, who wrote her notes addressed to "Dear M.M." and signed "W.W." Edwin Lahey of the *Chicago Daily News* told her "good to see you on the news side honey," and syndicated columnist Doris Fleeson encouraged Mary and invited her to parties to meet influential people in Washington. Over the years McGrory and Fleeson became good friends. Later in 1954 when Congress censured

Mary McGrory at far left seated next to Newby (Newbold) Noyes Jr. at a Sunday editorial staff meeting, ca. 1955. D.C. Community Archives, *Washington Star* Papers, D.C. Public Library.

McCarthy, reporters looked for juicier stories, the lights of TV cameras went out, and he faded from favor and allure.[7]

Newby Noyes's brother Crosby opened the *Star*'s first foreign bureau in Paris in 1954, which added insightful firsthand foreign news reporting to the *Star*'s columns so crucial to understanding the world after World War II. Noyes was attracted to reporting on how power was shifting in the global landscape and relished the chance to live in Paris. Ben Bradlee was *Newsweek*'s Paris correspondent at the time and had many fond memories of his friendship with Crosby while they both worked in Paris. In the summer of 1954, Bradlee, Noyes, and Bill Edgar, who ran Press Wireless in Paris, shared a nineteenth-century chateau in the village of Bolssy-Saint-Léger, France, along with their wives and children. Tish Noyes, Crosby's wife, made terrific spaghetti, and Barbara Sulzberger, the wife of Arthur Ochs Sulzberger, who was working in the *New York Times* Paris Bureau, taught them all how to "jitterbug in the ballroom." Just after Noyes opened the Paris Bureau, he reported from Geneva on the Indo-China talks where sources told him that the United States threatened to never sit down with communist leaders in the region. The accords established a provisional division of Vietnam at the 17th parallel to facilitate a ceasefire, withdrawal of troops, and elections to reunify Vietnam in two years. In the end, the conflict did not end. Ho Chi Minh did not withdraw troops in the south, and the Vietnam government in the south refused to hold elections. The United States was not a signatory to the Geneva Indo-China accords. By the 1960s America had sided with the South Vietnamese government against the communist north, which would fuel a decades-long war in Southeast Asia. Crosby Noyes's thoughtful and erudite commentary on the communist threat in world affairs drove the paper's coverage for nearly two decades. Noyes returned from Paris in 1956 to help cover the presidential campaign and soon after wrote a five-part series titled "The Red Challenge," which analyzed the Soviet strategy for dominance in Europe, the Middle East, and Africa.[8]

While on the campaign trail with Adlai Stevenson in September 1956, Crosby sent a light-hearted telegram to Mary McGrory and Blair Clark of CBS News who were in Eugene, Oregon, with Stevenson's vice presidential running mate Estes Kefauver. Mary and the tall and handsome Blair planned to celebrate their shared birthdays together. Noyes, who knew Blair Clark from Paris, warned Mary that the year before in Brussels, Clark exhibited "his international reputation for conduct so spectacularly outrageous that few respectable members of society care to invite him to birthday parties." Mary remembered fondly crisscrossing the country on the Kefauver plane with a "young-spirited, happy group of reporters . . . all of whom wrote songs and gag lines." Although McGrory was one of only two female reporters on the plane, she never felt excluded, enjoyed the camaraderie, worked hard, and "as long as I was allowed to go out and write stories that was what I wanted." Mary also gently cajoled her male colleagues to carry her bags—a practice that became a tradition with her. McGrory was an admirer and friend of Stevenson, but by late October 1956, she lost enthusiasm for his chances of winning and wired her editor Bill Hines, "Both Stevenson and his sparse audience seemed to be wishing they were elsewhere." Hines tele-grammed McGrory sometime later in October and suggested "you may desert Adlai and visit there (i.e., Baja, Califor.) . . . canonical objections against divorced men entirely aside." McGrory joined the campaign of Eisenhower's vice president Richard Nixon and left the divorced Adlai Stevenson. In 1956 Cecil Holland visited thirty-two states with Steven-son, Nixon, and Eisenhower, and just before the election, he predicted Eisenhower would win. Bob Walsh covered Kefauver and Stevenson, Jim Newton was on the campaign trial with Stevenson and Nixon, and White House correspondent Jack (Garnett) Garner stayed with Eisenhower on and off the campaign trail. Walsh said in those days the *Star* rotated re-porters through campaigns because "you get sick of the fellow or you get to like him too much"—neither was good. Walsh, who stayed with Ste-venson much of the 1956 campaign, said of him, "He played right in with what young people liked, the liberalism, the idealism, though he was a little too much like Hamlet" for most ordinary Americans in the 1950s. The World War II hero Eisenhower was the quintessential president for the 1950s and was reelected in 1956.[9]

Jack Horner replaced Joe Fox as White House correspondent two years after Eisenhower was elected in 1952. Horner, a Tennessean, came to the *Star* in 1938 from UPI, and after serving during World War II returned to the paper. Horner was among a select few "newspaper people who are friends," said Eisenhower in 1959, who the president routinely invited to private dinners for briefings at the White House. The Republican-leaning, easy-going, malleable, portly forty-something and balding Horner was just the kind of reporter Eisenhower preferred. Horner was purported to have routinely asked questions planted by Eisenhower at press conferences. Horner was elected president of the White House Correspondents' Association in 1959 and covered presidents from Eisenhower to Nixon and knew them all well. Bob Walsh, the House of Representatives reporter, covered the White House when Garner was elsewhere. Walsh viewed the Eisenhower years as pretty boring for re-porters. The president was either golfing or recuperating from his heart attacks and "hadn't done anything in particular" but was elected for two terms because he "could do it very well" and the economy was booming. McGrory once said that Eisenhower's press secretary Jim Haggerty could make "trivia seem like something that should be graven on tablets of stone," but Walsh also remembered Eisenhower's volatile temper when angry. Eisenhower's "eyes would just get cold and icy" and "at press conferences, he'd look at a guy and he'd freeze him." In the post–World War II era Newby Noyes nurtured budding talents like McGrory, and later political reporters Haynes Johnson, David Broder, and Paul Hope. Noyes recruited young reporters, some of whom were Korean War veterans in the late 1950s. They would report the political news of a far more cataclysmic decade led by more dynamic presidents to come after Eisenhower left office.[10]

At first Bob Walsh—a Catholic himself—thought Jack Kennedy's Catholicism would be a huge impediment to him winning the 1960 presidential election. Walsh believed Nixon was the better bet because as Eisenhower's vice president, he ran on the coattails of a popular president. Walsh first met Kennedy when he was elected to Congress in 1947 about a year after he came to the *Star*. *Star* reporters were routinely asked to divide up new congressional members among themselves to interview and profile. Walsh saw the assignment as an "awful headache" but agreed to handle four congressmen in the alphabet from H to M. Walsh introduced himself to Jack Kennedy in his congressional office, who "looked like a kid" and was "just getting over one of his many illnesses." Walsh never imagined this young, skinny kid would be president one day, although he was "running for President, I'm sure, even then." Mary McGrory first saw Jack Kennedy in 1946 at the Parker House in Boston when he campaigned for the vacant Massachusetts 11th congressional district seat. When one of Jack Kennedy's handlers she knew invited her to a campaign event for the newest member of the "glamorous clan" of Kennedy's, she went. Kennedy made a speech about Ireland, "but mostly I remember the smile and thinking how yellow he was from the malaria and how thin and how attractive," McGrory later recalled. When Kennedy ran against Massachusetts senator Henry Cabot Lodge in 1952, McGrory saw no real difference between the two, but when she attended a debate in Waltham, Massachusetts, she clearly saw that Lodge was no match for Kennedy, who was "like a prince of the blood, . . . very suave . . . debonair . . . this handsome, graceful, articulate creature," who won over everyone. Still when Kennedy chose to run for the presidency in 1959, McGrory thought he was still too young and hadn't earned his chance yet.[11]

Charlie Seib was a husky man of forty with a rim of thick, black hair surrounding his bald head and piercing eyes behind large, dark glasses when he took charge of both 1960 political conventions as assistant managing editor. At both political conventions McGrory reported on the people behind the politics, Cecil Holland wrote articles on the candidates, Bob Walsh roamed the convention halls and backrooms for stories, and Betty Beale wrote about personalities and social hobnobbing. Senior congressional correspondent Jeremiah O'Leary Sr. worked his sources in Congress. David Broder was at the Democratic Party convention in Los Angeles and covered its preliminaries. The tall, gangly David Broder came to the *Star*'s national desk from the *Congressional Reporter* in early 1960 and immediately was sent out to cover Kennedy. Broder would earn the Washington Newspaper Guild's award for his interpretive reporting of Kennedy's run to win the Democratic Party presidential nomination. In 1960 at age eighty, Gould Lincoln did not hit the campaign trail but attended both political conventions to write his "Political Mill" column. Lincoln heard rumors that Lyndon Johnson, Senate majority leader who had run unsuccessfully for the Democratic Party presidential nomination, might be Kennedy's vice presidential pick, so he headed over to the Biltmore Hotel to talk to Johnson. Lincoln found LBJ's secretary monitoring visitors to Johnson's hotel suite when he arrived, but she easily admitted the respected veteran reporter. Lincoln found Johnson alone and seated on the bed. When Lincoln asked LBJ if he was going to accept the vice presidential nomination, Johnson got up from the bed, began pacing up and down, and said, "You know, Jack Kennedy is going to have a terrific struggle to win this election, and I am going to do my very best to see that he's elected." It was exactly the confirmation Lincoln needed, so when he returned to the *Star*'s convention headquarters, he had his scoop. Bob Walsh had no personal connection to LBJ like Lincoln. Senator Sam Rayburn insinuated to Walsh in the convention hall that he thought LBJ didn't have a chance and Kennedy would pick Scoop Jackson instead. Over the years, commentators have speculated whether Johnson was Jack Kennedy's second choice, but when Lincoln later asked Bobby Kennedy if that was true, Lincoln said Kennedy "assured me . . . that Johnson was his [President Kennedy's] choice, his first choice, and his only choice."[12]

Bob Walsh, Cecil Holland, Jack Horner, David Broder, and Mary McGrory shared the coverage of the presidential campaigns in the fall. Kennedy and Johnson ran on the Democratic ticket, and Nixon and Henry Cabot Lodge Jr. ran for the Republicans. Walsh covered JFK in New England where Kennedy was the natural favorite, but Walsh also found that large crowds in the Midwest came to hear Kennedy, whose natural charisma charmed people everywhere. Cecil Holland was on the trail with Nixon much of the fall, and McGrory was constantly on the campaign trail and writing about Kennedy, whom she admired, and Nixon, whom she did not. Holland reported that Nixon viewed Kennedy's stand on helping Cubans who opposed Fidel Castro as "irresponsible." Nixon also objected to the projected budget required to implement policies in the Democratic Party platform, joking that it was "a whale of a lot of money— even . . . to a Kennedy." Walsh observed that Holland, a conservative southern Democrat, grew to admire Nixon and speculated that Holland may have even voted for Nixon twice but never revealed that to anyone. Despite McGrory's nearly decade-long friendship with Jack Kennedy, she often felt left out of Kennedy's inner circle of press favorites. On the day of the election, McGrory was on a press plane scheduled for Hyannis Port when the last press pool of reporters granted the closest access to Kennedy was announced and she was not on it. Mary believed the Kennedy men, including Jack, didn't take women political reporters seriously and saw politics as a rough game in which "you didn't want your wife or any of your womenfolk" to be involved, said Mary. Mary, however, balked at the stereotype, and when the president's entourage landed in Hyannis Port, she stomped over to JFK in a huff among a huge crowd of other reporters and asked him, "What do you have to do to become a pool reporter in this cavalcade? I have followed you for four years, and I have never so much as ridden in the pool car," to which he replied, "Mary, we'll never be parted again." Mary went to bed not knowing the outcome of the race, but at 5 am the next morning Kennedy's press secretary, Pierre Salinger, announced she would be in the final pool of reporters. McGrory greeted Kennedy that morning, who was in a playful mood carrying his young daughter, Caroline, piggyback on the lawn of the Kennedy family home in Hyannis Port. Later that day McGrory saw Kennedy display the "only emotion he ever revealed in public." With tears in his eyes, Jack said to his pregnant wife standing next to him "not much longer, Jackie," referring to both their expected child and his presidency. David Broder wrote "a victory without a verdict and a majority without a mandate were Senator Kennedy's today." Yet Kennedy had "reconstructed the old 'Roosevelt coalition,'" wrote Broder, that brought northern urban centers and southern rural areas together and pulled out a win, but by the closest margin since 1916. Broder also pointed out president-elect Kennedy would be the youngest president in history and the first Catholic. Kennedy's brief time in office would be pivotal in the history of the nation.[13]

The *Star*'s January 20, 1961, edition was overwhelmed with seventeen pages of articles, photographs, and words devoted to President John F. Kennedy's inauguration. Revelers at the inaugural parties the night before had trudged through the bitter cold and a snowstorm of more than seven inches, but inauguration day was bright and sunny. The front-page photograph of Kennedy's swearing-in by Supreme Court Chief Justice Earl Warren surrounded by former and future presidents Eisenhower, Truman, Johnson, and Nixon taken by *Star* staff photographer Ranny Routt is an iconic image of the moment. Haynes Johnson's intimate portrait of the inaugural introduced readers to his talents as a young reporter on the edge of a bright career in a brand-new political era. Johnson's observations about America's future when JFK took office were prescient, although he could never have foreseen Kennedy's fate. To Johnson, JFK's oath marked "more than a change in administrations: it meant that an era in American history was ending—an era beginning before World War II" when FDR, Eisenhower, and Truman "governed America from depression to war and peace and a new form of conflict, the cold war" emerged. JFK with his trademark "boyish good looks, the rapid gestures with chin thrust upward, the quick delivery of phrases," wrote Johnson, honored the New Deal's legacy in his speech but called for "a new frontier for America in the 1960s . . . to restore the Nation's place of leadership in the world." Not long after JFK took office, Ranny Routt tagged along with Cecil Holland, who was writing an inconsequential piece on the new president's daily routines. Caroline Kennedy showed up unannounced to visit with her dad, and Routt shot a series of endearing photographs of father and daughter that ended up on the AP wires and in newspapers across the country. Routt's photographs would be among the many iconic images of the Kennedy era.

In the spring of 1961 President Kennedy made an historic trip to Paris to meet with French president Charles de Gaulle and then to Geneva for talks with Soviet prime minister Nikita Khrushchev. McGrory went but was not part of JFK's exclusive press pool. McGrory, however, was among the reporters invited to the reception given by de Gaulle in honor of Kennedy at the Palace of Versailles. During a break between acts, a small party of guests gathered in the foyer behind the presidential box at the Palace's theater. McGrory was not really part of the exclusive gathering but got swept up in the crowd. Kennedy laughed when he saw Mary, and she casually asked the president how he was getting along with de Gaulle. Kennedy just shrugged but then asked her if she would like to meet de Gaulle. Kennedy introduced Mary to de Gaulle, who barely acknowledged her. Mary observed later that Kennedy, however, genuinely seemed more pleased to chat with her than his unfamiliar and formal hosts. McGrory reported the event with her usual wit, describing it as "a quiet evening up in the suburbs" where the de Gaulles invited the Kennedys to dinner "with 146 other guests in the famous Salle De Glaces, which is walled entirely with mirrors," followed by the "small diversion" of a ballet in a five-hundred-seat theater "which proved superior to showing slides of family scenes." The talks between Kennedy and Khrushchev in Vienna were to focus on the future of Berlin and nuclear détente. In April 1961 the CIA had orchestrated a covert attack by Cuban exiles at the Bay of Pigs in Cuba in hope of inciting an anti-Castro rebellion. It failed miserably, the exiles were imprisoned, and the United States was publicly humiliated. The talks between Kennedy and Khrushchev in Vienna from June 3 to 4, 1961, were tense, an embarrassment for the president, and ended in a stalemate. Kennedy's first year in office was not going well, but in February 1962 the Kennedy administration was able to boast a small victory in the cold war over the Soviets when John Glenn became the first American to orbit into space. A Russian had been first in space, but Kennedy made a serious commitment to the US space program in order to surpass the Soviets. Bill Hines as the *Star*'s new science editor covered the ticker-tape parade for Glenn in Manhattan. While Hines was in Manhattan he learned that a passenger plane had crashed at Idlewild Airport, killing ninety-four. Hines, who was notorious for his high-speed dictation, dictated the Glenn story on the way to the airport, the crash story ten minutes before the paper went to press, and an hour later a final story on a top oil executive who died in the crash.[14]

On Monday, October 22, 1962, from Puerto Rico *Star* reporter Dick (Richard) Fryklund reported that he doubted the US Navy's claims that it had canceled a large-scale amphibious exercise due to Hurricane Ella. Naval officers told Fryklund in confidence that "they had been ordered by the Navy in Washington not to discuss Cuba either 'militarily or politically' with reporters." Pentagon officials withheld from the press and public for almost two months that secret aerial reconnaissance maps showed missile sites in Cuba. The Pentagon also issued a twelve-point plan detailing the limits of what civilian personnel could discuss with the press. On Monday night President Kennedy made a nationally televised speech announcing a military quarantine to stop Soviet ships from moving nuclear weapons any further into Cuba. Fryklund was the primary defense department reporter in the era, and Jerry O'Leary Jr. assisted when needed. Fryklund started at the *Star* in 1952, and was Crosby Noyes's successor as the *Star*'s European correspondent when Noyes returned to the states from 1956 to 1958. When Fryklund returned home, the *Star* assigned him to the Pentagon, where he found "a mess" with "4 services . . . at war with each other." O'Leary was a tough Marine Corps reservist and World War II veteran who had covered hotspots in Latin America and claimed he once was held in a Cuban prison. Press Secretary Pierre Salinger cautioned reporters and editors to be judicious in reporting the crisis so as not to escalate tensions. Newspaper editors "accepted the temporary situation because they had no alternative," wrote the *Star* later. The Pentagon's press liaison Arthur Sylvester was the key Kennedy administration official tapped to control the public message throughout the crisis. Administration officials sincerely believed an unfettered press might threaten their ability to manage the situation and lead to a cataclysmic global confrontation. Kennedy also hoped to improve his image with the public as a strong leader after the Bay of Pigs debacle.[15]

On Tuesday morning after Kennedy's televised speech, Khrushchev discreetly ordered all ships carrying missiles to Cuba to turn around because even he was sobered by the reality of a nuclear confrontation.

Khrushchev, however, chose not to tell the White House. The Soviets kept only civilian tankers and freighters in the waters headed for Cuba. In the *Star*'s Tuesday afternoon edition, State Department reporter Earl Voss told his readers that more than twenty Soviet ships were streaming toward Cuba and may end up in a "possible clash with American warships." Voss was a solid reporter whose concise and interpretive reporting on foreign affairs for the *Star* had extended back to reporting from Vietnam on the Indo-China War in 1953. Early Wednesday, Kennedy still was receiving inconclusive and contradictory intelligence on the location of Soviet ships. Later that day, however, Central Intelligence Agency (CIA) director John McCone told JFK their best intelligence showed all inbound Soviet ships had turned around or that US forces had stopped them. As a result, Secretary of State Dean Rusk made his infamous statement that the Soviets and the United States were "eyeball-to-eyeball, and the other fellow just blinked," which media outlets repeated and the Kennedy administration never corrected. On Wednesday, Pentagon reporters were convinced that the interception of a Soviet ship was imminent, but Sylvester repeatedly refused to confirm or deny rumors that US ships had turned back five to six Soviet ships. O'Leary characterized official Pentagon sources as being vague about any US and Soviet military confrontation and wrote "it was learned elsewhere the ship was not boarded." On Saturday, October 27, the Soviets shot down a U-2 reconnaissance plane and killed its pilot, Major Rudolph Anderson. Pentagon officials told reporters the plane and its pilot were "presumed lost."[16]

On October 30, Voss was in New York reporting from the United Nations that the "dismantling of Soviet rocket bases in Cuba has already begun," with no mention of the secret, high-level bargain that ended the crisis. Bobby Kennedy and Soviet ambassador Anatoly Dobrynin conducted backdoor negotiations in which Kennedy and Khrushchev exchanged confidential correspondence that ended in a secret agreement for the United States to quietly remove missiles in Turkey in exchange for the Soviets removing the Cuban missile installations. Kennedy and his team told the press no secret deals were made between Khrushchev and him. A day after Voss's report and the US blockade was temporarily suspended, the *Star* felt free to speak out and publicly castigated the Kennedy administration's severe restrictions on news gathering during the crisis. The administration, by censoring the press during the crisis, the *Star* wrote, "in our opinion, recklessly and thoughtlessly forfeited a confidence that in this country that has been the rule, rather than the exception" that government will tell its citizens the truth. The editorial concluded we now have a world where the truth "is that part of the truth selected by officialdom to piece together a desirable image" and having "tasted the fruits of a use of power more readily identified with

the Soviet Union, with Hitler, Mussolini and a long string of lesser dic-
tators . . . those in high places will now realize that this fruit is poison
and discard it." Fryklund also judged that "by carefully timing and
wording announcements about blockade activities, the administration
attempted to control the image of the action" presented to the Russians,
Cubans, and the world. Fryklund reported that the Associated Press and
United Press International censored or killed certain stories while other
"questionable stories" were printed or broadcast, but "none was worth
a protest or cautionary word from the Defense Department." Reporters also bitterly complained about not being allowed to report from the
scene of the blockade. Sylvester admitted that even during World War
II and the Korean War, such press restrictions were not imposed, but in
the "peculiar kind of military action that was neither war nor peace, the
administration policy was not only justified but helped materially to carry
out a difficult confrontation." Fryklund corrected some crucial aspects of
his reporting when he learned from "a completely qualified source" that
a Soviet B-130 Soviet submarine had surfaced because it ran out of air and
not, as he reported earlier, because of the blockade. In addition, his report
that the Soviet ship *Marucla* was boarded by the United States because
it intended to run the blockade and carried rockets or bombers he now
knew was untrue and conducted strictly for publicity. On November 20,
Kennedy held a press conference where he justified controlling the press
so the administration could "speak with one voice" and keep secret intelligence inside "the highest levels of government." At first the press was
impressed with Kennedy's willingness to conduct live press conferences
on TV and not even prescreen questions. Ironically, two years earlier
Newby Noyes had written Kennedy to thank him for meeting with him
and Bill White (Emporia, *Kansas Gazette* editor and CBS correspondent) on
the eve of his inauguration to express their dislike for televised news conferences because, according to Noyes, "a really good conference makes a
dull show and vice versa." Yet Noyes conceded if they "are here to stay,"
he suggested to JFK, at least, to solicit written questions from the press
first. President Kennedy wrote Noyes that because he could not match
the esteem in which President Eisenhower was held, "I am compelled
to depend on a greater communication with the public" such a conference gives. After the Cuban crisis, however, Kennedy's usual charm and
humor did little to dispel reporters' criticisms. Then the *Saturday Evening
Post* published an article written by Stewart Alsop and Charles Bartlett,
journalists and friends of the president, based on their exclusive access to
the "men who steered the course of the United States in the shadow of
nuclear war." The story glowed with praise for the ExComm (Executive
Committee) members who advised JFK, and the president's steely determination while portraying Ambassador Adlai Stevenson as weak and

an appeaser. In order to salve the wounds of reporters justifiably jealous over Alsop and Bartlett's exclusive access, Salinger invited a group of five reporters to answer questions about the rumors swirling around the *Saturday Evening Post* story. The *Star*'s David Broder was among them. Broder reported that Salinger claimed the president did not suggest the story to Alsop and Bartlett and told them he and "President Kennedy 'played no role whatever' in the controversial magazine article." The *Star* countered, "Competent sources told the *Star* that Mr. Kennedy did tell his advisers to co-operate, and that some of them refused to do so." Whatever the *Star*'s sources knew, a December 13 *Star* editorial put to rest its challenge to JFK's repeated denials, writing, we "join Mr. Kennedy in leaving this question to the historians," where it still remains.[17]

Sylvester finally agreed to allow a select group of Pentagon reporters firsthand access to Cuban waters after the Soviets began sending their missiles back. On November 10, Orville Splitt, who ran Sylvester's information office, came to the press room without any prior notice with a surprise announcement. Those reporters lucky enough to pick six winning slips out of one hundred in a Pentagon lottery bucket would have thirty minutes to board a navy patrol plane headed for Cuba. Jerry O'Leary was one of the lucky ones that morning. *Post* reporter George Dixon did not win the lottery but offered K-rations to the apprehensive reporters with just thirty minutes to spare. O'Leary reported from the cramped plane two hundred miles east of Havana that he "looked at what seemed to be five missiles on the deck of the ship" under a tarp on a Russian freighter with the American destroyer *Vesole* just behind. Without official confirmation, however, O'Leary could only speculate about what he saw. Near the end of November, the Pentagon allowed some reporters into Guantanamo Naval Base, including O'Leary. O'Leary reported from Guantanamo Bay on the return of wives and children of American marines to the base after their evacuation and Cuban exiles' claims of seeing Cuban missile sites. O'Leary also reported on the release of one thousand prisoners to Guantanamo caught in the Bay of Pigs invasion and interviewed D.C. attorney E. Barrett Prettyman Jr. to learn about his negotiations with Fidel Castro to release the Cuban prisoners in exchange for food and drugs to Cuba. O'Leary later that year would be the *Star*'s reporter on the scene of a much bigger story involving President Kennedy that this time would change the course of history.[18]

David Broder was in Dallas for the *Star* covering Kennedy's trip to Texas to fundraise and generate support for the reelection of southern Democrats in November's midterm elections. JFK came after many entreaties from Texas governor John Connally, vice president Lyndon Johnson, and other Texas Democrats. The press was keenly aware of Dallas' reputation for right-wing fanaticism, fierce opposition to black civil rights, and general nastiness toward the Kennedy administration. Broder knew about Republican women who had cornered and yelled insults at their fellow Texan Lyndon Johnson during the 1960 campaign, a prominent Baptist pastor who warned his flock about the dangers of electing a Catholic president, and Edward M. Dealey, publisher of the *Dallas Morning News,* who once told Kennedy "you and your administration are weak sisters." Yet Broder and his fellow reporters were surprised when enthusiastic crowds were "standing 10 deep" as president and Mrs. Kennedy and Texas governor John Connally and his wife reached downtown Dallas in their dark blue Lincoln Continental convertible headed for the Trade Mart Hotel. Texans were especially enthralled by the dazzling young First Lady Jacqueline Kennedy, who her husband joked to a Fort Worth crowd that morning, "Nobody wonders what Lyndon and I wear." Broder saw lots of friendly signs along the parade route in Dallas like "please stop and shake our hands," or "Hurrah for JFK," but also one that read "I hold you and your blind socialism in complete contempt," which Broder wrote showed "Dallas was living up to its reputation for wackiness." Reporters thought trouble might erupt but never envisioned the horrific tragedy that would happen next. Broder was in one of two press buses several vehicles behind President Kennedy's limousine when the motorcade reached the Triple Underpass and "suddenly a shot rang out and then two more." Reporters on the buses were too far back to see the president's car clearly but saw motorcycle patrolmen racing around and the president's car picking up speed. Broder arrived at Parkland Hospital to chaos and uncertainty knowing only that the president had been shot. Then in a nurses training room in the basement of the hospital at 1 pm central time at a hastily improvised press conference, Broder heard Dr. Kemp Clark, "a balding 38-year old with horn-rimmed glasses," announce the president was dead. When Broder called the *Star*'s newsroom with his story, he got a young Carl Bernstein, who was on the dictation desk. Bernstein remembered his hands shaking the whole time he took Broder's dictation, and as a result he misspelled "Parkland" hospital in the lead. In the Saturday edition Broder wrote about the burden of shame Dallas residents might carry for years. John Latham, an eighty-one-year-old blind news vendor, told Broder, "Why did it have to be us? This will mark Dallas for years and years and years," or a local cabbie who said, "I sure hope it turns out to be that guy . . . not one of our local Baptists." A Methodist minister spoke plainly, "There is a coldness, a callousness and a ruthlessness that surpass belief here . . . now we must pay the price . . . admit our sins and begin to make amends."[19]

On Friday after news of Kennedy's death came over the AP wires, reporters and editors silently reappeared in the newsroom and an uncharacteristic quiet enveloped the newsroom over the next few sad and fearful days. Mary McGrory later recalled that reporters worked twenty-hour shifts or more, sent out for sandwiches for sustenance, were kind to each other, and quickly returned to the newsroom after an assignment to write their story and just be with each other as they put out the news about this momentous time in history. McGrory was at Our Lady of Mercy Catholic School in Potomac, Maryland, in a French class when she learned of Kennedy's death. Mary immediately went back to the *Star*'s newsroom, where she wrote a tribute to Kennedy in the extra that day. McGrory went to Andrews Air Force Base around 6 pm to view the return of Kennedy's body. McGrory saw the airfield "garishly lit . . . by landing lights and television light," as it usually was for presidential arrivals, and a crowd of "high officials of the New Frontier" ashen faced, grief stricken, and standing silently "unseeing and unhearing in the nightmarish light and noise." Among them were historic figures like Averill Harriman, Majority Leader Mike Mansfield, Majority Whip Hubert Humphrey, Secretary of Defense Robert McNamara, Kennedy's young Special Counsel Theodore Sorensen, and George McBundy. A little after six, an honor guard of six young, enlisted men marched forward as *Air Force One*, "all white and blue, landed amid a deafening roar." The door swung open and McGrory saw that "this time there was no familiar graceful figure, gingering a button of his jacket, waiting to smile, waiting to wave." After the casket was placed in the hearse, Jackie and Robert Kennedy entered and silently closed the door behind them. McGrory then turned and saw "with tears on their faces, the leaderless men of the New Frontier who went up to greet" their new president, Lyndon Johnson, and his wife, Lady Bird, as they walked down the ramp. When Mary returned to the newsroom, she went straight to her desk in the very back and far away from editors to write an editorial and news story for the Saturday edition. Newby Noyes was anxious to get her editorial and began pacing in front of McGrory's desk from a distance for a time, but then he moved closer, standing over her ready to pull the copy from her typewriter. Newby asked Mary, "Well?" to which she replied, "I'm going to write for the news side first and then I'll do his editorial" as tears streamed down her face. McGrory was able to finish her tribute for the editorial page in forty-five minutes after finishing the news story. McGrory wrote that Kennedy:

> brought gaiety, glamour and grace to the American political scene in a measure never known before. The lightsome tread, that debonair touch, that shock of chestnut hair, that beguiling grin, that shattering understatement— these are what we shall remember. He walked like a prince and he talked like a scholar . . . His public statements were always temperate, always measured. He derided his enemies, he teased his friends . . . When the ugliness of yesterday has been forgotten, we shall remember him smiling.[20]

Jerry (Jeremiah) O'Leary Jr.'s contacts in the military, Latin American community, and FBI would prove useful in reporting the Cuban missile crisis and President Kennedy's assassination in Dallas. In this photo he is with military historian Forrest Pogue, ca. 1963. D.C. Community Archives, *Washington Star* Papers, D.C. Public Library.

Kennedy's death blanketed the country with a huge sadness, but it also engendered great fear and apprehension. The public was hungry for news about Kennedy's killer. Who was Oswald, did he have co-conspirators, what were his motives, and how did carry out the murder? Broder was an excellent political reporter, but he had no real experience covering

crime stories. City Editor Sid Epstein argued, "This is a murder" and so
who do you send to cover a murder, "You send a police reporter," and
Jerry O'Leary Jr., was just that person. O'Leary was an experienced police
beat reporter, had useful FBI connections, and his understanding of Latin
America would prove helpful too. O'Leary was at his desk in the newsroom working on a rewrite when news of Kennedy's death came over the
wires. Jerry had struggled with alcoholism for years, but by 1963 he had
stopped drinking, attended Alcoholics Anonymous, and remained sober
the rest of his life. O'Leary's sobriety and reporting experience coincided
with covering one the most important news stories of his career. O'Leary
arrived in Dallas on a chartered flight from D.C. around 8 pm CST Friday
and took a taxi immediately to the city's granite and limestone Beaux-Arts
old City Hall building that housed the jail and Dallas Police Department
offices. When O'Leary exited the elevator around 9 pm, the third-floor
police offices were crammed with more than one hundred newsmen,
cameramen, photographers, two large TV cameras, and floodlights that
swept in any direction with "eye-searing glare." Cables zig-zagged everywhere—down the third-floor hallway, in windows, through police offices,
and even down the side of the building. O'Leary also encountered a man
dressed in a flashy sports coat and felt hat not long after he arrived who
was chatting up newsmen and giving out business cards for "his tawdry,
burlesque-type nightclub, the Carousel." O'Leary waved the man off and
paid him little attention at the time, thinking he was just a bail bonds-
man, or a "hanger on" at the station. Ike Pappas, a radio reporter, who
Jerry would get to know in Dallas, did take one of the man's cards, and
O'Leary discovered later the irritating man was Jack Ruby. Each time Oswald was taken from his cell for questioning that night and the next day,
a half dozen homicide detectives all wearing broad-brimmed cowboy hats
would escort Oswald in handcuffs down a twenty-foot corridor from the
jail elevator to the third-floor interrogation room. The police pushed newsmen back into lines on either side of the third-floor hallway and instructed
them repeatedly not to ask the suspect questions. Just an arm's length
away from Oswald, TV newsmen couldn't resist thrusting microphones
in the prisoner's face as photographers hopped on tables for the best shot,
and a deafening roar of questions emanated from reporters like "Why
did you do it, Lee?" or "Have you got a lawyer?" wrote O'Leary. O'Leary
never heard Oswald's answers clearly in the den of screeching voices, even
when reporters in the front repeated what they heard to those in the back
of the crowd. Dallas Police Chief Jesse Curry would later testify to the
Warren Commission that he had good relations with the press and wanted
to cooperate with them but if he could do it over, he would restrict their access. Curry also testified that he heard accusations from some in the press
of police mistreatment of Oswald, so "in order to avoid being accused of
using Gestapo tactics," he acquiesced to them. O'Leary freely used the

phone in Curry's outer office and had easy access to police officers and
their chief. O'Leary characterized Curry as a "large, soft-spoken man . . .
unfailingly polite" who "was bending over backwards" to allow the full-
est possible news coverage as possible, but he became "overwhelmed by
events as an official can," and "let things get out of control by inertia."
Except for guards posted outside the Homicide and Robbery Division offices, O'Leary rarely encountered officers who checked his or anyone else's
press credentials. The Warren Commission would later also conclude that
"part of the responsibility for the unfortunate circumstances following
the President's death must be borne by the news media." After a judge
brought formal charges against Oswald for President Kennedy's murder
near midnight, a press conference was hastily held in the basement of
the old City Hall Building. O'Leary again saw Ruby, who had earlier attempted to hand out his business cards, at the midnight press conference
but took little notice of the nondescript man. Oswald stood in the witness
area rather than behind the screen for a usual lineup. O'Leary described
Oswald as he was led onto an illuminated stage as a "slightly built suspect
whose light brown hair is thinning in the front" and who "had a cut over
his left temple and the beginning of a blackened right eye," which police
claimed he received during the scuffle at the theater. Oswald blinked in
the glare of the lights and denied that he had killed the president. When
the press shoved and pushed too close to the suspect, the police aborted
the press conference and removed Oswald.[21]

O'Leary returned to his hotel and dozed off from around 4 to 6 am
on Saturday after the midnight press conference. Jerry then returned
to the Dallas police station, where he remained for almost twenty-four
consecutive hours. For the *Star*'s Saturday edition, O'Leary detailed evidence gathered by police against Oswald, including paraffin tests that
police claimed showed Oswald fired a gun shortly before his arrest. Police also found a rifle "similar to a Mauser" with a telescopic sight near
a window at the Texas School Book Depository where the fatal shots
were fired, and eyewitnesses saw Oswald carry a long package that
may have concealed a gun to the Book Depository where he worked.
O'Leary also wrote a warm tribute to slain Dallas police officer Private
J. D. Tippitt, "a husky man with coal black hair and high cheek bones
. . . the prototype of the Western law man," who left behind a young
family when Oswald shot him as he approached the suspect on a busy
street an hour after the president was shot. District Attorney Henry
Wade told reporters that four investigators had fifteen witnesses that
would give "sufficient evidence to prove he [Oswald] killed the President." On Saturday O'Leary learned that Dallas police had linked a gun
Oswald purchased through a mail order house to the one used to shoot
the president. O'Leary investigated Oswald's communist connections

and found that he had renounced his US citizenship and lived in the Soviet Union where he married his Russian wife, Marina. O'Leary talked with Cuban exile Carlos Bringuier, who met a suspicious man in New Orleans named Lee H. Oswald who "tried to infiltrate" an anti-Castro organization and distributed pro-Castro literature on the streets. Police also found a photograph of Oswald holding a rifle in one hand and a pistol in a holster during a search of Marina Oswald's rented rooms in Irving, Texas. O'Leary told readers he personally viewed the photo and saw Oswald holding two newspapers, "one the *Worker* and the other *The Militant*, organ of the Trotskyite Socialist Workers Party," and a rifle with a telescopic sight that "appeared to be a bolt-operated weapon similar to the gun believed to have slain President Kennedy." The photograph was printed in the *Star* and appeared in many newspapers. The Warren Commission concluded that "neither the press nor the public had a right to be contemporaneously informed" of evidence against the accused. The Dallas authorities gave the media erroneous information, and the press gathered its own information that together jeopardized Oswald's chances of a fair trial.[22]

Chief Curry told reporters Saturday night that he planned to transfer Oswald to the county jail around 10 am on Sunday morning. District Attorney General Wade in the early morning hours of Sunday gave full details of the state's case against Oswald despite the FBI's objections. O'Leary slept a few hours at his hotel and returned to police headquarters around 8 am. O'Leary estimated about fifty-three newsmen were in the building that morning and assumed the rest of the press were "in states bordering on nervous and physical exhaustion" and chose to skip the transfer and sleep-in since the main story was winding down. Chief Curry told a small group in his anteroom around 10:20 am that he had considered taking Oswald overnight "without fanfare" but he didn't want to "double-cross 'you people.'" O'Leary asked Curry about security for Oswald during the transfer since the prisoner had received many death threats. Curry told O'Leary that the police had hired an armored car, which O'Leary later learned was a decoy. Police instead planned to use an unmarked blue sedan to drive Oswald on an alternate route to jail. O'Leary generally preferred to work alone but partnered with Icarus M. Pappas, a radio reporter for WNEW in New York, who had a car that O'Leary offered to drive so they could trail Oswald while Pappas broadcasted. Around 9:30 am O'Leary and Pappas timed how fast they could race down the stairs from the third floor to the basement to see Oswald as he left the interrogation room and be in the basement in time to see him escorted to the armored car. Around 11:30 am O'Leary, Pappas, and other reporters were in an anteroom outside Curry's office when they heard a commotion in the hallway and then someone shout "Here he comes." O'Leary immediately positioned himself near the "lee of a television rig, hoping to use it as a blocking back protects a runner." O'Leary saw Oswald, unshaven with orange mercurochrome antiseptic on his facial cuts and dressed in his usual drab clothes walk barely a foot from him flanked by two western-clad homicide detectives manacled to the prisoner's hands. Although police ordered reporters not to ask Oswald questions, they still shouted incessant questions, but the "arrogant and intransigent" prisoner, wrote O'Leary, said little except, "Yes, I want to get in touch with the American Civil Liberties Union about . . . " just before entering the elevator. O'Leary raced with Pappas down the stairs three rungs at a time to the basement where he found a small crowd of newsmen and police officers in a "curving double line" from the basement door to two parked cars on the right. In seconds, O'Leary chose a position in the crowd facing "the basement door about 12 feet and slightly toward the ramp" and "tethered on my toes from excitement" when he heard Oswald was on his way. O'Leary was momentarily startled when the officer behind the wheel of the unmarked blue sedan "suddenly lurched backwards," ramming people until its "tailfins came to rest waist high" on him. O'Leary leaned against the car and when he looked up, he saw Oswald coming through the basement door with his two guards. Oswald seem to pause, and then O'Leary "saw a dark figure glide, rather than run, out of the line about five feet to my right" and a second later "the dark figure barreled into the center of the trio, shoved the pistol into Oswald's midsection and there came the hollow explosion a firecracker makes in a tin can." O'Leary saw Oswald instinctively raise his manacled hands to protect himself as his "face contorted with pain and surprise . . . and his mouth opened in an unheard howl," and then he toppled over his assailant. The next few seconds "were a kaleidoscope of tangled bodies, amid shouts of rushing men in the wildest scene any reporter is ever likely to witness," O'Leary wrote. Less than an hour after the shooting, the FBI questioned O'Leary and would follow up with a second interview a few weeks later. Eight months later a Warren Commission investigator also interviewed O'Leary. O'Leary was convinced that Oswald never saw the gunman nor recognized him "in that moment of doom" when "the confusion was indescribable" as men swore and struggled all around him. O'Leary wrote the Star's managing editor Bill Hill later about his testimony to the Warren Commission while on Naval Reserve duty in July 1964. In hindsight Jerry told Hill, he remembers few things in the immediate aftermath of the shooting, except telling himself not to put his hands in his pockets as he heard shouts of "Get Him!" with guns drawn and pointed all around him. As a good newsman, however, "I made sure to look at my $15 Timex and said over and over to myself 10:19 a.m., 10:19 a.m." The official time of the murder was 11:21 am EST. O'Leary said he "walked slowly and I trusted, majestically, toward the elevator trying very hard to look like a cop" rather than a suspect. When the elevator came, O'Leary stepped inside alone and was so unnerved, he kept hitting the wrong buttons until after three tries, he finally mashed the third-floor button. Chief Curry sat alone and calm while he composed correspondence in his office. O'Leary entered the office and said, "Chief, something terrible has happened. Somebody shot Oswald." Curry dropped his pen and "uttered one vulgar Anglo-Saxon word that, in all truth, still seems to cover the situation best," O'Leary told Hill. At 1:30 pm Sunday Curry announced Oswald's death to the press but refused to respond any further to their questions then or later. Curry also refused to cooperate with Prosecutor Wade, who held a lengthy press conference on his own Sunday evening despite the FBI's objections. O'Leary with few notes phoned in his story that afternoon feeling he just had to tell someone the story even though there would be no more press runs for Sunday.[23]

On Monday O'Leary traveled to Fort Worth to report on Oswald's funeral, where he ended up being a stand-in pall bearer along with other newsmen. In late November O'Leary interviewed many who knew Oswald and Ruby and searched public records into Oswald's past for a special report published in the *Star* about the assassination. O'Leary talked with Ruth Paine, who gave free lodging to Marina Oswald in Irving, Texas; Earlene Roberts, who was the housekeeper at Lee's boarding house; Oswald's Book Depository supervisor R. S. Truly; and Jack Ruby's sister and housemate. O'Leary revealed new details about Oswald's trip to Mexico and his contentious dealings with the Cuban and Mexican embassies, gave an account of Ruby's early life in Chicago that lead him into the underworld, and recounted the days and hours before Ruby shot Oswald. O'Leary would win the Washington Newspaper Guild's award for National Reporting that year for his reporting from Dallas. O'Leary also attended Private Tippit's funeral, where he observed the officer's wife, Marie, "as composed as Mrs. Jacqueline Kennedy proved to be."[24]

On Saturday evening *Star* city editor Sid Epstein accompanied Mary McGrory to a sort of wake in the East Room of the White House with other press members. Mary then returned to the newsroom to compose a remembrance of Kennedy as promised for the Sunday paper. Prickly managing editor Bill Hill read it and told her to rewrite it in the first person. Despite Hill's contrariness, she agreed he was right and reworked it. On Sunday McGrory stood in the long public lines to see the president as he lay in-state at the Capitol Rotunda and wrote about that experience. McGrory's column for Sunday gave homage to Jacqueline Kennedy's grace and courage and the crowd that tried to "reward her heroism with a heroism of its own," as people from all walks of life patiently waited for hours to enter the Rotunda to pay their respects. McGrory saw Mrs. Kennedy stop to talk with a group of nuns and look into almost every face she saw in the crowds. The young widow, McGrory wrote, "has borne herself with the valor of a queen in a Greek tragedy" and "everything she has done seems to be a conscious effort to give to his death the grandeur that the savagery in Dallas was calculated to rob it of." Mary was exhausted by Sunday evening and felt like "the world was falling apart" after reeling from an emotional day coupled with news of Oswald's murder. As Mary prepared to leave, she told John Cassady she would cover the funeral the next day. Cassady asked Mary, "You're sure you're not too tired?" She simply responded, "No." McGrory was grateful for Cassady's calm presence in those few harrowing days when he often provided a sandwich, a cup of coffee, or word of encouragement to tired and sometimes "incoherent" *Star* reporters. At 11 am on Monday, November 25, Cardinal Cushing conducted a requiem mass at the St. Matthew's Cathedral for John Kennedy, and Mary McGrory was there. After the funeral ended, McGrory and William Walton, a Kennedy family friend, went to the bar at the Hay Adams Hotel to have a brandy. They talked about Kennedy and for a few moments almost forgot that he was dead because his passing still seemed so unreal. Walton told her, "Do one thing for him, no crap," and she said she would try. When she returned to the newsroom, her emotions about the last few days and memories of Kennedy seemed overwhelming and her first attempt was too long and ponderous, so she went back to what she had learned over the years about writing emotional pieces: "Keep the sentences short, otherwise, it'll sag." Mary's front-page column the next day was headlined "He Would Have Liked It: The Funeral Had That Special Kennedy Touch." Kennedy would have liked Mary's touch too. Reading Mary's words can bring a reader to tears but also elicit a wry smile too when she writes of Kennedy, who would have liked that "nobody cried out, nobody broke down . . . Excess was alien to his nature . . . he would have seen every politician he ever knew" and as "an old campaigner, [he] would have loved the crowd." It was a day, McGrory wrote, with "so much grief nobly borne that it may extinguish that unseemingly hour in Dallas, where all that was alien to him—savagery, violence, irrationality—struck down the 35th President of the United States."[25]

The violent end to President John Kennedy's life marked the start of a decade of tortuous changes, more assassinations, social unrest, and violent divisions in America. The nonviolent civil rights movement had already awakened Americans who far too long had ignored racial injustices in the country. The commitment to nonviolence to bring social justice would be seriously challenged in the coming decade. As US military involvement in the Vietnam War escalated and the death toll mounted, the first large, organized, antiwar movement in America grew. The 1960s also marked the downward spiral of the *Star* and the fight to save the paper. Those at the *Star* who covered politics would have little time to contemplate their fate as they reported some of the most important political stories and debates of the twentieth century.

8

Covering Politics and Presidents in the Vietnam War Era, 1964–1974

On the same day President Kennedy was struck down by an assassin's bullet and Lyndon Baines Johnson was sworn in as president, Don B. Reynolds, an obscure Maryland insurance agent, testified before a Senate Rules Committee in closed session about bribery and kickbacks involving two men with very close political connections to Lyndon Johnson. Reynolds told the Committee that Bobby (Robert G.) Baker, the Senate secretary and a protégé of LBJ, had recommended him to Walter Jenkins, a longtime aide to Johnson, as an agent to sell Senate Majority Leader Lyndon Johnson in 1957 a high-value life insurance policy after he suffered a heart attack. In exchange, Reynolds claimed that Jenkins expected him to buy advertising for another business on the Johnsons's Austin TV station and purchase an expensive stereo for LBJ. Lyndon Johnson's legacy as a consequential and talented politician has been forever tainted in the history books by stories of corruption and cronyism. Still Johnson's commanding personality, prodigious political skills, and southern roots made him the perfect president to push through historic civil rights legislation and Great Society programs. Johnson's many successes as president however, were tragically scarred by the escalation of the war in Vietnam, major divisions in the country, and violence in the streets. The *Star*'s slide into financial ruin would begin in the same era President Johnson's presidency fell apart. Yet as this tumultuous era unfolded, the paper remained steadfast, tireless, and at times brilliant in its reporting of the important political stories of those years as its financially prosperous past began to fade.[1]

In September 1963 Republican Delaware senator John Williams began investigating charges of kickbacks and influence peddling by Bobby Baker. Williams was a tough and independent-minded senator intent on rooting out political corruption in government since taking office in 1946. By October, the Baker scandal had leaked out and hit the newsstands, forcing Baker to resign as Senate secretary. Paul Hope was in Alabama covering the tragic murder of four young girls in a Birmingham, Alabama, church in the fall 1963, when Charlie Seib asked him to go to South Carolina where Baker grew up to get reaction from locals to the scandal. When Hope returned to the newsroom, he was taken off the civil rights beat and asked to focus on the Baker story. Hope asked for John Barron to assist him. Hope had worked with Barron on the *Star*'s state desk and saw him as "a very competent reporter" and thought Barron's investigative skills and doggedness were needed on the Baker story. Barron had been an intelligence officer in Berlin, where his wife, Patty, said he "ran spies into East Germany" before coming to the *Star* in 1957. John and Patty met at the University of Missouri Journalism School where they both graduated in the early 1950s with their friend Haynes Johnson, who came to the *Star* around the same time.[2]

The Democratic Party controlled the Senate Rules Committee and blocked release of Reynolds's testimony until January 1964. On Tuesday, January 21, 1964, the *Star* reported on a score of Baker's crooked business deals revealed by the release of Reynolds's testimony, including one directly affecting D.C.—payoffs to push passage of a bill for construction of the D.C. Stadium. The *Star* also printed excerpts from Walter Jenkins's interview at the Executive Office Building in December directly contradicting Reynolds's sworn testimony. The weekend before the transcripts were officially released, the *Star* asked for a response from the White House on the conflicts between Jenkins's and Reynolds's testimonies. Andy Hatcher telephoned Jenkins and, as President Johnson explained later to his friend, Texas newspaperman Marshall McNeill, "Well Walter said now tell them the transcript will be available on Monday and there is no conflict. I said that I knew nothing about the arrangement made by Reynolds" and there was no conflict since "a fellow named . . . Young"—not Jenkins—had bought the advertising. LBJ complained to McNeill after the article was published that "the *Star* changed their story that they'd written, that they turned over to Hatcher . . . rewrote it and left that part of it out." McNeill told Johnson that the *Star* was "just trying to make a name" for itself. For the next two months Barron and Hope continued to talk with Baker's business associates and friendly Republicans, and to report on a complex web of corruption spawned by Baker. The *Star*'s March 12 editorial called the Senate investigation a "Whitewash" by Democrats who were leaving "in the public mind a deep and fully justified suspicion" that the Senate Rules Committee was attempting to cover up a major scandal. In response, President Johnson telephoned Deke DeLoach, FBI director J. Edgar Hoover's assistant and the Bureau's liaison to the White House, to tell him "the *Star* has got a hell of a mean editorial today. I thought you had better influence in the *Star* than that," to which DeLoach replied, "The *Star* is closing up its doors too on that . . . they've called up their boys and reassigned them." DeLoach was either misinformed or engaged in wishful thinking. Barron and Hope appear never to have been reassigned, didn't get the message or ignored it, and persevered with unraveling the Baker scandal for almost a year.[3]

The Bobby Baker scandal made the press curious about the extent and nature of the Johnsons's wealth. *Life* was the first news outlet to devote money and resources to the subject, but the story was never published since it collided with JFK's assassination and LBJ's rise to the presidency. The *Wall Street Journal* and *U.S. News and World Report* both published stories on LBJ's wealth, but Barron's story on June 9, 1964, included the most shocking detail that the Johnsons's wealth may be worth as much as $9 million. President Johnson told his press secretary, George Reedy, "that 9 million thing . . . that has the circulation to pick it up. The rest of it, I think, is too complicated for anybody to read or understand." LBJ understood to voters so much wealth "sounds like a helluva lot of money to John Doe on the street." LBJ and Reedy were both perplexed with the amount of time and money the *Star* had spent "for just a news story . . . it's not quite worth it for them." Reedy thought he might know why. Reedy attended a party hosted by Charlie Seib, whom he had known for many years. All the "*Star* people" at the party were "pretty friendly except maybe Newbold Noyes," who wasn't unfriendly but "he was a little cool," Reedy told Johnson, and "I have a hunch from the way that Charlie talked to me Sunday that he may have gotten overruled on a couple of things." Johnson was bewildered that the *Star*, which "is not a Goldwater paper, and not a mean Republican paper and has always been friendly to me," would publish "this Barron story . . . it's very vicious . . . a very mean one" and "it's pure planted lie." Reedy knew LBJ's longstanding animosity toward Bobby Kennedy and suggested that "Bobby and his group . . . there's no question that they've got the *Star*." Deke DeLoach would later report to the president that the FBI found no link suggesting Bobby Kennedy had influenced the *Star* on the Baker case. Johnson was right to assume Barron and Hope depended on leaks, but not from Robert Kennedy. As Paul Hope said, "John had a good friend down at the FBI who steered us to a lot of things," and Senator "Williams also confirmed a lot." Patty Barron remembered her husband became really good friends with Senator Williams, in "a father-and-son sort of way." Patty judged Williams as "straightforward, decent and kind of down home," whom John trusted completely. Williams's unimpeachable integrity had earned him the nickname "conscience of the Senate." Patty said John talked with Reynolds too and believed a lot of what he said was true but just as much was "brouhaha," as John called it. Hope saw Reynolds as "not a very reputable character but he knew where the bodies were buried." After LBJ won the presidency in a landslide and nearly a year after the Baker scandal surfaced, Barron and Hope in January 1965 wrote a wrap-up article. Their biggest indictment was of the Democratic majority, which had "done next to nothing" in what they called a "major case of influence peddling." They cautioned the public that "the questions still pending go to the very heart of the legislative process and involve the integrity of Congress." The laundry list of charges included payoffs, improper pressure to influence legislation, questionable political contributions, and even the use of call girls by "highly placed persons." Patty Barron was suspicious that the Internal Revenue Service's audit of them in 1964 might have come from the Johnson administration. The audit didn't amount to much since the Barrons ended up owing only $6.76, according to Patty. During Deke DeLoach's investigation of possible undue influence by Robert Kennedy on the *Star*, he "discretely" met with Newby Noyes and "four other officials at the *Star*." Jerry O'Leary reported to DeLoach at that meeting that overall the *Star*'s articles were more pro than con but had to admit the Bobby Baker articles were the most critical. DeLoach explained to Clyde Tolson, assistant to Hoover, that "the *Star* has always been Republican in political philosophy," but when Goldwater won the nomination, it "faintly" supported Johnson. "Old timers" at the *Star*, DeLoach wrote, are "basically against big government and give-away type programs of big government" that FDR and LBJ alike fostered. But to the paper's credit, DeLoach observed, "The *Star* unlike the *Washington Post* . . . is more or less independent in its thinking and does not hesitate to take a slap at the President if the situation presents itself." LBJ's attempt to court his friend and former *Star* editor Ben McKelway was a waste of time, DeLoach judged, because Noyes is in charge now. Barron and Hope would win the George Polk Award in National Reporting in 1965 for "breaking and developing the story of the Bobby Baker controversy in the face of counter pressure from high government officials" and the Raymond Clapper Award from the American Society of Newspaper Editors. As Hope said later, he and Barron were unable to delve into "lot of stuff . . . because Congress was controlled by the Democrats," and Senator Williams, who was a great help to them, had no subpoena power.[4]

Paul Hope (L) and John Barron (R) receive congratulations from Morris L. Ernst (center), attorney and cofounder of the American Civil Liberties Union, after winning the 17th Annual George Polk Award for their coverage of the Bobby Baker political scandal, March 31, 1965. D.C. Community Archives, *Washington Star* Papers, D.C. Public Library.

By the time John Barron received his awards for the Baker story in 1965, he had already accepted a position at *Reader's Digest*. Barron's decision to leave the *Star* was the direct result of another Johnson administration scandal he discovered. This time, however, Barron was thwarted by top *Star* editors in his desire to publish what he knew. On Tuesday evening, October 13, 1964, Barron was attending his naval reserve meeting and Patty Barron was on her way to a separate meeting when she got a call from an unnamed source who left his number and a message for John to call him as soon as possible. When John arrived home, he called the source, who told him that he had seen Walter Jenkins's name on the police blotter a week earlier for a solicitation arrest at the G Street YMCA men's room, a notorious spot for gay men to discreetly meet, which the police often surveilled. Jenkins had been a Johnson aide since LBJ's US House and Senate years and an essential member of the White House staff. Jenkins and his wife had attended a party hosted by Ben Bradlee on the night of October 7 to celebrate the opening of *Newsweek*'s new office while the president was away campaigning. Jenkins left the party and escorted his wife to her car for her to drive onto another party, and then set out to walk to the White House. On the way Jenkins stopped by the G Street YMCA, where he was arrested for solicitation. Jenkins was fined and released at the jail and afterward returned to the White House to work until midnight. Early the next morning, Barron called the *Star*'s police reporter to confirm Jenkins's recent arrest and also learned of a previous one in 1959. Around 10 am Charlie Seib called Liz Carpenter, Mrs. Johnson's press secretary, who was on duty in the absence of the president's press secretary George Reedy. Seib told Carpenter that a police blotter showed that Jenkins "has been arrested on a morals charge, and we are going to use the story." Seib then asked her, "Is he in a hospital? Is he under medical treatment? What is the story? We want the White House to say something. I've tried to get hold of George Reedy, and he's in New York." Carpenter couldn't believe it. The Jenkins she knew was a dedicated family man with six children who worked long hours without complaint for a demanding boss and shunned the limelight. Carpenter said such charges must be a case of mistaken identity and she would get back to Seib after checking into it. Liz called Walter, who was still at home, but he did not respond directly to her questions and only said, "I'll handle it." Carpenter would later say of the *Star*, "I must say I look back on that phone call and think of Charlie Seib sitting there with the story ready to go, and throwing me the possible excuse that there was a medical reason. I will always think more of him and the paper because of the way they handled it." Seib later said the *Star* only wanted "to be sure about it before going ahead. A grisly story like that is impossible to retract. A man's life was at stake." Jenkins immediately called Abe Fortas, a respected Washington lawyer and friend of the Johnson administration, to ask for his help. By the time Jenkins reached Fortas's home, he was so traumatized that the story of his arrests was out that he was in "a state of emotional collapse and asking for help," Fortas recalled. Fortas called Clark Clifford to tell him that Jenkins was in bad shape, gave no specifics, and requested they meet. Fortas's chauffeur arrived at Clifford's office, and as the two drove slowly around town, they both agreed they needed to talk to local newspaper editors to stall publishing the story until they could speak with Jenkins's wife and family. They first visited *Star* editor Newby Noyes that morning. John Barron was angry when he saw the two highly influential lawyers friendly to the White House enter the *Star*'s newsroom and head for Noyes's office. Fortas and Clifford asked Noyes to consider carefully if the *Star* was "obliged to publish a report of this nature concerning a married man with young children" until the facts were absolutely confirmed, his family notified, and Jenkins had entered a hospital for treatment. The *Star'*s editors were sure of their facts and believed the Jenkins's story would surface soon but agreed to hold off as long as other publications did the same. Fortas and Clifford also visited John T. O'Rourke, *the Washington Daily News* editor, whose reporters had already partly confirmed the story, and he too agreed to hold off publishing. J. R. Wiggins at the *Washington Post*, who first heard the news of Jenkins's arrest from the two attorneys, made no commitment to hold the story. Fortas and Clifford called President Johnson late Wednesday afternoon to tell him about Jenkins, and by 8 pm the president asked for Jenkins's resignation. UPI broke the story on the wire that evening after receiving a tip from an unnamed reporter at "a Washington newspaper" and a second anonymous tip. The story appeared in most morning newspapers, including the *Washington Post*. The *Star* and the *Daily News* published the story that afternoon. According to Patty Barron, John was livid when he returned home the next day complaining that his bosses had squelched his scoop. Barron began looking for other jobs, and when *Reader's Digest* offered him one, he accepted. Fortas said of the *Star'*s editors, "I shall always honor these men at The *Star* . . . They had a scoop," but chose not to print it right away. As Noyes explained after the story became public, the *Star'*s decision not to publish was not the result of pressure from the White House but "wholly on the grounds of the effects on Jenkins, his family, his condition." The editorial also told its readers that "arrests of perversion," as it characterized the incident in a time far less open and accepting of homosexuality, regularly come to the paper's attention, but they usually choose not to report them because "we believe the individuals concerned in these pitiful cases need not be pilloried before the world."[5]

In 1964 the *Star* gave President Johnson a lukewarm endorsement with its "fingers crossed" because he "seems to us the lesser evil" after Goldwater won the Republican Party nomination. Newby Noyes met with Governor Scranton early in the campaign and pledged to support him, but after Goldwater won, Noyes and other top editors abandoned the Republican Party. The *Star* confessed in its LBJ endorsement it would have preferred William Scranton, George Romney, Richard Nixon, or "even a Rockefeller," and although Goldwater was not "a bad man, . . . doubts and fears are not the stuff of which an effective program can be fashioned," and Goldwater appeared to be against many things like "communism, big government, and immorality" than for anything positive. Paul Hope joined Broder and Haynes Johnson to cover the 1964 campaign and spent a lot of time with the Scranton campaign during the Republican primary. Hope, who was a self-described "registered Republican," said in the 1964 campaign, "I got my eyes opened to how the press operated." To Hope the press corps was dominated by Democrats who would sit "around the bars after a day's campaigning and tell people in the Scranton campaign, for instance, how to run their campaign to beat Goldwater . . . I thought that was really strange." Hope traveled with the Goldwater campaign after the conventions and thought he "was a really interesting guy to cover" and "the granddaddy of the modern conservative movement" but also a "very controversial" candidate "who told it like it was, or at least like he thought it was but, of course, he got really swamped by Johnson." The *Star*'s senior political analyst Gould Lincoln, whose writing always showed a preference for moderate Republican Party values, was blunt in his criticism of Goldwater. After LBJ's landslide win, Gould castigated Republican political leaders for supporting Goldwater whose views had "nothing whatever to do with the Lincoln concepts of liberty, dignity, and equality." After the election in November, Lincoln retired from the *Star* after more than fifty years of covering politics, and David Broder went to the *New York Times*. Paul Hope became the paper's chief national political correspondent. Broder stayed only eighteen months at the *Times* and then took a job with the *Washington Post*. Longtime *Star* congressional reporter Jeremiah O'Leary Sr. retired in 1964 too, but the *Star*'s longtime White House correspondent Jack Horner stayed. According to political columnist Stewart Alsop, Horner was one of a few select reporters who Johnson saw "on a business" basis. In fact, soon after Johnson's gall bladder surgery in 1966, Horner is photographed standing next to the president's hospital bed taking notes from him for the *Star*'s next edition. According to the caption, the president chose the *Star* to catch up on the latest news—it was a shameless plug for the paper. Johnson, however, never accepted the *Star*'s invitations to attend its "Celebrity Lunch" but preferred instead to invite political reporters and editors to the White House Cabinet Room for background sessions. At one such meeting, Johnson was late, and as everyone waited, Mary McGrory spotted four buttons in front of the president's chair and joked to everyone at the table that maybe they were the buttons that launched nuclear missiles to Russia, but as she leaned in closer, she discovered they were for Coca-Cola, 7-Up, Diet Pepsi, and coffee.[6]

Johnson's astute political abilities combined with Democratic Party majorities in both houses of Congress resulted in enactment of historic civil rights legislation and the introduction of a host of new federal domestic programs for a "War on Poverty" to create a "Great Society" in America. Medicare and Medicaid, the Public Broadcasting Corporation, the Department of Housing and Urban Development, and federal student loans, among others, have stood the test of time. When Congress passed Johnson's Medicare bill in July 1965, however, the Sunday *Star*'s editorial was skeptical, describing it as "a tasty bit of icing on the cake" for the Johnson administration's "vast, sprawling social legislation." The editorial thought the original Medicare bill was a more "sensible proposal" because it stuck to covering hospital stays and nursing home care that helped seniors pay onerous medical bills but argued new legislation was far too expensive at approximately $7.5 billion. When Goldwater labeled LBJ's "Great Society" programs as socialism, however, a *Star* editorial countered that LBJ's policies are "still light years away from the 'cradle to grave' security sponsored by contemporary socialism," and "more like ordinary human concern for human distress than like an ideology." John Cline's moderate politics had guided the *Star*'s editorial pages since the 1940s when he became editorial page editor. Cline was a trained lawyer and a political moderate who had an almost religious commitment to presenting all sides of an argument, which often led to a squishy balance. Through the 1960s, Cline's staff included editorial writers John C. Henry, Truman Temple, and Bob Walsh, who focused on business and politics; Crosby Noyes, who was a foreign affairs columnist; and *Star* editor Newby Noyes. Everyone at the table had a say in shaping an editorial, according to Walsh. Despite Lyndon Johnson's ability to enact historic civil rights legislation and domestic programs, his handling of the Vietnam War would be his undoing.[7]

In 1965 Johnson sent the first American combat troops to Vietnam and began aerial bombing of North Vietnam. The change in policy began less than a year after Congress passed the Tonkin Resolution instigated by an unconfirmed torpedo attack on a US military ship in the Gulf of Tonkin by the North Vietnamese. That same year Crosby Noyes returned to the states to write a foreign affairs column for the *Star*. Crosby and his brother, Editor Newby, along with many senior editors and reporters, supported the Vietnam War largely fueled by their World War II experiences and Cold War ideology. *Star* reporters had been traveling to Southeast Asia since the early 1950s. Earl Voss toured the Far East and reported from Vietnam during the Indo-China War in 1953, and James E. Roper was there in 1955 when a mass exodus of anticommunists from communist-occupied North Vietnam took place after the Geneva Accords were signed. In September 1963 Dick Fryklund had written from Saigon when Kennedy was still in office about Defense Secretary Robert McNamara's tour of American military advisers on the battlefront after "the Kennedy administration . . . wavered on the brink of junking the war here a month ago during the shocking wave of protest suicides" by Buddhist monks against President Ngo Diem's government. Fryklund saw McNamara's decision to continue the fight as the "best of a poor lot of options" in this "important war with the Communists." The corrupt Diem government would fall in a bloody coup two months later. Richard Critchfield, the *Star's* first official Asian reporter based in New Delhi, wrote from Tan An, South Vietnam, during his own battlefront tour in 1965 for a series titled "The Lonely War." Critchfield met a young captain who he thought epitomized the quandary many American advisers faced. As the captain looked out over the Mekong Delta, he told Critchfield "it looks peaceful, does it not," but as they saw five men in "mollusk hats" and "black pajamas" walk down a country road in the distance, the captain countered, but "you never know," they could be either enemy guerillas planning an attack later or ordinary villagers. Critchfield later wrote about the uncertain battlefront landscape in Da Nang where US soldiers faced "elephant grass higher than a man's head, leeches, scorpions . . . mantraps eight feet deep and floored with bamboo spikes and the whole bag of dirty tricks" as they do "the gritty job of ferreting the Viet Cong out hamlet by hamlet amidst an often hostile civilian population." Critchfield was a graduate in Far Eastern Studies at the University of Washington and Columbia's School of Journalism, and it showed in his knowledge of the region. In 1966 Critchfield wrote critically about land reform and pacification, where he saw landlords in the south "bloodsucking" the peasant with high rents and in the north the "Viet Cong tax collectors who shoot first, and collect later." In 1966 Harrison Salisbury, *New York Times* assistant managing editor, became the first journalist to report from inside North Vietnam by invitation of its leaders about the US bombing of North Vietnamese civilians. Crosby Noyes thought it incredible that the US government, while sending 400,000 men to fight in Vietnam, allows "reporters, handpicked by the enemy" to write "straight-faced dispatches what they are seen and told by the enemy." Fryklund too thought Salisbury's reporting questionable since he believed that what Salisbury saw was strictly controlled by the North Vietnamese while "in the south the good and the bad of American and South Vietnamese actions are accessible to reporters who want to dig them out." After two years of almost continuous US bombing of North Vietnam, the *Star's* editorial staff reversed its support of the policy in a May 21, 1967, editorial titled, "It's Time to Stop Bombing in the North." Letters to the *Star's* editors about its reversal ranged from "many thanks for your brave and true stand" to "it was to be expected from the ultra-liberal 'rag' commonly known as *The Evening Star*, the noted anti-anticommunist paper." The *Star* urged the halt without any quid pro quo because the bombing simply wasn't working and thought it might be a spur to peace negotiations, as the North Vietnamese had hinted. On March 31, 1968, Lyndon Johnson called a halt to the bombing in North Vietnam and announced he would not run for reelection as president but instead focus his attention on seeking peace talks with the North Vietnamese communists. Johnson's announcement followed his arch political enemy Robert Kennedy's entry into the presidential race.[8]

The *Star*'s Asian correspondent Richard Critchfield reporting from Vietnam in 1966. D.C. Community Archives, *Washington Star* Papers, D.C. Public Library.

The presidential election of 1968 at its core became a referendum on peace or war in Vietnam. Racial politics and Richard Nixon's promise to the so-called silent majority to restore law and order in an increasingly violent and divided country played a crucial role too. Paul Hope covered the campaigns of George Romney, Richard Nixon, Hubert Humphrey, and Robert Kennedy. Haynes Johnson was on the campaign trail early with Senator Eugene McCarthy and in March broke the story that Robert Kennedy was entering the race. Kennedy's personal assistant, Angie Novello, called Haynes Johnson at 2 am at home one morning to tell him Bobby had asked him to fly to New York City the next morning where Kennedy planned to announce his candidacy. Johnson described his friendship with Kennedy as "very close" since first meeting Bobby Kennedy in the early 1960s when Johnson was writing his book on the Bay of Pigs and consulted Kennedy, who was in charge of intelligence at the CIA. When Kennedy saw Johnson the next day, he asked the reporter to accompany and advise him during his campaign, but Johnson declined the offer in order to remain an impartial commentator. Mary McGrory covered Eugene McCarthy but later confessed she lost her journalistic objectivity during his presidential run. By 1968 McGrory and McCarthy had been friends for almost twenty years, and his campaign manager Blair Clark was a close reporter friend with whom she had a private and likely unconsummated romantic relationship for years, according to her biographer John

Norris. Mary's greatest attraction to McCarthy was the candidate's strong and early opposition to the Vietnam War and the young campaign volunteers she befriended. Mary, however, had not been an early McCarthy supporter. When she heard Gene McCarthy was running in the New Hampshire primary, she said, "I was not only disbelieving but embarrassed." Mary instead encouraged her friend Bobby Kennedy to enter the presidential race, but when he stalled and entered late, she became highly critical of his run. By 1968 Mary was a friend of Bobby and Ethel Kennedy, who she visited in Hyannis Port. Bobby regularly sang camp songs at Mary's infamous parties. The Kennedys also offered their Hickory Hill estate's swimming pool during the summer for children at the St. Ann's orphanage—a cause Mary had supported since moving to Washington. Haynes Johnson and Paul Hope were at the Ambassador Hotel the night Bobby Kennedy won the California primary. Johnson was in the ballroom where Kennedy addressed his supporters, and Hope was in the hotel's press room adjacent to the ballroom writing his story about Kennedy's primary win. Hope and the other reporters in the press room heard a "pop pop pop" coming from the kitchen nearby. They all jumped up and raced toward the noise. When Hope and Jules Witcover entered the room, they glimpsed Kennedy's bloodstained body on the floor through a chaos of screams and jostling bodies. A moment later they saw the "big old football player" Rosey Grier, recalled Hope, tackle and land on top of a small, dark man the reporters learned later was the shooter Sirhan Sirhan. Hope and Witcover jumped on top of a steam table but quickly hopped down when they saw a gun in Sirhan's hand pointed upward. They later learned there were no more bullets in the chamber of Sirhan's gun. Long after the rush of reporting the story, Hope in a more reflective mood called those months of assassinations and violence as "a pretty sad time." Hope and Haynes Johnson remained in Los Angeles three days until Kennedy died from his wounds. Bobby Kennedy's premature and shocking death was particularly difficult for Mary McGrory because it had occurred during a time of estrangement between the two friends. McGrory joined Haynes Johnson to attend and report on Robert Kennedy's funeral mass at St. Patrick's Cathedral in Washington on June 7.[9]

Richard Nixon emerged as the clear frontrunner for the Republican Party's presidential nominee in 1968 and won on the first ballot at the party's convention in Miami Beach in August. News from the Republican convention paled in comparison to the drama that would unfold at the Democratic Party convention in Chicago. An organized antiwar movement came to Chicago to protest for peace outside the convention hall but were denied a permit to demonstrate by Chicago authorities. Thousands of armed US Army and National Guard troops joined nearly six thousand Chicago police officers, who were under strict orders from Chicago mayor

Richard Daley to keep order. The standoff between the protesters and police inevitably escalated into repeated violent clashes in Chicago's streets
during the convention. Chief political reporter Charlie Seib headed the
team of national political reporters that included Paul Hope, Bob (Robert) Walters, Bob Walsh, and Lyle Denniston with Haynes Johnson and
Mary McGrory providing commentary. A day after the convention began,
McGrory and Johnson wrote side-by-side profiles on the two rivals. Mc-
Grory satirized Humphrey as the "Happy Lodge Brother" who "moves
in a bubble of security and approval" while outside is a "grim, embattled
city full of cops and kids who hate each other." Humphrey had not been
on the ballot in any of the primaries, but party bosses maneuvered to
make him the nominee during the convention. Haynes Johnson saw Mc-
Carthy as the "unconventional politician" who stood "serenely apart"
from convention politicking and offered voters no specific policies other
than ending the Vietnam War. The street protests stoked heated conflicts
between party leaders supporting Humphrey and the antiwar delegates
who, from the podium and the floor, voiced strong opposition to the war
and Daley's virulent response to the antiwar demonstrations. The *Star*
team setup a temporary newsroom inside the convention hall. Although
the hall was less violent than the streets, angry protests and manhan-
dling by security of delegates and the media occurred on the convention
floor. *Star* staff had rooms at the Conrad Hilton with other press and
convention delegates. Demonstrators from nearby Grant Park marched
to protest outside the Hilton the night Humphrey was nominated, which
precipitated some of the most violent clashes between police and protesters. Protesters set off stink bombs that drifted into the lobby and halls of
the Hilton, remembered some reporters. Mary McGrory was with Gene
McCarthy in the Hilton that night, and together they went to the hotel's
fifteenth floor where McCarthy volunteers had set up a makeshift first-aid
station, where they comforted and talked with injured protesters. When
McGrory submitted her copy for the next edition, *Star* editors quarreled
over how much prominence to give her column and eventually chose
to print it inside the paper rather than on its customary front-page slot.
Assistant managing editor Burt Hoffman came to Mary's defense and
impulsively resigned in protest but returned later. Mary wrote, McCarthy
was "being politically tear-gassed and beaten" the night he lost the nomination, just like young protesters who "were suffering the same fate in
actuality beneath his eyes" and hers too, as they watched the disturbing
scenes below from his hotel room window. After the convention ended,
McGrory concluded that the violence was caused by the heavy-handed
tactics of LBJ and Chicago mayor Daley, neither of whom "has a high
degree of trust in his fellow man, and both suffer from a fatal penchant
for over reaction," and in the end "the system which beat Gene McCarthy

may well have beaten itself in the process." McGrory's column again did not appear on its usual first page but on the *Star*'s editorial pages.[10]

In October, the *Star* endorsed Richard Nixon, although it conceded his "qualifications do not come from his charm. He is neither a television matinee idol nor a comforting father figure . . . He lacks charisma." Despite Nixon's shortcomings, the writers concluded he was the best candidate to deal with "the problems and crises that will confront the nation over the next four years." Nixon emerged as the choice of what he labeled the "silent majority." Young *Star* reporters felt far less sanguine about Nixon than did the *Star*'s more senior staff. Bob Walsh, who was a self-identified FDR Democrat, said after retiring from the *Star* in 1970, "Newspaper people in their late twenties or early thirties, from what I see are mostly liberally inclined, and they would tend to support a Democratic candidate for President . . . many are against Nixon almost instinctively." Boris Weintraub and Joy Billington as young reporters were definitely not Nixon fans when they were assigned to cover his inaugural parties in 1969. When Joy was revived by Weintraub after fainting in an overcrowded ballroom, he decided they should "just get the hell out," but the doors were locked. Weintraub described later that "the definition of hell is stuck in a room with 5,000 Richard Nixon supporters celebrating his election and no way to get out." In 1969 the *Star*'s editorial page editor John Cline retired after nearly twenty years in that position as Nixon took office. Smith Hempstone, another Theodore Noyes grandson, became the new editorial page editor. Hempstone was a staunch Cold War–era conservative who supported the Vietnam War to stop the spread of communism. Hempstone had forged a separate career in international affairs studying in Africa and then covering the region for the *Chicago Daily News* before coming to the *Star*. Newby Noyes younger brother Tommy (Thomas E.) joined the editorial board in 1967 and held more leftist views than his two older brothers, according to Newby's son Terry (Newbold Noyes III). By the end of 1969 Haynes Johnson would leave too to work for the *Washington Post*. Johnson began his remarkable career as a novice reporter at the *Star* in 1957. Newby Noyes soon recognized Johnson's hunger and talent for exploring news outside normal boundaries and nurtured that drive. Noyes gave Johnson time off to write books and a separate budget to work on special investigative projects for the paper, ranging from an Alaskan earthquake, impoverished Appalachia, and foreign conflicts. Johnson won a Pulitzer in 1966 for his coverage of civil rights, and by the time he left the *Star*, he was a highly respected journalist. Johnson was grateful for the support and freedom the *Star* provided but by 1968 saw the *Post* as a more dynamic newspaper with a promising future and political opinions more palatable to his own views on the Vietnam War and civil rights. The *Star* and *Post* maintained a tacit agreement not to actively pursue each other's reporters, but as Paul Hope saw it, Bradlee understood "when horseflesh like that comes on the market, you don't turn it down." When Johnson told Newby Noyes he was leaving for the *Post*, Newby was especially furious that he chose the *Post* and told him, "Then I want you to clean your desk out and be out in two hours." The relationship between Haynes Johnson and his mentor Newby Noyes was never mended. Noyes soon hired Jim Doyle, who was then Washington Bureau Chief of the *Boston Globe*.[11]

Mary McGrory characterized the *Star*'s newsroom in the Nixon era as "a boiling caldron of dissent and protest and so forth." Smith Hempstone, as editorial page editor during Nixon's presidency, believed that many on the news staff opposed the paper's position on the Vietnam War. Even Newby Noyes's college-age son Terry Noyes fiercely argued with his father against the war. Terry remembered his father telling him once, "this is the great war of your generation, you're gonna feel terribly left out if you don't go." To Terry and many of his generation this was a very different war than their fathers had fought. On October 15, 1969, antiwar organizers called for a nationwide strike or "Moratorium" on campuses to end the Vietnam War, and Haynes Johnson, just months before leaving the *Star*, wrote that Georgetown students' "solemn and serious" march through the "old city" by candlelight was a "moving spectacle." The *Star*'s editorial that same day, however, concluded, "It is clear that this demonstration is enthusiastically welcomed in Hanoi" and harmful to President Nixon's efforts to end the war for the "silent majority" he represents. Johnson would be gone by the time the May 1970 demonstrations exploded on campuses across the country in the wake of Nixon sending combat troops into Cambodia and Laos to stop the North Vietnamese from using the two countries as a sanctuary for military supplies and personnel. Smith Hempstone said, "A group of perhaps 30 *Star* reporters, headed by Jim Doyle, signed a letter attacking our position in Vietnam" at the time of the Cambodian invasion. The *Star* published the letter but did not change its position in support of the war. On May 5, 1970, four young students were shot and killed at Kent State University when National Guard troops opened fire on student protesters. The *Star*'s editorial concluded "the peace movement needs no martyrs" because "there will be no massive shift of opinion because of the blood spilled on the campus" at Kent State and that "dissent in the street can produce nothing more than violence." In 1970 when Joseph Goulden of the *Washingtonian Magazine* wrote a profile of the *Star*, he asked Newby Noyes about ideological conflicts at the paper. Noyes responded, "Look . . . I know the newsroom is filled with young reporters who are liberal Democrats. Well I'm not, but that's none of their business. All I expect of them is that they do an objective job of reporting." Haynes Johnson said much the same when he told Goulden that he agreed with little on the editorial page, "but what was there didn't affect my work, and not a line was ever changed in a story I wrote because of editorial policy." McGrory said of the editorial page, "it's perfectly dreadful," but she regularly ignored it and wrote whatever suited her. Mary's columns at the time were so antithetical to the opinions of the editorial writers that scores of readers wrote caustic letters to the editor critical of her opposition to the Vietnam War. Mary offered her resignation to Newby Noyes, but he didn't accept it and just told her, "I don't care what you write, just keep writing it for us." Mary and Newby had political differences but remained good friends throughout their lives. McGrory admired Noyes as a "magnificent editor, terrific with a pencil" who, along with his brothers Crosby and Tommy, "could all write" and "could all sing." In fact, Newby's brother Tommy was a Broadway actor in the 1950s before becoming a journalist. Newby once told a newsman of McGrory, "I love her but she constantly is causing me headaches." In 1974 when Newby Noyes resigned as *Star* editor, Mary wrote to apologize for "having screeched at you" too much and to tell him how much she missed him and his guidance. Mary bestowed many praises on her friend Newby in the letter, but the one that best exemplified their mutual respect and admiration was, "I've always been proud you were our editor—even when we disagreed. I was proud that you never changed a word of mine even when you hated what I was saying."[12]

By the late 1960s the respected veteran foreign correspondent and columnist Crosby Noyes was making annual trips to hotspots around the world to help him write his foreign affairs column. A week before the Moratorium began, Noyes wrote from Saigon on October 7, 1969, that "even skeptics . . . agree that things are coming under control" by the South Vietnamese government and there is "mass participation in the political life of the country " According to Henry S. Bradsher, the *Star*'s longest-serving Asian correspondent, the South Vietnamese government considered the paper a strong supporter due in large part to Noyes's positive columns about their government and its policies. Bradsher had worked in New Delhi and then Moscow for the Associated Press before coming to the *Star*. Bradsher sometimes accompanied Noyes on his annual world trips, and once sat in on an interview with South Vietnamese president Nguyen Van Thieu, which Bradsher thought "produced little hard news." Bradsher later said, "I never thought I had any special access because of the *Star*" to the South Vietnamese government and besides, "my role was not to express opinions—supportive or otherwise."* In any case, Bradsher found political figures in Saigon relatively easy to access, plus he developed his own key sources such as the US ambassador to Vietnam Ellsworth Bunker and US Information Agency head

Barry Zorthian, both of whom he had known while working at the AP's New Delhi Bureau. Bradsher also developed friendships with the "Voice of America People" who "would tip me off on things they were hearing." Zorthian ran press briefings for Saigon reporters they sarcastically dubbed the "five o'clock follies." By the time Bradsher began visiting Vietnam regularly, he found "the briefings had developed into contentious affairs, often confrontations between briefers and skeptical reporters." Reporters "were all skeptical about the assertions the military was claiming . . . everything was going well, and getting better and so forth . . . I was skeptical too," recalled Bradsher. Bradsher's part-time translator and guide, Hoang Ngoc Nguyen, whom he hired on his first visit to Saigon, became a trusted friend and valuable link for introductions to the Buddhists and student leftists who opposed the Catholic-oriented government, although Nguyen was not a leftist himself.[13]

Henry Bradsher's predecessor Don (Donald) Kirk had worked for the *Star* since 1967 and was still overseas when Bradsher was hired. Don Kirk had reported for newspapers in the states, held a masters in International Relations from the University of Chicago, and at age twenty-nine had been a Fulbright Scholar at the Indian School of International Studies in New Delhi when the *Star* hired him. Kirk and his wife had an apartment in Hong Kong, but he spent most of his time reporting from Saigon in the field, especially during the Tet Offensive in 1968 when the Viet Cong conducted one of the deadliest campaigns in which they overtook villages and cities throughout South Vietnam. In the wake of Tet even the esteemed broadcaster Walter Cronkite expressed grave doubts the US military could ever defeat the North Vietnamese. President Nixon began the first of a series of troop withdrawals in 1969 and began placing greater reliance on South Vietnamese forces to fight the war (aka "Vietnamization"). *Star* editors saw Nixon's foreign policy focus moving to Communist China as an emerging power in Cold War politics. The *Star* invited Bradsher to one of its famous luncheons to share his views on the Soviet Union after he served as AP's Moscow Bureau Chief. Newby Noyes took the opportunity to tell the very tall and lanky, thirty-something, dark-haired Bradsher, who towered over the editor, that the paper was looking for a new Asian correspondent. Bradsher at the time was studying China as a Neiman Fellow at Harvard and was frustrated with the AP's empty promises for a new overseas assignment. When Newby Noyes offered Bradsher the job as its Asian correspondent with a primary focus on China and occasional reporting trips to Vietnam and Laos as needed, he jumped at the chance. Bradsher wanted to "put the bigger picture together" by analyzing the politics and economics of each country rather than just covering "the day-to-day stories" in Vietnam. Don Kirk had written those kinds of stories, but Bradsher judged the public got news on the battlefront from nightly newscasts, the wire services, and other papers and he wanted to write more in-depth articles about the region. Don Kirk was offered a job in the *Star*'s newsroom, but he chose to stay in Asia to write a book and freelance.[14]

Bradsher arrived in Hong Kong with his family in December 1969, and within a month his editor, Burt Hoffman, sent him to Saigon on the anniversary of the Tet Offensive in January 1970. Saigon looked very different from the city Bradsher had first seen in 1962 while at the AP. There were no more outdoor cafes and quiet streets but bombed-out buildings and Saigon residents constantly rushing around the city precariously perched on speeding motorbikes. Bradsher got his press credentials and visited his old colleagues Peter Arnett and Malcolm Browne at the AP bureau near the shelled-out old French governor's palace. Over the next five years Bradsher would visit the AP Bureau daily when in Saigon. On that first visit Bradsher learned how easy the military made it for the press to go into the field—just sign up in downtown Saigon the night before for a helicopter or transport plane flight headed for a military base and show up on time the next morning. So Bradsher hitched a ride on a helicopter to Bangkok, Thailand, and then onto Vientiane, Laos, where he met Scotsman Tammy Arbuckle, a stringer for the *Star*, who was "quite a character . . . a very daring reporter" who "went into areas that were pretty tough and nasty" and "one of the best stringers in Vientiane, Laos but not very organized," recalled Bradsher. Bradsher discovered Tammy knew the "ways of the Pathet Lao" and "had cultivated relations with CIA people" who ran the war at a compound outside Vientiane. Bradsher, however, found nothing during his visit to report to Hoffman about a new North Vietnamese offensive. The next time Bradsher visited Vietnam in May 1970, twelve thousand US troops were conducting an offensive into neighboring Cambodia to destroy North Vietnamese sanctuaries of weapons and supply caches. Bradsher was in Pakistan when Hoffman called him to cover the fighting. Bradsher traveled with the US 11th Air Calvary Division in early May behind armored personnel carriers and truckloads of soldiers with other reporters along Cambodian Route 7 into Snoul north of the Fishhook area Nixon designated for searches. Bradsher hitched rides or hiked to interview soldiers and their officers in the field, like the Battalion commander James L. Anderson at Firebase Terri Lynn, named after Anderson's nine-year-old daughter back in Ohio. Anderson told Bradsher that the battalion had found a communist base camp with supply caches and "enough mess halls to feed more than 2,000 men at a time." Bradsher's report would be on the front page of the *Star*'s May 5, 1970, edition next to the tragic news and images of five students killed at Kent State during antiwar protests. After two days in the field, Bradsher caught a military plane back to Saigon to file his dispatches, and the next day he discovered that the 11th Armored Cavalry Regiment with which he had just traveled had been attacked the previous night. Bradsher recalled later "hitchhiking back from such places like Danang could get a little dicey, but I never got stuck when trying to get back to Saigon to send my report." Bradsher saw his reporting from the battlefield as the exception while his interpretive summaries of Vietnamese politics and economics as his usual and preferred topic. Bradsher experienced some danger, like the time he dodged incoming fire at a fire base but Bradsher downplayed these incidents as minor mishaps compared to colleagues and friends who experienced much worse danger or lost their lives.[15]

In the spring of 1971 one of the largest and most confrontational antiwar demonstrations took place in Washington over three days. Protesters nearly shut down the city, and more arrests occurred during the May Day demonstration in 1971 than in any other day in US history. Young *Star* beat reporters like Lance Gay, Duncan Spencer, and Angus Phillips and photographers Bernie Boston, Brig Gabe, and Kenneth Heinen were among those on the street covering the news. Angus Phillips, with long hair and a full beard, was even mistakenly arrested while observing the demonstrations. The week before Vietnam War veterans had demonstrated en masse for the first time against the war. The front page of the *Star*'s April 23, 1971, edition carried a powerful photograph of a "tall scraggy Vietnam war veteran [who] shouted before he flung his presidential citation, Purple Heart and Bronze *Star* that had become symbols of dishonor, shame and inhumanity" clanging onto the Capitol steps. He was first in a line of many that day. Opposition in the media and on the streets to America's involvement in the Vietnam War was at a crescendo. A month later the *New York Times* on June 13 began publishing excerpts from the Pentagon Papers, a classified report commissioned by former defense secretary Robert McNamara to examine the history of US involvement in Vietnam. The study by defense analysts revealed that presidents from Truman to Johnson had hidden from the American people its deep misgivings about ever winning the war and the rampant corruption and unpopularity of the South Vietnamese government with the Vietnamese people. Despite those doubts, the US military continued to escalate the war and cost the lives of scores of Americans and Vietnamese in the hope of containing communism in Southeast Asia and, if not winning, then at least "not losing face" among nations. The *Times* received the Pentagon Papers from Daniel Ellsberg, who helped write the Papers. By the late 1960s Ellsberg had switched from supporting to opposing the war. Just days after the *Times* published the documents from the study, the *Washington Post* too began publishing sections of it and was followed by another fifteen or so newspapers, but never the *Star*. Ellsberg initially approached sympathetic members of Congress, but when they refused to help, he chose the *Times* and then the *Post*, most likely because their editorial pages opposed Nixon's policies in Southeast Asia and he saw them as willing partners in making the findings public. Although Ellsberg shut the *Star* out, Ron Sarro focused on Congressman Pete (Paul Norton) McCloskey's disclosure of about six hundred pages of documents Ellsberg gave McCloskey as part of the much larger study. McCloskey, a decorated Marine Corps veteran, was a California Republican and outspoken opponent of the Vietnam War. Sarro wrote articles about McCloskey's revelations in the documents and the congressman's efforts to persuade Congress to look into the study's findings and call Ellsberg to testify. Sarro would later cover Ellsberg's speech to Congress. Among the most damning findings in the papers Sarro reported was that "the United States 'encouraged, authorized, aided and abetted' the overthrow of South Vietnamese President Ngo Dinh Diem" in 1963 despite Robert Kennedy's doubts about the coup. Court reporter Lyle Denniston thoroughly covered the Pentagon Papers case until the Supreme court ruled in favor of the *Times* and *Post*. After the ruling, the *Star* in an editorial agreed that "no newspaper should have to run the risk of harassment, intimidation or persecution for its opposition to official policy," nevertheless, a "newspaper should be held accountable for breaches of national security with the possibility of fines and jail sentences." Yet the *Star* agreed no such breach had actually occurred in the Pentagon Papers case. Nothing in the Papers, however, changed the *Star*'s support for Nixon's policy on the Vietnam War on its opinion pages. The 1972 presidential campaign again would largely be a referendum on the Vietnam War and racial politics as it was in the last election, but now in an even more sharply divided American electorate.[16]

In 1972 George Wallace, who had declared "segregation now, segregation tomorrow, and segregation forever," in 1963 as Alabama governor, made his third run for president and his second attempt to be the Democratic Party candidate. Some in Nixon's so-called silent majority preferred Wallace to Nixon because of his tough stand on race in America. State editor Ludy Werner Forbes was on the desk the afternoon of May 15, 1972, when a call came in that Wallace, who was campaigning in Maryland, had been shot during a rally in Laurel, Maryland, just outside Washington. Ludy was exasperated because the *Star* had chosen not to cover that particular Wallace campaign event. She immediately dispatched Prince George's County, Maryland, reporter Bill Taft to check out the story. Meanwhile, when Ron Sarro learned Wallace was shot and had been taken to Holy Cross Hospital in Silver Spring, Maryland, he went to the hospital where his wife, Mary, was a shock trauma nurse in charge of the emergency room. The *Star*'s presses were holding the late edition for a headline until they knew for sure about Wallace's condition. Sarro briefly met with his wife and asked her one question, "Was he going to live or die?" Sarro called Newby Noyes, who was waiting in the *Star*'s newsroom with reporters, editors, typographers, printers, pressmen, and other staff to get word from Sarro, when he spoke one word to Noyes, *live*, and the presses began rolling. Wallace even won the Maryland Democratic primary but was confined to a wheelchair with a dramatically diminished political career for the rest of his life. Wallace was in a crowded slate of candidates in 1972 campaigning for the nomination of a Democratic Party in disarray running against a sitting president that was popular with a majority of Americans. George McGovern was nominated at the Democratic Party convention in Miami, but the drama there centered more on reforms to the party than with McGovern's nomination. Duncan Spencer canvassed delegates pushing the reforms and got mixed reviews from "kids [who] gave us the benefit of their inexperience" to others who complained that delegates were more concerned with reform than winning. Paul Hope, who covered McGovern's campaign that year, thought the candidate was so far left and the party so far in shambles that McGovern had no chance of winning the election. Hope was right. Nixon won in a landslide election, and for the second time the *Star* had endorsed him.[17]

In February 1972 President Nixon made a groundbreaking trip to Communist Red China. The *Star* chose Henry Bradsher to cover Nixon's visit, who thought maybe the regular White House correspondents were a little "peeved." Bradsher's strong interest and study of China coupled with his understanding of Marxist systems while working as AP's Moscow Bureau Chief showed in his perceptive analyses of the hidden power struggles in Beijing at the time of the Cultural Revolution. In the spring of 1974 Bradsher learned just how much his perceptive reporting angered the Chinese when its foreign ministry's press office gave his fellow journalists this message to pass along, "Journalists are a despicable bunch and Bradsher is the most despicable of them all. He will never be allowed to visit China again." But in 1972 Bradsher was not yet banned and the *Star* arranged for him to fly to Guam and then onto Beijing on *Air Force One* with Nixon—not the chartered press plane. The press corps was "herded along from one place to another," remembered Bradsher, and they all stayed in the same small hotel and received regular briefings in a makeshift press room. The press was allowed to attend the Great Banquet where they saw Chou En-lai, but the news was largely "second hand," recalled Bradsher. President Nixon's historic trip to China was a major foreign policy success and greatly enhanced his image with voters before the 1972 election. The president's foreign affairs adviser Henry

Kissinger hoped to add to Nixon's vote margins by negotiating peace in Paris to end US military involvement in Vietnam before election day. On October 26 the *Star* reported, like many other papers, that Kissinger had declared that "peace is at hand" in Paris between the warring parties. Bradsher reported from Saigon that South Vietnamese president Nguyen Van Thieu "told a demonstration of government officials today that any peace agreement lacking his signature is invalid." The South Vietnamese government strongly objected to terms in the agreement not requiring the North's troops to withdraw, eliminating nearly all US military aid, and imposing an outside organization to oversee new elections. Kissinger was "pretty mad," according to Bradsher, and called Newby Noyes to ask that he either bury or, better yet, not print Bradsher's story fearing it could undermine Kissinger's statement that peace was imminent in Vietnam. Bradsher said Noyes "stood up for me" as he had before on other controversial stories, and the story appeared on the front page the next day. Denis Horgan, who was foreign editor at the time, remembered "essentially they told him [Kissinger] . . . we will take that into consideration and have a nice day. They weren't going to get pushed around by this season's blowhard in the White House," and maybe top *Star* editors were uncomfortable with it "because they could do things to you, it was a different time" but "we always felt that they would stand by us." Despite the conflict between Kissinger and the *Star*, the Nixon White House considered the *Star*'s op-ed pages overall pretty friendly to him at that point.[18]

Just days before the 1972 election, President Nixon wrote Newby Noyes, "I want you to know how much your thoughtful and perceptive editorials have meant to me over the last four years." The *Star* endorsed Nixon in 1968 and again in 1972. *Star* editor Newby Noyes's admiration for Nixon stretched back to when he was a young reporter in the early 1950s covering the Alger Hiss trial. Ironically, one of Noyes's closest friends was Mary McGrory, who had strongly disliked Nixon almost as long as Noyes had admired him. In 1962 McGrory famously wrote a blistering account of Nixon's behavior when he addressed reporters after he lost his run for California governor. McGrory sketched Nixon's dark side, writing, "he stood there with hands jammed in his pockets" and spoke for seventeen minutes "in a finale of intemperance and incoherence perhaps unmatched in American political annals" in a voice "curling with rage and scorn" every time he mentioned the press. McGrory's piece brought her lots of both praise and scorn from the public. The journalism profession, however, judged it excellent enough to give her the George Polk Award for national reporting in 1962, singling out her comments on Nixon's farewell. In July 1970 the *Star* invited Nixon to one of its luncheons to celebrate Gould Lincoln's ninetieth birthday. Nixon's press secretary, Ron Ziegler, suggested that the lunch be limited to the all-male editorial board and referred to it as "stag." Women reporters sent protest telegrams to the White House, including one signed by some *Star* female reporters, for excluding women. McGrory did not sign any of the telegrams, but neither did she give Nixon a warm welcome. After the luncheon, Newby Noyes led Nixon on a tour of the newsroom where *Star* staff greeted the president with handshakes and smiles. McGrory continued to type away at her desk in the back of the newsroom until Noyes took Nixon to her desk. The conversation between the two was laced with tense jibes. McGrory would later learn she had been on Nixon's official enemies list. It is a testament to Newby Noyes's diplomacy and good humor that he remained friends with two sworn enemies for many years. Noyes and McGrory remained friends throughout his life, but Noyes's admiration and respect for Nixon began to dim after his reelection.[19]

On December 18, 1972, Nixon ordered B-52 pilots to begin around-the-clock heavy bombardment of North Vietnam in hopes of getting the communist leadership back to the negotiating table. The bombing resulted in devastating not only military targets but also the North Vietnamese civilian population. Sometime in late December 1972, Daniel Patrick Moynihan called to thank Newby Noyes for the *Star*'s recent positive editorial on his appointment as ambassador to India. Their conversation was soon dominated by Noyes's anger over the heaviest bombing in North Vietnam since the war began. When Moynihan wrote to Nixon expressing his own opposition to the bombing, he mentioned that Noyes had told him that "they had had it at the *Star*" and "were turning against the administration on the issue of the war." Two days after the bombing began on December 18, a *Star* editorial called it a "regrettable and dangerous step" despite the Nixon administration's understandable frustration with North Vietnam's "maddening negotiating tactics." When the White House called for a pause in the bombing and renewed peace negotiations, the *Star* editorialized, "Mr. Nixon must inevitably—and soon—reach a conclusion that the time had come when this slaughter of civilians had to stop" and "begin anew the search for an end to a cruel war which has cost all those involved in it so dearly." At the time many condemned the bombing, including religious leaders, scientists, European countries, and a Democratic Party–controlled Congress that threatened to cut off funding if the war continued. Still, for Noyes and the *Star* it was a significant reversal of past support for Nixon. Conservative columnists in the *Star*, like Gould Lincoln, David Lawrence, and Noyes's cousin and columnist Smith Hempstone, remained steadfast in their support of Nixon and the Vietnam War. A heavily edited, handwritten, and undated draft editorial found in Newby Noyes's personal papers that was never published reveals the heart of his opposition to the policy. It read: "If we cannot bring ourselves to extend this happy New Year pause, are we perhaps finally

. . . hooked irrevocably on a commitment to bomb North Vietnam to extinction? Is that an acceptable solution to our dilemma? Can we—can the world live with it?" On January 27, 1973, *Star* foreign correspondent Andrew Borowiec's dramatic front-page headline from Paris read "Cease-Fire Begins in Vietnam at 7 P.M." as a direct result of peace accords signed in two separate ceremonies that he wrote "were an anticlimax to years of dying, torment and bitter negotiations." US prisoners of war and combat troops in Vietnam began coming home as a result. A violent civil war in this small Southeast Asian country was far from over, though. Henry Bradsher reported in November 1974 on the "increasingly chaotic and violent political situation" by a "corrupt government" in Saigon. Bradsher later characterized his reporting in 1974 as "very downbeat" and "very skeptical that any of these countries"—Vietnam, Cambodia, Laos—would survive without US help. The *Star* called Bradsher back to Washington from Hong Kong in December 1974 as Newby Noyes prepared to depart, Jim Bellows arrived, and Allbritton became the *Star*'s publisher. As the North Vietnam army moved closer to Saigon, Bradsher asked his editors for permission to go to Saigon to cover its fall because "I thought that was a story that needed to be covered first-hand and their attitude was that it could be covered out of the Department of Defense . . . they didn't feel it was worth sending me." Nixon's historic trip to China, the signing of the Anti-Ballistic Missile Treaty with the Soviet Union, and the end of US military involvement in the Vietnam War during his second term were major foreign policy achievements. Those achievements, however, would be overshadowed by a scandal in the Nixon White House that began germinating the previous summer after news of a break-in at the Democratic National Committee (DNC) headquarters at the Watergate building was reported in the two local Washington dailies.[20]

On Saturday, June 17, 1972, Barbara Cohen arrived at the city desk around 5:30 am and as usual called the police reporter Gus Constantine first thing. Constantine rattled off a string of arrests until one got her attention—four burglars who were arrested at 2:30 that morning for breaking into the DNC headquarters offices. Barbara's first thought was who would be dumb enough to burglarize the cash-strapped DNC. By the time Cohen left at the end of her shift that afternoon, she was pretty excited about how far the story might go. That night Barbara and her husband at the time, Richard Cohen, invited Carl Bernstein, their friend and Richard's colleague at the *Post*, to dinner. Barbara would later divorce Richard, and after marrying again she has been Barbara Cochran for the last twenty-five years of her personal and professional life. Barbara, Richard, and Carl talked about the Watergate break-in story over dinner, and as Barbara later recalled, she and Carl, "both of us start saying 'this goes right to the White House; we know this goes right to the White House,'" but Richard was very skeptical that Nixon would take such a risk. The next day AP reported one of the men arrested was James McCord, who was the security coordinator for the Committee to Reelect the President (CRP). *Star* reporter Bob Walters perused public records, talked to James McCord's neighbors in suburban Maryland as well as DNC and CRP officials, and wrote a thorough report on McCord but revealed little beyond what the public already knew. Experienced *Star* political reporters like Fred Barnes, Paul Hope, Dana Bullen, Ron Sarro, and others, reported on the break-in's implications for a while, but most senior editorial staff moved on to other stories. In June, *Star* management was distracted by the final negotiations to purchase the afternoon *Washington Daily News* in hopes of attracting its 200,000 readers to the *Star*. That summer editors incorporated *Daily News* staff into the newsroom, including Joe Volz and Pat Collins. Volz, at forty, had covered organized crime in D.C., and Collins at twenty was a young crime reporter who had covered Watergate a little at the *Daily News*. Volz and Collins got the Watergate break-in story because they had gumshoe experience investigating crime stories. As Volz later said, "What surprised both Pat and me was we were given the story right away, my God all these *Star* reporters; why did they give us the story? . . . Bob Walters, Fred Barnes were more experienced reporters and they had covered it a little bit but they didn't want to touch it." Volz tried to interview the Watergate burglars' first lawyer Doug Caddy but could not even get him to open the door to his P Street apartment. Volz also went to G. Gordon Liddy's home in Oxon Hill, Maryland, but instead ended up talking to a *Star* paper boy about Liddy. Bob Woodward later called Volz asking him if was trying to pay off the kid to spy on him. When Hurricane Agnes caused major damage in Pennsylvania in late June, managing editor Charlie Seib pulled Volz off the break-in story and sent him to cover the aftermath of the storm. Collins was alone on the story for a while, but then he went off to army reserve camp. In early August, Woodward and Bernstein broke their first big exclusive that directly connected a $25,000 campaign check from CRP official Kenneth Dahlberg, Nixon's Midwest campaign chair, to a Miami bank account of a Watergate burglar. Lyle Denniston, world editor at the time, called Volz back to cover Watergate, but metropolitan editor Scott Smith thought Collins could make better use of his time covering crime. Smith lost his argument this time, and Volz and Collins became a team again for a while but without much enthusiasm from Seib. Volz and Collins visited Hugh Sloan, CRP's treasurer, on a number of occasions at his home, but he revealed nothing about the source of the $25,000 campaign donation. When the two reporters asked Sloan if his recent resignation from CRP was connected to the FBI's investigation of the break-in, he claimed he left for "purely personal reasons"—his wife was expecting their first child in a month and needed him home. They viewed his answer as specious since she was still working at the White House.[21]

Volz saw Watergate as one of the biggest stories in the country in the summer of 1972 and was puzzled that few *Star* editors and reporters showed any interest. The scuttlebutt in the newsroom was the *Star* just didn't have the money to pursue it like the *Post*. Volz said he and Collins "laughed at the second-newspaper mentality because" to them "it was the best story going!" Barbara Cohen, who was principal assistant national news editor by August, believed experienced reporters on the national desk were uninterested in the story because they thought "why would Nixon, who was so far ahead, do something like this?" but reporters on the city desk were more suspicious and convinced Watergate was a potentially big story. Volz believed the *Star* "had nobody like Bradlee" among its top editors, and both Volz and Cohen agreed that most top *Star* editors thought Watergate was just a crime story. Denis Horgan, who moved to the national desk in 1972 to be Cohen's deputy, later said that although the *Star*'s leadership was conservative, at "no point did he or anyone . . . interfere with the coverage, or tone it down . . . they may not have encouraged it in a dramatic way but they didn't get in the way . . . we just never got the handle on the thing." Volz and Collins got help from a few national desk staff like Jim Polk, who helped them investigate campaign finance violations, and Jerry O'Leary, who had excellent FBI contacts. In fact, Polk's stories about the Securities and Exchange Commission's fraud and campaign finance violations case against millionaire Robert Vesco, a major campaign contributor to Nixon, earned him a Pulitzer for National Reporting in 1974. Jerry O'Leary looked into the Latin American angle since many of the burglars had connections to Cuba and wrote a few interesting side stories, but nothing key to the scandal. O'Leary's FBI contacts paled in comparison to the *Post*'s "Deep Throat," later revealed as Mark Felt. Volz knew Mark Felt, but Felt chose Woodward, not him, to tell his secrets. Volz and Collins instead got a lot of leaks from the CRP's spokesperson DeVan L. Shumway, who steered them wrong every time. The White House once used the *Star* to leak a false story published in its July 7, 1972, edition implying that the burglary may have been funded by a right-wing group of anti-Castro Cubans.[22]

After the Watergate burglars were indicted in mid-September, Seib went on vacation and returned Collins to the city desk because he thought the story was winding down and only one reporter was needed until the trial began in January. Then on September 29, Woodward and Bernstein reported that "reliable sources" revealed that former attorney general John Mitchell controlled a secret fund of cash that high-level CRP officials used to fund secret intelligence against the DNC. Volz and Collins were reunited and spent many frustrating days that fall covering the Watergate scandal. The *Star* was never able to confirm the link between Mitchell and the fund. After the *Post* story revealed Mitchell's secret fund, Volz protested to Shumway, "Don't you feel bad about week after week misleading us?" Lyle Denniston, a veteran political and court reporter, was frustrated that the *Star* was not breaking any stories about Watergate and used a little reverse psychology on "his tired team" in a meeting when he speculated that if Volz and Collins couldn't confirm facts on their own, "We'll have to run stories quoting the *Post*," which any good reporter saw as "the highest possible journalistic heresy," according to Volz. The *Post* broke another explosive story in early October—FBI investigators found Republican Party staff tried to recruit operatives with payments from Mitchell's secret fund to conduct "dirty tricks" to sabotage Democratic Party candidates and singled out Donald H. Segretti as a particularly ambitious recruiter. Collins and Volz pursued a separate lead about a former FBI agent named Lou Russell, who had worked for Nixon periodically over the years. At the time of the break-in, Russell worked security at the Watergate complex and was also employed by James McCord to run security checks on CRP staff. The two reporters interviewed Russell, who was at the Howard Johnson's across the street from the Watergate the night of the break-in. They wrote an interesting story about Russell, but neither the reporters nor the FBI could definitively connect him to the burglary. When the wire services picked up the story, their headline was "Lou Russell Linked to the Break-In," which Volz said "we specifically did not say." The *Star* and both reporters were sued for the mistake, but the judge blamed the wire services and dismissed the case. *Star* editor David Kraslow grew increasingly "edgy" about the *Post* beating the *Star* almost daily on the Watergate story. Kraslow, a fine investigative reporter himself, came to the *Star* in 1972 as an assistant managing editor after he was fired as the *Los Angeles Times* Washington Bureau Chief during a power struggle at the *Times*. Exasperated for a scoop, Kraslow sent Volz to California to track down Segretti to interview him or at least find another angle on the story. Volz never found Segretti and instead settled for an interview with his college roommate Larry Young, but the story was mostly just a rehash of what the *Post* had written. Denis Horgan, looking back on Watergate, said of the *Star*'s coverage, "It wasn't like we were just buffing our nails. . . . the sad piece is that the *Post* did so very well that everyone else appeared to have done nothing which wasn't the case. We tried but we simply just weren't able to do it."[23]

Ben Bradlee years later said the *Post*'s coverage of Watergate "felt lonely" until near the end of October 1972 when other newspaper editors began to take the story more seriously. Volz took issue with some of Bradlee's assessment, calling it "overly dramatic . . . they weren't alone" in those first few months. Volz saw lots of papers struggling to get the story, but "once October came along and they got inside the White House, they were alone because nobody else could match 'em." By October, Volz and Collins were working ten-to-twelve-hour days exclusively on the Watergate story, but with little additional help. Volz judged they needed a "staff of ten reporters, at least" and about five researchers to phone Capitol Hill and CRP staff, but the *Star* was struggling financially. The two reporters unsuccessfully attempted to get leads from *Star* staff. For example, *Star* society columnist Isola McClendon knew Martha Mitchell and Barbara Cohen, who along with her husband, Richard Cohen, at the *Post*, were friendly with their young bachelor friend Carl Bernstein. Neither offered any help. Senior White House correspondent Jack Horner was their biggest roadblock. Volz found that Horner didn't believe anything the *Post* was reporting, refused to help them, and was far too close to the president to be objective in any case. Nixon granted Horner an exclusive interview after his reelection, but with so many restrictions from the White House, it was borderline propaganda. When *Newsweek* asked Horner if he thought he was being singled out for privileges by the president above other reporters, Horner admitted, "I am . . . it's a very pleasant thing." Horner boasted he wasn't like "activist members of his profession" who "give the impression that they know more about running the country . . . I would not be interested in reading what some reporter thinks," which *Newsweek* concluded is the kind of reporter Nixon preferred. The *Star*'s pro-Nixon reputation strongly mitigated against Volz and Collins cultivating sources or leads, and top editors mostly agreed with Nixon's press secretary Ron Zeigler's line that Watergate was "just a third-rate burglary." Still Volz never felt any pressure from anyone at the *Star* to drop the story. He just thought some editors, particularly Seib, "didn't know what to do with it." Volz was convinced Watergate was really a police investigation that required a number of hard-driving reporters to "get down and dirty . . . go out in the street and talk to people." As Volz reflected later, "You can't imagine [David] Broder going to some girl's house at 9:00 o'clock at night" to coax out information from her, despite him being an excellent political reporter at the *Post*. Woodward and Bernstein, however, were not shy about making a lot of light night house calls. Volz and Collins did too, but no one inside the CRP was willing to give them information. By December, Seib threatened to fire Volz because "he hadn't gotten the story." Volz agreed with Seib, telling him, "You damn right Charlie, and neither have 2,000 other people in the country. I've gotten more exclusives than any other reporter except for Woodward and Bernstein but I didn't get these big stories." Volz was disappointed in himself and admitted to Seib, "This is the first time . . . where I tried so hard and I got whipped by a couple of other guys." Kraslow came to Volz's defense and Seib backed down, but within three months Volz left when he was offered a job with the *New York Daily News*.[24]

In February 1973, Volz, Collins, O'Leary, and Polk were subpoenaed to testify along with Woodward and Bernstein, Katharine Graham, and other reporters and editors at the *Washington Post*, the *New York Times*, and *Time* in connection with a libel case brought by Maurice Stans, finance chair for the CRP, against Democratic Party officials. In an effort to find libelous statements from DNC officials, the CRP requested reporters who covered Watergate to turn over their notes, which to everyone in the *Star*'s newsroom elicited lots of laughs because Volz and Collins didn't have any. Collins and Volz loved getting the subpoenas, but according to Volz, Newby Noyes thought if Katharine Graham was undeterred by threats of jail, "he would go to the slammer too." The two protested: "If anybody goes to prison it's gonna be us . . . I mean that's the ultimate tribute . . . the President wanting to throw you in jail." No one went to jail or produced any notes because in short order Judge Charles Richey dismissed the subpoenas for all ten journalists based on their "qualified privilege." By April 1973 four senior White House staff resigned as a result of the Watergate scandal, and in May the Senate Watergate Committee began its televised hearings. As Watergate was fought out publicly in the courts and in Congress, political reporters on the *Star*'s national news desk took charge of the coverage. Norman Kempster and Robert Walters reported on the Nixon White House response to Watergate press coverage; Ron Sarro and Shirley Elder wrote about the House Judiciary Committee's work; Lyle Denniston, Jim Doyle, Barry Kalb, Walter Taylor, and Martha Angle covered the televised Watergate hearings and court cases. Around this time Noyes hired Jack Germond, an astute veteran political reporter and Bureau chief with Gannett News for twenty years, as the *Star*'s new chief political reporter after Noyes asked the paper's longtime chief political reporter Paul Hope to write for the editorial page and regularly contribute to its "Washington Close-Up" column. Germond claims he convinced Noyes and others he could match the *Post*'s David Broder. Jack Horner, who had been the *Star*'s senior White House reporter for years and was close to Nixon, retired from the *Star* in March 1974.[25]

Mary McGrory went to the Watergate hearings every day and took notes about the dominant personalities and the most interesting things said. Although she spoke with her editor John Cassady daily, she received little direction from him or others, and the editing was very light. Most *Star* editors just watched the hearings on TV, she later recalled. In 1975 McGrory won a Pulitzer for "her trenchant commentary spread over more than 20 years as a reporter" and in particular her columns on Nixon's "fall and ultimate disgrace." Mary was thrilled when she learned she was on Nixon's "enemies list." Art Buchwald was jealous he did not make the list but still took McGrory to the Sans Souci, a popular French restaurant in Washington, to celebrate, where she received a standing ovation from friends and colleagues. McGrory wrote an open letter to Charles Colson on July 1, 1973, in the *Star*, thanking him with a heavy dose of sarcasm for making her "an 'enemy' of the people" when "all these years I thought you didn't care." Mary also begged for a subpoena like the "four other *Star* reporters" who "were insufferable, posturing around here about being martyrs for the free press." Still, she congratulated Colson for fooling her for so long but was relieved to now know who orchestrated her repeated IRS audits, the phone taps, and the thefts of her apartment.[26]

The *Post*'s groundbreaking reporting of Watergate that brought down a president made it a national celebrity. Across town the *Star* was struggling just to survive as the only remaining daily newspaper in the city. In order to save the *Star* from sinking under its debts, the Kauffmann, Noyes, and Adams families, who had owned the paper for more than one hundred years, began negotiating the sale of the paper to millionaire Texan Joseph Allbritton in 1974. It was a difficult time for Newby Noyes as he saw the newspaper his ancestors had worked so hard to make an enormous success and a highly respected newspaper in the city decline so far under his watch. In addition, in Noyes's last year as *Star* editor, he saw President Nixon, a man he once admired and considered a friend, fall into disgrace. According to the *Star*'s editorial page editor Smith Hempstone, the paper backed Nixon throughout the Watergate scandal until the twenty-one-minute gap in the Watergate tapes emerged. Upon Nixon's resignation, the *Star* editorialized "there is a sick strain in this man's character that poisoned the atmosphere of his White House" and "for any man, the difference between victory and defeat can be the breadth of an eyelash. . . . The lesson is humility which Nixon never learned." Noyes's character was the antithesis of Nixon's. Despite Noyes's anxieties and disappointments at a difficult time, he showed the kind of generosity, graciousness, and fairness that epitomized the integrity he showed throughout his life. The Pulitzer Prize jurors did not recommend Woodward and Bernstein or the *Post* for a Pulitzer for its Watergate coverage in 1973. The Pulitzer advisory board had the authority to override the decision of the jurors, but Ben Bradlee, who was on the board, kept silent when he heard the news, even though he was furious. As Bradlee entered the Columbia Journalism School Library for the advisory meeting, Newby Noyes and Scotty Reston of the *New York Times* told him they were going to override the jurors and award the *Post* the Pulitzer's Public Service Award, because as Noyes told him, "You damned well deserve it." In July 1974 Bradlee wrote to Noyes as the *Star* was slowing slipping away from him:

> I have thought often of what must be your anguish in the last few months .
> . . it must seem to you—as it seems to me—unfathomably unfair that virtue
> is not always its own reward; that your virtues—fairness, decency, compas-
> sion and commitment and more . . . have not rewarded you with at least the
> solvent permanency enjoyed by so many who can't hold your socks. You
> have been rewarded with the great respect and affection of your peers and
> your friends, including this one.

The loss of the *Star*, according to his Newby's son Terry Noyes, was a tragedy his father never quite got over and saw as a personal failure. Closer inspection of the *Star*'s history, however, shows business decisions made long before Newby Noyes became editor were the foundation of the *Star*'s demise. After the families sold the *Star*, the new owners tried to correct the paper's downward spiral, but they too would fail. The story of the *Star*'s long demise from one of the most financially successful newspapers in the country to abject bankruptcy is a heartbreaking but necessary story to tell.[27]

9

+

The Long Demise

Newbold Noyes Sr., grandson of patriarch Crosby Noyes, recalls that as a boy of six in the first decade of the twentieth century he spent many idyllic summers with his siblings, cousins, parents, aunts, and uncles at Alton Farm, the Noyes summer estate in Silver Spring, Maryland, near Washington. "From a small boy's viewpoint there was a splendid stream, along the banks of which cows grazed, and where one could wade and catch tadpoles and minnows. . . . All of the grandchildren who spent summers there always will remember our life there." Crosby Noyes originally purchased one hundred acres of farmland in 1882 and expanded a modest house to a gracious three-story Queen Anne–style mansion. Newbold's cousin Ruth as an adult described the house as having "a sixteen foot wide veranda," a "tremendous hallway with a huge fireplace and ceiling of giant height . . . flanked by a 30 foot x 40 foot living room on one side, a library and study on the other," and a dining room that could seat as many as thirty people. Distinguished friends and guests such as President Theodore Roosevelt came for weekend picnics, parties at the mansion, and horseback riding. Newbold Noyes, who was lucky enough to have known his venerable grandfather as a young boy, captured the love and esteem all Noyes descendants must have felt for their beloved patriarch when he wrote of that time:

> My grandfather used to tell me stories in the evening before bedtime, in his study behind the library. The room was lined with books. There was a green shaded reading lamp upon the desk beside where he used to sit. He seemed tremendous to me in his specially upholstered lounge chair as I sat in a small

chair beside him. In fact, he was not a very large man. There was, however, no question as to his almost superhuman qualities in my eyes. . . . For years after we last sat there in his study together I boasted to all who would listen that Crosby Noyes was the loudest, most forceful and most virile sneezer in all the world. It is the sober truth that when I was six or seven years old and he was some seventy years of age he could and did extinguish the green-shaded lamp when he sneezed in the midst of our story-telling. After such a cataclysmic explosion we would sit together in the darkness while he quietly handkerchiefed his beard and then found matches that smelled of sulphur and I marveled in reverential awe and adulation over the might and brawn and devastating prowess of this giant among men.[1]

This portrait of Crosby Noyes captures the quiet but forceful personality of a man through the force of his imagination, hard work, and fierce ambition achieved great success. Noyes was born into hard-scrabble New England poverty, but with little money and slim opportunities, he came to Washington in 1849 alone seeking a better life. In 1867 Noyes boldly grabbed his chance for wealth and influence when he and Samuel Hay Kauffmann with the help of three other investors purchased the *Star* from William Wallach. Within ten years of purchasing the *Star*, Noyes and Kauffmann were running the most financially successful newspaper in the city, with three times as many subscribers as any other daily paper published in Washington. A reporter doing a feature about the *Star* in 1879 described Crosby Noyes as "a small slightly-built man, with a slow deliberate manner of speaking" laced with occasional humor who dressed in "dark, gray clothes, a soft felt hat," had "a slight stoop as if from much desk-work," and worked in a "plainly furnished second floor front office . . . of one of the most influential newspapers in Washington." Noyes retained the modest dress and manner of his Yankee roots throughout his life, but the legacy of the great newspaper he built with Samuel Kauffmann was not modest, nor were the family dynasties they sired. Yet a century later the successful newspaper Crosby Noyes and Samuel Kauffmann built and left to their children at their deaths was sold to Texas businessman Joseph Allbritton. The story of the squandering of that legacy is a long, multifaceted, and tortuous tale.[2]

Critics inside the *Star*, owning family members, as well as those who saw its failures from a distance claimed family nepotism contributed greatly to the *Star*'s demise. Of the three owning families, the generations of Noyes and Kauffmann family members who ran the paper included talented journalists, writers, businessmen, musicians, actors, and influential civic leaders, but also ne'er-do-wells, inept businessmen, unremarkable journalists and editors, drunks and womanizers, the insulated wealthy, and self-indulgent elites with social prejudices. The first generation was relatively industrious and successful. Crosby Noyes's son Frank took his

Noyes family patriarch Crosby Noyes at the height of his success and influence in the nation's capital as the respected publisher of the *Evening Star*, ca. 1900. Reprinted with permission
of the D.C. Public Library, *Star* Collection, © *Washington Post*.

first job with the *Star* when he was thirteen selling copies of the paper
behind the circulation desk during the summers and after school. In 1877
Crosby's eldest son Theodore graduated at age nineteen with a degree
from Columbian College (now George Washington University) and began working as a reporter for the *Star* while attending law school. At age
twenty-five Theodore Noyes moved to Sioux Falls in the Dakota Territory
in 1883 to practice law and help with statehood efforts. He was eventually elected to public office but returned home four years later to help his
aging father run the paper. Frank Noyes attended Columbian College too
but left at age seventeen to start full-time work at the *Star* in the business

office. Frank Noyes left the *Star* in 1901 to become publisher and editor of the *Chicago Record Herald*, and while there he played a major role in establishing the Associated Press and served as its president until 1938. Theodore and Frank were striking young men with stylish handlebar mustaches and attire, intense eyes and handsome faces, much like their father, Crosby, when he was a young man. In fact, Frank's niece Eleanor Noyes Hempstone called her Uncle Frank a bit of a "ladies' man" when he was young, with his "beautiful blue eyes" and "very sweet expression."[3] The bespectacled, slight, clean-shaven youngest son Tom Noyes was more free-spirited than his older brothers. Tom was a talented writer and editor at the paper, but he also pursued his passions by building a baseball club and Masonic Lodge in Washington. Tom tragically died at age forty-four in 1912. Samuel Kauffmann's son, Rudolph, came to work at the *Star* in 1875 after graduating from Amherst and was managing editor by 1893, a position he kept for more than thirty years. Rudolph's younger brother Victor started working as a cub reporter in 1889 and was Sunday editor and finally the *Star*'s treasurer until his death in 1941. Family nepotism contributed to the ruin of the *Star*, but the story of the its eventual demise is far more complex.

Samuel Kauffmann died in 1906, and Crosby Noyes in 1908. The descendants of Crosby Noyes and Samuel Kaufmann in the first five decades of the twentieth century ran a respected and hugely profitable newspaper when nepotism for good or ill was not much of a factor because the tastes and worldview of local residents and advertisers greatly favored the *Star*. Frank Noyes returned to the paper as its president after his father's death. A year after Frank took charge the *Star*'s circulation was 48,000, and by 1948 when he retired, it was 211,000. During the 1920s the *Star* printed greater advertising lineage than all other district dailies combined and would retain that lead until the 1950s. By 1933 the *Star* was ranked first among all newspapers in the country in advertising lineage and held that distinction for more than decade until the *New York Times* battled it for first place during World War II when newspaper print was rationed. In 1916 Theodore Noyes had been so confident in the *Star*'s advertising lead that as a staunch teetotaler, he was willing to reject liquor advertisements even before Prohibition began in D.C. The policy continued until 1957—more than twenty years after Prohibition ended and ten years after Noyes died. During the worst of the Great Depression, the financial losses for newspapers across the country on average were near 10 percent, but the *Star*'s losses were around 1 percent. Despite the hard times of the 1930s, the *Star* started the Blue Streak prenoon edition, added Associated Press wire photos a month after AP began the service and a rotogravure pictorial tabloid, and invested $250,000 in purchasing twelve "electrically driven, completely automated printing presses." In

1938 Victor Kauffmann urged the *Star's* Board to purchase WMAL radio station, an NBC affiliate, from M. A. Leese Radio Corporation, and in 1947 the Evening Star Company (the "Company") purchased and started broadcasts on WMAL-TV. These purchases would later sustain the *Star* in hard times and prove to be one of the wiser decisions made by the *Star's* owning families. By 1952, the *Star* was flush with advertisers, carried more than 40 percent of the advertising in the city, and was among the five richest newspapers in the nation. As Katharine Graham said of the *Star* at the time, "The *Evening Star* seemed to own the market and the town. It was the respectable establishment paper, overflowing with ads" through the 1950s.[4]

The *Star's* owning families shared their success with staff and offered some of the best salaries, working conditions, and benefits in the industry. In 1919 the Company began offering mortgage loans to employees, sick pay, disability benefits, pensions, and life insurance based on years of service. The *Star* built a new Annex to the Evening Star Building at a cost of more than $1 million, which opened in 1922 with a new modern newsroom, an employee cafeteria that ran at a loss, elevators, a free medical and dental clinic with professional medical staff, and a furnished club room for the Evening Star Club. Male staff founded the Evening Star Club in 1898 for white men only over age twenty-one who paid a small initiation and monthly fee. The club held biennial dinners in downtown hotels and published the *Morning Star* through the 1920s. In a male-dominated paper and racially segregated era, white female staff were allowed to enter the smoke-filled men's club room by invitation only, but black employees were never permitted inside the club room. The Company furnished the club room with "a billiard table, card tables, a Victrola, big comfortable chairs and lounges . . . [and] a removal stage for entertainments" in 1922. Two years later the *Star* expanded employee benefits to include a staff savings plan with a one-fifth match from the Company, gave its first Christmas bonus, and began selling coal to help employees heat their homes. Route boys and later paper girls got special rewards for hard work and ingenuity and annual excursions through the 1960s. In the 1930s when many employees lost their jobs at struggling newspapers, the *Star* maintained a policy of "no layoffs during periods of depression," and when a reporter questioned one *Star* official about the policy, he replied, "It's profitable, as well as humane and decent to let the *Star* employees know that they are considered as something more than a piece of machinery, to be thrown out if they are no longer useful." Jerry O'Leary remembered that despite the *Star's* low wages during the depression, he thought he was the luckiest kid around to have a steady, six-day-a-week job as a copy boy, as did many at the paper. In a wave of union organizing across the country, the American Newspaper Guild organized the

Star's newsroom in 1938. Although unions for blue-collar workers, like typesetters and printers, had negotiated contracts with the *Star* since the 1880s, a union for editorial staff was new. O'Leary, a cub reporter at the time, said he joined the Guild right away and got a welcomed raise from $10 to $15. In January 1941, four hundred guests attended the Evening Star Club's annual "Family Dinner" at the Willard Hotel, where District of Columbia commissioners John Russell Young and David McCoach Jr. were the guests of honor. Benjamin McKelway was the toastmaster, and guests were entertained by Ray Heatherton and his band with swing vocalist Judy Clark, the Capitol's Rhythms Rockets dancers, a skating act, a comedian, and an entertainer from the Earle Theater who led the crowd in singing. The *Star* was flush with cash, generous to its employees, and the top money-making newspaper in the city.[5]

The next generation of Noyes after Frank and Theodore Noyes were disappointments to their fathers and had few positive effects on the *Star*'s future. Consistent with the prejudices of the era, the families never considered daughters for leadership positions. Teddy (Theodore Prentice) Noyes was Theodore's only son, and Newbold Noyes was Frank Noyes's only son. Teddy Noyes died in 1933 at the age of thirty-seven. Theodore Noyes judged his son Teddy would never have the qualities and abilities required to lead a major newspaper, so he never pushed him in that direction. One family member characterized Teddy as a bit of "a wastrel" and another "a playboy and sportsman" who appeared to be seduced by the easy life that great wealth afforded him. Nieces and nephews were very fond of his wife, Adelaide, and one family member called her a bit of a "good time gal" who formed a group called "the Outlaws," for those who had married into the Noyes family. Smith Hempstone Jr. described his cousin, Ted Jr., Ted and Adelaide's only son, as a lot of fun, but like his father he unfortunately never outgrew the aimless life of his youth. John Thompson, Smith Hempstone's half-brother, fired Ted Noyes Jr. from the *Star*-owned TV station for some unknown malfeasance, and he eventually wound up broke at the end of his life. Newbold Noyes, Frank Noyes's only son, began his career at the *Star* in 1919 as associate editor, a position he held until his death at age fifty in 1942. Newbold's Uncle Theodore was critical of his nephew's abilities and reluctant to turn over the reins of leadership when he retired. Theodore Noyes instead favored Ben McKelway, who was not part of the family. Noyes saw McKelway as someone with the qualities and intelligence able to retain and grow the success and reputation of the *Star* after his death. McKelway joined the paper in 1920 and was first a proofreader, then city editor, news editor, managing editor, and finally associate editor. As Noyes's health failed in his last three years of life, he was editor in name only, with McKelway performing the actual daily tasks of *Star* editor. Theodore Noyes died at his home on New Hampshire Avenue in 1946, and in 1949 McKelway was officially named *Star* editor—a job he held until 1963. McKelway was the first person outside the owning families to own *Star* stock, sit on the Board, and the first editor who was not a Noyes. In February 1948 Frank Noyes resigned as president of the Company, and by the end of the year he died. Frank's brother-in-law, Fleming Newbold, was appointed president after Frank's death, but he too died a year after the appointment in January 1949 after which Sam (Samuel H.) Kauffmann II, grandson of founder Samuel Hay Kauffmann and son of Victor Kauffmann, became president. In 1952 when the *Star* celebrated its centennial at an anniversary party, Sam Kauffmann told the audience, "Tonight, not only are we looking back over the past 100 years with a feeling of honest pride; we are also looking forward to the next 100 years with an equally strong feeling of hope." Sam Kauffmann's failures in the next few years during a crucial time in the *Star*'s history would contribute greatly to the paper's eventual demise. The seeds for the paper's demise in the D.C. newspaper market, however, had been planted nearly two decades before.[6]

In the early 1930s no one imagined that the *Washington Post* would ever become a respectable newspaper, much less overtake the *Evening Star* as the most profitable newspaper in the city. The *Post* was a distant fourth in circulation and advertising revenue behind the Hearst-owned newspapers in the city and the *Star*. The genesis of the *Post*'s eventual success began when wealthy New York banker and Hoover Republican Eugene Meyer bought the *Post* for the low price of $825,000 in 1933 at a public auction on the steps of the *Post*'s old offices at 13th and E Streets from the financially and morally bankrupt Ned McLean. Victor Kauffmann and Fleming Newbold were there to witness the auction with Evalyn Walsh McLean (Ned's estranged wife), McLean's two sons, Alice Longworth, and Andrew Mellon's son-in-law David Bruce. Meyer and William Randolph Hearst Jr. did not come but sent bidders to represent their interests. After Meyer bought the *Post*, he spent most of his money in the 1930s hiring editors and writers to make the paper's editorial pages one of the finest in the nation. Despite the boost in the *Post*'s integrity and intellectual vigor, the paper would continue to lose money until World War II when it finally earned a small profit. In 1946 Eugene Meyer became president of the World Bank and turned over the *Post*'s operations to his son-in-law Phil (Philip) Graham, a liberal Democrat, who used the paper to promote progressive political views to which the city's population was slowly turning. Phil Graham also was intent on finding a way to end the *Star*'s phenomenal run of economic successes. Graham would be greatly assisted in his effort by the apathy and shortsightedness of Sam Kauffmann. In 1939 Cissy (Eleanor Medill) Patterson bought Hearst's two Washington

newspapers and merged them to form the *Times-Herald*. Cissy Patterson
successfully ran the *Times-Herald* as a scandal and gossipy tabloid until
1948 when she died. Patterson bequeathed the *Times-Herald* to seven loyal
staff members, but they couldn't replicate her success and began losing
lots of money. Phil Graham with the consent of Eugene Meyer in secret
offered the *Times-Herald* owners $4.5 million to buy the paper. At the
time Phil told his wife, Kate, as they were vacationing in Narragansett,
"I know getting the *Times-Herald* would be too good to be true," but if he
succeeded, "the first thing I'd like to see is Sam Kauffmann's face when he
hears the news." Cissy's cousin Robert McCormick, owner and publisher
of the *Chicago Tribune*, instead decided to buy the *Times-Herald* to keep it
in the family and retain its conservative stands. By 1954, however, Mc-
Cormick at age seventy-three was tired of running a failed newspaper.
McCormick viewed the moderate Republican Eugene Meyer as a man
of his generation with whom he could do business and discounted the
influence of Meyer's younger, left-leaning son-in-law Phil Graham. Sam
Kauffmann made no attempt to buy the *Times-Herald*, which he considered a second-rate tabloid that appealed to a small segment of blue-collar
residents and sensation seekers. So in 1954 Eugene Meyer at seventy-eight
purchased the *Times-Herald* from his contemporary Robert McCormick
for $8.5 million. After the merger, top *Star* leadership thought the *Post*
would not retain that many of the *Times-Herald*'s morning readers. They
were wrong. The *Post* gained 180,000 new subscribers from the former
250,000 *Times-Herald* subscribers, and within four months nearly doubled
its daily circulation from approximately 203,000 to 383,000. Jack Schoo,
who worked in the *Star*'s advertising department, remembered the pep
talk Sam Kauffmann gave all the advertising executives and sales people
after the merger. Kauffmann told them, "Boys, for every dollar they bring
in, we're gonna bring in two," but when the circulation figures came in,
they were all "stunned," according to Schoo. One year after the merger,
the new *Post-Times Herald* exceeded the *Star* in profits and circulation but
not yet in advertising. Despite the *Post*'s successes, Sam Kauffmann and
much of the paper's top management remained relatively sanguine about
the *Post*'s ability to overtake the *Star*'s perennial lead in advertising lineage. The *Post* still only carried twenty-five million advertising lines compared to the *Star*'s forty-two million one year after the merger. For years
members of the Noyes and Kauffmann families had leveraged their close
personal and professional connections with the business elites in Washington to build a commanding lead in advertising. By 1959, however, the
Post squeaked out a small lead over the *Star* in advertising lineage, which
it never lost but only increased in the years to come. At the time of the
merger, the *Star* had an almost two-to-one lead over the *Post* in advertising lineage, but by 1971 the reverse was true.[7]

The same year the *Post* purchased the *Times Herald*, Sam Kauffmann underwent surgery to have a lung removed and the wound never properly healed. Kauffmann took prescription drugs for his condition, which led to near deafness and pain for the rest of his life. Rudy Kauffmann or other family members who sat next to Sam Kauffmann during business meetings would write on a slate the gist of the discussion for Sam, but he rarely got the full import of the give and take at meetings and his own arrogance wouldn't allow him to admit any weakness or take much advice. Kauffmann's anti-Semitism, which even his own daughter, Joan Lamphere, recognized, antagonized local Jewish business owners upon whose advertising business the *Star* depended. Newby Noyes, the *Star*'s editor in the last decade before the families sold the paper, saw up close Kauffmann's failings and laid the blame squarely at his door, telling *Post* reporter Stephen Klaidman in 1976 that he "refused to respond in any competitive way when the *Post* bought the *Times Herald*. He wanted to play it cool, sit back and watch the balance sheet." In the decades after World War II, suburban growth, the popularity of TV evening news, and new commuting habits had deleterious effects on afternoon papers. In addition, the *Star* had its own unique problems—family nepotism, complacency, and a lack of imagination among top management. Instead of attacking the competition head on, Kauffmann focused all his energy on overseeing the construction of a $15 million new plant in southeast Washington. The building opened in 1959, just four years after the *Post-Times Herald* merger, and the timing could not have been worse, even though plans for a new plant had been in the works for years. As early as 1940, the owning families began looking for sites to build a new modern, more efficient, and larger building to house their staff and equipment to replace the historic but un-airconditioned and smaller building located in the heart of congested downtown Washington. In 1949 top *Star* management purchased land at Virginia Avenue and Second Street, SE on the assumption that the paper's afternoon delivery trucks could easily access the proposed southwest freeway and deliver papers to subscribers in the city and suburbs more rapidly. The site also offered the opportunity to build a railroad spur to the main tracks under Virginia Avenue to allow rail cars to deliver newsprint and supplies directly into the building's lower level. The new plant was certainly more spacious than the old building, with five stories and a basement totaling 397,000 square feet of space compared to 124,000 square feet in the old building. At the building's dedication in May 1959, the *Star* boasted in an employee handout that it had a roof garden, a staff cafeteria opened "24 hours, 6 days a week," an employee lounge, a "mailroom longer than a football field," a soundproof teletype room, air conditioning, and space for more improvements. The old Evening Star Building located in the

heart of Washington, D.C. just blocks from the US Capitol and the White
House on Pennsylvania Avenue was built in the classic Beaux-Arts
architectural style, with carved stone, painted frescoes, a mahogany-
paneled newsroom, and a relaxing club room. The new building had
none of those features but instead, as described to staff, was designed
to offer the "ultimate in speed and efficiency" with offices of "light gray
slag walls," "brown vinyl asbestos" floors, and ceilings of "enameled
acoustical metal tiles . . . in line with modern industrial practice." The
exterior was gray ceramic brick with windows fronting only on Virginia
Avenue and a lobby of "St. Genevieve Rose marble" walls, terrazzo tile,
and aluminum figures representing the *Star*'s history. Star sports writer
Morrie Siegel succinctly described why the new plant was "one of the
worst mistakes it made . . . the *Star* owners thought the city was going
to grow into Southeast," but it didn't. The eastern leg of the southwest
freeway was never constructed, thereby cutting off freeway access for
trucks to quickly deliver newspapers to northwest D.C. and Maryland
as Kauffmann had hoped. Sam Kauffmann's tenure ended in 1962 when
the family-dominated *Star* Board elected Crosby Noyes Boyd, Frank
Noyes's grandson, as president. Boyd would inflict no major damage on
the paper like his predecessor, but his maintenance of the status quo did
nothing to reverse the paper's sharp decline in advertising and revenue.
The *Star* made a number of other changes in top management in 1962 but
stuck to its same perennial model of choosing family members to lead.
The Board retained Rudolph Kauffmann II as production editor, elected
Bin Lewis as production manager, and John H. Thompson and Godfrey
Kauffmann as vice presidents. On the editorial side, Ben McKelway left
and Newby Noyes became executive editor. Noyes continued to publish
a well-respected newspaper with a reduced staff and budget constraints.
Newby's son Terry Noyes as a young man remembers his father stress-
ing to him more than once the sentiment that "nepotism has destroyed
the paper." Terry suspected his father was tacitly discouraging him from
working at the *Star*. The families had their share of talent, but overall
nepotism at the paper by the 1960s was inhibiting fresh ideas on how to
compete for business in the new competitive landscape of Washington,
D.C. By the late 1960s the *Star* settled into second place behind the *Post*,
and its once great financial successes and fortune were only a memory
to veteran *Star* staffers. Jack Schoo, who worked in the paper's advertising department in the 1950s and stayed until 1980, fondly recalled "all
we had to do was open the transom and let the business in," or Jerry
O'Leary, who remembered when the *Star* "owned the town" and *"The
Washington Post* was chopped liver as were our three other rivals." Those
days were only memories by the 1970s.[8]

An *Evening Star* board meeting in the boardroom on Virginia Avenue, ca. 1965; all but two—Robert Cleveland and Ben McKelway—were members of either the Noyes or Kauffmann families (l–r around table): John Thompson, Director Robert Cleveland, Bin (Willmott) Lewis, Crosby Stuart Noyes, Sam (Samuel H.) Kauffmann, Crosby Noyes Boyd, Newby (Newbold) Noyes, Ben (Benjamin) McKelway, Rudolph Kauffmann, Jack Kauffmann, and Godfrey Kauffmann. Reprinted with permission of the D.C. Public Library, *Star* Collection, © *Washington Post*.

The *Star* plant by the late 1960s was located in a run-down neighborhood, isolated from the heart of the city, and in shabby condition. The plant was surrounded by failed housing projects, a rundown liquor store nearby, and card and dice games on the streets, according to one senior editor. Reporter Cristine Russell described the building in the 1970s when she worked there as "industrial," with "tiled yellow and linoleum floors," "careless chain smokers [who] were always lighting the wastebaskets on fire," and staff who ran to the parking lot to avoid getting mugged but sometimes failed despite their swiftest efforts. Despite the *Star*'s mounting financial troubles and its unattractive surroundings, Mary McGrory recalled, "Even when we were going down, there was that great lifeboat feeling and people pulling for each other and sticking together." Jerry O'Leary fondly remembered the camaraderie among staff, and when "drinking was very much a part of the lives of some reporters" at a string of local bars near the old Evening Star Building, like Gendelman's and the Chicken Hut and later Mr. Henry's or the Class

Reunion when the plant moved to Virginia Avenue. *Star* reporters who were around during the paper's last thirty years when it struggled financially experienced the newsroom as a fun place to work, full of humor, practical jokes, mutual support, and devoid of hierarchy in the generally competitive workplace of a newsroom. There was plenty of shouting and arguments but in the end everyone got along for the good of the paper. The *Star* had a reputation for being a "reporter's paper"—a newspaper where reporters had the independence as well as the responsibility to write their own stories with little interference from an editor. Many *Star* employees whether in the newsroom, business offices, or production side were rarely fired and were content to remain at the paper until retirement. The paper had a softball team, a glee club, annual summer outings for newsboys, and an employee newsletter titled *The Family Star*, begun in 1960 with chatty news about staff weddings, birthdays, retirement parties, and professional accomplishments. The *Star*'s owning families actively promoted and created an environment where staff felt they were part of a family. This intense loyalty would sustain the *Star* through good and bad times, even as employee numbers dwindled and staff benefits were squeezed. Some who left, like Haynes Johnson, however, saw the easy-going chumminess and life-time job security as having both positive and negative impacts. The atmosphere was wonderful for employee morale and a reporter's independence, but he believed it sometimes undermined the competitive tension needed in the *Star*'s ranks and leadership necessary to meet the formidable challenges facing the paper in its last two decades.[9]

In 1968 Jack (John Hoy) Kauffmann, Sam Kauffmann's son, replaced Crosby Noyes Boyd as the *Star*'s president. Jack Kauffmann was an Army Air Corps World War II veteran and Princeton graduate when he began working in the paper's business offices in 1949. When Kaufmann became president in 1968, he was a handsome, golden-haired forty-something man of privilege and wealth with a flair for the good life among the powerful and rich in Washington. Kauffmann was more energetic, outspoken, and willing to take risks to save the paper than his predecessors in the job. In 1970 the *Star* ran a deficit for the first time and continued to increase its debts into the millions every year the families owned the paper. Kauffmann in early 1972 made a risky bet to save the *Star* when he began negotiations to purchase the *Washington Daily News*, the only other afternoon newspaper in D.C. The *Daily News* was a financially shaky six-day-a-week afternoon tabloid sold at many newsstands that was popular with government employees and black Washingtonians for its concise, on-the-spot news coverage, sports, and breezy style. The *News*, however, had been operating at a loss for more than five years by 1972. The *News* was a distant third behind the *Post* and *Star*, with an average weekday daily circulation of approximately 217,000 compared to the *Star*'s 302,000 and around 526,000 for the *Post*. The Scripps-McRae (later Scripps-Howard) Syndicate established the *Daily News* in 1921, but by the 1960s the Syndicate's bankrolling of the paper had substantially diminished. Sam Kauffmann and others at the *Star* for many years tried to convince Scripps-Howard's top executives to sell the *News* to them, but they declined until advertising lineage at the *News* began to dramatically fall. Jack Kaufmann began periodically traveling to New York City to the Scripps-Howard's offices on Park Avenue to discuss buying the *Daily News* with Jack Howard and other top management in 1972. Rumors circulated about the sale, but Kauffmann denied any knowledge of it. Staff at both newspapers learned about the sale just hours before the official announcement was made on July 13, 1972. The *Star* paid the low price of $5 million for the *News* and borrowed the money from American Security and Trust Company Bank to make the payment. In the end the *Star* hired thirty-three of the *Daily News*'s seventy-seven-member editorial staff. Jack Kauffmann and Newby Noyes both announced to the press they expected to increase circulation by one hundred thousand after the purchase and end their financial dependence on the Company's broadcast holdings for the past two years of losses. After the sale, the *Star* changed its first run to 9 am to compete with the *Post*, moved from hot to cold type, and within a year changed its name on the masthead to the *Washington Star-Daily News*. The *Star*'s owning families established Washington Star Communications (WSC) as a holding company for a newspaper subsidiary and another subsidiary for its broadcasting holdings. WSC acquired the Scripps-Howard news service and new syndicated features. Daily circulation increased to more than 415,000 by the fourth quarter ending in September 1974, but significant gains in advertising lineage did not materialize. By 1974 the *Star*'s daily circulation gains had slipped back and its percentage of advertising lines in the city was at 33.2 percent, a small improvement since the *Daily News* purchase, but still lagging far behind the *Post*'s more than 60 percent of advertising lines. In addition, the *Star* had amassed $15 million in debt between 1970 and 1974 and had only half the circulation of the Sunday *Post*. Local advertisers still viewed the *Post* as the better choice for reaching youth and suburban consumers where markets were growing. The *Star* continued to attract mostly older city residents familiar with the paper rather than the affluent and hip young professionals moving to D.C. and its suburbs by the 1970s. In addition, labor costs only metastasized when the *Star* added former *Daily News* staff to its payroll. Jack Kauffmann's gamble did not end the paper's deficits or substantially increase advertising revenue as he had hoped. By 1974 John Thompson, president of the Evening Star Broadcasting Company subsidiary, and other family members wanted to stop draining profits from the broadcast stations to make up for the newspaper's losses. Kauffmann admitted to a *Post* reporter two years after selling the *Star* that the owners should have purchased the *Daily News* years ago when the *Star* was flush with cash or at least more stable, not "when we were going to hell." Jack Kauffmann and the paper's owning families knew they had to find a financial backer or face bankruptcy for themselves and the 123-year-old newspaper they owned.[10]

According to Newby Noyes's son Terry, and one other Noyes family member, "someone who represented South African interests" wanted to buy the paper. Conservative Republican and media tycoon John P. McGoff was the South African who wanted to buy the newspaper but not the broadcast properties. The families turned down McGoff because, according to one family member, they didn't want to give control of the newspaper to a "foreigner." Other accounts report McGoff's financial bid was just too low for the families or McGoff was a much too controversial figure. In 1974 the investment banker John Clifford Folger introduced Jack Kauffmann to Joseph L. Allbritton, a prospective buyer who appealed far more to Jack and the family. Allbritton was a self-made millionaire and Texas banker with extensive real estate holdings and profitable businesses whose wealth had allowed him to acquire an impressive art collection, two Rolls Royces, palatial homes, and his own private jet. The wealthy Texan tycoon now wanted to increase his stature and influence among elites by owning a major metropolitan daily newspaper. Joe Allbritton offered to purchase shares in WSC's holdings that included both the newspaper and broadcast stations. Allbritton understood he needed the substantial profits from the broadcast holdings to offset the *Star*'s losses. Allbritton established Perpetual Corporation of Delaware (Perpetual) to purchase WSC stock, and in July 1974 Perpetual and WSC entered into an agreement for him to buy a 10 percent share in WSC. The agreement was approved by WSC shareholders at their annual meeting in September. Allbritton acquired 1,982 shares of WSC common stock for just under $5 million and loaned the WSC another $5 million with a note secured by a mortgage and security interest in WSC properties. The agreement also gave Allbritton "operational control" of the newspaper and "an irrevocable proxy to vote 67 percent of the stock of the newspaper subsidiary." On November 19, 1974, Allbritton filed a petition with the Federal Communications Commission (FCC) to transfer control of WSC to Perpetual and for a waiver of a new FCC rule that prohibited cross ownership of a newspaper and broadcast holdings in one market. The FCC started hearings on Allbritton's petition, but in the meantime, he did not wait to move forward on changes he hoped would improve the paper. Allbritton began to weed out family members in top leadership positions. One family member who stayed through the 1970s, however, was Bin Lewis.

Lewis oversaw production of the daily paper expertly because of his fine management skills and knowledge of new technology. Newby Noyes signaled his intention to resign after Allbritton found a new executive editor. Newby Noyes resigned on December 18, 1974, and Jim (James G.) Bellows, then associate editor of the *Los Angeles Times*, became the *Star*'s new editor. A reporter who worked for both Noyes and Bellows characterized Noyes as "a smart man who was over his head" and another as "a very thoughtful guy . . . someone who believed in good journalism" but who in the end could not save the newspaper he loved. In December WSC directors chose fifty-seven-year-old Godfrey Kauffmann as WSC's new president, who was a more unassuming member of the Kauffmann family than his cousin Jack.[11]

When Jim Bellows came to the *Star*, he found a newsroom demoralized by the *Post*'s spiraling success after its groundbreaking Watergate coverage. Bellows was not cowed by the *Post*'s success but judged it as "dull and flabby, a typical concomitant of financial success," so his strategy for attracting new readers to the *Star* was to publish a sprightly and sassy alternative. One of the first things Bellows did was to put "two things that were not dependent on news happening btw 6am–10am" on the front page that were "unique to the *Star*, interesting and different that made you want to read it," recalled Barbara Cohen, the *Star*'s national news editor at the time. Those two things were the "Q&A" section, a verbatim transcript of interviews conducted by *Star* reporters with famous people "coming through town," and the "In Focus" column, which probed deeper into news stories involving politics, sports, the arts, and local issues. Bellows created the position of special projects editor and picked Denis Horgan for the job. Horgan managed these seven-day-a-week, front-page features as well as the stories inside the paper that supported them. Horgan thought it one of the hardest jobs he ever had during his career, but one of the most rewarding. In addition to Bellows's front-page changes, he asked the paper's metro desk editor George Beveridge to cut back on coverage of the "court, the council, commissions and officialdom . . . we need to cover the school, more than the school board . . . we can't repeat what they [the *Post*] are doing but go to people out there to see how they are coping." In *Straight from the Washington Star*, a new "Monthly Publication for the Washington Business Community," Bellows was still pushing this idea and others a year later to attract business when he explained "we need to get back in touch with the people by covering them and not just government" and "put out a paper that's 'a delight to read— that people can laugh, cry and be open with,'" with "a middle-of-the-road editorial position with no knee-jerk ideology to either side." When the conservative Smith Hempstone resigned as lead editorial writer after the Allbritton purchase, Bellows wooed the forty-year-old, free-thinking Ed

(Edwin M.) Yoder Jr. to make the paper's editorial pages less predict-
able and ideological. Yoder was a Rhodes Scholar who had earned a BA
degree with honors from Oxford University and had been editorial page
editor at the *Greensboro Daily News* for a decade. *Star* political reporter Jim
Dickenson described Yoder as "a moderate southerner. He wasn't liberal
but he wasn't conservative either" and preferred writing about ideas,
not political ideology. Ed Yoder would win a Pulitzer for distinguished
editorial writing in 1979, and he told a reporter at the time, "we try to
be a bit unpredictable without being cranky," politically independent,
and as much as possible create editorial pages that are "lively, irreverent, forceful, and principled." Bellows also made a prescient decision to
start a Washington gossip column that would prove wildly successful but
would not have been as popular if he had not picked the right team of
people to write and edit it. One of Bellows's great strengths was his ability
to spot individual talent whether outside or inside the *Star*. Bellows chose
the young Mary Anne Dolan as Portfolio editor not long after he arrived,
and she suggested Diana McLellan to write the gossip column. McLellan
in turn picked Louise Lague to assist in writing "The Ear." Dolan also
oversaw a "Writers in Residence Program" to bring well-known writers
like Jimmy Breslin, Dick Schaap, Jane O'Reilly, Willie Morris, and Michael Novak to write for the *Star* for a time. Bellows hired the irreverent
and controversial political cartoonist Pat Oliphant to get the attention of
readers if not always their admiration. Bellows made the paper's type-
face lighter and changed its name simply to *The Washington Star*. Bellows
didn't just make smart changes, he inspired the troops through difficult
times with his own quirky personality and style. Bellows was not your
typical suit-and-tie, take-charge, big-city editor. Bellows was particularly
infamous, according to one editor, for giving "Delphic" instructions. Political reporter and editor Ron Sarro said Bellows "would give you a direct
order and never finish the sentence so that the actual solution came out
of your brain," and Denis Horgan joked that Jim's "brain worked faster
than his mouth." Barbara Cohen remembered the time Bellows came
to the newsroom to ask her to assign someone to write a piece on Patty
Hearst's kidnapping. Bellows "always talked with his hands by holding
them about 12 inches apart and moving them up and down in a chopping
fashion so picture this, he's standing by me saying 'Patty Hearst, Amelia
Earhart, Judge Crater, In Focus' and then walks away," recalled Barbara.
The scary part to Barbara was she actually understood him—he wanted
a story for "In Focus" about famous disappearances in American history.
Political reporter Jim Dickenson, who worked for both Ben Bradlee and
Bellows, considered them "two of the great American editors of the twentieth century" who were equals but "very different in style." According
to Ron Sarro, *Star* staff were loyal to Bellows in hard times because his

attitude was "I'm in the foxhole with you" and was a leader they "would have followed to hell." Bellows sometimes "compared us to the Viet Cong," Barbara Cohen fondly recalled, which was not a great analogy in that era, and "would say, 'yes we were fewer in number and didn't have the resources but by doing things really smart, we could attract attention to the paper . . . and tweak the nose of the *Post*' . . . we loved being the underdog and we loved it when we did better."[12]

At the same time Bellows was making changes to attract readers, Allbritton began taking steps to improve the paper's finances by reducing payroll costs and cutting some of the generous benefits the families had provided since the 1920s. Newby Noyes never had the heart to make the staff cutbacks and play hard ball with the unions to save money. As Terry Noyes said, "My father was basically a nice guy. He believed in keeping his word" to the men and women who worked at the *Star*, so he never found a way to cut back on staff or benefits to reduce costs, particularly the long-term obligations of generous pensions or deep reductions in craft union jobs when automation arrived. When Allbritton obtained full rights to operate the paper in 1974, he signaled to the *Star*'s unions that he needed to renegotiate current union contracts in order to cut around two hundred staff positions to reduce payroll costs. Allbritton reached separate agreements with the crafts unions. Brian Flores, Phil Kadis, Warren Howard, and other Newspaper Guild officers suggested a four-day workweek to the Guild membership as an alternative to staff cuts in the newsroom, and the Guild voted 347 to 44 to accept the compromise in December 1974. Ron Sarro recalled there was little resistance from Guild members because "the way *Star* people felt about one another I think they really thought we owed it to one another." Three months after negotiating new union contracts, the Company suspended its contributions to employee savings and pension plans. The four-day workweek in practice did not work well, though, because reporters were regularly working five days for four-days' pay. As Barbara Cohen later said, "everybody was completely dismayed, disgusted, and bummed out" about the rule, and most beats on the national desk "worked for free a lot." Despite exciting changes to the paper's columns, financial cutbacks, and sacrifices from the staff during the first year with Allbritton as publisher, the *Star*'s future was still uncertain.[13]

In late August 1975, the FCC announced it was postponing its decision on whether to waive the rule that disallowed a single person or entity to have joint ownership of a newspaper and broadcast station in one market until it held public hearings and gathered additional information, which might take a year. Treasury Secretary William Simon told a *Newsweek* reporter the FCC's action was "a coward's way out," and Mary McGrory spoke for many at the *Star* and in the news media when she said, "The

FCC seems to want to kill us to preserve competition . . . How in the hell do you figure that?" The *Star* most likely would not survive without the revenue from WSC's TV and radio stations. In the 1974 agreement with the families, Allbritton stipulated that in "the absence of any material adverse changes" and if FCC authorized the waiver, Perpetual at final closing would purchase "37.85 percent of outstanding common stock" in the WSC for slightly more than $16 million and make another secured loan to WSC of $4.3 million. Allbritton was increasingly frustrated with the FCC's inaction, the huge losses at the paper, and his dealings with the Noyes and Kauffmann family members who outvoted him on the WSC's board and continued to be paid "substantial cash dividends," despite the newspaper's large losses. Allbritton tendered a stock offer on August 18 to purchase all remaining shares of WSC common stock at $1,600 per share for a total cash value of $28.5 million. He released the offer to the press without prior notice to the shareholders. The price was low especially for the valuable broadcast properties, but with the debt the *Star* was accruing, some family members thought it might be fair. Jack Kauffmann personally told a reporter he thought the offer was "too low," but if stockholders agreed "I wouldn't buck them." Newby Noyes declined to comment until he looked at the details, but Rudy Kauffmann thought the offer "might meet with approval." Godfrey Kauffmann as WSC's president counseled stockholders not to act on Allbritton's offer until the Board had a chance to review it and advise them. Of the twelve directors, only J. Clifford Folger (Allbritton's nominee to the Board) and family member Bin Lewis voted to accept Allbritton's offer, while the remaining nine asked for changes to protect against the paper's future losses. The deadline for acceptance or rejection of the offer was August 27, but negotiations were extended. On September 3 Allbritton issued an amended tender offer to satisfy the objections of the nine directors. Godfrey Kauffmann and the other directors agreed to tender 52 percent of WSC stock and advised other shareholders to tender theirs too. Not long after the final sale to Allbritton, Newby Noyes in a letter to Allbritton wrote "whatever happens, and whatever the future may hold, I and my family and associates will always owe you a debt of deep gratitude for having the courage to take up a battle which had (so far as I am concerned . . .) exhausted and defeated us." Noyes's trust and confidence in Allbritton would be sorely tested in the next few years. In January 1976 Allbritton became sole owner of WSC for $28.5 million, which included the *Star* newspaper and TV and radio stations in D.C., Virginia, and South Carolina. However, Allbritton in Perpetual's final offer "reserved the right" to sell either the Washington broadcast stations or the *Star* based on "economic and financial conditions" beyond its control.[14]

While Allbritton negotiated for sole ownership of the *Star*, he wrote representatives of the paper's eleven labor unions on September 19, 1975, to ask them to extend current wage scales until September 1976. These unions negotiated for 1,800 of the 2,100 *Star* employees. In exchange, he offered employees a stock ownership plan and an end to the four-day workweek for editorial and advertising staff. Normally local unions negotiated contracts jointly with all district newspapers, but in 1975 the *Star* chose to negotiate separately with its craft unions because its financial situation was much more precarious than the wealthier *Washington Post*. Bin Lewis, who oversaw production and was trusted by the men in the press room, counseled them to compromise their benefits because if costs were not curtailed, the *Star* was headed for big trouble. As one union representative said, "Everybody was treated with respect; it was a fully unionized newspaper," so compromises were reached. Katharine Graham, however, took a much tougher stand with the craft unions than ever before because she believed they were unfairly draining money from the *Post* since modern automation required a smaller production staff. Contracts with seven hundred employees in the *Post*'s craft unions expired on September 30, 1975, and Pressman Union Local No. 6 called a strike. On the morning of October 1, 1975, pressmen burned and destroyed the *Post*'s printing presses, started a fire, and injured the night foreman. Jim Dugan, head of the local pressmen's union at the time, said "the men temporarily went insane over their treatment and it wasn't premeditated" but fueled, he claimed, by the uncompromising stand of *Post* negotiators Lawrence Wallace and John Prescott. The pressmen had heard rumors that the *Post* was sending nonunion workers to what Dugan called a "scab school" in Oklahoma City in anticipation of a strike. Mrs. Graham and *Post* management countered that the pressmen's violent actions warranted taking a tougher stand with the strikers. Not long after the *Post*'s presses shut down, Mrs. Graham went to see Allbritton to ask if the *Post* could use the *Star*'s presses or, at the very least, if he would shut down the *Star* in sympathy with a fellow publisher. Allbritton refused because he didn't want to instigate a strike or violence among pressmen working at the *Star*. According to Bellows, Allbritton, as a new publisher and uncertain of his proper role among fellow publishers, was a bit hesitant at first to refuse Kay Graham's requests. Bellows told Allbritton about his own experience as the *New York Herald Tribune*'s editor during a similar pressman's strike. *Tribune* reporters had counseled the publisher not to shut down in sympathy with the *New York Times*, but the publisher ignored them, which Bellows believed eventually led to the *Tribune* closing. Bellows assured Allbritton that he was right for refusing Graham because the *Star* was struggling financially. The *Post* then asked six nonunion suburban newspapers to print the paper and used trained management to run the presses. Two days after the strike, Scotty (James) Reston in a *New York Times* editorial on October 3 opined that despite the *Star*'s financial problems, the "tragedy is that the *Post* and the *Star* could not get together, even if they had to go down together on this issue." The *Star* republished Reston's editorial the following day next to one written by the *Star*'s Writer in Residence, Jimmy Breslin. Breslin had worked at the *Tribune* when Bellows was editor and was bluntly critical of his colleague Scotty Reston, writing, "I am not reading the gentle, friendly man I have known in the writing business" but "Mo Annenberg" at a typewriter who threatens "if the other side doesn't do the right thing, then we'll put the bums out of business." Reston wrote the editorial after *New York Times* publisher Arthur Ochs Sulzberger lunched with Allbritton and Bellows at the F Street Club in Washington and encouraged Allbritton to stop publishing in sympathy with the *Post*, even though the *New York Times* was not making a similar sacrifice. Breslin wrote "Apparently, the idea of these powerful publishers, Sulzberger and Kay Graham, was for the *Star* to behave and seek the warmth of the more powerful *Post*." As Bellows candidly wrote in his memoir, the *Post* strike was "a golden opportunity" for the *Star*, and the paper took advantage. The *Star* published a series of articles on the *Post* strike, lampooned the paper in "The Ear," and published "An Open Letter to the *Washington Post* and the Striking Newspaper Unions" from the ad hoc "Committee for a Fair Settlement" signed by politicians, clergy, and union leaders who asked that the Federal Mediation Service negotiate a settlement. *Star* cartoonist Pat Oliphant also drew an insensitive and sexist caricature of Kay Graham's horribly stretched breast caught in a printer, which garnered lots of attention but also sharp criticism. Although the *Post* struggled to print and went to half its size for a few weeks, by the end of October the paper was profitable again, according to Kay Graham. The *Post* hired replacement workers in January 1976 and never rehired the striking pressmen. Tragically, one of the striking pressmen committed suicide in February. Some *Post* reporters crossed the picket lines with reservations, and some stayed out in solidarity with strikers. The Newspaper Guild's membership voted by a small margin to oppose the strike because of the press operator's vandalism and violence. *Star* editor and Guild leader Ron Sarro, who attended the Guild meetings during the strike, said "the *Post* management got more support from *Post* Guildsmen than *Star* Guildsmen," but in the end "it was a monumental incident in labor because the *Washington Post* stood up to the union . . . in the end it weakened the union."[15]

The *Star* substantially increased advertising lines and ran in the black in October at the start of the strike, but only temporarily. The increase was a small blip in the *Star*'s efforts at chipping away at the *Post*'s substantial lead in advertising. Allbritton had hired James Daly in early 1975 to be

vice president for advertising. Ironically, Daly led the *Post* in the years
the *Star* lost its commanding lead in advertising but was now working
to reverse his success. Allbritton also hired Kaufman & Associates as its
marketing firm, but Daly early on was not impressed with their work and
Bellows thought the campaign to attract younger readers was a "cliché."
Robert Denny of the Kaufman firm wrote to Allbritton when they lost the
contract to argue "regardless of your entrepreneurial brilliance, Joe, troika
management won't work. It was one of the basic faults of the old *Star* family. No matter how capable Jim Daly is as an advertising sales manager,
how outstanding Jim Bellows is as an innovative editor, or how solid Bin
[Lewis] is on the production side, you're still a coach without a quarterback." Denny may have been onto something since Bellows's constant
but undefined refrain of wanting to attract the "affluent . . . well-educated
and most importantly young" readers frustrated Daly because he believed
targeting subscribers where they lived—city or suburb—defined their
tastes as much as their age. The *Star* also had a basic problem with just
keeping its subscribers, much less attracting new ones, since its daily editions were not getting to subscribers' doorsteps on time or at all. In late fall
1975 Circulation Director William Merritt and Production Manager Fred
Loskamp provided Allbritton with their explanations for the delays. Loskamp blamed mechanical problems in the press room like web breaks and
Merritt concluded traffic problems slowed distribution, but neither offered
workable solutions. Bill Merritt looked at the *Los Angeles Times* and the
Washington Post's practice of hiring independent contractors to only deliver papers while solicitation and collection for subscriptions were strictly
done by mail or electronically. Merritt and Bruce Kinsey, who were hired
to tackle the distribution problem, concluded these new delivery systems
over time would fail, and besides, "rearranging route boundaries would
pose enormous problems" under the current union contracts. Distribution
problems would plague the *Star* until the end, and many believed it was a
major factor in depressing circulation and advertising revenue.[16]

The national news desk, despite all the cutbacks, sacrifices, and turmoil
at the paper, managed to do some of its best work covering the 1974 midterm elections and the 1976 presidential campaign under Jack Germond
and the staff of reporters and editors he assembled. It all began when assistant managing editor for national news Dave Kraslow left the paper to
become publisher of the *Miami News* just before Bellows arrived. To save
money, Jack Germond was asked to take over Kraslow's duties as well as
remain the paper's chief political reporter. Henry Bradsher returned from
Hong Kong as the paper's last foreign correspondent stationed overseas
in December 1974 to save money as well. Germond, who was stretched
pretty thin with the job of both national news editor and chief political
reporter, had seen how well the thirty-year-old Barbara Cohen as assistant

national news editor had handled coverage of the crucial 1974 midterm elections. The elections revealed voters were turning against Nixon and the GOP in the wake of Watergate. Barbara remembered Germond telling her bluntly, "Well, kid you did a great job on the election-day stuff and you haven't had much reporting experience and you're too young but I'm going to make you the national editor." Cohen was elated with the opportunity to work closely with Germond, who she admired "as a fabulous political reporter" and with whom she "got along like a house on fire." Barbara was a talented young woman, but until Germond and Bellows came, she experienced minor slights, and in one instance an editor stymied her career based on his traditional view of gender roles. Barbara was hired as a copyeditor in 1968 for a training program specifically designed for editors begun by Ray Dick to invigorate the editor pool with a younger, more racially and gender diverse group of people. Cohen moved through the ranks relatively quickly. Yet despite her talent and hard work, when she was on maternity leave in 1972, the Metro editor Scott Smith phoned her at home to tell her that the promotion to principal assistant editor on the city desk, for which she was fully qualified, was going to someone else because, as he told her, "we're just not sure when you return . . . you're going to be as you were before." Barbara thought it unfair but took it in stride and just worked harder because in those days there were few, if any, official channels where complaints of possible sex discrimination could be aired. With Germond at the helm, however, Cohen's talents flourished, as well as "a whole shift of younger reporters, people who were aggressive, people who had an investigative mindset so that there was a big change of what the staff was like." Reporters included health writer Cristine Russell, congressional reporter Martha Angle, White House reporter Fred Barnes, energy reporter Roberta Horning, foreign policy reporter Ozy Johnson, Norman Kempster, Gloria Borger, John Fialka, Ed Pound, and Phil Gailey. Veteran reporters who rounded out the raft of talents included Lyle Denniston, who covered the Supreme Court with legal precision; Walter Taylor, who covered the White House; and Lee Cohn, who was the resident expert on labor and economics and wrote with such precise prose his copy needed little editing, remembered Cohen. Despite cutbacks, Germond brought in new people as well. One of his first new hires was his friend and colleague Jim Dickenson, a twelve-year veteran political reporter at the *National Observer*. Dickenson arrived in the *Star*'s newsroom the day after Nixon resigned from office and was immediately asked to write a story about President Ford's vice presidential choice Nelson Rockefeller. Germond referred to the three years Bellows was editor as "the best years I ever had in the newspaper business," and Cohen judged the national desk in the Bellows's years as the "high water mark for that group of people." Ed Yoder, the new editorial page editor, saw Bellows as less "political," as

compared to other newspapermen and editors he had known, and more a
"man of style and intuition . . . an authentic genius" who preferred to leave
political coverage to editors he trusted. Cohen also experienced Bellows as
someone who "didn't mess around much with national news because . . .
he trusted Jack [Germond] and Jack trusted me . . . it was kinda up to us to
do the very best job we could." In 1976 Germond's prescient reporting of
Jimmy Carter's potential to win the Democratic presidential nomination,
when few other political reporters saw it coming, garnered lots of respect
and attention for the *Star*. Allbritton was so pleased with the national news
desk's coverage of the 1976 presidential election, he invited them to his
Georgetown home for a catered dinner and presented Germond with an
inscribed Tiffany sterling tray and national desk reporters with "inscribed
Steuben paper weights." Earlier in the 1976 presidential campaign, Allbritton had not been so pleased with some of his top staff, especially his editor,
Jim Bellows. Although Bellows was agnostic on political news, Ed Yoder
realized the one thing Bellows was intent on doing right away when he
came to the *Star* in the wake of Nixon and Watergate was to rid the paper of the reputation of being too close to any president or ideology, and
Yoder agreed. That principle would be tested in the summer of the 1976
presidential campaign.[17]

Joe Allbritton was not always comfortable with the role of a hands-off
publisher after years of being a successful entrepreneur who was accus-
tomed to controlling the operations and people who ran his businesses.
This became painfully true during the Independence Day bicentennial cel-
ebrations of 1976. At a hot dog roast in the rear garden of the Allbrittons's
rented N Street home in Georgetown during the July 4th weekend, Allbritton asked Bellows to reserve space for him on the front page of Monday's
paper. When Bellows asked Allbritton why, he laughed and said he wasn't
saying because "you would try to talk me out of it." Allbritton was elated
that he and his wife, Barbie, were invited to dine at the White House with
President Ford, Vice President Rockefeller, and their wives on Sunday,
July 4th, and after dinner to gather on the Truman Balcony to watch the
bicentennial fireworks. Allbritton conceived the idea of publishing an editorial endorsing Ford and asked Steve Richard, whom Allbritton had appointed the paper's communications director, to prepare a draft. On Monday morning assistant news editor Ray Dick, who was on duty that night,
received the editorial from Richard with instructions to put it on the front
page. Dick called Bellows for his advice, and Bellows told Dick to hold
the editorial but to leave space for it or an alternative story and he would
call the desk in the morning with further instructions. When Allbritton
learned about Bellows overriding his decision, he was furious with his editor undermining his authority. Bellows tried diplomacy to ease the conflict
between Allbritton and him by suggesting the endorsement appear on the

editorial page, but Bellows remained firm in his initial decision. Bellows hoped to impress upon Allbritton that although a publisher had the right to decide on presidential endorsements, it was customary for a publisher to consult with editors first. The normally even-tempered Bellows called Yoder that morning around 7 am a bit vexed as he recounted the night's frustrating events, and then asked him if he knew anything about the Ford endorsement. Yoder told Bellows he was completely in the dark and was as troubled as him that Allbritton would do such a thing. Tensions only escalated over the next few days in the newsroom, so Yoder telephoned Allbritton's working counsel, Berl Bernhard, to see what he could do to negotiate a compromise between the *Star*'s publisher and editor. Within a few days Allbritton invited Bellows, Yoder, Bernhard, and Richard to meet at his Georgetown home to discuss the editorial. Bellows and Yoder both agreed with the substance of the editorial because they too opposed Ronald Reagan's candidacy, but at the meeting Yoder argued that a front-page endorsement of a candidate before a party's official nomination was the "nuclear weapon" of newspaper journalism and rarely used. In any case, Yoder argued that an editorial inside the paper would serve the same purpose and offered to rewrite the endorsement and place it on the editorial pages. Allbritton agreed to the compromise. Yoder never explicitly expressed his distaste for the endorsement Richard and Allbritton had concocted but was pleased when the compromise gave him the chance to rewrite what he considered a pretty poorly written piece of prose. Bellows would later write about all the things he had wanted to say to Allbritton at the meeting but didn't. Bellows especially believed that "fighting for our credibility" by not being the "patsy" of any president, as he judged the *Star* had been with Nixon, was crucial to the paper's survival and the paper's need to appeal to those "beyond Republican Precincts." Coincidentally or deliberately, Newby Noyes wrote to Allbritton around this time about "the problem of the proper relationship between a publisher-owner and his editor," to advise Allbritton, "that he (the publisher) loses face and status if he tries to use his newspaper to help his friends or hurt his foes."[18]

Allbritton was given the Polk Award in January 1976 in recognition of his efforts to save a great but failing newspaper. A year after Allbritton's Polk Award, the *Washingtonian Magazine* named Jim Bellows "Washingtonian of the Year" for 1976 in its January 1977 edition because he "has worked miracles to keep the *Star* alive and growing" and "inspired and rebuilt the *Star*'s staff and the *Star* has become perhaps the best afternoon newspaper in the country." Allbritton had some success in gaining entrance to the powerful and elite in Washington but remained an awkward novice among established newspaper publishers and jealous of Bellows's popularity. Ed Yoder, who liked both Allbritton and Bellows, witnessed and clearly understood why the two were

often "poles apart . . . Their ambitions for the *Star* were radically different. Jim wanted it independent and readable. Joe wanted success but
also wanted a platform to be a shaker in Washington. He had no idea
what the function of a publisher was." McGrory saw Allbritton "like
a kid with his face pressed against the candy store" he couldn't enter.
Denis Horgan recalled how "it would break your heart" to see the friction between Allbritton and Bellows, and although "they didn't fight
and yell at each other," their relationship "was cold" and "it always
had an element of fear." Early one cold, dark morning in February 1977,
Allbritton called the night desk editor from Los Angeles to remove his
name from the masthead. News of Allbritton's name being removed
from the masthead hit the newsstand, and publicity for the *Star* was not
pretty. Yoder and Bellows thought Joe took offense at being ignored,
and similarly McGrory observed, "He felt he was not being listened to
and treated with respect which may have been true because nobody
was treated with much respect around there anyway." In the middle
of this controversy, Mary recalled years later that Bellows kept repeatedly appearing at her desk to ask if she had heard from Allbritton after
he had not been in D.C. or at the paper for some time. Mary had willingly and successfully been the chief conciliator at the paper for years
when a reporter was in trouble for some odd offense and needed her
to cajole and console their irate boss. Mary was liked and respected by
both Allbritton and Bellows, so she told Bellows if he needed her help
to find Allbritton, she would try. McGrory recruited Ed Yoder, whom
Bellows and Allbritton also liked and respected, and together they located Allbritton with the help of his wife, Barbie. Allbritton agreed to
come back and have lunch with McGrory, Bellows, and other top editors because he was meeting with the unions anyway. Mary hosted a
lunch at her apartment, served lasagna, and led everyone in singing the
Baptist hymns Allbritton liked. Tensions between the paper's publisher
and editor eased, but not for long.[19]

In March 1977, Allbritton hired James Smith from the *Sacramento Bee*
newspaper as the *Star*'s president in charge of operations to fill the va-
cancy left by Richard Stakes, who had resigned in December 1976. Smith
was a tough manager who made drastic budget cuts to reduce costs and
increase profits when he came to the *Star*. WSC reported the paper's first
operating profit of $582,000 for the quarter ending in June 1977 as well as
a $5 million profit from the broadcast stations that helped offset its losses.
Despite the good financial news, Smith's sharp cutbacks were wildly
unpopular among the staff and with Bellows as well. Most editorial staff
had not received a raise in three years, and further cuts pushed some to
leave despite all the progress Bellows and loyal staff had made in creat-
ing a more popular newspaper. When Allbritton called a hiring freeze in

September, Jack Germond protested and even threatened to leave because the recent job offers he had made to Phil Gailey from Knight Ridder and Ed Pound from the *Chicago Sun Times* would have to be rescinded. Allbritton recanted slightly on the hiring freeze to allow Germond to hire Gailey and Pound only. In early November Bellows learned that Smith had recommended to Allbritton there be a 10 percent cutback, which meant approximately 140 of 1,400 *Star* employees would go. Bellows let his staff know about the staff cuts, and as time wore on, he became increasingly frustrated with the financial cutbacks, policy disagreements, and personal conflicts with Allbritton. Soon rumors of the staff's beloved editor's imminent departure spread in a gossipy newsroom and among the larger news media. Staff morale was pretty low. Finally, Jim Bellows left the *Star* to take a job as editor of the *Los Angeles Herald Examiner* in November 1977. Bellows's loyal Portfolio editor Mary Anne Dolan followed him to the *Herald Examiner* not long after he left. Bellows in his book *The Last Editor* graciously described his decision to leave the *Star* as a "mutual agreement" between Allbritton and him and not as a "firing, or a resignation." As a parting peace offering, Allbritton gave Bellows a sparkling silver Cadillac Seville, but he was not invited to Bellows's going-away party at the Sheraton Carlton Hotel attended by many *Star* editorial staff and significant personalities in Washington's newspaper world, including Ben Bradlee, Sally Quinn, Mark Shields, Bob Novak, and Kay Graham. Just days after Bellows's departure, Allbritton confirmed to a *Post* reporter that the 10 percent reduction in staff was eminent, that circulation had dropped, but he was hopeful that the *Star* would have a modest profit in 1978. Sid Epstein, a respected editor with deep roots at the paper, took over as interim editor. In December 1977, Allbritton rescinded the staff cuts and invited a select list of top staff to his house in Houston to regroup and strategize about the paper's future. Barbara Cohen attended the meeting and distinctly recalled the awkwardness of being the sole woman in the group but not much about the strategy discussed. Cohen, however, was keenly aware of Allbritton's wife, Barbie, saying to her husband over dinner "well why would you sell the TV station, that's what's making money." Barbara thought to herself "uh-oh." Cohen was right to be concerned. The FCC's final ruling in December 1975 gave Allbritton until 1978 to dispose of the broadcast properties. The deadline was approaching. Behind the scenes Allbritton had already begun making tentative overtures to Time, Inc. to buy the *Star*.[20]

In the 1960s when Time, Inc. was buying newspapers, it expressed interest in the *Star*, but the families were not yet ready to sell. In 1974 when the families began looking for a potential buyer, Scotty Reston urged Time, Inc.'s chairman of the board Andrew Heiskell to take another look at the *Star*, but after reviewing the paper's finances, operations, and labor costs, Time Inc. decided against the purchase. In the fall of 1977 Allbritton made a proposal to Heiskel through an intermediary. Soon after Jim (James) Shepley, Time, Inc.'s president and chief operating officer, and its editor in chief Hedley Donovan, plus Heiskell met with Allbritton to discuss his proposal over dinner in New York. Allbritton proposed a sale price of $35 million in cash or stock, $10 million of which would be Time, Inc.'s assumption of a loan. A few months later, however, Allbritton rescinded the offer after obtaining concessions from the *Star*'s unions and decided to continue publishing the paper. In March 1977 Allbritton also reached an agreement with Combined Communication Corporation of Phoenix (CCC) to trade WMAL-TV in Washington for KOICO-TV in Oklahoma City, plus receive $65 million in preferred CCC stock, but he needed the FCC's final approval of the trade. In January 1978, the FCC gave a less than clear approval of this trade of TV stations, so Allbritton reluctantly chose to sell the *Star* to Time, Inc. In a round of tough negotiations by phone over four days in relative secrecy, a deal was hashed out with Time, Inc. After Time, Inc.'s executive committee approved the sale, Allbritton flew to New York on February 2 to seal the deal with a handshake. Time, Inc. agreed to pay $20 million for controlling stock in the Evening Star Newspaper Company and to assume $8 million in debts with Allbritton remaining as publisher. When a reporter asked Allbritton in a news conference on February 4 if he had made money on the purchase and sale of the paper, he claimed, "I have not made any money purchasing the *Washington Star* if you accept my words as an old banker, that's my understanding." On February 16 the Board of Time, Inc. ratified the agreement, and in March when Time, Inc. purchased the stock, it paid $16 million—not $20 million as originally offered—since a careful review of the books showed a $4 million projected loss rather than a profit as stated in the original offer. Not long after selling the newspaper, Allbritton moved to stop the sale of the WJLA-TV, Channel 7 (formerly WMAL-TV), and instead sold WMAL's FM and AM radio stations to the American Broadcasting Company for $16.6 million. Allbritton invested an estimated $58 million in purchasing WSC and underwriting the *Star*'s losses over four years, and he netted approximately $32 million from the sale of the paper and the two Washington radio stations. At the time of the sale of the *Star* to Time, Inc., Allbritton appears to have lost money, as he said in his news conference on the sale of the newspaper alone. In the end, however, he profited greatly by retaining WSC's most valuable assets— WJLA-TV in Washington and TV stations in Virginia and South Carolina worth more than $100 million in 1978. In the years to come WJLA in particular would prove to be one of Allbritton's most lucrative holdings. One former *Star* reporter expressed the skepticism many felt about Allbritton's motives and the enormous profits he reaped from its sale when he said,

"I believe the Noyes and Kauffmann families had collective suicide when they learned how snockered they had been" by Allbritton. Newby Noyes wrote two years earlier to Allbritton when he bought WSC outright that the families had wanted a publisher "who understood the difference between a newspaper and a shoe factory—someone who instinctively recognized that you do not associate yourself with a newspaper for what it can do for you, but what you can do for it, and through it for the community." Walter Diercks, the *Star*'s general counsel and secretary, who was privy to the depth and complexity of the *Star*'s economic problems, saw Joe Allbritton's motives for owning the *Star* slightly differently than both Noyes and his harshest critics. Diercks did not believe Allbritton bought the *Star* just to end up with WSC's profitable broadcast properties but instead saw a man who wanted to be "the head honcho of a big city newspaper" which "made you a really big deal in Washington. Joe liked that sort of thing . . . and giving that up was hard." Diercks also said, "I think Joe did try to make it work. I think his intentions on the front end were honorable" but "he didn't have a deep enough pocket . . . to sustain the losses . . . at some point you got to conclude that maybe somebody else can make this work but it ain't me." *Star* national reporter Jim Dickenson, who admired the work of Yoder, Germond, and Bellows during the Allbritton years, stated succinctly much the same thing when he said: "The underlying economic problem couldn't be changed . . . All the improvements at the *Star*, pardon the expression, were like putting lipstick on a pig." Allbritton stayed on as publisher for a few months after Time, Inc. took over, but Diercks saw Allbritton getting increasingly frustrated and testy at board meetings because he "was always used to being his own guy and now he was reporting to a bunch of guys from a big company" who on a "net worth basis, Joe was probably worth more than all of them and Joe wasn't used to taking orders from anybody." Even more importantly, Allbritton knew he could not stay on as the *Star*'s publisher and retain the more profitable WJLA under FCC rules, so he resigned as publisher in May 1978.[21]

Time, Inc. as a media giant with a reported $90 million in profits in 1978, appeared to have the financial resources to challenge the *Post*'s enormous lead in circulation and advertising. Although Time, Inc. had never run a major daily newspaper, Jim Shepley and Hedley Donovan, editor in chief at Time, Inc., desperately wanted to try. Both had connections to Washington when they were young, aspiring reporters. Donovan began his newspaper career in the late 1930s as a novice reporter at the *Washington Post* and Shepley as a young Washington Bureau chief in the 1950s. After Allbritton's abrupt departure, Time, Inc. named the more affable and slightly paunchy George Hoyt as publisher to tackle the business side. Hoyt had run seventeen suburban Chicago newspapers for

Pioneer Press that Time, Inc. owned. Soon after Time, Inc. bought the paper, Jim Shepley chose Barbara Cohen and Phil (Phillip) Evans for a new position as comanaging editors. Cohen was in charge of news, and Evans oversaw production. Time, Inc. hired Murray Gart, assistant managing editor for Time, Inc.'s weekly news chain, as the *Star*'s editor in June 1978. Gart, with thick dark-rimmed glasses, dark eyes, and a slightly receding hairline at forty-three, was your stereotypical suit-and-tie, middle-aged corporate executive who had spent more than twenty years ascending Time, Inc.'s corporate ladder. Soon after Gart arrived, he asked Time, Inc. executives for permission to hire sixty new editorial staff at the paper. The editorial staff had been winnowed down to 225 as compared to 490 editorial staff at the *Washington Post*. Gart eventually got permission to hire just twenty new editorial staff, but enough he believed to start new suburban editions. Gart and Hoyt's first joint initiative was to establish five zoned editions at the *Star*—one for the district and one each for the four surrounding counties. Both men had backgrounds in community news and saw the zoned editions as a way to attract new subscribers and market advertising to local businesses. Each edition had a managing editor and dedicated staff to gather and report the news from each office located in the community it served. Sheilah Kast, who had covered energy and the Maryland and Virginia state legislatures, was picked as editor for the first zoned edition, the *Arlington-Alexandria Star*. The *Star*'s zoned editions, however, had to compete with the suburban *Journal* newspapers, which were already familiar to readers, as well as three suburban editions published by the *Post*. The *Star*'s senior political writer Jack Germond was not a fan of the zoned editions, whose coverage of "every school board and sewer commission in the suburbs" he thought was sorry competition for the *Post*. *Star* reporters at the regional offices did their best with what they were given, but the strategy was underfunded. Denis Horgan recalled that when staff first learned that Time, Inc. had bought the paper, they were relieved to be "in the hands of professionals again with big money" and "not tired old families and then a banker" who "came in and he doesn't know anything about the game." When Gart traveled to California to meet with Jim Bellows as one of his first actions after he became editor, Horgan thought that was "a classy thing to do." Horgan and other veteran staff soon discovered, however, that Time, Inc. "was not such a good thing because they assumed we were all a bunch of bumpkins" and "pushed everybody around in a New York kind of way." Despite Gart giving Horgan the chance to reshape the Lifestyle pages as editor, over time Horgan experienced Gart as a "horrid individual to work for" who was "mean and vindictive" and "the quintessential bureaucrat, sycophantic to anyone above him and oppressive to anyone below him." Gart in appearance and temperament was the antithesis of the creative, unassuming, and supportive Bellows. Horgan and much of the editorial staff disliked that Gart had eliminated most of Bellows's innovations and chose to emphasize straight, factual news rather than investigative reporting. Gart kept Diana McLellan's popular gossip column "The Ear," but most of Bellows's other changes were dropped. Gart used Time Life's News Service to augment the paper's columns with national and foreign news stories. Barbara Cohen thought that copy from News Service reporters was too rough for a daily newspaper and better suited for editors who had time to polish it for a weekly magazine. Cohen also did not like how the News Service pushed aside veteran reporters and longtime overseas stringers. Gart went outside the paper to hire writers like Judy Bachrach, Nancy Collins, Jurate Kazickas, and Sandra McElwaine to improve the arts and society coverage. McElwaine and Bachrach both liked Gart because he hired them and treated them well but realized most veteran *Star* staffers did not appreciate Gart. Judy Bachrach knew longtime *Star* staff "resented all the new people . . . Who wouldn't that's understandable, I was new, I was from the *Post*—the enemy . . . but at the same time I have to say this—I didn't get any of the shit I got at the *Post*." Despite their resentments, Bachrach thought *Star* staff were always nice to her. Jim Dickenson, who Gart asked to be national news editor when Cohen was promoted, described Gart as "not a warm and cuddly guy" and "something of a bully," but once "I sort of stood up to him . . . after that we got along famously." Still Dickenson "never liked Time and its whole approach" and the people in charge, "their arrogance and the ignorance of Time . . . were really quite palpable." Managing editor for news Barbara Cohen had a good working relationship with Gart but disagreed with his choices to make the *Star* a serious newspaper and create regional editions. Mary McGrory's strong personality and motherly protectiveness of *Star* staff meant she often clashed with Gart, who she characterized as "power struck" and who thought "we were just rubes, that we didn't know anything about anything." Bachrach's more gracious view of Gart was as an outsider from humble origins who wanted to be part of the Washington establishment, but the *Star*'s irreverent staff ridiculed such sycophantic notions. Some in the newsroom found it odd and others just plain silly for Gart as an editor to spend such an exorbitant amount of time and money on decorating his office and riding around in a chauffeured car. Jack Germond, who took a "dead level" view of powerful people, saw Gart as way too impressed with Washington power. Germond and Jules Witcover, who began jointly writing the syndicated column "Politics Today" in 1977 for the *Star*, sometimes played jokes on Gart, like once making up meaningless words or acronyms that Gart would then pretend to know.[22]

By the fall of 1978 *Star* management anticipated a loss of $16 million for 1978. Top Time, Inc. executives thought controlling and managing the size of the paper's labor force, especially its unionized production staff and route carriers, was crucial to reducing its losses. The *Post* had conducted a bitter strike in 1975 but as a result was financially healthier because it had winnowed down its production staff and contracted with nonunionized, independent route carriers. Hoyt wanted flexibility in work rules, a reduction of the number of printers, and five-year contracts to ensure labor stability. Barbara Cohen was among the editors who attended a meeting Jim Shepley convened in the editors' conference room overlooking the SE/SW freeway sometime that fall critical to the *Star*'s future. Shepley informed the editors that Time, Inc. would invest $60 million over five years, but if the *Star* couldn't make a profit by then, it would close the paper. Shepley also said they would accomplish this by summoning unions to negotiate new contracts with favorable terms to ensure labor stability. Cohen as a young, successful editor was less concerned about her own future, but as she told Shepley, she didn't want to tell "people who have been here so long and turned down dozens of jobs . . . who were loyal to the *Star*" that Time, Inc., "which we had all thought of as a savior," was only staying for a limited time unless the paper could "turn the corner." Barbara recalled Shepley's response was "'well you know,' this is a paraphrase to the effect 'if they are so great, why are they still here.'" When she singled out Lee Cohn as a fine veteran reporter, Shepley responded bluntly, "Lee Cohn could go work someplace else," and she realized at that moment "the newer people were going to be the stars and the older people were going to not be treated so well and I personally was going to find that very difficult." On October 23 George Hoyt asked leaders of the eleven *Star* unions to reopen negotiations on contracts that did not expire until the next year. At the time, Cohen thought staff might get small raises, but as she and the unions soon discovered, Time, Inc. had decided to play hardball. After a month of talks, Hoyt called a meeting of union leadership on November 22 to issue an ultimatum that Time, Inc. would invest $60 million over five years only if all unions ratified five-year contracts by December 31, 1978, but without new contracts, management would shut down the *Star* permanently on January 1, 1979. Dorothy Strizinski, administrative officer for the Washington-Baltimore Newspaper Guild, told the press in early December that Hoyt had agreed in writing in October that if new contracts were not renegotiated the current ones would remain in force and the ultimatum had breached that promise. On December 15, Jim Shepley met with officers and representatives of the unions to implore them to end their stalemate "before irreversible events overtake us." Shepley candidly told them that "we paid a low price for the *Star*, backed by some solid real estate assets," but without the flexibility to manage our staff to fix distribution problems that have led to lost subscriptions and to hire "the hottest editorial staff we can train and assemble" where "seniority cannot be the sole basis for reward," we will "close down operations, put the real estate on the market and pay off the creditors." When union representatives asked why negotiations couldn't wait until the contracts expired in 1979, Shepley told them that prospective advertisers were aware of the *Star*'s losses and "they need evidence of a commitment by both of us." Shepley ended by saying, "I stand ready to give you and the *Star* whatever contribution of blood and sweat the job requires but I decline to bleed and sweat in vain." Management "put a gun to our heads," said Ron Sarro, who was a *Star* Guild representative on the negotiating team in 1978 and told us "we are in charge of the rudder" of your lifeboat and "are going to sink your boat unless you do it our way." The unions considered striking, but a strike on a business slated to close made no sense. One by one the unions agreed to Time, Inc.'s conditions, except for the pressmen and printers who held out until the evening of December 31, 1978. Barbara Cohen and her husband, Richard Cohen, at the time were celebrating New Year's Eve at home with friends when she was called into work. The printers and pressmens' unions with the most to lose filed a lawsuit to stop the closing but failed when Hoyt told the judge that the *Star* would immediately file for bankruptcy if he ruled against Time, Inc. Finally, at 11 pm the printers' union, as the last holdout, agreed to the contract. Shepley, however, refused to print the *Star* until he saw the signed contracts the next day, so the paper was not published on New Year's Day 1979. Cohen returned home feeling "so depressed," and as a result she began seriously to reconsider Frank Mankiewicz's recent offer to be news director at National Public Radio's new show, *Morning Edition*. Barbara Cohen left the *Star* in April 1979, and Phil Evans, her co–managing editor left in June after four years at the paper. The new contracts allowed *Star* management to sharply reduce the 185 printer jobs over time by eliminating eighty printers in the first six months through buyouts and more over the next five years. The contracts also allowed management to alter driver's delivery routes to improve distribution, phase out certain jobs, and implement a new merit system to reward employees based on performance. Time, Inc. informed the public in a January 2, 1979 editorial that the *Star* "is here to stay" because "the restoration of authority to those who must manage the *Star* as a business is an intrinsic part of every one of the contracts."[23]

Time, Inc. restored travel budgets and increased the editorial staff that had been decimated by hiring freezes and attrition under Allbritton. When Time, Inc. took charge, young reporters like Michael Isikoff, Howard Kurtz, Lisa Myers, Jane Mayer, and Fred Hiatt were hired for the Metro

In *Star* newsroom Murray Gart stands behind reporter who struggles at Logicon computer, and behind Gart are (L–R) George Hoyt, Sidney Epstein, and Bill McElwain. Reprinted with permission of the D.C. Public Library, *Star* Collection, © *Washington Post*.

Desk and launched into successful careers. More experienced writers like Betty Cuniberti from the *Post* and Howard J. Smith from the Associated Press were hired to beef up sports coverage. New hires in top leadership positions from outside the *Star* included William McIlwain, formerly a newsman at *Newsday* and editor at the *Boston Herald American*, was hired as deputy editor; Eileen Shanahan, a former *New York Times* Washington bureau reporter, filled the newly created job of projects editor; and designer Eric Seidman, who came from the *New York Times* in 1979, redesigned the layout of the *Star*. Time, Inc.'s purchase of a computer system called Logicon, however, was a big mistake and a headache for the editorial staff. On the other hand, one of Time, Inc.'s smartest business moves was to obtain the popular comic strip *Doonesbury* drawn by Garry Trudeau in 1979. The *Star*'s general counsel, Walter Diercks, who was involved in the business deal, called it a "pretty inspired deal . . . a really shrewd thing" for Time, Inc. to maneuver. Established in 1916, the Washington Star Syndicate by 1979 distributed the columns of Mary McGrory, James Kilpatrick, James Beard, Fulton Sheen, and William Buckley. Time, Inc. exchanged assets of the Star Syndicate for a substantial minority interest in UPS (United Press Syndicate), which distributed the popular comic strips *Doonesbury*,

Cathy, and *Tank McNamara.* To be sure that Ben Bradlee was personally
handed the thirty-day cancellation notice of *Doonesbury* at the *Post's* offices, Walter Diercks waited in a phone booth across from the *Post* building
and dictated a blow-by-blow account over the phone to the *Star's* office
so they could publicly make the announcement when he saw the private
messenger deliver it to Bradlee. Unfortunately, Diercks realized sometime
into his recitation that he had chosen the wrong spot since there were no
windows on the front of the building to peer through. When Bradlee received the cancellation, he was pretty angry, so he and other top editors
chose to immediately stop running *Doonesbury* in the *Post* on June 4 before
the contract officially expired, and didn't notify the public. The *Star's* publication of *Doonesbury* was scheduled to start on June 24, so district residents, including a disgruntled Jimmy Carter White House, were without
Doonesbury and other UPS strips for three weeks. *Post* ombudsman Charlie
Seib told the public that the *Post* simply made "a business decision" not to
promote its competitor's products but had to admit the decision not to
inform the public was "cavalier, if not arrogant." Ironically, in 1975 Seib
was enticed by Ben Bradlee to leave as the *Star's* managing editor to take
the job of the *Post's* ombudsman after a twenty-year career at the *Star.* To
the public, Bradlee's actions appeared petty and unresponsive, and his
answers to numerous press inquiries afterward only generated more negative press. The *Star* took advantage of the *Post's* bad publicity and aggres-
sively marketed its *Doonesbury* coup in headlines and stories for the three
weeks before the strips resumed. The *Star* temporarily got some terrific
publicity and enjoyed poking fun at the *Post,* which delighted *Star* staff
who for years bristled at the *Post* in print, calling its paper "the financially
troubled *Star.*" Despite all the hype and fun, the financial rewards were
minimal and temporary.[24]

The *Star* began publishing an AM edition in July 1979, which was sold
at newsstands and in coin boxes. The *Star* told advertisers in a circular
promoting the AM extra that it would contain later news than the other
morning paper, including West Coast sport scores and closing market
tables popular with white-collar professionals. In a press release in June,
Hoyt told readers and advertisers that the AM edition will make the
Star an all-day newspaper but emphasized "the *Star* will remain in the
afternoon field" because "reading newspapers in the evening is still a
basic reading habit in Washington." Behind the scenes, however, Hoyt
and Gart knew all too well that suburban commuters preferred the *Post*
over the *Star* because it gave them the most current news and delivered
papers on time before dawn and rush-hour traffic. After labor contracts
were renegotiated, Hoyt and Bill Merritt, vice president for circulation,
gained greater flexibility in streamlining routes and delivery times, but
problems persisted. Heavier daytime traffic and midmorning deadlines

for news meant even if readers got their papers on time, they contained little fresh news. In 1980 Gart was so distressed by the *Star*'s losses that he suggested to Hoyt that shifting the *Star* to a weekday morning newspaper without weekend editions was the only way for the paper to survive. Hoyt thought Gart's idea would look weak and defeatist to advertisers, and besides overhauling the paper's distribution system for morning delivery he judged was almost insurmountable. Hoyt and Gart rarely saw eye to eye and had a contentious working relationship. The *Star*'s circulation increased slightly in 1979 but then dipped when the recession hit, and after three years of Time, Inc.'s ownership, the paper's circulation was at 323,000—lower than when Time, Inc. bought the paper. As a consequence, retail businesses chose to spend a greater percentage of their advertising budgets at the *Post*. The *Star*'s percentage of advertising revenue in the city was dangerously low in 1978 at 28.1 percent when Time, Inc. bought the paper, but in three years it had dipped even lower to 25 percent. The *Star* tried giving deep discounts to advertisers, which attracted some retailers for a while, but the paper discontinued them in 1980 when it began losing too much money. The gains from discounts were never enough or enduring because advertisers continued to get better results from advertising in the *Post* at even higher rates. Jack Schoo as advertising manager was charged with initiating a new incentive plan and a rotating assignment system for salesmen under the new union contracts, but Carol Khan, retail advertising manager, thought the system never worked well. A rotating salesman never had enough time to build trust with an advertiser or learn the business. Advertising sales staff were decimated and demoralized by the changes, and as a result, their successes were few.[25]

Gart's insistence that reporters rein in investigative reporting and analysis sapped the initiative of many in the newsroom. Gart claimed the *Star* just didn't have enough staff to do investigative reporting or analysis well. Increasingly, more gifted political reporters and editors, young and old alike, started leaving the *Star* under Time, Inc.'s management when they had stayed through tough times in the past. Time, Inc.'s management style, Gart's abrasive personality, and editorial decisions were the main reasons. Among those who left before the *Star* closed were Fred Barnes to the *Baltimore Sun*, Robert Pear to the *New York Times*, national news editor Jim Dickenson to the *Post*, Jonathan Fuerbringer to the Washington Bureau of the *New York Times*, and deputy editor Bill McIlwain to the *Arkansas Gazette*. Ron Sarro, who started at the *Star* in 1966 and moved up the ranks to become an assistant national news editor, reluctantly left the newspaper he loved in 1980 because Gart "was not my friend . . . his leadership was horrible. He was not a friend of the *Star*. He's why I left." Editorial page editor Ed Yoder bitterly resented Gart's constant meddling in his authority to independently manage the editorial pages, telling Gart after a particularly fractious disagreement, "I cannot function as a cipher . . . It seems to me the *Star* can have only one editorial page editor at a time. You must decide who that editor is to be." In addition, Gart made repeated last-minute changes to page proofs, and according to Yoder had an "impulse for boiling the personality and spontaneity out of the copy, when my own idea was to allow small divergences of taste" to keep the "flavor of personality and idiosyncrasy in the copy." Gart refused to back down or change so he and Yoder continued to clash, but Yoder stayed until the end. After Time, Inc. took over, journalists also noticed that an uncharacteristic amount of stories about Time, Inc. executives began appearing in the *Star*. Mary McGrory later told an interviewer, "Every now and then, seems like someone had to write a long piece about an 'exalted Time personage.'" Jim Dickenson as national news editor was generally left alone to manage the news on the national desk, but when Gart asked him to write a "puff piece" on Hedley Donovan when he retired and became a White House advisor in the Carter administration in 1979, Dickenson refused. Gart got another reporter to write it, and Dickenson edited the piece down considerably but "still I didn't think it was appropriate to even do the story." Mary McGrory stayed until the end, but she too often sparred with Gart. Gart tried more than once to move McGrory's front-page column to the opinion pages. Gart wrote McGrory in November 1980, "I feel quite strongly that some columns must move and perhaps, be replaced by others. Yours is one." McGrory threatened to leave so Gart recanted, but in April 1981 he tried to move her column again and she wrote, "Now, for me, the end has come," but she remained.[26]

By 1981 Time, Inc. had invested nearly $85 million, which was far larger than the $60 million it originally promised to invest over five years. Jim Shepley and Hedley Donovan, who had been the most ardent proponents of buying and investing in the *Star*, had retired as president and editor in chief, respectively, at Time, Inc. by 1980, although Shepley remained chairman of the Washington Star Company. Time Inc.'s new president, Richard Munro, and editor in chief Henry Grunwald, were less enthusiastic about losing any more money on their predecessors' investment and began looking for a way out. Time, Inc. tried to negotiate a Joint Publishing Agreement (JPA) with the *Post* under the Newspaper Preservation Act, but it failed in mid-July. The JPA would have allowed each paper to run its own news and editorial functions but combine business, circulation, and production operations, which would have saved millions of dollars, but as the *Star*'s general counsel Walter Diercks said, "a JPA for a dominant paper" like the *Post* "made no business sense." Diercks saw Shepley as being genuinely disappointed that Time, Inc. pulled the plug on the *Star* when it did, and he tried to convince the Board to give the paper more time to succeed but failed in the attempt. Diercks said of Time, Inc., "It turned out to be a much more daunting thing than they thought it would be," plus "the economy tanked in 1981." In a *Washingtonian Magazine* article scheduled for publication in August 1981, Time, Inc. vice president Charles B. Bear told the writers, "We'll stick with it whether it's $40 million or $60 million or $80 million, or whatever." The article also profiled editor Murray Gart, who defended his "less is more" style against the "excess verbiage, superfluous facts, the wandering sidebars" of the *Post* he derisively called "Pravda on the Potomac"—an allusion to what he considered its liberal bias. Gart also repeatedly made allusions to a recent scandal involving *Post* reporter Janet Cooke's Pulitzer Prize–winning story about an alleged child drug addict in D.C. she referred to as Jimmy. Cooke's Pulitzer had to be withdrawn when the story proved to be patently false. The *Post*, however, suffered little damage except a loss of face while the *Star* continued to sink deeper in debt. On July 22, Time, Inc.'s Board voted to close the *Star* and settled on a closing date of August 7, 1981. At 6 am on July 23, 1981, Murray Gart called Ed Yoder and asked him to arrive by 7 am for a meeting in his office. When Yoder arrived, he found the rest of the editors as apprehensive as he was and prepared himself for the worst. Gart "looked stricken" and Shepley was "sad and fidgety," recalled Yoder. Shepley announced that the *Star* would close on August 7 unless a substantive buyer with good credentials and financial resources to operate the paper came forward because Time, Inc. had invested far more than it had anticipated in just three years. Gart asked the editors to hold off on announcing it to staff before 8 am when the press release went out. Many of the editors objected at not being able to offer their reporters more advance warning. Some staff heard the jarring news on the radio, while others received personal calls from editors that softened the blow only a bit. TV cameras and the working press descended on the *Star*'s offices and newsroom. Munro, Grunwald, Shepley, Bear, and Time, Inc. Chairman of the Board Ralph P. Davidson held a press conference in a Washington hotel that morning, and *Star* reporters spoke to fellow journalists and broadcasters in the newsroom despite instructions from higher-ups not to do so. Job recruiters for other newspapers came to the newsroom as well. Reporters openly wept at the shock of losing a more than century-old newspaper. McGrory remembered that later afternoon when Gart told staff how sorry he was but that "you are all very desired," there "were snickers around the edges" of the crowd. Gart kept trying to appease the hostile crowd but had little luck until finally a "compassionate desk man," wrote McGrory, said, "Well here's to you Murray," after which a toast was drunk by all. Then Gart gave his well wishes to executive director Bill McIlwain, who was leaving for a new job. McGrory remembered Bill hopped on a desk with a foot still healing from recent surgery to say to the crowd, "I can't tell you how much I admire you" and then his voice broke. Staffers gave McIlwain hearty cheers, and according to McGrory, everyone "began to drink in earnest" after that. Phil Gailey retrieved his auto harp from home, and Timothy O'Leary, a third-generation O'Leary at the paper, found his guitar and together they played while everyone sang along. Walter Diercks remembered the staff was pretty angry at Time, Inc. for reneging on its commitment, but after "having interacted with Jim Shepley on the day it was announced; I know the grief that was felt there," and believed that "senior people on site" like Hoyt and Gart tried very hard to make it work. McGrory's Sunday, July 26 column left no doubt of her shabby opinion of Time, Inc. "To us, they were Roman generals, who came to the provinces and found natives who had their own ideas and not the slightest hesitation in expressing them. We acted as if we thought we owned the paper. That's because, in a way, we did." Mary also expressed some pent-up anger at Washington readers, lecturing, "Don't worry, I'm not going to weep all over you. I've just lost a newspaper and so, people of Washington have you . . . We're sad. But we're mad too . . . the outrage of it—the capital of the Western World a one-paper town."[27]

In the three weeks between announcing the closing on July 23 and the actual closing on August 7, 1980, some sixty buyers approached Time, Inc. to purchase the *Star*. In the end none were committed to operate the *Star* long enough and meet certain obligations to staff that satisfied Time, Inc. despite meeting their asking price. One of the more interesting offers was an effort by the *Star*'s unions led by the Newspaper Guild to find investors to buy the paper and allow the unions to operate it. All the unions agreed to make sacrifices to their contracts to make it work, according to union leader Carlos Sutton. Sutton and Raymond Dick approached Robert Linowes, former president of the Washington Board of Trade, among others, to help them find investors, but Time, Inc. never really took the unions seriously. The impending closing induced a number of prominent journalists across the country to express their regrets and belated praise for the *Star* before it closed. *Washington Post*'s David Broder and Haynes Johnson, who got their starts as young political reporters at the *Star*, wrote about what the paper meant to them. Broder wrote, "I'm not objective about the *Star*. I worked there for five happy years. I have many friends on the staff" and "it embodies one of the great journalistic traditions in America . . . No paper in America had a clearer sense of its own values . . . This capital and this country need the kind of newspaper it has been." Haynes Johnson, who won a Pulitzer at the *Star*, had a deep respect for editors who gave him the freedom to explore and write the stories he wanted. Johnson also expressed a keen affection for the "old fashioned . . . sober . . . prosperous . . . paternalistic paper" it once was, where all its employees were treated extremely well and paid top dollar. Johnson posed the question to his friend David Broder, who he met at the *Star*: "Did you tell them . . . what fun we had" and how much we enjoyed "sticking it to the *Post*." *Nightline* TV show host Ted Koppel told his audience that closing the *Star* "deprives many of us of some of the finest journalists and editors ever to work together in one place," and *New York Times* columnist James Reston blamed Washingtonians for killing "the best afternoon newspaper in the country." The *Post*'s Richard Cohen gave the *Star* one of its truest and most enduring compliments when he wrote it was a "thoroughly honest paper. If you read it in the *Star*, you knew it was true."[28]

The *Star*'s "Final Edition" was published on August 7, 1981, and contained the news of the day, but mostly it was a memorial full of testimonies from those who celebrated the paper's 129-year history and mourned its loss. Mary McGrory had already received a secure job offer from the *Post* but refused to discuss her new job until the *Star* closed. Mary instead spent the last two weeks helping and cheering on dazed and mournful staff who were still searching for new jobs. Finally, Mary wrote her last column, which poured out her long and genuine affection for the people and newspaper she considered the "Home and the Luck of My Life." Mary remembered the *Star* in 1947 when she came as a book reviewer as a "large, untidy, noisy operation" full of generous, gossipy, and cheeky people like national news editor Chuck Egan in the 1940s, who she called "a rock-jawed giant who knew everyone's middle initial" as well as most Kentucky Derby winners. The *Star*'s editor Ben McKelway through the 1950s, she wrote, "was revered for his probity, his dignity, his fairness and the whimsy that glinted through his shy sternness," who she always felt compelled to respectfully address only as "Mr. McKelway." Jerry O'Leary regrettably was not in the newsroom when the end came but at a Reagan administration briefing in Santa Barbara, California, where White House deputy press secretary Larry Speakes led reporters in a chorus of "For He's a Jolly Good Fellow" and toasted O'Leary with coffee and sweet rolls to ease the pain. *Star* veterans Mary Lou Forbes and George Beveridge prepared a synopsis of the *Star*'s history, and sportswriters Steve Hershey, Joe Kelly, and Morrie Siegel wrote some of their best behind-the-scenes stories never printed before. The last edition carried images of historic front pages, historic events, and the paper's own past. *Star* political cartoons by the Berrymans, Gib Crockett, Bill Garner, and Pat Oliphant were there too. Three pages of letters to the editors from the public were printed, and a reprint of a letter from President Reagan, whose closing words were "there is a great silence today in Washington. A fine newspaper is gone and a noble tradition ended." Letters to the editor were sent by politicians, journalists, former *Star* staff and their children and grandchildren, former newsboys and newsgirls, and many from loyal subscribers. Florence S. Berryman, daughter of *Star* cartoonist Clifford Berryman and sister of Jim Berryman, who herself worked for the *Star* for twenty-two years, wrote, "It will be like a death in my family. I've lived with the *Star* all my life. My parents subscribed to it before I was born, and I have since they died. . . . So there will be a big hole in my life." A father wrote of his sons who as boys with *Star* paper routes "first learned public relations, public service and the reward of doing a good job." Some writers were angry at Time, Inc. and some at Washingtonians, like the subscriber who wrote, "The *Star* is not being closed because of too-tough competition from the *Post* . . . it is being closed because of lousy out-of-town, out-of-touch management!" and another who asked, "Why, if the staff at the *Star* is so good and talented . . . is the newspaper going out of business? Is it that the tastes of us Washingtonians are getting to be so deplorable that we don't even recognize talent anymore?" An eighty-one-year-old wrote to say she had been reading the *Star* since 1910 and would miss it a lot, and another loyal subscriber said she "cried this morning when the announcement was made." There were also newer subscribers, like the mother who replied, "No, it can't be" when her sixteen-year-old daughter told her the *Star* was closing, and for her "the day went downhill after that," or another who begged, "For God's sake, don't do it. I would pay for two subscriptions if it would help," but it was too late. A pressman and World War II veteran unsure of his future told Phil Gailey, "I think I'm going see a few grown men cry today," and one of those men was Denis Horgan. Horgan, who had reluctantly resigned from the paper just weeks before, cried when he heard the news, and years later said with sadness "the *Star* has a piece of my soul forever and I miss it so." A *Star* switchboard operator who, after answering calls from hundreds of well-wishers, finally broke into tears herself after hearing a caller cry over the phone. Bailey Morris, a young female staffer, wrote, "Losing a newspaper is like having a death in the family. Most of all, it hurts," and for those without a job "who are older and less mobile—it may mean accepting something less." The public ordered 425,000 copies of the final edition—one hundred thousand over the normal press run and slightly above the highest record set by the *Star*. On August 7, 1981, the presses shut down for the final time at the *Star*'s plant, and the lights went out in the *Star*'s newsroom forever. Some *Star* staff went to Capitol Hill bars to commiserate with one another and soothe their sorrow in drink, and others just went home to find solace. On that summer evening at dusk the final edition of the *Star* was seen on Washington's streets as night fell over the city. As starlight has sprinkled the evening sky in the nation's capital ever since, countless named and unnamed ghosts from the *Star*'s past that haunt the places where its history was made ensure that the story of a great newspaper once published there is never forgotten.[29]

Notes

CHAPTER 1

1. "Execution of Brown at Charlestown," *Evening Star* (hereafter ES), December 2, 1859.

2. "*Evening Star*–Draft Historical Sketches" [ca. 1938 and 1952], Papers of the *Washington Star* Newspaper, 1852–1981, Washingtoniana Division, Special Collections, D.C. Public Library (hereafter *Star* Papers); Hal P. Denton, "The Homes of the *Evening Star*," *Fiftieth Anniversary Supplement*, ES, December 16, 1902, 21–22.

3. Newbold Noyes, "Crosby Stuart Noyes: His Life and Times," *Records of the Columbia Historical Society* 40–41 (1940): 197–225; William Bowman, written answers to author's questions, April 11, 2005.

4. Crosby S. Noyes, "Washington Journalism, Past and Present," *Anniversary Supplement*, 38.

5. Ibid.

6. Ibid.

7. Samuel H. Kauffmann, "*The Evening Star* (1852–1952): A Century at the Nation's Capital" (address to the Newcomen Society, Washington, D.C., March 28, 1952), 13, *Star* Papers; "The Inauguration of Abraham Lincoln President of the United States," ES, March 4, 1861.

8. Noyes, "Crosby Stuart Noyes: His Life and Times," 207; J. Cutler Andrews, *The North Reports the Civil War* (Pittsburgh: University of Pittsburgh Press, 1955), 410–11.

9. W. D. Wallach to C. S. Noyes, October 4, 1867; C. S. Noyes to W. D. Wallach, October 7, 1867; W. D. Wallach to C. S. Noyes, October 9, 1867; and Samuel Hay Kauffmann to Benjamin Harrison Kauffmann, October 30, 1867: in *Star* Papers.

10. "Historical Sketches," *Star* Papers.

11. *"The Evening Star," Progress: A Weekly Journal Devoted to Advertising and the Business Interests of Washington, DC* (July 9, 1894): 241; Autobiography of Gideon Lyon, n.d.; and Rudolph M. Kauffmann, "Reminiscences by R. M. Kauffmann, 1952": in *Star* Papers.

12. F. DeWolfe Miller, "Struggling Walt Whitman Had Press Agent's Skill," ES, July 30, 1961; "The Evening Star," *Progress*, 245.

13. Denton, "Homes of the *Evening Star*," *Anniversary Supplement*.

14. Ibid.

CHAPTER 2

1. Samuel H. Kauffmann, "A Century at the Nation's Capital," 12, *Star* Papers.

2. "Historical Sketches," *Star* Papers; James H. Whythe, "The District of Columbia Territorial Government," *Records of the Columbia Historical Society* 51–52 (1955): 87–102; William M. Maury, "Alexander 'Boss' Shepherd and the Board of Public Works," *George Washington University Studies* 3 (1975); Tom Dowling, "Alexander Shepherd: Model 19th Century Go-Getter," *Washington Star* (hereafter WS), November 25, 1976.

3. Whythe, "The District of Columbia Territorial Government"; Maury, "Alexander 'Boss' Shepherd."

4. Theodore Noyes, "Some of Washington's Grievances: No Votes, Yet No Grievance?" ES, March 10, 1888.

5. Editorial, ES, December 7, 1889.

6. Oswald Garrison Villard, "Washington, a Capital without a Thunderer," in *Some Newspapers and Newspaper Men* (New York: Alfred A. Knopf, 1923), 178–79; Grover W. Ayers, *A City-State in the United States: Proposed? Opposed*, Pamphlet (Washington, D.C.: Ten Miles Square Club, n.d.) in Vertical Files, Washingtoniana Division, DCPL; Anthony Thompson, *The Story of the 23rd Amendment* (Senior Thesis, Princeton University, 1965), 21.

7. Katharine Graham, *Katharine Graham: Personal History* (New York: Alfred A. Knoff, 1997), 188; Editorial, *Washington Times*, November 22, 1897; Theodore Noyes to Theodore Roosevelt, August 11, 1902; and Crosby Noyes to Theodore Roosevelt, August 15, 1902, in Theodore Roosevelt Papers, Library of Congress (hereafter LC).

8. Graham, *Personal History*, 189; "Benjamin McKelway Dies; Retired Editor of the Star," WS, August 31, 1976; Mary McGrory, transcript of oral history interviews by Kathleen Currie, August 4, 1991, and July 26, 1992, 12, Women in Journalism Oral History Project, National Press Club Archives, Washington, D.C.; Senator Estes Kefauver, Statement before Senate Committee on Expenditures, June 7, 1951, in Jessica Elfenbein, *Civics, Commerce and Community: The History of the Greater Washington Board of Trade, 1889–1989* (Washington, DC: Center for Washington Area Studies, George Washington University, 1989), 65; Editorial, "Senator Kefauver's Mistakes," ES, June 10, 1951.

9. Editorials, "Redevelopment Issues," and Editorial, "Upgraded Area B," ES, December 19, 1952, and May 2, 1953.

10. Mary Lou Werner-Forbes, interview by author, June 24, 2006; Patricia Barron, interview by author, March 23, 2007.

11. Thompson, *The Story of the 23rd Amendment*, 24–41; Editorial, "The Past Is Prologue," ES, March 30, 1961; Morton Mintz, "D.C. Suffrage Victory Upsets Foes of Home Rule," WP, April 13, 1961.

12. Martha Derthick, "The Press," in *City Politics in Washington, D.C.* (Cambridge, MA: Harvard University Press, 1962), 111; Remarks by Benjamin McKelway, January 10, 1964, Greater Washington Board of Trade Archives, Special Collections, George Washington University.

13. Harry N. Hirshberg, notes, March 7, 1966; Harry N. Hirshberg to F. Elwood Davis, March 10, 1966; William Press to Elwood Davis, March 15, 1966; "Memorandum for the Record re: Officers' Meeting Concerning SNCC Home Rule Activities," n.d.; and Harry N. Hirshberg, statement re: "Retail Boycott Threat," March 10, 1966: in Washington Board of Trade Archives.

14. Ronald Sarro, interviews by author, November 23, 2009, and January 25, 2010; Paul Delaney, interview by author, March 16, 2007.

15. Diane Brockett, "Lack of Promised Funds Slows Forest Haven Reform," "Forest Haven's Retarded Sorely Need More Teachers," and "Here's Why Queene Resigned as Forest Haven Boss," WS, February 2, 1976, April 29, 1975, and November 4, 1976.

16. Ned Scharff, interview by author, November 23, 2015; Scharff, "Four Yeldell Relatives Are on DHR Payroll," WS, November 18, 1976; Philip Shandler, "Yeldell Defense: Everybody Does It," and Kenneth Walker and Gloria Borger, "Yeldell Defense . . . : The Rally," WS, November 24, 1976; Michael Kiernan, "Analysis: The Mayor and How He Handles Crisis," WS, November 25, 1976.

17. James B. Rowland and Jerry Oppenheimer, "Friends Gather with Mandel for a Bourbon," WS, November 25, 1975; Editorial, "Indictment of a Governor," WS, November 26, 1975; Rowland, "Mandel's Dream: To Leave His Mark on Maryland's History," WS, November 25, 1975.

18. Rowland, "Governor Mandel Calls Federal Indictment a Fraud," WS, December 1, 1975.

19. Editorial, "Low Drama in Baltimore," WS, December 9, 1976.

20. Kiernan, "The Waning Political Power of D.C.'s First Elected Mayor," and "The Washington Decade," WS, January 3 and September 4, 1977.

21. Kiernan, "Candidate John Ray," and "Judging a Campaign by the Headquarters It Keeps," WS, August 26, and July 16, 1978; Michael Kiernan, interview by author, November 2015; Editorial, "The Next Mayor," WS, September 10, 1978; Editorial, "Marion Barry for Mayor," WP, August 30, 1978.

22. Michael Davis with contributions from Laura Murray, "Barrys Get Break on Home Loan," WS, December 7, 1979; Lurma Rackley, interview by author, November 24, 2015; Rackley, "He Loved Us and We Loved Him Back: A Remembrance of Marion Barry," *Washington Informer*, December 19, 2014.

CHAPTER 3

1. "The *Washington Star*," *Washington Bee*, April 27, 1918; Villard, "Capital without a Thunderer," 172, 179; "1st Separate Battalion Played Heroic Part in Defeat of Huns," ES, February 14, 1919; C. Vann Woodward, *The Strange Career of Jim Crow*, 2nd rev. ed. (New York: Oxford University Press, 1966), 114–15.

2. Editorial, "Outbreak of Devility," ES, July 7, 1919; "Statement about the District of Columbia Branch of the NAACP Activities as of July 23rd in Connection with the Riots," n.d., Records of the National Association for the Advancement of Colored People, LC; "Colored Citizens' Paper Demands That Criminal Be Caught and Punished," ES, July 9, 1919.

3. "Woman Attacked on Way from Work," ES, July 19, 1919; "Negroes Attack Girl," WP, July 19, 1919; "Men in Uniform Attack Negroes," ES, July 20, 1919; Arthur I. Waskow, "The Washington Riot," chap. III in *From Race Riot to Sit-In: A Study in the Connections between Conflict and Violence* (Garden City, NY: Doubleday & Company, Anchor Books, 1967), 23.

4. "Four Shots Fired at Convalescents and Four at Marine from Auto," and "Military Authorities Co-Operate with Maj. Pullman to Bring Order," ES, July 21, 1919; "Crime Stirs Citizens: A Mobilization for Tonight," WP, July 21, 1919; John Shillady, Secretary of the NAACP, to US Attorney General A. Mitchell Palmer, July 25, 1919, NAACP records; Louis Brownlow, *A Passion for Anonymity: The Autobiography of Louis Brownlow, Vol. 2* (Chicago: University of Chicago Press, 1958), 84.

5. Transcript of July 20, 1919, Sunday night meeting, NAACP records; "Civil War Times Recalled by Wild Night's Tumult," "Scores Injured during Riots Are Treated at Hospitals," and "Disorders Numerous Despite Combined Forces thought to Be Ample," ES, July 22, 1919; William G. Haan to Major General Thomas H., July 30, 1919, William George Haan Papers, 1864–1924, Wisconsin State Historical Society cited in Waskow, "Washington Riot," 28–29; Editorial, "A Climax of Mob Crime," ES, July 22, 1919.

6. "Marian Anderson Wins Tribute of 75,000 at Concert," ES, April 10, 1939.

7. Ben W. Gilbert, "Towards a Color Blind Newspaper: Race Relations and the *Washington Post*," *Washington History* 5, no. 2 (Fall/Winter 1993–94): 14–16; "Krug, Commissioners to Meet Tomorrow on Recreation Problems," ES, June 30, 1949; Benjamin C. Bradlee, *Ben Bradlee, A Good Life: Newspapering and Other Adventures* (New York: Simon & Schuster, 1995), 125–27; Editorial, "What Next Mr. Krug," ES, June 30, 1949; Editorial, "D.C. Swimming Pools," WP, June 30, 1949.

8. Gilbert, "Towards a Color Blind Newspaper," 9–16, 21–22; Michele F. Pacifico, "Don't Buy Where You Can't Work: The New Negro Alliance of Washington," *Washington History* 6, no. 1 (Spring 1994): 74; "Daily Paper Is Charged with Bias," *Pittsburgh Courier*, June 14, 1952; Mara Cherkasky, "For Sale to Colored: Racial Change on S Street, NW," *Washington History* 8, no. 2 (Fall/Winter 1996–1997): 51.

9. "The Ban on Segregation," ES, May 18, 1954; "Emancipation," WP, May 18, 1954; "On Segregation," *Washington Daily News*, May 18, 1954; "Let's Give Thanks," *Pittsburgh Courier*, May 29, 1954.

10. Harvie Wilkinson III, "Massive Resistance, 1954–1960," chap. 5 in *Harry Byrd and the Changing Face of Virginia Politics, 1945–1966* (Charlottesville: University Press of Virginia, 1968), 113–33; Benjamin Muse, *Virginia's Massive Resistance* (Bloomington: Indiana University Press, 1961), 25–34; James W. Ely Jr., *The Crisis of Conservative Virginia: The Byrd Organization and the Politics of Massive Resistance* (Knoxville: University of Tennessee Press, 1976), 30–31, 44–46; Werner-Forbes, interview; "Pulitzer Winners," ES, May 5, 1959.

11. Werner-Forbes, interview.

12. Ely, *Crisis of Conservative Virginia,* 20, 61–62; Werner-Forbes, interview; Mary Lou Werner, "Virginia Sues to Test Its Own School Law," ES, September 14, 1958; John D. Morris, "Virginia to Test School Closings in a State Court," *New York Times* (hereafter NYT), September 14, 1958.

13. Werner-Forbes, interview; Ely, *The Crisis of Conservative Virginia,* 62; Wilkinson, *Harry Byrd,* 142–47.

14. "Crowd at School Jeers Newsmen," NYT, September 10, 1957.

15. Haynes Johnson, interviews by author, November 20, 2006, and April 7, 2007; "Observations on Our Series: 'Negro in Washington,'" ES, June 16, 1961.

16. Taylor Branch, "Baptism on Wheels," in *Parting the Waters: America in the King Years, 1954–1963* (New York: Touchstone, Simon & Schuster, Inc., 1989), 412–50; Gene Roberts and Hank Klibanoff, *The Race Beat: The Press, The Civil Rights Struggle, and the Awakening of a Nation* (New York: Alfred A. Knopf, 2006), 243–55; Miriam Ottenberg, "White House Orders Action to Keep Order," ES, May 21, 1961.

17. Cecil Holland, "U.S. Warned to Stay Out of Race Fight," "Mississippi Comes Next for Students," "11 Aboard for Trip to Mississippi," "27 Jailed Riders Reject NAACP Offer of Bail," and "Cities in Contrast: Police Hold Key to Order," ES, May 22, 23, 24, 25, and 28, 1961; Miriam Ottenberg, "Governor Acts After Night of Violence," and "Robert Kennedy Asks Restraint in South," ES, May 22 and 24, 1961.

18. Ottenberg, "Going to Be Enrolled, Robert Kennedy Says," ES, September 29, 1962; Holland, "Meredith Registered; Two Die, Scores Hurt," ES, October 1, 1962; David S. Broder, "The Star Deserves to Live," WP, July 29, 1981.

19. P. Barron, interview.

20. Paul Hope, "Two Students Will Enroll, U.S. Promises," ES, June 11, 1963; Editorial "The Door Is Open," ES, June 12, 1963.

21. Hope, "Justice Aide Helps Stop Race Clash in Jackson," ES, June 15, 1963; John Barron, "Talks Snagged in Cambridge," ES, June 16, 1963.

22. Editorial, "Don't Chance It," ES, July 12, 1963; Clarence Hunter, "Rights Groups to See Police on D.C. March," "Special Communication Net Slated for August 28 March," and "Parking for Marchers Remains Big Problem," ES, August 10, 11, and 22, 1963; Editorial, "Wednesday's March," ES, August 26, 1963; McGrory, "Born in Protest, Freedom March Flowers in Civility," Myra MacPherson, "Javits Party Buzzes with March Successes," Jeremiah O'Leary Jr., "Rights Crowd Melts Quickly," John McKelway, "The Rambler: Above It All," and David Broder, "Successful March Pleases Leaders of Civil Rights Drive," ES, August 29, 1963.

23. Paul Hope, interview by author, April 9, 2007; Hope, "Birmingham Buries Its Dead," ES, September 18, 1963; Editorial, "The Church Bombers," ES, September 16, 1963.

24. Barron, "Keep 'Meddlers' Out Mississippi Whites Ask," ES, June 28, 1964.

25. P. Barron, interview; Barron, "Negro Couple's Story of a Night of Terror," ES, June 30, 1964; Editorial, "Bill Passed," ES, July 3, 1964.

26. Johnson, interviews; Roberts and Klibanoff, *The Race Beat,* 379; Johnson, "Selma's Serene Appearance Belies Racial Turbulence," ES, February 7, 1965.

27. Johnson, interviews; Johnson, "Battle Hymn Welcomes Dr. King," ES, March 9, 1965.

28. Johnson, interviews.

29. C. Hunter, "People Together in a Single Purpose" ES, March 25, 1965; Johnson, "Quiet Withdrawal Winds up March in Montgomery," and "Selma Revisited: 4 Months After Their 'Finest Hour' Rights Forces Are in Disarray," ES, March 26, and July 26, 1965.

30. Delaney, interview.

31. Ernest Holsendolph and Michael Adams, "1,000 Turn Out to Hear H. Rap Brown in District," ES, July 28, 1967; "Negro Youths Go on Rampage in Mid-City," ES, August 1, 1967; Delaney, interview.

32. Crosby S. Noyes, "Riot Threat Requires Calling Off King's March," ES, April 4, 1968; Delaney, interview.

33. Delaney, interview; Harry Jaffe, *Dream City: Race, Power, and the Decline of Washington, DC* (New York: Simon & Schuster, 1994), 71–80; Delaney, "Mayor Witnesses Looting," ES, April 5, 1968.

34. Delaney, interview; April 5, 1968 edition, ES; "Riots Bring Best from Star Staff," *The Family Star*, May 1968.

35. "Riots Bring Best from Star Staff"; Steve Hershey, "The Biggest Story Produced No Words," ES, August 7, 1981; Looting and Arson by Crowds Spread to Center of City," ES, April 5, 1968.

36. "Fauntroy, Carmichael Reactions to Slaying," ES, April 5, 1968; Winston Groom, interview by author, February 2, 2007; Groom, "A Close-Up: Washington's April Riots," *The Family Star*, May 1968.

37. "Riots Bring Best from Star Staff"; Groom, interview.

38. Johnson, interviews; Johnson, "A Washingtonian Travels His Ravaged City," and "150,000 Attend Rites for King," ES, April 7 and 9, 1968.

39. Editorial, "Trial by Fire," ES, April 9, 1968; Martin Weil, "Newspaper Coverage of Blacks Criticized," WP, June 15, 1969.

40. Newbold Noyes Jr. to President Richard Nixon, handwritten letter, January 8, 1973; Newbold Noyes Jr., handwritten notes of White House Oval Office meeting with President Nixon and John Ehlichman, March 8, 1974, in Noyes family private papers (hereafter Noyes Papers).

CHAPTER 4

1. Tom Kelly, "General Sickles Cuts a Swath in Lafayette Park," in *Murders: Washington's Most Famous Murder Stories* (Washington, DC: Washingtonian Books, 1976), 73–82.

2. "The District Courts: Ten Years' Progress," *Fiftieth Anniversary Edition*, ES, December 16, 1902; "Police Affairs" and "Inquest," ES, November 2, 1859.

3. John W. Lynch, *800 Paces to Hell: Andersonville, A Compilation of Known Facts and Persistent Rumors* (Fredericksburg, VA: Sergeant Kirkland's Museum and Historical Society, 1999), 340; Alexander Gardner, "Witnesses for Wirz Hanging," photo reprint in *The Washington Star's First 100 Years in the Nation's Capital, Centennial Anniversary Special Section*, December 16, 1952, 7; Mark Katz, *Alexander Gardner, Witness to an Era: The Life and Photographs of Alexander Gardner* (New York: Viking Press, 1991), 196; "Extra: Execution of Wirz: Last Hours of the Condemned

Man. Conduct on the Gallows . . . " ES, November 10, 1865; Autobiography of G. Lyon, *Star* Papers.

4. Crosby S. Noyes, "Journalism since Jamestown" (Address to the National Editorial Association, Jamestown Tercentennial Exposition, Jamestown, VA, June 13, 1907); and Kauffmann, "Reminiscences": in *Star* Papers.

5. "Rowboat Ferry Service in Capital In '89 Is Recalled," ES, March 18, 1936.

6. Kauffmann, "Reminiscences" and "Historical Sketches": in *Star* Papers; George Kennedy, "He Was There When Ford Theater Fell," ES, July 25, 1951.

7. Smith Hempstone, written answers to author's questions, April 22, 2005; "Enter Prohibition," Star*'s First 100 Years,* 19; "King Booze Quits Throne in Capital," ES, November 1, 1917; Chalmers Roberts, The Washington Post: *The First 100 Years* (Boston: Houghton Mifflin Company, 1977), 154; Linda Wheeler, "The Day It Poured," WP, February 27, 1994.

8. Pete Martin (aka Philip C. Kauffmann), "Star Reporter, in Jail, Find District Prison No Paradise," and "Prisoners in Jail Here Herded Like Animals in Dirty Germ-Landen Cells," ES, March 7, 1926; "Zihlman to Offer Bill Remedying Jail Conditions," and "Members of House Call for Remedy of Jail Conditions," ES, March 8 and 10, 1926.

9. "Roof Collapses under Snow and Balcony Falls," ES, January 29, 1922; Woody West, "50 Years Ago Today, a Disaster," ES, January 28, 1972; Gerard O. Herndon, "Knickerbocker Tragedy 40 Years Ago Recalled," ES, January 28, 1962.

10. Cy Perkins, "Away Back When," *The Family Star,* December 1960–January 1961; John H. Cline, "Linking Gambler to Wilson Killing," ES, October 24, 1935; "Jury Is Guarded for Wilson Probe" and "Four Are Indicted in Wilson Killing," ES, January 20 and 21, 1936.

11. Carter Brooke Jones, "Startling Jump in D.C. Crime, Blamed on Numbers Race . . . ," ES, January 2, 1938; *The Family* Star, February to March, 1961; Jones, "'Numbers' Ring Heads Face Tax Fraud Charge," and "The Lawyer Blamed the Newspapers and the *Star* Accepts the Blame," ES, March 30, 1938, and February 26, 1939.

12. Joseph C. Goulden, "The *Evening Star*: The Good Grey Lady Is No. 2, and Not Really Trying Harder," *The Washingtonian* (January 1970): 69; Harriet Griffiths, "Faces Made to Order," ES, August 27, 1961; Mattson Kidnaper Drawn by *Star* Artist," ES, February 3, 1937.

13. Teresa and Timothy O'Leary, joint interview by author, July 10, 2006; "Priest Freed Boy of Possession by Devil, Church Sources Say," ES, August 19, 1949; "'The Exorcist': The Story That Almost Wasn't," *Washington Star-News* (hereafter SN), December 29, 1973.

14. Haynes Johnson, "Peanuts on Payday" in "*Washington Star* Memories: Newsroom Nostalgia and Legends of the *Washington Star*," WP, August 7, 1981; J. O'Leary Jr. and Dana Bullen, excerpts in *The Day America Dropped the Adam Bomb, and Other Memories, Confessions and Lore from the Crew of the Late, Great* Washington/Evening Star: [for] *Tenth Year Reunion* (September 28, 1991): 7, 14; Elsie Carper, "Reporter Miriam Ottenberg of the *Washington Star* Dies," WP, November 10, 1982; Ottenberg, *The Federal Prosecutors* (New York: Giant Cardinal edition, November 1963), "Dedication page."

15. Edwin Tribble, draft report to Rudy Kauffmann, January 16, 1953, Tribble Bio file, *Star* Papers; Harry Bacus, excerpt in *America Dropped the Adam Bomb*, 17; Editorial, "Union Station Wreck," January 16, 1953; "Edwin Tribble, Editor at *Star*, Dies," WP, May 28, 1986.

16. Ottenberg, "The Parking Lot Murder" ES, March 1, 1953; Alfred E. Lewis, "Detectives Question 5000," WP, April 7, 1953.

17. Ottenberg, "Five-Man Council Will Map Juvenile Crime Probe . . . ," "New Juvenile Court Waiver Setup Urged," and "U.S. Attorney Supported on Juvenile Trials," ES, October 9, 1953, January 18 and January 26, 1954; Ottenberg, "Legal Ruling Blocks Mental Health Program," "District General Mental Case Impasse Ends," and "Bill Curbing Phony Pleas of Insanity Become Law," ES, October 17, 1954, March 13 and August 10, 1955; Ottenberg and Sam Eastman, "Code Book Bars $1 Million-a-Year Abortionist Rings," ES, July 6, 1958; Ottenberg, "Mallory Case Matches Speed . . . " ES, January 12, 1958; Editorial, "As Clear as Mud," ES, January 15, 1957; Editorial, "Cutting Corners," WP, November 25, 1957.

18. "Statements of Prisoners: Robert E. Martz and Frederick C. Sampson," "Letter Upholds *Star* Reporter," "Prisoners Fear Police Reprisal," and "Police Brutality Probe Tops 1932 Local News," ES, August 25, August 28, and December 27, 1931; Ottenberg, "How the 'Secret Seven' Laid Trap for Police . . . ," ES, September 19, 1954.

19. Miriam Ottenberg to Bill Hill, n.d.; Ottenberg to John A. S. Cushman, September 3, 1964, in Miriam Ottenberg Papers, Wisconsin Historical Society; Attorney General Robert F. Kennedy, "Foreword," in Ottenberg, *The Federal Investigators*, ix.

20. Ottenberg, "Special Report: The Haters," ES, March 9, 1965.

21. "7 Slayings Laid to Muslim Feud," SN, January 19, 1973; Michael Satchell and Chris Lorenzo, "7 Indicted in Sect Killings," SN, August 16, 1973; Paul Delaney, "Survivor Tells of Killings of 7 Moslems in Capital," NYT, February 23, 1973; Winston Groom, interview by author, August 17, 2011; Paul Delaney, unpublished manuscript excerpt, n.d. (mailed to author); Groom, email to author, August 4, 2011.

22. Groom, "Muslim Murder Trial to Begin," "3 Muslims Identified as Killers," "Survivor Assaults Muslims at Trial," "Hanafi Is Found Not in Contempt," and "New Probe Due in Hanafi Killings," SN, February 10, February 28, March 1, March 5, and May 18, 1974.

23. Groom, "Prison Told of Fear for Informer's Life," WS, January 23, 1975; Ned Scharff, "Slain Man Put with a Killer He Helped Convict," WS, January 5, 1975; Groom, "7 Life Sentences to Muslim Killer," WS, January 7, 1975; Toni House, "Anguish Puts a Crimp in Hanafi Trial," WS, October 13, 1976.

24. Mary Ann Kuhn, "In Focus: How to Face-to-Face Turned the Crisis Around" and Walter Taylor, "The Hard Luck Story of 'Eddie the Painter' and Family," WS, March 11, 1977.

25. Brad Holt, "Cameras Seized: Police Rough Up Two Cameramen," SN, June 15, 1974; Mike Adams, "Adams and Sterba Tell 'The Story Behind the Story,'" *The Family Star*, May–June–July, 1967.

CHAPTER 5

1. Kauffmann, "Reminiscences"; and "A Valediction to a Departing Member of the *Star*'s Staff, John P. Miller, 1899": in *Star* Papers; Gore Vidal, *1876* (New York: Random House, 1976), 147–48; Helena McCarthy, "Social Gaities before the War," *Fiftieth Anniversary Supplement*, 39; H. H. Fry, "The Star and Sports," *Fiftieth Anniversary Edition*; "The *Evening Star*," *Progress*, 246–47.

2. Bowman, answers to questions; Shirley Povich, *The Washington Senators* (New York: G. P. Putnam and Sons, 1954), 41, 61–62.

3. J. Ed Grillo, "Johnson Alone Must Decide Whether He Will Play Here," ES, December 2, 1914; Povich, *Washington Senators*, 89–91.

4. "The Rambler Writes of Virginia Ancestors," ES, January 15, 1919.

5. Cy Perkins, "Away Back When," *The Family Star*, December 1960–January 1961; "Just a Timely Word as to the Wedding Invitations," and "Happy the Bride the Sun Shines On," ES, February 10, and February 17, 1906.

6. Perkins, "Away Back When"; "Katharine M. Brooks," ES, March 29, 1979; *The Family Star*, January–February 1967.

7. "City Goes Insane in Carnival Sport," and "Griff's Tear Loose After Game and Celebrate Like Schoolboys," ES, October 11, 1924; Francis E. Stann, "Cronin Will Vary Offensive," ES, April 17, 1933; Merrell Whittlesey, "Over 43 Years Stann Covered All the Bases," ES, May 26, 1973; Oliver Owen Kuhn to Theodore Noyes, memorandum, March 28, 1934, *Star* Papers.

8. Whittlesey, " . . . Stann Covered All the Bases"; Morris Siegel, "Starstruck," *Regardies* (August 1984): 57–58; Burton Hawkins, "Dissension Over Bluege Blamed for Nat's Flop," and "All Again Sweetness and Light Among Nats," ES, August 20, and August 22, 1947; "Nats' Pilot, Scribe Again Are 'Pals,'" ES, August 23, 1947.

9. Bill Dismer Jr., "Gridiron Finese Is Redskins' Need," ES, September 7, 1937; Lewis F. Atchison, "Football Expert Lew Atchison to Cover Redskins' Training," ES, July 28, 1948; "Atchison Wins McCann Award," ES, January 16, 1972.

10. Kuhn to Noyes, March 28, 1934, *Star* Papers; "Nice Lady," letter to the editor, ES, July 16, 1958.

11. "Critic Carmody Retires May 1," ES, April 5, 1964; Jay Carmody, "Hitchcock's Touch Is Evident in Making of His Movies," ES, September 22, 1952; Woody West, "Jay Carmody, Longtime Critic for the *Star* Dies," SN, June 19, 1973 ; Carmody, "So This Can Happen to a Tragic Drama," ES, March 29, 1960; Al Horne, "Actor Berates Drama Critic in After-Monologue," WP, April 3, 1960; "A View from the Footlights," *Washington Daily News*, April 2, 1960.

12. "Woman of the Year: Eleni Epstein" brochure (American Legion Post No. 18: Washington, D.C., 1972), Epstein bio file, *Star* Papers; Betty Beale, *Power at Play: A Memoir of Parties, Politicians and the President in My Bedroom* (Washington, D.C.: Regnery Gateway Publishing, 1993), 2–31; Ami Stewart, "Betty Beale: Washingtonian by Birth, Georgetowner by Bent," *The Georgetowner* (January 5, 1956): 1; Tom Kelly and Judy Hennessee, "The Remarkable Betty Beale," *The Washingtonian* (March 1967): 33.

13. George Kennedy, "The Rambler Observed a Birthday," ES, March 23, 1962; John McKelway, "The Rambler Has an Announcement," ES, November 3, 1964; Myra McPherson, "The Rambler" in *"Washington Star* Memories."

14. Betty Beale, "Perle Gives Whirl on River . . . ," ES, July 13, 1959.

15. Isabelle Shelton, excerpt in *America Dropped the Adam Bomb*, 18; Isabelle Shelton, "A Mad Day with LBJ," ES, February 16, 1964; "Likes and Dislikes," letter to the editor, ES, August 14, 1966.

16. J. O'Leary Jr., "Curmudgeons and Poets, They Were the Splendid Star," WS, August 7, 1981; George Kennedy, "The Rambler Will Never Forget," ES, July 20, 1963; Dick Heller, "Bill Peeler, Newspaperman," *Heller's Corner* (blog), February 14, 2014, http://www.dickheller.wordpress.com; Carl Sell, email to author, February 25, 2016.

17. Michael Tomasky, "The Racist Redskins," review of *Showdown: JFK and the Integration of the Washington Redskins* by Thomas G. Smith, *The New York Review* (November 20, 2011): 51–52; Atchison, "Court Action May Follow Udall Warning to Marshall," ES, March 25, 1961; Editorial "Kickoff," ES, August 17, 1961; Atchison, "Redskins Sign First Negro, Ron Hatcher . . . " ES, December 10, 1961; J. Gordon Hylton, "Who Was the First Black Redskin?" *Marquette University Law School Faculty Blog*, November 8, 2009, http://www.law.marquette.ede/facultyblog.

18. Atchison, "Crystal Ball Is Cloudy, Game Will Be Rowdy," ES, December 24, 1964; Promotion "Byline: Sports," ES, September 2, 1960"; *Family Star*, October–November 1962 and August–September, 1966; Russ White, "Egos Ride Air Waves," ES, February 27, 1972; Siegel, "Star Struck," 54, 55.

19. Charles Tracewell, "This and That" column, ES, February 14, 1957; Fifi Gorska, "Twirlathon," ES, March 5, 1966.

20. Beale, "Guess Who's Going to Be Married!" "Exclusively Yours" column, ES, January 1, 1969; Beale, *Power at Play*, 34, 54–57; "The Ladies Who Cover Washington: 'The Greatest Snobs Are Men,' Betty Beale," "Close-Up" column, *Life Magazine* (February 28, 1969): 32; Kelly and Hennessee, "The Remarkable Betty Beale," 33.

21. Beale, "The Other Side of the Picture," "Exclusively Yours," column, ES, September 1, 1968; Joseph Volz, "Star Sold: As Time Goes Buy . . . " *Washington Journalism Review*, (April/May, 1978): 22; *Editorial*, "White House 'Pools,'" SN, December 21, 1972; Katharine (Kay) Graham to Newbold Noyes Jr. (Newby), December 19, 1972, Noyes Papers.

22. Judy Bachrach, interview by author, September 7, 2010.

23. Steve Guback, "The Best of All Was New Year's Eve Game," WS, August 7, 1981; "The Sacking of Coach Allen," Letters to the Editor, WS, January 15, 1978; George Beveridge, "George Allen, the Press and the Rest of Us," ombudsman column, WS, January 24, 1978.

24. James Bellows, *The Last Editor, How I Saved the* New York Times, *the* Washington Post, *and the* Los Angeles Times *from Dullness and Complacency* (Kansas City, KS: Andrews McMeel Publishing, 2002), 174; Mary Anne Dolan, "Bellows Remembered by Mary Anne Dolan" (remarks by Ms. Dolan at Bellows memorial service), Kevin Roderick, ed., *L.A. Observed*, Editor's blog, March 19, 2009, http://www.laobserved.com/archives; Lynn Rosellini, interview by author, June 16, 2010.

25. Rosellini, interview.

26. Rosellini, interview; Rosellini, "The Double Life of a Bisexual Pro Football Star," and "Dave Kopay—Out in the Open," WS, December 9 and 11, 1975; Jane O'Reilly, "On the Sport Pages, Tell It Like It Isn't," WS, December 14, 1975.

27. Diana McLellan, interview by author, July 6, 2010; Steve Daley, "Secrets of the Town's Biggest Gossip," *The Washingtonian* (July 1978): 65.

28. McLellan, interview; Louise Lague, interview by author, June 30, 2010; Daley, "Secrets of the Town's Biggest Gossip," 65; David Braaten, "Earwigs Let Their Hair Down and Have a Ball," WS, June 21, 1976.

29. McLellan, interview; Lague, interview; Bellows, *The Last Editor*, 23–25.

30. Rosellini, interview.

31. Rosellini, interview. Bellows, *The Last Editor*, 200; Charles Seib, "A Bid for Washington Attention," ombudsman column, WP, November 24, 1978; William Safire, "Here's to Media Wars," NYT, November 27, 1978.

32. Edwin Yoder, email to author, November 20, 2016; Bachrach, interview; Sandra McElwaine, interview by author, April 27, 2007; Dennis Horgan, interview by author, November 14, 2016; Tom Dowling, "'Star Wars' Sequel: Empire-Building Act," WS, May 18, 1980; Richard Lee, "Society Wars: The Arrival of Murray Gart, the Resurrection of Betty Beale and Other Reporters from the Champagne and Caviar Battles Between the *Post* and *Star*," *The Washingtonian* (November 1, 1978): 148.

33. Bachrach, interview; Bachrach, "A Classic English Scandal of Politics, Sex, Money and Ambition," "Close-Up," column, WS, November 6, 1978.

34. Bachrach, interview; Betty Cuniberti, "Following Ups and Downs of a Star Named Al King," and Tim Kurkjian, "The Day-to-Day Routine Was Anything but Ordinary," WS, August 7, 1981.

CHAPTER 6

1. Kauffmann, "Century at the Nation's Capital," 13 *Star* Papers; Villard, "Washington, a Capital without a Thunderer," 181.

2. Historical Sketches, *Star* Papers; "The *Evening Star*," *Progress*, 245–48; Helen Thomas, *Front Row at the White House: My Life and Times* (New York: Simon & Schuster, 1999), 124; "News Bulletins: How the *Star* Informs the Public of Great Events," *Fiftieth Anniversary Edition*.

3. Lucy G. Barber, "'Without Precedent,' Coxey's Army Invades Washington, 1894," chap. 1 in *Marching on Washington: The Forging of an American Political Tradition* (Berkeley and Los Angeles, CA: University of California Press, 2002), 11–26; "The *Evening Star*," *Progress*, 247; "Coxeyites in Low Spirits," and "Coxey's Men Afloat," ES, April 11 and 17, 1894.

4. Carl Browne and William McDevitt, *When Coxey's "Army" Marched on Washington, 1894* (San Francisco, CA: 1944), Maryland Room, Special Collections, University of Maryland Libraries; Barber, "Without Precedent," 30–36; "Coxey's March Ends," ES, May 1, 1894; George Kennedy, "Met a Man Out of History," "The Rambler" column, ES, March 21, 1962.

5. "Talk with Cisneros," and "Visit to Gen. Gómez," ES, January 20 and 25, 1896.

6. "Expelled from Cuba," and "Back from Cuba," ES, February 4, and March 30, 1896; Charles H. Brown, *The Correspondents' War: Journalists in the Spanish-American War* (New York: Charles Scribner's Sons, 1967), 29, 110–12; "Topic of the House: The Alleged Letter of the Spanish Minister," ES, February 10, 1898.

7. Brown, *Correspondents' War*, 112–14; "No News from Pepper," "Receiving the News," "Officers Puzzled," "Discussing the Theories," and "Evidence of a Torpedo," ES, February 16, 17, and 18, 1898.

8. A. J. Clarke, "News Gathering in War Time," *Fiftieth Anniversary Supplement*, 33–34; Theodore Noyes, "Oriental America and Its Problems (Washington, DC: Press of Judd & Detweiler, 1903), v, in Theodore Noyes Papers, Washingtoniana Division, Special Collections, D.C. Public Library.

9. "Berryman, Dean of Cartoonists, 80 Today," ES, April 2, 1949; Noyes, "Journalism since Jamestown"; Philip H. Love, "C. K. Berryman: His Work Is Fun," ES, April 3, 1949; Gould Lincoln, transcript of oral history interview by Jerry N. Hess, August 10, 1967, 15, Truman Presidential Library.

10. Gould Lincoln, transcript of oral history interview by Dorothy Pierce, September 28, 1968, 12–13, Lyndon Baines Johnson Presidential Library; Thomas, *Front Row at the White House*, 124; David Braaten, "Gould Lincoln Is Dead at 94: Dean of City's Political Writers," SN, December 2, 1974.

11. Editorial, "The President on Censorship," ES, April 27, 1917; "Publishers Attack Spy Bill," ES, April 23, 1917; President Woodrow Wilson to Breckinridge Long and Wilson to George Creel, November 20, 1917; and George Creel to Wilson, November 28, 1917: in Ray Stannard Baker, *Woodrow Wilson: Life and Letters, War Leaders, April 6, 1917–February 28, 1918*, Volume 7 (New York: Doubleday, Doran & Company, 1939), 367–68; Editorials, "Evidence of German Spying," and "Working for Germany," ES, May 26 and 31, 1917.

12. Woodrow Wilson to Joseph P. Tumulty, July 20, 1917 in Baker, *Wilson: Life and Letters*, 178; Roberts, *The Washington Post*, 153; Christine A. Lunardini, "Politics, Prison, and Revolution," in *From Equal Suffrage to Equal Rights: Alice Paul and the National Women's Party, 1910–1928* (New York: University Press, 1986), 123–49; "Copies of Orders and Communications Relating to Conduct of 'Pickets,' While Prisoners at Occoquan Workhouse," *Report of the Board of Charities of the District of Columbia, 1917*, 54–60.

13. George Kennedy, "The Rambler . . . Fondly Recalls an Old City Editor," ES, December 9, 1957; "Dan E. O'Connell . . . Dies," "Complain of Being Kept from Room," and "Cold Landlords Facing Warrants," ES, December 6, 1957, October 7 and October 12, 1918.

14. "Oliver Owen Kuhn Dies in Hospital," ES, July 19, 1937; Oliver Owen Kuhn, "Shrapnel: Sidelights on the War," and "Make Germany Pay Says Kuhn to French," ES, October 23, 1917, and March 31, 1919; Editorials, "Defeat or Ratification, "Ratification and Reservation," and "The Victors' League Survives," ES, October 31, and August 30, 1919, and October 18, 1920.

15. Paul Dickson and Thomas B. Allen, *The Bonus Army: An American Epic* (New York: Walker Publishing Company, 2004), 28–38.

16. Thomas E. Henry, "The Army of Bewilderment," and "Army Strangely Mute," ES, June 5 and 6, 1932; Dickson and Allen, *The Bonus Army*, 81–104, 127–30; Editorial, "Threats of Disorder," WP, July 9, 1932; Editorial, "Send the Marchers Home," ES, July 8, 1932.

17. Dickson and Allen, *Bonus Army*, 137, 145–46, 158.

18. Dickson and Allen, *The Bonus Army*, 153–83, 184–85; Thomas R. Henry, "City of Hovels Is Wiped Out by Fire and Swords of Troops," ES, July 29, 1932;

"Thomas R. Henry of *Star* Staff Wins Mention for Bonus Army Stories," ES, March 2, 1933.

19. Donald A. Ritchie, *Reporting from Washington: The History of the Washington Press Corps* (New York: Oxford University Press, 2005), 14–15, 17; Braaten, "Gould Lincoln Is Dead at 94"; Lincoln, transcript of interview, September 18, 1968, 11, 14.

20. Editorial, "The First Year," ES, March 4, 1934.

21. Theodore Noyes memorandum to staff, ca. summer, 1934, *Star* Papers; Oswald Garrison Villard, *The Disappearing Daily: Chapters in American Newspaper Evolution* (New York: Alfred A. Knopf, 1944), 193; Ritchie, *Reporting from Washington*, 244–45.

22. Editorial, "The Constitution Reestablished," ES, May 28, 1935; Lincoln, transcript of interview, September 18, 1968, 14; Editorial, "Liberals and Pay Rolls," and "Confirmation of Young as D.C. Head Due Soon," ES, July 11, 1937 and March 30, 1940; J. O'Leary Jr. "Curmudgeons and Poets"; "Jeremiah O'Leary Sr., Capitol Leaders Eulogize," ES, May 1, 1969.

23. Thomas R. Henry, "Capital Retains Outward Calm Despite Shock of War News," ES, December 8, 1941.

24. J. O'Leary Jr., excerpt in "The Day America Dropped the Adam Bomb," 7; *Star's First 100 Years*, 24; "E. Blair Bolles, 78, a Retired Journalist . . . ," NYT, January 29, 1990; "War Correspondent Expected 'Milk Run' on Steyr Raid," ES, November 23, 1944; *The Morning Star*, 1946, *Star* Papers.

25. "Overseas *Star* 'Retires Today," and "Paper Salvage Grows into Big Business for Schools," ES, August 14, and May 26, 1946.

26. Joseph A. Fox, transcript of oral history interview by Jerry N. Hess, October 5, 1970, 2–12, Harry S. Truman Library, http://www.trumanlibrary.org/oralhist/foxja.htm; "*Star* Staff Rushes Four Extras to Throng of Late Shoppers," ES, April 13, 1945.

27. Thomas E. Henry, "Henry Visits a Camp Where Nazi Doctors Killed Humans in 'Scientific Tests,'" ES, April 24, 1945; B. M. McKelway, "Buchenwald Stands as Symbol to World of Nazi Indecency," ES, April 29, 1945; "Tour of 'Horror Camps to Be Made by Editors,'" AP, ES, April 22, 1945.

28. McKelway, "Buchenwald . . . World of Nazi Indecency" and "Editors' Report Says Brutal Master Plan Governed Nazi Camps," AP, ES, May 6, 1945; "Nazi Atrocity Pictures," ES, June 24, 1945.

29. George Kennedy, "The Rambler . . . Recalls Exciting Moment," ES, March 11, 1960; Werner-Forbes, interview.

30. "500,000 Here Celebrate Peace with Noise and Merrymaking," ES, August 15, 1945.

CHAPTER 7

1. *Evening Star* official press release, July 29, 1948, Thomas G. Buchanan bio file, *Star* Papers.

2. David McCullough, *Truman* (New York: Simon & Schuster, 1992), 551–52; Newbold Noyes Jr., "The Story of Dorothy Bailey," ES, March 27, 1949; "*Star*

Reporter Wins $100 News Award," WP, June 1, 1949; J. Montgomery Clift to Newbold Noyes Jr., October 8, 1973, Noyes Papers.

3. Fox, transcript of interview, 22–24; "Mr. Fox Returns to Washington," ES, November 6, 1948; Robert K. Walsh, transcript of oral history interview by Jerry N. Hess, October 12, 1970, 60–61, Harry S. Truman Library, http://www.truman library.org/oralhist/walshr.htm.

4. Walsh, transcript of interview, 96–97; Walsh, "Apartment Residents Fail to Remember Hiss or Chambers," ES, August 20, 1948.

5. Walsh, transcript of interview, 97; Noyes, "Hiss Found Guilty of Perjury," ES, January 22, 1950; Noyes to President Richard Nixon, handwritten draft letter, n.d., Noyes Papers.

6. "Applause for McCarthy," "Long Hearing," and "Replacement for Mc-Carthy," Letters to the Star, ES, March 21, 1950, May 5, 1954, and March 24, 1954; Editorial, "On Curbing McCarthy," ES, March 2, 1954.

7. McGrory, transcript of interviews, 1, 10–18, 21–22; McGrory, "The Big Stars Appear in Setting of Drama . . . ," and "The Buildup Was Great . . . ," ES, April 23 and 27, 1954; McLendon and Smith, *Don't Quote Me!: Washington Newswomen and the Power Society* (New York: E. P. Dutton & Co., 1970), 34–35.

8. Bradlee, *A Good Life*, 158; Crosby Noyes, "United States, May Walk Out of Indo-China Geneva Talks," and "The Red Challenge . . . ," ES, May 5, 1954, and July 14, 1956.

9. Crosby Noyes to McGrory, September 21, 1956, telegram; McGrory to Bill Hines, October 20, 1956, telegram; and Hines to McGrory, n.d., telegram: in Mary McGrory Papers, LC; McGrory, transcript of interviews, 28, 23; Walsh, transcript of interview, 182, 137.

10. "News Source Was President," ES, July 22, 1959; Stephen Bates, *If No News, Send Rumors: Anecdotes of American Journalism* (New York: Henry Holt and Company, 1989), 95; Mary McGrory, Peter Lisagor, and George Herman, White House Correspondents' Press Panel, transcript of oral history interview by Fred Holborn, August 4, 1964, 91, John F. Kennedy Library; Walsh, transcript of interview, 122, 99–100.

11. Walsh, transcript of interview, 63, 94–95; McGrory, Press Panel transcript, 2–6, 14.

12. Gould Lincoln, transcript of oral history interview by Jerry N. Hess, August 10, 1967, 6 & 9, Harry S. Truman Library, online: accessed February 28, 2006, at http://www.trumanlibrary.org/oralhist/lincolng.htm; Walsh, transcript of interview, 175–76.

13. Cecil Holland, "Nixon Pushes Attack on Foe's Cuban Position," and "Nixon Charges Religious Issue Used as a Smear," ES, October 22 and 24, 1960; Walsh, transcript of interview, 183–84; McGrory, Press Panel transcript, 49, 101; McGrory, "Vast Change Came with New Frontier," ES, November 24, 1963; Broder, "Kennedy's Majority Appears no Mandate," ES, November 9, 1960.

14. McGrory, Press Panel transcript, 37; McGrory, "Kennedys Entertained in Splendid 'Suburb,'" ES, June 2, 1961; *The Family Star*, April–May 1961.

15. Eric Alterman, "John F. Kennedy and the Cuban Missile Crisis," in *Why Presidents Lie: A History of Official Deception and its Consequences* (New York: Viking Press, Penguin Group Publishers, 2004), 136; Laurence Chang and Peter Korn-bluh, eds., *The Cuban Missile Crisis: A National Security Archive Documents Reader*

(New York: The New Press, 1991), 364; Richard Fryklund bio file, *Star* Papers; Editorial, "'World We Live In,'" ES, October 31, 1962; Michael Dobbs, *One Minute to Midnight: Kennedy, Khrushchev, and Castro on the Brink of Nuclear War* (New York: Alfred A. Knopf , 2008), 135, 146–47.

16. Dobbs, *One Minute to Midnight*, 91, 85–87, 105; Earl Voss, "Offensive Arms Are Believed on Some Vessels," ES, October 23, 1962; J. O'Leary Jr., "No Arms Found . . . ," and "Swift Action Follows Loss of Photo Plane," ES, October 25 and 28, 1962.

17. Voss, "U.S. Suspends Air Surveys," ES, October 30, 1962; Chang and Kornbluh, *The Cuban Missile Crisis*, 376–83; "World We Live In"; Richard Fryklund, "Control of Cuba News Seen as a U.S. Weapon," and "Crisis Footnote: Navy Flushed Out Red Subs Near Cuba," ES, October 29 and 30, 1962; Dobbs, *One Minute to Midnight*, 135–36, 146–47; Harold W. Chase and Allen H. Lerman, eds., "News Conference of Nov. 20, 1962," in *Kennedy and the Press: The News Conferences* (New York: Thomas Y. Crowell Co., 1965), 336; Newbold Noyes to President John Kennedy, January 27, 1961; and Kennedy to Noyes, n.d.: in Noyes Papers; Stewart Alsop and Charles Bartlett, "In Time of Crisis," *The Saturday Evening Post* (December 8, 1962): 15–21; Broder, "Broad News Curbs Opposed by Salinger," ES, December 9, 1962; "Kennedy Opened Files to Newsmen, Life Says," ES, December 10, 1962; Editorial, "Still No Answer," ES, December 13, 1962.

18. George Dixon, "A Bank of Heroes," WP, November 13, 1962; J. O'Leary Jr., "41 of 42 Missiles Seen on Red Ship . . . ," "Dependents Return to Cuba," "Exiles Tell of Missiles . . . " and "D.C. Attorney Played Vital Role in Havana," ES, November 11, December 8, November 6, and December 26, 1962.

19. Broder, "Dallas Is Haunted by Sense of Guilt and Shame in Wake of Assassination," and "John F. Kennedy's Last Day" ES, November 23 and 24, 1963; Tom Wicker, "Kennedy Killed by Sniper . . . ," NYT, November 23, 1963; Carl Bernstein, "The Dictationists," in *"Washington Star* Memories."

20. McGrory, transcript of interviews, 49, 53; McGrory, "They Were Waiting at the Airport," and "What We Shall Remember," ES, November 23, 1963.

21. Siegel, "Star Struck," 57; O'Leary's, joint interview; Jeremiah O'Leary Jr. to Bill Hill, August 17, 1964, J. O'Leary Jr. bio files, *Star* Papers; "FBI Report, Interview of Jeremiah O'Leary at Dallas Texas, Dictated and Taken 12/3/63" by Special Agent; "FBI Report, Interview of Jeremiah O'Leary at Washington, D.C., Dictated and Taken 12/8/1963" by Special Agent: in HSCA (House Select Committee on Assassinations) Transcripts of Interviews, Records of the US House of Representatives, Record Group (RG) 233, National Archives (NARA), College Park, Maryland (duplicated as Commission Exhibit 2052 in *Hearings Before the President's Commission on the Assassination of President Kennedy, Vol. XXIV*, 460–74): *Report of the Warren Commission: The Assassination of President Kennedy* (New York: New York Times Company, October 1964), 189–93, 222–24; J. O'Leary Jr., "Killing Suspect Had Fired Gun, Tests Reveal," ES, November 23, 1963.

22. J. O'Leary Jr. to Hill, August 17, 1964; J. O'Leary Jr., "Killing Suspect Had Fired Gun," "Death Makes a Hero of Obscure Policeman," and "Police Say They Know Where Oswald Got Gun," ES, November 23 and 24, 1963; "Lee Harvey Oswald" file, *Star* Photo Collection, Washingtoniana Division, Special Collections, D.C. Public Library; John P. Mohr, Assistant to FBI director J. Edgar

Hoover, to Cartha P. (Deke) DeLoach, Assistant Director for Crime Records Division, memorandum re: "Assassination of the President, Photograph of Lee Harvey Oswald with Rifle and Revolver 'Life' Magazine, Feb. 21, 1964," HSCA FBI Liaison with Warren Commission series, RG233, NARA; Warren Commission Report, 221, 213–24.

23. J. O'Leary Jr., to Hill, August 17, 1964; "FBI Report, Interview of Jeremiah O'Leary," HSCA Transcripts of Interviews; J. O'Leary Jr., "Oswald's Fateful Shooting Seals Lips of Key Figure in President's Killing," ES, November 25, 1963.

24. J. O'Leary Jr. "Sharply Contrasting Texas Funerals Complete Two Dramatic Roles," "The Oswald Story," and "The Story of Jack Leon Ruby," ES, November 26, November 29, and December 1, 1963.

25. McGrory, transcript of interviews, 50–52; McGrory, "A Young Widow Brings Meaning to Tragic Chaos," "John Cassady: A Gem of a Newspaperman," and "He Would Have Liked It: The Funeral Had That Special Kennedy Touch," ES, November 25, 1963, April 8, 1978, and November 26, 1963.

CHAPTER 8

1. Robert A. Caro, *The Years of Lyndon Johnson: The Passage of Power* (New York: Alfred A. Knopf, 2012), 284–85, 299.

2. Hope, interview; Patricia Barron, discussion with author, *Star* 25th Reunion Party, August 12, 2006, National Press Club, Washington, D.C.

3. Telephone conversation between Lyndon Johnson and Marshall McNeill, January 22, 1964, 6:30 p.m., Citation#2090, Tape WH6401.18, Program #14; Telephone conversation between Johnson and Deke DeLoach, March 12, 1964, 2:15 p.m., Citation# 2489, Tape WH6406.09, Program #16, in Recordings and Transcripts of Conversations and Meetings, Presidential Papers, LBJ Library.

4. Caro, *The Passage of Power*, 296–98; Telephone conversation between Johnson and George Reedy, June 9, 1964, 12:31 p.m., Citation 3647-48, Tape WH6406.04, Program #1, Recordings and Transcripts . . . , LBJ Library; Deke DeLoach to Clyde Tolson, re: "The *Washington Evening Star*'s Animosity toward President," June 17, 1965, File #92, Official and Confidential Subject Files of J. Edgar Hoover, Records of the Federal Bureau of Investigation, RG65, NARA, College Park; Hope, interview; P. Barron, interview; Hope and Barron, "The Fallen Angel: Questions Still Abound as Senate Wrestles with Baker Case," ES, January 10, 1965; P. Barron, discussion with author, *Star* 25th Reunion Party; *The Family Star*, April–May 1965.

5. P. Barron, interview; "FBI Report on Investigation of Jenkins," October 22, 1964, Office Files of Walter Jenkins, 1955–64, Presidential Papers, LBJ Library; Elizabeth Carpenter, transcript of oral history interview IV by Joe B. Frantz, August 27, 1969, 33–35, Internet copy, LBJ Library; Charles B. Seib and Alan L. Otten, "Abe, Help!—LBJ," *Esquire*, June 1965, 87; Clark M. Clifford, transcript of oral history interview IV by Joe B. Frantz, August 7, 1969, 14–15, Internet Copy, LBJ Library; Editorial, "Reporting on the Jenkins Case," ES, October 17, 1964; "Johnson Friends Call on Press," NYT, October 16, 1964; Cecil Holland, "Fortas Defends Role in Walter Jenkins Case," ES, August 5, 1965.

6. Editorial, "The Presidential Choice," ES, November 1, 1964; DeLoach to Tolson, "Star's Animosity to the President," RG 65, NARA; Hope, interview; Gould Lincoln, "Capitol Hill GOP to Lead Party," "The Political Mill" column, ES, November 7, 1964; Stewart Alsop, *The Center: People and Power in Political Washington* (New York: Harper & Row, 1968), 205; "Immediately Upon Arising, Take One Star . . . " *The Family Star*, January–February, 1967; Thomas E. Noyes, "Celebrity Lunch," in *"Washington Star* Memories."

7. Editorials, "Medicare Assured," and "Socialism in the Campaign," ES, October 19, 1964, and July 11, 1965; Walsh, transcript of interview, 192.

8. Richard Fryklund, "No Reason to Pull Out: Viet Nam Findings," ES, September 28, 1963; Richard Critchfield, "The Lonely War: A Night of Tragedy in the Precarious Life of a Viet Nam Village," "The View from Hill 278 Da Nang Can Be Lovely," and "The People's War," ES, January 24 and May 12, 1965, and January 24, 1966; Crosby Noyes, "Journalistic War Likely to Escalate Sharply," column, ES, January 3, 1967; Fryklund, "Interpretive Report: Hanoi Press Control Tight," ES, January 13, 1967; "It's Time to Stop Bombing . . . " Letters to the Editor, ES, May 25, 1967.

9. Haynes Johnson, "Kennedy Will Run for President: To Announce Decision . . . ," ES, March 15, 1968; Johnson, interviews; John Norris, *Mary McGrory: The First Queen of Journalism* (New York: Viking Press, 2015), 24–25, 60–61, 67, 97, 102–16; McGrory to Richard Stout, *Newsweek* reporter, April 24, 1970, McGrory Papers; McLendon and Smith, *Don't Quote Me!*, 37; McGrory, transcript of interviews, 52; Hope, interview.

10. McGrory, "Humphrey: Happy Lodge Brother," and Johnson, "McCarthy: Serenely Apart," ES, August 27, 1968; Hope, interview; Norris, *Queen of Journalism*, 126–27; McGrory, "McCarthy Comforts Unhappy 'Army,'" and "A Militarized Nightmare," ES, August 19 and September 1, 1968.

11. "For the Crucial Test Nixon's the One," ES, October 27, 1968; Walsh, transcript of interview, 180; Boris Weintraub, comments to audience, *Star* 25th Reunion Party; Newbold (Terry) Noyes III, interview by author, April 13, 2011; Johnson, interviews; Hope, interview.

12. McGrory, transcript of interviews, 12, 67; T. Noyes, interview; Johnson, "Good Manners Open Moratorium," ES, October 15, 1969; Editorial, "The Moratorium," ES, October 15, 1969; Smith Hempstone, answers to questions; Editorial, "Tragedy at Kent," ES, May 5, 1970; Goulden, "Good Grey Lady Is No. 2," 67, 33, 68; McGrory, transcript of interviews, 67, 12; McGrory to "Newby" Noyes, December 18, 1974, Noyes Papers.

13. Henry S. Bradsher, *The Dalai Lama's Secret and Other Reporting Adventures: Stories from a Cold War Correspondent* (Baton Rouge: Louisiana State University, 2013), 246, 280; Henry Bradsher, interview by author, August 16, 2016.

14. Bradsher, interview.

15. Bradsher, interview; Bradsher, *Dalai Lama's Secret*, 244–49, 280–82; Bradsher, "Thrusts into Cambodia Productive,'" ES, May 6, 1970.

16. Sarro, interviews; Sarro, "Papers Tie U.S. to Diem's Fall," ES, June 22, 1971; Editorial, "The Court, the Press, and the Prosecutors," ES, July 11, 1971.

17. Mary Lou Werner-Forbes, comments to audience, *Star* 25th Reunion Party; Sarro, interviews; Duncan Spencer, "Delegates Assess Reform Results" ES, July 14, 1972; Hope, interview.

18. Bradsher, interview; Bradsher, *Dalai Lama's Secret*, 203; Bradsher, "3 Major Objections Listed by Saigon," ES, October 27, 1972; Horgan, interview.

19. Nixon to Noyes, November 3, 1972, Noyes Papers; McGrory, "Nixon Turns on Friend and Foe Alike," ES, November 8, 1962; Myra MacPherson, "President Attends Stag Luncheon," WP, July 24, 1970.

20. Daniel Patrick Moynihan to Richard Nixon, reprint of letter, December 28, 1972, in Steven R. Weisman, ed., *Daniel Patrick Moynihan: A Portrait in Letters of an American Visionary* (New York: Public Affairs, Perseus Books Group, 2010), 270; Editorials, "Setback for Peace," "The Bombing Halt," and "Back to Paris," ES, December 20 and 31, 1972, and January 1, 1973; Bradsher, "Saigon Protests Worry Hanoi," ES, November 1, 1974; Bradsher, interview.

21. Barbara Cochran, interview by author, October 14, 2014; Robert Walters, "O'Brien Denounces 'Political Spying,'" ES, June 19, 1972; Joseph Volz, interview by author, April 4, 2011; Volz, "None of the President's Men," *The Washingtonian* (July 1975): 46; Carl Bernstein and Bob Woodward, "Bug Suspect Got Campaign Funds," WP, August 1, 1972; Volz and Pat Collins, "GOP Aide Quit at Time of Quiz," ES, August 2, 1972.

22. Volz, "None of the Presidents Men," 46; Cochran, interview; Volz, interview; Horgan, interview.

23. Volz, interview; Volz, "None of the Presidents Men," 47–48; Woodward and Bernstein, "Mitchell Controlled Secret GOP Fund," and "FBI Finds Nixon Aides Sabotaged Democrats," WP, September 29 and October 10, 1972; Volz and Collins, "Lou Russell's Dual Hats," ES, October 11, 1972; Horgan, interview.

24. Benjamin C. Bradlee, "Watergate: The Biggest Story," WP, June 14, 1992; Volz, interview; "Horner's Corner," *Newsweek* (December 25, 1972): 52.

25. Volz, "None of the Presidents Men," 50; Volz, interview; Barry Kalb, "Federal Judge Kills Newsmen Subpoenas," ES, March 22, 1973; Jack Germond, *Fat Man in the Middle: Forty Years of Covering Politics* (New York: Random House, 1999), 111.

26. McGrory, transcript of interviews, 36–37; Norman Kempster, "Mary McGrory Wins a Pulitzer Prize," ES, May 6, 1975; McGrory, "Happiness Is Chuck's List," ES, July 1, 1973.

27. Hempstone, answers to questions; Editorial, "President Nixon's Farewell," ES, August 9, 1974; Bradlee, *A Good Life*, 366–68; Bradlee to Noyes, July 26, 1974, Noyes Papers; T. Noyes, interview.

CHAPTER 9

1. Newbold Noyes, "Crosby Noyes: His Life and Times," 220–21; Robert Oshel and Marilyn S. Slatick, *Home Sites of Distinction: The History of Woodside Park*, (Silver Spring, Maryland: Woodside Park Civic Association, 1998), 30.

2. "Washington Journalists," *The Republic* (July 29, 1879), 368, *Star* Papers.

3. Bowman, answers to questions.

4. Joseph P. McKerns, ed., *Biographical Dictionary of American Journalism* (Westport, CT: Greenwood Press, 1989), 517–18; "The Star's Centennial," and Editorial, "No Distilled Liquor Advertising," ES, January 1, 1952, and February 14, 1934; "Advertising, 1920–1958" and "Historical Sketches": in *Star* Papers; "Star's Battery of Latest

Type Printing Presses," ES, May 13, 1934; Audit Bureau of Circulations (ABC) Audit Reports, six months ending September 30, 1952; Graham, *Personal History*, 85.

5. "New Annex Gives the *Evening Star* Newspaper One of the Best Equipped Plants in the World," ES, May 10, 1922; Henry G. Hanford to Mr. Casebeer, memorandum re: "Employees Pension, Disability Benefit and Death Benefit Plan," August 12, 1924, *Star* Papers; George Manning, "Daily Proves Firms Need Not Wait for 'Official' Welfare Programs," *Editor and Publisher*, September 26, 1931; J. O'Leary Jr., "A Career Began 55 Years Ago," *Washington Times*, June 4, 1992; "400 Members Attend 'Family Dinner' of Evening Star Club," ES, January 9, 1941.

6. Bowman, answers to questions; Smith Hempstone, answers to questions; Kauffmann, "A Century at the Nation's Capital," 25.

7. Graham, *Personal History*, 58–59, 182, 187, 217–18, 232; Donald Richey, "Company Town Papers," in *Reporting from Washington: The History of the Washington Press Corps*, 243–47; Joseph M. Winski, "Why Washington's *Star* Fell," *Advertising Age* (September 21, 1981): 56; ABC Audit Reports, six months ending September 30, 1953, 1954, 1955, and 1971; Goulden, "Good Grey Lady Is No. 2," 32–33.

8. Stephen Klaidman, "A Tale of Two Families," WP, May 9, 1976; "New Building Fact Sheet," ca. 1959; and "Welcome to Family Day Open House," *Star People* (May 24, 1959): in *Star* Papers; Siegel, "Starstruck," 55; T. Noyes, interview; Winski, "*Washington Star*'s Fall," 56; J. O'Leary Jr., "55 Years Ago."

9. Cristine Russell, "Still Seeing Stars after Thirty Years: A Venerable Paper Is Gone, but Not Forgotten," *Columbia Journalism Review* (August 8, 2011), http://www.archives.cjr/behind_the_news/still_seeing_stars_after_thirt.php; McGrory, transcript of interviews, 12; J. O'Leary Jr., "Curmudgeons and Poets; Johnson, Interviews.

10. ABC Report ending March 31, 1972; William H. Jones and Paul W. Valentine, "The News Is Closed" and "News Was Sold After Years of Negotiations," WP, July 13, 1972; Joseph C. Goulden, "Can Jack Kauffmann Save the *Star News*?" *The Washingtonian* (October 1972): 74; ABC Report ending September 30, 1974; Klaidman, "A Tale of Two Families."

11. T. Noyes, interview; Bowman, answers to questions; Peter Benjaminson, "He Came to Do Good and He Did Well," in *Death in the Afternoon: America's Newspaper Giants Struggle for Survival* (New York: Andrews, McMeel & Parker, 1984), 91; Letter to the Editor from John P. McGoff, WS, August 7, 1975; "Amended Offer to Purchase 17,846 Shares of Stock of *Washington Star* Communications, Inc. for Cash at $1,600 Per Share by Perpetual Corporation of Delaware," September 3, 1975, *Star* Papers; Cochran, interview.

12. Bellows, *The Last Editor*, 26; Cochran, interview; Horgan, interview; Beveridge to Bellows, memorandum, June 17, 1975, *Star* Papers; James Dickenson, interview by author, February 28, 2011; "*Star* Editor Wins Pulitzer for Distinguished Editorials," WS, April 17, 1979; Sarro, interviews.

13. T. Noyes, interview; Benjaminson, "He Came to Do Good," 94; "Guild Votes 347 to 44 . . . " SN, December 10, 1974; Sarro, interviews; Cochran, interview.

14. "Perils of the Star," *Newsweek* (August 11, 1975): 81; "Amended Offer to Purchase . . . by Perpetual"; and Godfrey Kauffmann to Shareholders of Washington Star Communications, August 19, 1975, in *Star* Papers; "Allbritton Offer to

Buy Up Star Stock, Settle FCC Issue," WS, August 19, 1975; Washington Star Communications (WSC) Press Release, August 21, 1975, *Star* Papers; Noyes to Allbritton, n.d., Noyes Papers; Stephen M. Aug, "FCC Approves Allbritton's Purchase of Star Properties," WS, December 18, 1975.

15. "Allbritton to Representatives of the Labor Unions at the *Washington Star,*" memorandum, September 19, 1975, *Star* Papers; S. Aug, "Wage Freezes Urged on Unions at Star," WS, September 20, 1975; Carlos Sutton, interview by author, December 12, 2007; Philip Nobile, "High Noon at the *Washington Post,*" NYT, November 14, 1975; Bellows, The Last Editor, 175–80. Graham, *Personal History,* 521, 539–44, 554, 567–69; "An Open Letter to the *Washington Post* and the Striking Newspaper Unions," WS, December 31,1975; Sarro, interviews.

16. Bellows to Allbritton, memorandum, November 10, 1975; Denny to Allbritton, November 7, 1975; Daly to Allbritton, memorandum, November 13, 1975; Merritt to Allbritton, memorandum, December 4, 1975; Merritt to Daly, memorandum re: "Los Angeles," November 18, 1975; and Merritt to James R. West, memorandum, August 12, 1975: in *Star* Papers.

17. Bradsher, interview; Cochran, interview; Dickenson, interview; Germond, *Fat Man in the Middle,* 128, 139–44; Edwin M. Yoder, "*Star* Wars: Adventures in Attempting to Save a Failing Newspaper," *Virginia Quarterly Review,* http://www.vqronline.org.printmedia.php.

18. Bellows, *The Last Editor,* 169–72; Yoder "*Star* Wars"; Yoder, email to author, November 4, 2016; Noyes to Allbritton, ca. 1975, Noyes Papers.

19. Yoder, answers to author's questions, email, November 20, 2016; Horgan, interview; Yoder, "*Star* Wars"; McGrory, transcript of interviews.

20. WSC Press Release, July 28, 1977, *Star* Papers; "Shootout at the *Star,*" The *Washingtonian* (January 1978): 61; Jim Bellows, *The Last Editor,* 184–90; Cochran, interview.

21. Curtis Prendergast with Geoffrey Colvin, *The World of Time, Inc.: The Intimate History of a Changing Enterprise, Volume Three: 1960–1980,* edited by Robert Lubar (New York: Atheneum, 1986), 512–19; *The Inside Straight: A Monthly Publication for the Employees of the* Washington Star, April 1977; and Joseph Allbritton press conference recording, February 4, 1978: in *Star* Papers; Benjaminson, "He Came to Do Good," 106; John Morton, "Saving the *Star*: Another Episode, the Most Critical of All, in the Life of Washington's Second Newspaper," *The Washingtonian* (November 1975): 108, 165. Dickenson, interview; Noyes to Allbritton, n.d., Noyes Papers; Walter Diercks, interview by author, November 14, 2014.

22. Prendergast, *The World of Time, Inc.,* 524; "*Star* Announces Plans for 5 Local Editions," WS, September 26, 1978; Germond, *Fat Man in the Middle,* 148–49; Horgan, interview; Cochran, interview; Bachrach, interview; McElwaine, interview; Dickenson, interview; McGrory, transcript of interviews.

23. "The *Star* Stays," *Time Magazine* (January 15, 1979): 57; Cochran, interview; Prendergast, *The World of Time Inc.,* 526–27; Dorothy Strizinski, "Unions to Save the *Star,*" press conference recording, December 9, 1978; and James R. Shepley, "Remarks by . . . Shepley to a Joint Meeting of Officers and Representatives of the Unions Representing Employees of the *Washington Star,*" December 15, 1978: in *Star* Papers; Sarro, interviews; Editorial, "We Are Here to Stay," WS, January 2, 1979.

24. Diercks, interview; Charles B. Seib, "How *Doonesbury* Disappeared," WP, June 8, 1979.

25. "The A.M. Extra Means Extra Readers Extra Opportunity for You," ca. July 1979; and *Star* Press Release, June 1, 1979: in *Star* Papers; Prendergast, *The World of Time, Inc.*, 531; ABC Reports, six months ending September 30, 1979, and 1981; George Johnson, et al., "The Underdog *Washington Star* Is Growling," *The Quill* (July–August 1979): 27–28; Winski, "Why Washington's *Star* Fell," 56.

26. Sarro, interviews; Yoder, "*Star* Wars"; McGrory, transcript of interviews; Dickenson, interview; Norris, *The First Queen of Journalism*, 182; McGrory to Gart, April 6, 1981, McGrory Papers.

27. Prendergast, *The World of Time, Inc.*, 531–34; Diercks, interview; Richard T. Stout and Joseph Tinkelman, "Is Time Running Out on the *Washington Star*?" and "An Interview with *Star* Editor Murray Gart," *The Washingtonian* (August 1981): 129–30, 207; Yoder "*Star* Wars"; Dale Russakoff et al., "The Death of the *Washington Star*," WP, August 18, 1981; McGrory, "Thursday, July 23, in Newsroom for Press Conference at 10:30 am from Richard Munro . . . Who They Had Never Seen Before," Notes, July 23, 1981, McGrory Papers; O'Leary's, joint interview; McGrory, "A Paper Worth Saving," column, WS, July 26, 1981.

28. Prendergast, *The World of Time Inc.*, 534; Sutton, interview; Broder, "The *Star* Deserves to Live," WP, July 29, 1981; Johnson, "Star Follows Long Trend of Declining Evening Papers" and "Death in the Afternoon," WP, July 24 and 26, 1981; Ted Koppel, Transcript, *Nightline* broadcast on ABC-TV with Mary McGrory and Jeremiah O'Leary Jr., aired on WJLA (D.C. affiliate channel), July 23, 1981, McGrory's Papers; James Reston, "The Evening Star," NYT, August 4, 1981; Richard Cohen, "Through Newspaper Graveyards," WP, July 26, 1981.

29. McGrory, transcript of interviews; McGrory, "It Was Home, and the Luck of My Life," column; "Readers Say Goodbye to the *Star*"; Phil Gailey, "Telephones Jammed by Wellwishers' Calls"; and Bailey Morris, "The End of the *Star*: A Death in the Family": in the last edition, WS, August 7, 1981; Horgan, interview.

Biographical information for Star staff not specifically cited in the Notes is taken from the biographical files and clippings in the Star Papers at the D.C. Public Library.

Bibliography

Abernethy, Lloyd M. "The Washington Race War of July 1919." *Maryland Historical Magazine* 58, no. 4 (December 1963): 309–24.

Alterman, Eric. *When Presidents Lie: A History of Official Deception and Its Consequences.* New York: Viking Press, Penguin Group Publishers, 2004.

Audit Bureau of Circulation Reports, 1954–1981.

Baker, Ray Stannard. *Woodrow Wilson: Life and Letters, War Leader, April 6, 1917–February 28, 1918,* Volume 7. New York: Doubleday, Doran & Company, 1939.

Barber, Lucy G. *Marching on Washington: The Forging of an American Political Tradition.* Berkeley and Los Angeles, CA: University of California Press, 2002.

Bates, Stephen. *If No News, Send Rumors: Anecdotes of American Journalism.* New York: Henry Holt and Company, 1989.

Bayley, Edwin R. *Joe McCarthy and the Press.* Madison, WI: University of Wisconsin Press, 1981.

Beale, Betty. *Power at Play: A Memoir of Parties, Politicians, and the President in My Bedroom.* Washington, DC: Regnery Gateway Publishing, 1993.

Belford, Barbara. "Mary McGrory." In *Brilliant Bylines: A Biographical Anthology of Notable Newspaperwomen in America.* New York: Columbia University Press, 1986.

Bellows, James. *The Last Editor: How I Saved the* New York Times, *the* Washington Post, *and the* Los Angeles Times *from Dullness and Complacency.* Kansas City, KS: Andrews McMeel Publishing, 2002.

Benjaminson, Peter. "He Came to Do Good and He Did Well," and "A Flawed Attempt." In *Death in the Afternoon: America's Newspaper Giants Struggle for Survival.* New York: Andrews, McMeel & Parker, 1984.

Bradlee, Benjamin C. *A Good Life: Newspapering and Other Adventures.* New York: Simon & Schuster, 1995.

Bradsher, Henry S. *The Dalai Lama's Secret and Other Reporting Adventures: Stories from a Cold War Correspondent.* Baton Rouge: Louisiana State University Press, 2013.

Brown, Charles H. *The Correspondents' War: Journalists in the Spanish American War.* New York: Charles Scribner's & Sons, 1967.

Brownlow, Louis. *A Passion for Anonymity: The Autobiography of Louis Brownlow, Second Half.* Chicago: University of Chicago Press, 1958.

Caro, Robert A. *The Years of Lyndon Johnson: The Passage of Power.* New York: Alfred A. Knopf, 2012.

Chang, Laurence, and Peter Kornbluh, eds. "John V. Kennedy and Cuban Missile Crisis." In *The Cuban Missile Crisis, 1962: A National Security Archives Reader.* New York: The New Press, 1992.

Daley, Steve. "Secrets of the Town's Biggest Gossip." *The Washingtonian* (July 1978): 65.

The Day America Dropped the Adam Bomb: And Other Memories, Confessions and Lore from the Crew of the Late, Great Washington/Evening Star, *Tenth Year Reunion,* September 28, 1991. Compiled by Jeffrey Frank.

Derthick, Martha. *City Politics in Washington, D.C.* Cambridge, MA: Harvard University Press, 1962.

Dickson, Paul, and Thomas B. Allen. *The Bonus Army: An American Epic.* New York: Walker Publishing Company, 2004.

Dobbs, Michael. *One Minute to Midnight: Kennedy, Khrushchev, and Castro on the Brink of Nuclear War.* New York: Alfred A. Knopf, 2008.

Elfenbein, Jessica. *Civics, Commerce and Community: The History of the Greater Washington Board of Trade, 1889–1989.* Washington, DC: Center for Washington Area Studies, George Washington University, 1989.

Ely, Jr., James W. *The Crisis of Conservative Virginia: The Byrd Organization and the Politics of Massive Resistance.* Knoxville: University of Tennessee Press, 1976.

Felsenthal, Carol. *Power Privilege and* The Post: *The Katharine Graham Story.* New York: G. P. Putnam's Sons, 1993.

Germond, Jack. *Fat Man in a Middle Seat: Forty Years of Covering Politics.* New York: Random House, 1999.

Gilbert, Ben W. *Ten Blocks from the White House: Anatomy of the Washington Race Riots of 1968.* New York: Frederick A. Praeger, 1968.

———. "Toward a Color-Blind Newspaper: Race Relations and the *Washington Post*." *Washington History* 5, no. 2 (Fall/Winter 1993–94): 5–27.

Goulden, Joseph C. "*The Evening Star*: The Good Grey Lady Is No. 2, and Not Really Trying Harder." *The Washingtonian* (January 1970): 28–69.

———. "Can Jack Kauffmann Save the *Star News*?" *The Washingtonian* (October 1972): 74–139.

Graham, Katharine. *Katharine Graham: Personal History.* New York: Alfred A. Knopf, 1997.

Greater Washington Board of Trade Archives. Special Collections, George Washington University.

Green, Constance McLaughlin. *Washington: A History of the Capital, 1800–1950.* Princeton, NJ: Princeton University, 1976.

Harry S. Truman Presidential Library. Oral History Collection.

Hoover, J. Edgar. Confidential Subject Files. Federal Bureau of Investigation Records, National Archives, College Park, MD.

House Select Committee on Assassinations. Transcript of Interviews. U.S. House of Representatives Records, National Archives, College Park, MD.

Jenkins, Walter. Office Files. Presidential Papers, Lyndon Baines Johnson Presidential Library.

Kauffmann, Samuel H. "*The Evening Star* (1852–1952): A Century at the Nation's Capital." Paper presented before the Newcomen Society, Washington, D.C., March 28, 1952.

LBJ Library. Oral History Collection.

———. Recordings and Transcripts of Conversations and Meetings.

Lunardini, Christine A. "Politics, Prison, and Resolution." In *From Equal Suffrage to Equal Rights: Alice Paul and the National Women's Party, 1910–1928.* New York: New York University Press, 1986.

Maury, William M. "Alexander 'Boss' Shepherd and the Board of Public Works." *George Washington University Studies* 3 (1975).

McGrory, Mary. Papers. Library of Congress.

———. Transcript of oral history interviews by Kathleen Currie, August 4, 1991, and July 26, 1992. Women in Journalism Oral History Project. National Press Club Archives, Washington, D.C.

McGrory, Mary, Peter Lisagor, and George Herman, White House correspondents Press Panel. Transcript of oral history interview by Fred Holborn, August 4, 1964. John F. Kennedy Presidential Library.

McLendon, Winzola, and Scottie Smith. *Don't Quote Me!: Washington Newswomen and the Power Society.* New York: E. P. Dutton & Co., 1970.

Muse, Benjamin. *Virginia's Massive Resistance.* Bloomington: Indiana University Press, 1961.

National Association for the Advancement of Colored People. Papers. Library of Congress.

Norris, John. *Mary McGrory: The First Queen of Journalism.* New York: Viking Press, 2015.

Noyes, Crosby S. "Journalism since Jamestown." Address to the National Editorial Association, Jamestown Tercentennial Exposition, Jamestown, VA, June 13, 1907.

Noyes Family. Estate Files. Montgomery County Historical Society, Rockville, MD.

———. Private Papers. Sorrento, ME.

Noyes, Newbold. "Crosby Stuart Noyes: His Life and Times." *Records of the Columbia Historical Society* 40–41 (1940): 197–225.

Ottenberg, Miriam. Papers. Wisconsin Historical Society, Madison, WI.

Povich, Shirley. *The Washington Senators.* New York: G. P. Putnam and Sons, 1954.

Prendergast, Curtis, with Geoffrey Colvin. "Fallen Star." In *The World of Time Inc.: The Intimate History of a Changing Enterprise, Volume Three: 1960–1980.* Edited by Robert Lubar. New York: Atheneum, 1986.

Ritchie, Donald A. *Reporting from Washington: The History of the Washington Press Corps.* New York: Oxford University Press, 2005.

Roberts, Chalmers. The Washington Post: *The First 100 Years.* Boston: Houghton Mifflin Company, 1977.

Roberts, Gene, and Hank Klibanoff. *The Race Beat: The Press, the Civil Rights Struggle, and the Awakening of a Nation.* New York: Alfred A. Knopf, 2006.

Roosevelt, Theodore. Papers. Library of Congress.

Sasche, Michael Judah. *The D.C. Home Rule Movement, 1966–1973.* BA Thesis, Amherst College, 1999.

Siegel, Morris. "Starstruck." *Regardies* (August 1984): 54–58.

Smith, Thomas G. *Showdown: JFK and the Integration of the Washington Redskins.* Boston: Beacon Press, 2011.

Stout, Richard T., and Joseph Tinkelman. "Is Time Running Out on the *Washington Star?*" *The Washingtonian* (August 1981): 128–206.

Thompson, Anthony. *The Story of the 23rd Amendment.* Senior Thesis, Princeton University, 1965.

Villard, Oswald Garrison. *The Disappearing Daily: Chapters in American Newspaper Evolution.* New York: Alfred A. Knopf, 1944.

———. "Washington, a Capital without a Thunderer." In *Some Newspapers and Newspaper Men.* New York: Alfred A. Knopf, 1923.

Volz, Joseph. "None of the President's Men." *The Washingtonian* (July 1975): 46–51.

Warren Commission, Report of the: The Assassination of President Kennedy. New York: New York Times Company, October 1964.

Washington Star Newspaper. Papers, 1852–1981. Washingtoniana Division, Special Collections, District of Columbia Public Library (DCPL).

———. Photo collection, ca. 1930–1981. DCPL.

Waskow, Arthur I. "The Washington Riot." In *From Race Riot to Sit-In: A Study in the Connection between Conflict and Violence.* Garden City, NY: Anchor Books, 1967.

Wilkinson, III, J. Harvie. "Massive Resistance, 1954–1960." In *Harry Byrd and the Changing Face of Virginia Politics, 1945–1966.* Charlottesville: University Press of Virginia, 1968.

Winski, Joseph M. "Why Washington's *Star* Fell." *Advertising Age* (September 21, 1981): 55–60.

Yoder, Edwin M. "*Star* Wars: Adventures in Attempting to Save a Failing Newspaper." *Virginia Quarterly Review* (Autumn 1993). http://wwwvqronline.org/essay/star-wars-adentures-attempting-save-failing-newspaper.

NEWSPAPERS AND MAGAZINE PRIMARILY CONSULTED:

Evening Star, 1852–1972
New York Times
Washington Daily News
Washington Post
Washington Star News, 1972–1974 (successor to *Evening Star*)
Washington Star, 1974–1981 (successor to *Washington Star News*)
The Washingtonian Magazine

AUTHOR INTERVIEWS

Bachrach, Judy
Barron, Patricia
Bowman, William**
Bradsher, Henry
Cochran, Barbara
Delaney, Paul
Dickenson, James
Diercks, Walter
Groom, Winston
Hempstone, Smith**
Hope, Paul
Horgan, Denis
Johnson, Haynes
Kiernan, Michael
Lague, Louise
McElwaine, Sandra
McLellan, Diana
Noyes, Newbold, III
O'Leary, Teresa and Timothy
Rackley, Lurma
Rosellini, Lynn
Sarro, Ronald
Scharff, Ned
Sutton, Carlos
Volz, Joseph
Werner-Forbes, Mary Lou
Yoder, Edwin**

* The *Evening Star, Washington Star-News, and Washington Star* were accessed via microfilm at the D.C. Public Library before editions were available online. A smaller number of articles were accessed by the author only online at http://infoweb.newsbank.com/resources.
** Responses submitted as typewritten or email responses to author's questions.

Index

Khaalis, Hamaas Abdul, 101, 103–5
Khrushchev, Nikita, 185–87
Kiernan, Michael, 40–43
King, Billie Jean, 129–30
King, Martin Luther, Jr., 59–60;
  assassination of, 71–74, *74*, 75–78;
  "I Have a Dream" speech of, 64;
  Selma voter registration drive of,
  67–68, *70*
Kirk, Don (Donald), 216–17
Kissinger, Henry, 220–21
Klingman, Eliab, 13
Knickerbocker Theater collapse, 89–90
Kopay, David, 131
Koppel, Ted, 269
Kraslow, David, 126–27, 226–27, 251
Kuhn, Mary Ann, 105
Kuhn, Oliver Owen, 112, 114, 154–55
Ku Klux Klan, 47, 59, 66–67
Kurkjian, Tim, 139

Lague, Louise, 132–34, 246
Lansburgh's department store, 166–67
The Last Editor (Bellows), 135, 256
Layton, John, 71
League of Nations, 154–55
Lewis, Alfred E., 97
Lewis, Bin (Wilmott), 75, 240-41,
  244–45, 248
Lewis, Jesse, 71
Lewis, John, 64, 67
Lewiston, Maine, 11
liberals, Washington, D. C., and, 29–30
Lincoln, Abraham: assassination of,
  17–18, 82; *Star* on, 9–10, 14–15, 17
Lincoln, Gould, 149–50; FDR and,
  159–60, 162; Goldwater criticized
  by, 207; "Political Mill" column of,
  159, 161, 183
Lindbergh, Charles, 92–93, 155
Lindbergh child, kidnapping of, 92–93
literary coverage, 23, 136, 177
Little Rock, Arkansas, desegregation
  in, 57
Lodge, Henry Cabot, 182
Logicon computer system, 263, *263*
London, Jack, 51

Long, Breckinridge, 151
Long, John D., 147
Longworth, Nicholas S., 110
Louis, Joe, 50, 123
Love, Philip, 98, 100, 114
Lustig, Ray, 74–75
lynching, 47
Lyon, Gideon A., Jr., 20, 144–45

MacArthur, Douglas, 157–58
MacArthur, Harry, 116
MacPherson, Myra, 64, 124
Maine, USS, 147–48
Malcolm X, 101, 104
Mallory, Andrew, 98
Mallory Supreme Court decision, 98
Malone, Vivian, 62
Mandel, Marvin, 41–42
Mannix, William, 145–46
March on Washington for Jobs and
  Freedom, 63–64
Marshall, George Preston, 122
Maryland, 31; Mandel trial in, 41–42;
  Mt. Ranier, exorcism story in,
  93–94; racial violence in, 61–63;
  Wilson, A., murdered in, 91–92
Mason, Ed, 105
Maxa, Kathleen, 129
McCardle, Dorothy, 126
McCarthy, Eugene, 210–13
McCarthy, Helena, 107, 142
McCarthy, Joseph, 177–80
McCloskey, Pete (Paul Norton), 219
McCord, James, 224
McCormick, Robert, 238
McDonald, Edward (Mickey), 91
McDonald, John, 90
McElwaine, Sandra, 136–37, 260
McGoff, John P., 244
McGovern, George, 220
McGrory, Mary, 29, 68, 207, 247–48,
  255; on Eisenhower administration,
  181–82; Gart friction with, 260, 266;
  Kennedy, J. F., and, 182–84, 190–91,
  197–98; Kennedy, R., and, 211;
  March on Washington described
  by, 63–64; McCarthy, E., covered

of, 36; King, M. L., assassination
riots in, 71–74, *74*, 75–79;
Knickerbocker Theater collapse in,
89–90; Lansburgh's department
store in, 166–67; liberals in, 29–30;
March on Washington for Jobs
and Freedom, 63–64; mini riots in,
71–72; 1919 riots in, 47–50, 79; "Old
Washington" column, 109; Potomac
flooding, 21, 86; prohibition in,
88–89; race relations in, by 1970,
79–80; suffrage for, 26–28, 32–34;
suffragists in, 150–53; Union
Station train disaster in, 95–96;
urban renewal in, 30–31; War
Preparedness Parade in, 150
Washington, Walter E.: King, M. L.,
assassination riots and, 73–74,
78; *Star* covering administration
of, 37–42, 71; *Star* cultivating
administration of, 36–37
Washington-Baltimore Newspaper
Guild. *See* Newspaper Guild
Washington Bee, 46–48
Washington Daily News, Star
purchasing, 224, 242–44
Washington Metropolitan Police
Department: BEF and, 156–58;
Ottenberg, M., and, 97–98; race and,
37, 71; scandals of, *Star* covering, 98
Washington Nationals. *See*
Washington Senators
Washington Post, 78, 97; advertising
and, 237–38, 243, 250–51, 264–65;
Barry endorsed by, 44; city hall
reporting by, 37; on criminal
justice, liberal views of, 98;
Doonesbury and, 264; eventual
success of, 237–38, 240; on Free D.
C. and Board of Trade, 36; Gart
disparaging, 267; Graham, K.,
at, 126, 134–36, 228, 249; under
Graham, P., 30, 52, 98, 237–39;
home rule advocated by, 30, 33–34;
Johnson, H., at, 213–14; Meyer
and, 28, 52, 161, 237–38; Pentagon
Papers in, 219; pool integration

covered by, 51; on prohibition, 88;
sports coverage of, *Star* competing
with, 128; strike at, 135–36, 249–50,
261; with Time, Inc., JPA attempt
of, 266; *Times-Herald* acquired by,
30, 238–39
Washington Redskins, 113–14, 123,
128, 164; gay athletes of, 130–31;
racial discrimination of, 122
Washington Senators, 108–9, 111–13,
128
Washington Star. See specific topics
Washington Star Communications
(WSC), 243–45, 248, 257–58
Washington Star-Daily News, 243
Washington Times, 28–29, 152
Watergate scandal, 126, 253; press
subpoenaed in, 228; Pulitzer Prize
and, 229–30; Russell story in, 226;
Senate hearings on, 228–29; *Star*
covering, 224–29; Woodward and
Bernstein in, 223–25, 227–29
Weintraub, Boris, 213
Werner, Ludy (Mary Lou), 31, 94; civil
rights, desegregation covered by,
32, 54–57; Hiroshima bombing and,
171; Wallace shooting and, 219
West, Woody, 75, 90
Weyler, Valeriano, 146
Whig party, 8
White House Correspondents'
Association, 167, 181
Whitman, Walt, 20–21
Wilde, Oscar, 138
Williams, John, 201, 203–4
Williams, Maurice, 104–5
Wilson, Allen, 91–92
Wilson, Hank, 45
Wilson, Woodrow, 49, 96, 150–52, 154
Winchell, Walter, 179
Wirz, Henry, 82–83, *83*, 84
Witcover, Jules, 211, 260
WJLA-TV, 257–58
WMAL, 73; radio, 27, 50, 235, 257; TV,
235–36, 257
women reporters: society news
covered by, 107, 110–11, 116–18,

About the Author

Faye Haskins was archivist and then photo librarian in the Special Collections Division, Washingtoniana Collection at the District of Columbia Public Library where the papers of the *Washington Star* newspaper and the *Star* photo collection are held. She holds masters' degrees in history and library science from the University of Maryland and is the author of *The Art of D.C. Politics: Broadsides, Banners, and Bumper Stickers* and *Behind the Headlines: The* Evening Star's *Coverage of the 1968 Riots*, journal articles published in *Washington History*, a publication of the Historical Society of Washington, D.C. She is an independent author and historian who now lives in the Hill Country near Austin, Texas.